INTELLIGENCE AND ADAPTATION

INTELLIGENCE AND ADAPTATION

AN INTEGRATION OF PSYCHOANALYTIC AND PIAGETIAN DEVELOPMENTAL PSYCHOLOGY

by

STANLEY I. GREENSPAN

INTERNATIONAL UNIVERSITIES PRESS, INC.

New York

Library of Congress Cataloging in Publication Data

Library of Congress Cataloging in Publication Data

Greenspan, Stanley I
Intelligence and adaptation.

(Psychological issues ; v. 12, no. 3/4, monograph 47/48)
Bibliography: p.
Includes index.
1. Developmental psychology. 2. Intellect.
3. Cognition. 4. Emotions. 5. Psychoanalysis.
6. Piaget, Jean, 1896- I. Title. II. Series.
BF713.G73 155.4'13 78-13893
ISBN 0-8236-2718-7
ISBN 0-8236-2717-9 pbk.

Manufactured in the United States of America

CONTENTS

ACKNOWLEDGMENTS

Grateful acknowledgment is made to the following publishers for permission to use material from:

"Concept Development," by John H. Flavell, in *Carmichael's Manual of Child Psychology*, 3rd edition, edited by P. Mussen, © 1970 by John Wiley & Sons, Inc., Publishers, New York.

The Developmental Psychology of Jean Piaget, by John H. Flavell, © 1963 by Litton Educational Publishing, Inc. Reprinted by permission of D. Van Nostrand Company.

Ego Psychology and the Problem of Adaptation, by Heinz Hartmann, © 1958 by Heinz Hartmann, M.D., International Universities Press, Inc., Publishers, New York.

The Growth of Logical Thinking: From Childhood to Adolescence, by Barbel Inhelder and Jean Piaget, translated by Anne Parsons and Stanley Milgram, © 1958 by Basic Books, Inc., Publishers, New York.

The Construction of Reality in the Child, by Jean Piaget, translated by Margaret Cook, © 1954 by Basic Books, Inc., Publishers, New York.

The Psychology of the Child, by Jean Piaget and Barbel Inhelder, translated from the French by Helen Weaver, © 1969 by Basic Books, Inc., Publishers, New York.

The Structure of Psychoanalytic Theory: A Systematizing Attempt, by David Rapaport, © 1960 by International Universities Press, Inc., Publishers, New York.

"Toward a Theory of Thinking," by David Rapaport, in *Organization and Pathology of Thought: Selected Sources,* translation and commentary by David Rapaport, © 1951 by Columbia University Press, Publishers, New York. Reprinted by permission of Elvira Rapaport Strasser.

In addition, I would like to give special thanks to John Curry for his invaluable collaboration in co-authoring the "Review of the Literature" and for his overall assistance in researching, writing, editing, and conceptualizing the material.

INTRODUCTION

The development of a unified framework, in which the relationship between emotional development and cognitive or intellectual development can be understood, has been one of the major unresolved problem areas of modern psychology. Although there is an apparent parallel between the development of intellect and overall emotional maturity in the earliest stages of development, as development proceeds into later childhood, adolescence, and adulthood, major differences emerge in individual intellectual and emotional levels of functioning. A relatively brilliant person, for example, may function at a very primitive, immature emotional level. On the other hand, a person with marked intellectual limitations may function at a well-integrated, mature emotional level.

Research in understanding personality organization, especially in terms of assessment and outcome, has been hampered by our inability to evaluate both lines of development within a uniform framework. As a result, there has been a marked inability to reach a consensus about the types of programs, educational or social-emotional, that best facilitate overall development.

The two most comprehensive theories of human development, not surprisingly, stem from separate attempts to understand either emotional or cognitive development. Psychoanalytic developmental psychology has provided the most inclusive view of human experience from a psychological and emotional perspective. Piaget's cognitive developmental psychology has given us our most complete model for understanding the unfolding of human intellect. While many other schools of thought have contributed to understanding these two lines of development, the psychoanalytic and Piagetian approaches stand as our major theoretical models of distinctly human personality functioning.

This work attempts a full synthesis of psychoanalytic and Piagetian developmental psychology in the context of current clinical and research experience. And, in so doing, it develops an integrated approach to understanding emotion and cognition in human adaptation and intelligence. Earlier works on this subject, such as that of Peter Wolff (1960), carefully examine these two models, but stop short of developing the transformational bridges or functional relationships between emotion and intellect. In this work we shall first review the similarities and differences between psychoanalytic and Piagetian psychology and past attempts to bridge both theories. Following this, we shall explore the structural symmetry of the two models and the different stimulus worlds each encounters. It will be shown that Piaget's precise developmental model offers unique potential for our further understanding of the development and organization of human adaptation, and that this model can be integrated within the broader framework of a psychoanalytic approach.

Relationships will be examined between internal drives and affects, their related self- and object representations, regulating and mediating structures, and the various levels of mental operations (sensorimotor, preoperational, concrete, and formal operational), which for Piaget constitute intelligent human functioning. Realms of experience as different as those described by the "dynamic unconscious" and "rational intelligent thought" have been viewed as theoretically incompatible (particularly by Piaget). In the context of an integrated theory, however, they can be operationally defined, and their relative influence on behavior understood. A hierarchical model will be developed in which psychological structures at different organizational levels (somatic, representational, and derivative representational) provide a basis for understanding how the human organism deals symmetrically with inanimate and animate; cognitive and emotional; conscious, reality-oriented and unconscious, drive-colored experience. This model of intelligence and learning will be seen to take into account recent clinical and empirical findings regarding early personality development.

Understanding the relationship between the ego and the environment has long been an important goal for psychoanalytic ego psychology. In the effort to extend the theory of psychoanalysis beyond the limits of psychopathology and to reformulate it as a general psychology, psychoanalysts have had a persevering interest in theories of normal cognitive development. In particular, a number of attempts have been made to introduce the findings of Jean Piaget and his Geneva school of genetic psychology into a generally analytic framework.

As early as 1933, de Saussure published a paper relating the Freudian theory of libidinal development and superego formation to the development of logic in the child's thinking (A. Freud, 1951). Such a paper would be of great historical interest today, but radical changes in both theories severely curtail its current relevance.

Piaget himself presented a paper at the International Congress on Psycho-analysis in Berlin in 1922, in which he discussed the prelogical reasoning of children in relation to the shift from primary- to secondary-process dominance (Anthony, 1957). Following this brief encounter with Freudian theory, however, Piaget's research interests led him more and more in a strictly cognitive direction, and away from the psychoanalytic school. Anthony hypothesizes that different theories of infantile animism may have ended the early and very limited cross-fertilization between psychoanalysis and Piaget's genetic psychology. Freud attributed the child's tendency to view inanimate objects as alive to an emotional mechanism, namely, projection; Piaget, on the other hand, attributed animism to a lack of intellectual differentiation between the self and other objects. Whether or not this particular issue actually had a pivotal effect on future developments in Piaget's and Freud's thinking is less important than its symbolic value as an indicator of the directions these respective thinkers would take in constructing psychological systems. Freud and subsequent analysts developed a system based on the theory of drives, a system concerned primarily with the affective life of man. Piaget and his much smaller group of followers turned to the investigation of intelligence as the characteristically human form of adaptation to the environment.

Involved in their different projects, psychoanalysts and genetic psychologists paid one another little heed through the 1930s and 1940s. With the advent of psychoanalytic ego psychology, a new impetus was given to interaction between analysis and genetic psychology. Hartmann's (1939) postulation of a conflict-free sphere of the ego was particularly significant in this regard, since it opened psychoanalytic thought to a consideration of cognitive functions in their own right.

Hartmann and Kris (1945) stressed the importance of genetic propositions, in addition to dynamic ones, in analysis and called for further cross-fertilization between child psychology and psychoanalysis. They remarked: "The academic study of child psychology and child development has not sufficiently taken notice of the genetic approach in psychoanalysis. Psychoanalysts, on the other hand, have failed in many respects to take into account the data that child psychology has assembled; an omission that has led to many incongruities" (p. 13).

Hartmann (1950) pointed out that Freud had questioned the utility of direct child observation as practiced by psychologists because phenomena were not interpreted in their dynamic fullness of meaning. But Freud had also admitted the difficulties involved in founding an entire child psychology upon the method of adults' verbal reconstruction. According to Hartmann, the theoretical edifice of ego psychology made possible a fruitful combination of the methods of reconstruction and direct observation.

Anna Freud (1951) noted the significant contribution to this dialogue between analysis and child psychology made by psychoanalytic observers conversant with experimental and statistical methodologies. She mentioned, in particular, the works of David Levy, Margaret Ribble, René Spitz, Margaret Fries, and John Bowlby.

By 1950, then, psychoanalysis, at least in its ego psychological school, was open to direct child observations and to the insights of developmental psychology. Piaget, for his part, had made only occasional references in his works to Freudian thought. His most significant critique of analytic thinking was published in a book dealing with the formation of symbols in children's play, dreams, and imitations (1945). This criticism drew a partial response from Anthony (1957), and will be summarized below. At the outset it should be noted that Piaget's critique of psychoanalysis was not formulated with post-Freudian ego psychology in mind.

Since 1950, there have been numerous efforts to relate Piaget's theory of cognitive development to psychoanalysis. These works have varied greatly in scope, method of approach, and quality of results. Some have involved comparison or contrast between the psychoanalytic and the genetic systems as total theoretical approaches. Others have focused on relatively restricted topics that are within the scope of both theories in order to obtain a fuller perspective on a familiar subject.

The present work has been written in the conviction that there is a need within the psychoanalytic community for a single reference that will both clarify the present relationship of Piaget's genetic psychology to analytic thinking and offer a new integrated approach to the cognitive and affective aspects of human development. To date, efforts to relate the two schools of thought have not built upon one another in any sequential or programmatic fashion. Accordingly, part of the present work consists of a review of these efforts. While not totally comprehensive, this review covers all major comparisons of the two theoretical systems as such, as well as the most significant articles focusing on six areas of mutual theoretical interest.

Wolff's monograph on *The Developmental Psychologies of Jean Piaget and Psychoanalysis* (1960) is the best publication to date that compares and contrasts the two approaches, but it does not offer a true synthesis. It contains an excellent summary of Piaget's basic psychological principles and a review of the stages of development in the first two years of life from both the analytic and the genetic perspectives. In treating a system as vast as Piaget's, however, it is not surprising that Wolff's monograph does not touch upon all aspects of the system of potential importance for the expansion of psychoanalysis into a general psychology. Most notably, Wolff does not consider the periods of intellectual development beyond the sensorimotor period, which ends at approximately two years of age. Such topics as the formation of symbolic thought and the characteristics of childhood and adolescent thinking are thus omitted from his monograph.

Certain developments in the literature since 1960 make it opportune to present another look at Piaget's work from the perspective of psychoanalysis. Chief among these are the publications of Flavell (1963) and Furth (1969). The former is a comprehensive summary of the content of Piaget's psychological system; the latter examines the theoretical foundations upon which Piaget has built his vast research. If the former summarizes for the English-speaking audience what Piaget has discovered, the latter explains most effectively what he has been attempting to do, from a broader theoretical perspective.

The present work draws upon such secondary sources as Flavell and Furth and reviews primary research publications and theoretical statements by Piaget himself. No attempt is made to cover all the topics in Piaget's psychology. Flavell (1963) remains the best source for such a comprehensive survey. The present study excludes any detailed account of a great many subjects of Piagetian research, such as his work on perception and on certain concete operations of the intellect. Except for a short review of his theory of moral development, we have avoided references to Piaget's earliest research, which was marked by a highly verbal methodology, and has been superseded both by his systematic observations of his own children and by the closely reasoned studies with large samples that constitute his latest research endeavors.

We have chosen to discuss topics that convey the present status of Piaget's thinking. The selection of material has been designed to be representative, not comprehensive. It is our hope that the summary of the work of Piaget and his collaborators provided here will enable the psychoanalytic reader to grasp not only potentially relevant content within Piagetian research, but also the nature of Piaget's system as a unique theoretical edifice. In this sense, we believe that the genetic psychology of the Geneva school can continue to be a fruitful subject of discussion within the psychoanalytic community not only at the level of psychological content, but also at the level of model building.

1

REVIEW OF THE LITERATURE RELATING PSYCHOANALYSIS TO PIAGETIAN PSYCHOLOGY

with JOHN CURRY, Ph.D.

General or Multidimensional Comparisons

This chapter briefly reviews previous attempts to relate Piagetian and psychoanalytic theory. General theoretical works and works that focus on more than one point of comparison include those by Odier (1956), Cobliner (1967), Anthony (1956a), and Wolff (1960).

In this respect, Odier's book is the least substantial, as reviewers have pointed out (Anthony, 1957; Flavell, 1963). It relies on only a few constructs from Piaget's early thinking (chiefly *adualism* and *realism*) and utilizes them to elucidate case histories related to the author's own theory of neurosis. While Odier's attempt at synthesis falls short, his guiding principle—that theoretical accounts of emotional and cognitive development can be enhanced by cross-fertilization—remains valid.

In a more significant contribution, Cobliner cites certain "unmistakable parallels" between Piagetian and psychoanalytic constructs. On the Piagetian side he focuses on the developmental mechanisms of self-regulation: rhythm, regulation, and grouping (see Piaget, 1970), Each of these levels represents an advance in self-regulation over its predecessor. Three parallels are proposed between the Piagetian model and that of psychoanalysis. The first is that both theories hold that psychic energy is controlled by intrapsychic rather than by physical agents. The second is that both posit a developmental sequence from lesser to greater self-control. Just as the transition from rhythm to regulation to grouping leads to improved cognitive self-regulation, so the eventual predominance of the reality principle over the pleasure principle leads to the delay and modification of impulse discharge and the subservience of drives to rational thought. The third parallel is that between Piaget's notion of impulse control through values and the psychoanalytic construct of the superego.

Certain problems are apparent in Cobliner's scheme of parallels. The major one, perhaps, is the vast difference between the two theories in reliance upon drive or impulse as explanatory constructs. Piaget does not deal with these, and the type of self-regulation he considers pertains to perception and intelligence, rather than to personality or social behavior. When Cobliner criticizes Piaget's structures as too mechanistic because they do not deal with transformations of psychic energy, the argument is irrelevant because energy is not a construct in Piaget's system.

Cobliner's most cogent criticisms of Piaget's theory seem to be: (1) that it does not account fully for regression in logical thinking and (2) that it does not account for irrational or regressive aspects of human behavior. The second criticism pertains to the scope of Piaget's theory. If we accept it as a genetic epistemology, not a general psychology, we may then attempt to integrate Piaget's theory of cognition into a more general model.

The identification of parallels is a useful initial step toward theoretical integration. Cobliner's work is limited, however, in that he does not identify ways in which one theory actually complements or enriches the other. For example, one could ask whether Piagetian work contains constructs or data that would further explain the relationship of cognitive to affective development. To answer such questions it is necessary to go beyond parallels.

A major step in this direction has been taken by Anthony (1956a). Rejecting Odier's attempt to create a metatheory through a synthesis of Piagetian and psychoanalytic constructs,

Anthony focuses on six selected topics of mutual theoretical interest. His first two topics concern implications of Piaget's notion of object permanence for the psychoanalytic concepts of object relations and separation anxiety. The next two topics relate Piaget's cognitive stages to phenomena of childhood psychosis, namely, loss of object permanence and regression to infantile behavior patterns. Finally, Anthony discusses the Piagetian theory of conscience formation and preoperational thinking as these relate to analytic notions of moral development.

Anthony's utilization of these six Piagetian constructs varies somewhat within his article. Initially, he uses Piaget's empirical findings to verify certain analytic propositions and falsify others. The experiments regarding object permanence, for example, tend to favor orthodox analytic thought over Melanie Klein's notion of partial object relations from birth. Later, however, Anthony tends to focus on accommodating the two theoretical systems to each other. He attempts, for example, to reconcile the theories' conflicting accounts of conscience formation by identifying Piaget's autonomous morality with an ego, not a superego function. The limitation of this "accommodating" approach is that it involves a stretching and an oversimplification of constructs in both theories. Totally different causal factors are posited to account for "autonomous morality" and the postoedipal "superego," so that much more than a difference in terminology is involved.

Anthony's short article does show that Piaget's genetic psychology has relevance for psychoanalysis when applied to selected topics. The article's main contribution is in the use of certain empirical observations from Piagetian research to evaluate theoretical points in psychoanalysis. This approach is to be favored over that of attempting to "validate" constructs in one theory by accommodating them to constructs of another theory. Merely demonstrating that two theories agree does not validate either one.

To date, the most extensive and significant attempt to compare Piaget's developmental psychology and psychoanalysis has been Peter Wolff's monograph (1960), which focuses on the sensorimotor period. For each of the six sensorimotor stages,

Wolff gives several of Piaget's empirical observations, discusses the implications of stage-specific behavior for Piaget's major explanatory concepts, and compares Piaget's ideas to those of psychoanalysis. Thus, Anthony's use of empirical observations to critique analytic theory and Odier's goal of achieving a viable synthesis are both incorporated into this work, and carried to a qualitatively higher level of sophistication.

Wolff's fundamental method of achieving theoretical synthesis is the same for each of the six topical areas he discusses. First he points out a significant difference in the two theories' accounts of a phenomenon. Then he proposes three possible synthetic models. The first is a reduction of Piaget's model to the status of a subordinate component within a Freudian model. The second is a reduction of Freudian constructs to subordinate components ("derivatives") within a Piagetian model. The third, stemming from psychoanalytic ego psychology, avoids reductionism in either direction. Instead, it introduces the drive state of the organism as a mediating variable, and holds that a Freudian account of the phenomenon in question is valid under states of drive arousal. A Piagetian account, on the other hand, is valid under states of low drive arousal, or quiescence.

The six topics discussed by Wolff within this framework include motivation as a function of internal versus external stimulation and object relations as a function of drive tension reduction versus an invariant assimilation-accommodation process. Contrasting accounts are given of the relationship between goal-directed motility, diffuse motility, and affect. In addition, Wolff examines the conflict and adaptational models of the origins of reality-adaptive behavior, goal-oriented behavior as a function of autonomy from internal versus environmental forces, and thought as having its origins either in hallucinatory images of absent objects or in action schemes.

As implied above, Wolff's final theoretical synthesis appears to depend on the construction of a type of dualism involving two parallel systems. The Freudian theoretical system accounts for behavior under high drive states, while the Piagetian system explains adaptation under low drive states. Thus, the state of the organism is postulated as the chief explanatory link between the two major theories.

While we agree that the state of the organism is a motivational variable, we would also hold that a truly comprehensive theory must explore more fully than Wolff's does all the functional relationships among posited variables (Rapaport, 1959). Wolff does not deal, for example, with the relative relationships of drive to cognition, but states only that drive level (as though "all-or-nothing" levels or thresholds existed) is a precondition for the predominance of one or the other of two essentially independent, parallel systems. The nature of the connecting bridges between the two systems is thus not really explored. In addition, Wolff examines only the early phases of human development.

An adequate, comprehensive theory, to our mind, must be a structural theory in Piaget's sense; it must include, as a central construct, the notion of structure and give an account of the system's inherent laws of transformation. Although Wolff has made psychoanalysis and Piaget's genetic psychology compatible by postulating a parallelism held together by the concept of drive state, he has not brought dynamic and cognitive constructs together in a higher-level structural system, unified under a set of transformational rules.

In other publications, Wolff has maintained his interest in relating Piagetian constructs to psychoanalysis. He has developed a classification of infant behavior patterns, related these to internal need states, and shown that an infant's capacity for certain motor behaviors is a function of both need state and type of stimulation (1959). In a later work (1966), Wolff examines the potential effect of internal stimuli on the development of cognitive structures themselves. He points to classifications of infant behavior never considered by Piaget (e.g., affect-expressive reflexes), and argues that significant alterations in Piaget's theory would follow from incorporation of such affective schemes into the theory.

Empirical evidence is cited in the 1966 publication, supporting Wolff's view that certain behaviors essential to Piaget's developmental progression, such as visual and auditory pursuit of an object, occur only in certain drive states. Thus, the generalization and scope of Piaget's work is called into question, and the need to consider the state of the organism as a moderating variable is underscored. Later papers by Wolff have covered the self-regulating mechanism of rhythm (1967b, 1968) and the general relationship of psychoanalysis to child development research (1971).

Wolff, however, has never gone beyond proposing two parallel systems as a way to relate psychoanalytic and Piagetian psychology. As indicated, a complete theoretical integration involves postulating the transformational principles that account for how the phenemena each theory purports to explain interact throughout development. In this context, it is interesting to note that Wolff (1971) takes the stand that psychoanalytic propositions do not intersect "in any crucial way" with data culled from direct infant observation (p. 568). In his view psychoanalysis is not an empirical science, but a method of interpretation of symbols.

Specific Topics of Comparison

Object Permanence and Object Relations

A Piagetian notion of special import to psychoanalysis is the development of the scheme of the permanent object. Flavell (1970) gives a succinct account of the six stages of this development as inferred from direct observation of infants' pursuit behavior. Essentially, an infant originally has no concept that objects exist independent of himself or his actions. He is aware only of undifferentiated events in which his own efforts, actions, and perceptions are blurred together. By the end of the sensorimotor period, however, he has become aware that objects maintain their existence in space and time even when they are no longer in his perceptual field.

Replication studies utilizing large numbers of subjects have confirmed Piaget's discovery of this phenomenon, which was originally based on observations of his own children (Décarie, Corman and Escalona, 1969; Décarie, 1962; Uzgiris and Hunt, 1975). Consequently, psychoanalytically oriented writers have taken this finding seriously and investigated its implications for the analytic theory of object relations.

In an extensive study of 90 subjects, Décarie (1962) attempted to establish a chronological parallel between the development of object permanence and that of object relations. A scale of behaviors related to the former was devised based on Piaget's writings, while a scale of behaviors related to the latter was constructed from the writings of A. Freud, Spitz, and Hoffer. Object relations development was conceptualized as passing from a narcissistic period, through an intermediate period, to a period of true object relations.

Piaget's invariant sequence of stages in object permanence was validated by Décarie's study, but no such invariant sequence of stages was found in the emotional area of object relations. Thus, Décarie relinquished her major goal of demonstrating a clear correlation between the two realms of development. A general correspondence in development, however, was found for the 50 percent of her subjects who did develop object relations in the hypothesized behavioral sequence.

Décarie points out that the major theoretical disagreement between Piagetian and Freudian models here concerns the beginnings of mental representation. With regard to the theory of object relations, psychoanalytic writers have considered the child capable of mental representation and symbolic behavior as early as the intermediate period (three to six months), and capable of imitating an internalized model and having imaginative fantasies before twelve months. For Piaget, however, true mental representation, symbolic play, and imaginative thinking are all dependent on the development of the scheme of the permanent object, and are thus not possible prior to the last stage of the sensorimotor period (16 or 18 to 20 months). Décarie interprets her findings as supportive of Piaget's position and argues that analytic thinkers must distinguish between an affective attachment to a human object and the ability to represent mentally that object in its absence. She does not discuss, however, which cognitive structures are prerequisites for such an affective attachment.

Cobliner (1967) takes up the same issue. Accepting the position that the "object" referred to in object relations theory cannot develop unless certain aspects of Piaget's permanent object have already developed, he points out that Piaget's stage sequence is based on experiments with inanimate objects. Since the human object is the most stimulating and interesting in the child's world, Cobliner argues that it may have a certain priority in development, such that object permanence is achieved faster with animate than with inanimate objects. However, Cobliner, following Spitz (1965), places the attainment of some form of libidinal object constancy between the eighth and tenth month of life, a good ten months before Piaget is willing to attribute the scheme of the permanent object to his subjects. It is certainly questionable whether the probable priority of human over inanimate objects is sufficient to account for a ten-month gap between the achievement of object permanence for mother and its parallel for "things."

Since there is general agreement among analysts that stable object relations depend on the ability to retain a mental image of the absent object (Arlow et al., 1968), the disparity between analytic and cognitive psychology timetables of mental development is of significance. Cognitive psychologists' notion of *object permanence* refers to the child's awareness that objects continue to exist outside his perceptual field. This scheme is dependent on mental representation, or the child's ability to form an internal image of the object in its absence.

In an excellent article addressed to the relationship between object constancy and mental representation, Fraiberg (1969) illuminates the wide variety of usages and operational definitions of the term *object constancy* in psychoanalysis. The attainment of object constancy is postulated as early as six months and as late as 25 months, with concomitant variations in the type of mental representation deemed necessary to undergo this emotional development.[1]

One of Fraiberg's major contributions here is to point out Piaget's distinction between "recognition memory" and "evocative memory." While the latter is required for true object permanence, the former may be sufficient to account for early forms of object constancy. Fraiberg goes on to develop the position that certain mental images of infancy postulated by analysts are not really challenged by Piaget's notions of mental

[1] Later we will discuss Mahler's timetable, which places attainment of libidinal object constancy at three years (Mahler, Pine, and Bergman, 1975).

representation, since they are not "evoked" in the absence of a stimulus, but rather are generated under conditions of internal, or drive, stimuli.

Finally, Kaplan (1972) shows that a structural aspect of Piaget's theory, the notion of vertical *décalage,* can be used to organize the concept of object constancy as a subject-object relationship that is "reacquired in more complex and integrated ways at successive phases of development" (p. 323). Kaplan thus demonstrates that a formal characteristic of one theory may be useful as an organizing principle for data of the other theory. Analogously, it is possible to demonstrate that content generated from an analytic point of view (drive stimuli) may affect the cognitive structures which are the major organizing constructs postulated in Piaget's theory.

The Development of Mental Representation and the Genesis of Thought

Novey (1958) and Beres and Joseph (1970) have analyzed in detail the meaning of mental representation in psychoanalysis. A review of their works shows that the term has both a passive and an active meaning. In the passive sense, a mental representation is in internal replica of some external event, fulfilling a role similar to that of a *mediating variable* in learning theory. Furth (1969) has analyzed this concept with reference to learning theory and pointed out that Piaget's structuralism does not accord such a vital role to internal figurative representations.

On the other hand, *mental representation* may designate the process of reconstruction of a figurative image in the absence of an external stimulus, i.e., an active, evocative process. In this sense, there is a virtual identity between Piaget's *evocative memory* and psychoanalytic *mental representation.* However, Piaget's theory of the development of cognitive structures functions as a critique of the passive notion of mental representation. More specifically, it calls into question the epistemology involved in postulating such internal representation.

Wolff (1967a) has articulated this point at some length, demonstrating that the orthodox psychoanalytic theory of the genesis of thinking posits primitive hallucinatory images formed by processes of simple associational learning. The naïve realism implied in this associationist epistemology (images as copies of external events) is belied by Piaget's findings that young children "distort" incoming perceptual stimuli in accordance with their primitive mental structures. Wolff then argues that the marriage of psychoanalytic theory to an associationist theory of memory and learning is a mismatch, and that analysis would more readily fit with a truly genetic theory of cognitive development. Psychoanalytic assumptions favoring the postulation of organizing schemes of experience that would shape incoming data are outlined by Wolff; these already-postulated organizers include drives, congenital instinctual apparatuses, and drive-restraining structures. Finally, Wolff notes three implications of Piaget's findings for a renewed psychaoanalytic theory of learning: (1) rejection of the hallucinatory model of the genesis of thought; (2) reconsideration of certain types of infantile thinking as reality-adaptive, rather than as primary process; (3) inclusion of some *a priori* formal structures, analogous to schemes, within the model of memory, to serve as organizers of perceptual input and experience.

Two other articles by analytic writers are relevant to the issue of early mental representations and the development of thought, particularly in relation to primary and secondary processes. Silverman (1971) proposes a parallel between the transition from prelogical to logical classification, studied by Piaget, and the transition from primary- to secondary-process thinking. His speculations are interesting but also point to inconsistencies in the identification of the points of transition from primary to secondary process. Furthermore, his approach is based on the method of ascertaining parallels, while a more beneficial approach might be the utilization of Piagetian principles to clarify the actual functioning of primary- and secondary-process thinking.

In this direction, Holt (1967) offers a view of the primary process based on Piaget's structuralism, but greatly at variance with the usual psychoanalytic notion that primary process develops into secondary process as it becomes more reality-oriented. Holt proposes that the primary process be considered not merely a mode of energy organization, but a structural system in its own right. The nonarbitrariness of condensations and displacements involved in the construction of stable defenses, repetitiveness of dream elements, stability of neurotic symptoms, and the universality of certain symbols are all factors invoked to support the argument that there is a structural foundation and development to the primary process itself. Holt further argues that, contrary to Freud's theory, frustrated reality-adaptive thought leads to a regression that generates primary-process thinking.

In the works of Wolff and Holt, we see instances where input from Piagetian psychology calls forth significant alterations in the psychoanalytic model of thinking. Holt's paper is more speculative, while Wolff's, though theoretical, is grounded more in observational data. Beyond the theory building generated by the two papers, to fulfill the requirements of a comprehensive account of emotional and cognitive development, one still needs to show the interrelationships among the new variables introduced in the metatheory (e.g., *a priori* organizing structures of memory and internal stimuli, or reality-adaptive structures and primary-process structures). How, for example, do wish fulfillments and early action schemes become integrated so as to account for the structure and content of primary process?

Several psychoanalytic writers have been influenced by Piaget's emphasis on the connection between symbolic play and representational thinking. Galenson (1971), relying on the work of Furth (1966) and Vernon (1967), notes that language is only one aspect of symbolic thought and cannot be identified with operative thinking. She reviews Piaget's position on the relationship of symbolic play to cognitive development, using Piaget's theory to explain clinically observed sequences. She then proposes a theory of symbolic-thought development, ending with empirically testable hypotheses regarding a relationship between a dearth of ludic symbols and acting-out behavior.

To Galenson's contribution, McDevitt (1971) adds parallel causal hypotheses based on the psychoanalytic theory of object relations. Here is an example of theoretical cross-fertilization between the cognitive and object relations point of view, as writers attempt to clarify and relate the multiple determinants of symbolic thinking.

Finally, mental representation in the language and play of blind children has been studied by Fraiberg and Adelson (1973). Delays in the use of self-referential pronouns are observed in this handicapped population, and explained by reference to Piaget's theory of imitation as the basis of the symbolic function (which is responsible for aspects of mental representation). Piagetian theory is thus used to inform empirical observation. These authors' findings serve to expand the knowledge base to which an adequate theory of mental representation and the genesis of thought must conform.

Psychopathology

Psychoanalytically oriented writers have examined Piaget's findings in search of new insights into pathological processes. Anthony (1956b), for instance, discusses the relevance of preoperational thinking to clinical phenomena such as fears of death, magical fantasies about body function, and the development of a rigid, authoritarian personality structure. In a later article (1958), Anthony uses a scale of development of object permanence to differentiate primary from secondary autism and reports that psychotic children have significantly more difficulty with the Piagetian task of perspective-taking than do neurotic children. Thus, Anthony uses Piaget's notion to interpret and organize first-order clinical and research observations.

With a similar approach, Trunnell (1964, 1965) demonstrates that schizophrenic adults perform and reason on certain Piagetian tasks in a manner similar to that of preoperational children, as opposed to that of normal adults. Finally, an excellent empirical study by Norris, Jenes, and Norris (1970) delineates qualitative differences between the conceptual structure of obsessional patients and normal controls. The results are interpreted to suggest that obsessional patients may have a cognitive deficit related to poor development of the classification structures of propositional thinking, which normally emerge in adolescence.

These articles demonstrate that the data base of a truly general cognitive-affective psychology can be expanded using a

Piagetian heuristic framework. Several other attempts to generate empirical studies of psychopathology from a Piagetian perspective, however, are most notable for their weaknesses. Gratton (1971) sets out to demonstrate that psychotic development in the first two years of life correlates with failure to develop object permanence. He states his hypothesis in terms of correlation between impaired object relations and impaired object permanence, but fails to measure impaired object relations. Furthermore, Gratton's data show that object permanence is not deleteriously affected by childhood schizophrenia, as it is by autism. Gratton's work has its chief value in the development of a checklist capable of discriminating autism from schizophrenia and retardation.

In a case history report, Pivetta (1973) argues that Piagetian constructs (e.g., realism) have more explanatory power than Freudian constructs (e.g., repressed trauma) in accounting for an instance of obsessional neurosis. Her monograph, however, is exceedingly poorly written and full of *non sequiturs.* At its heart, Pivetta's argument seems to collapse when she reduces *realism,* a Piagetian construct of normal development, to a consequence of a "pre-traumatic trauma."

In addition to well- and poorly designed empirical studies or reports, there have been a number of speculative theoretical articles relating Piagetian notions to psychopathology. Bettelheim (1967) stresses Piaget's emphasis on action as the foundation of thought and speculates that an extreme rigidity, based on the belief that personal safety resides in sameness, keeps autistic children from acting on objects and thus developing normal thought processes. Unfortunately, Bettelheim restricts his theorizing to a solely psychogenic, and thus highly questionable, theory of autism, directing the causal sequence back to deficiencies in mothering.

Freeman and McGhie (1957) compare certain behavior patterns of adult schizophrenic patients to the behavior of infants studied by Piaget. Repetitive behavior patterns, reminiscent of Piaget's primary and secondary circular reactions, and failure to pursue desired objects outside the perceptual field, suggesting loss of object permanence, were observed in their patients. The authors argue that such schizophrenic symptoms should not be interpreted as meaningful in a symbolic sense, but as a breakdown in the cognitive functions of the ego.

Finally, Feffer (1967) has interpreted multiple symptoms of psychopathology in terms of Piaget's notion of decentering. This cognitive operation ordinarily enables the thinker to focus on more than one dimension of an object simultaneously. Decentering thus provides for a self-corrective feedback system, which reduces the distortion consequent upon unbalanced focusing on only one aspect of an object or person. Feffer suggests that concrete thinking, paleologic, and projective hallucinations are interpretable as instances of defective decentering.

Motivation

Several authors have written theoretical essays relating Piaget and psychoanalysts on the topic of motivation. Hunt (1969) points out that classical psychoanalysis relates all behavior to the motivating force of the drives, while Piaget does not relate cognitive behavior to any such independent motivating construct. Instead, the motivation of the children Piaget studied is said to be based on their "sensorimotor interaction with their environmental circumstances" (p. 28).

Indeed, the only "motive" in Piaget's equilibration model of intellectual development is an inherent "need to know." Wolff (1963) has contrasted this single notion with Rapaport's (1959) psychoanalytic concept of a motive as an internal force marked by peremptoriness, cyclical character, selectiveness, and displaceability. While admitting that the "need to function" is a sufficient construct *within* Piaget's model, Wolff calls into question the comprehensiveness of that model. Specifically, he argues that clinical experience attests to drive-motivated behavior; that affects are not only concomitants of cognitive structures, but structure-building forces themselves; and that such motivational factors as are postulated by psychoanalysis may exert a strong influence even on the structuralization of cognitive schemes.

A third author, Kessen (1971), has contrasted the "hot" motivational theory of psychoanalysis with the "cold" one of Piaget. He contrasts the two theories on four points: (1) the initial organizing apparatus attributed to the child; (2) the view of the environment; (3) the account of the origins of motivation; and (4) the view of what constitutes a satisfactory resolution of conflicting demands facing the infant. After each of these points of contrast, Kessen notes the limitations of or the questions arising from Piaget's equilibration model. To cite one example only, Piaget's answer to what constitutes a satisfactory resolution by the infant is his notion of a new balance between assimilation and accommodation. His theory, however, cannot predict the strategy an infant will adopt when faced with the option of maximizing either assimilation or accommodation, while minimizing its complement.

Other authors have either criticized Piaget's motivational constructs or used them as one basis for developing a broader model than that postulated by psychoanalysis. In the former vein, Mischel (1971a, 1971b) argues that Piaget's motivational constructs are teleological rather than mechanistic, and are not independent of the behavior they are used to explain. They thus differ qualitatively from most psychological theories of motivation, including that of psychoanalysis. Consequently, the two types cannot simply be linked in a unifying model, as Wolff has attempted with his "state of the organism" variable. Mischel also argues that Piaget's notion of motivation by equilibration cannot be tested empirically. Such investigators as Kuhn (1972) and Bandura and McDonald (1963) have, however, tested it against reinforcement models.

Both Hunt (1963) and White (1959) have developed models of "intrinsic motivation" or "effectance" which rely in part on Piagetian concepts and experiments. Although these two models differ, they both postulate a realm of motivational force which is independent of homeostatic need. Hunt's model proposes to account for behavior as either an intentional, repetitious interaction between the infant and the environment or the pursuit of novel solutions to problems. White's model attempts to account for similar phenomena, including learned motor and self-help skills, exploratory behavior, novel behavior, and behavior directed toward attaining higher levels of mental coordination.

White (1960) argues that his competence model of motivation, based largely on Piaget's observations, is a necessary complement to the psychosexual and interpersonal models of motivation common to psychoanalytic theory. While White's formulation is controversial, Zern's (1973) reply, arguing that the concept of "secondary process" already explains all the behavior cited by White as due to competence motivation, is weak and unconvincing.

In reviewing these articles, we note a general lack of empirical advance, but a substantial contribution to the clarification of theoretical differences between psychoanalysis and Piagetian psychology, as well as clarification of each theory's limitations. Much of the dialogue seems reducible to the issue of theoretical comprehensiveness. Classical psychoanalysis cannot fully account for the behavior White groups under his competence model, while Piaget has no constructs to account for behavior related to prior need states, definable without reference to the behavior itself.

Extension of the Piagetian Model

Obviously, two major blocks to higher-level theoretical synthesis between psychoanalysis and cognitive psychology are the former's underemphasis on cognitive determinants and the latter's general lack of interest in emotional development. Psychoanalytic ego psychology has rectified to some extent the lack in classical analytic theory of a full account of conflict-free cognitive development. On the Piagetian side, a comparable development has extended the cognitive theory into *potential* contact with psychoanalytic notions of emotionality and interpersonal relations. A cognitive developmental model is being used to investigate both the emotional correlates of cognitive development and the development of cognition in the interpersonal or social area. Only a few selected articles from each of these realms will be reviewed here.

RELATIONSHIP BETWEEN COGNITIVE AND EMOTIONAL DEVELOPMENT

Piaget holds that cognition and emotionality develop as parallel, interdependent processes. Goldschmid (1968), who studied the correlation between ten measures of cognitive conservation and a series of emotional and environmental factors, found that her results supported Piaget's general premise. Children with higher levels of cognitive development tended to see themselves more objectively, to be viewed more favorably by teachers, and to be more popular with peers.

Dudek (1972) and Dudek and Dyer (1972) also found a general positive correlation between cognitive and emotional development (the latter was measured by Rorschach protocols or by Cattell's Early School Personality Questionnaire). Furthermore, in the small segment of their sample where regression in cognitive functioning was noted over time, a characteristic defense pattern was isolated. In these children, their considerable imaginative and creative ability was overly constructed by obsessive-compulsive defenses.

A study by Brown, Matheny, and Wilson (1973) links the realms of intelligence, interpersonal cognition, and emotional maturity. In 14 pairs of twins, one twin of each pair was rated more mature in social cognition on the basis of more adultlike responses to a test measuring understanding of the social phenemonon of kindness. As a group these more interpersonally mature children also scored significantly higher than did their twins on cognitive measures (IQ) and on the emotional indices of length of attention span and paucity of temper tantrums.

The relationship between cognitive and emotional development in adolescence is treated in a theoretical essay by Looft (1971), following Elkind (1967). Pointing out that formal operational thinking enables the adolescent to give thought to his own thinking and to deal with hypothetical possibilities, Looft discusses two characteristic forms of cognitive-affective egocentrisms in adolescence: the *imaginary audience* and the *personal fable*. The proposed correlation here between cognitive and emotive factors is open to empirical verification.

SOCIAL COGNITIVE DEVELOPMENT

The fundamental process designated as central to the achievement of interpersonal knowledge is named and defined somewhat differently by the major researchers in the field. In developing a general theory of interpersonal behavior, Feffer (1970), for instance, uses as his central construct the notion of cognitive decentering, or the ability to switch focus from one to another aspect of an event in a balanced, simultaneous manner. Piaget (1936) has also shown how such a process underlies progress in impersonal cognitive development.

Feffer designed a projective technique measuring a subject's ability to shift perspectives and hold multiple social perspectives in mind. Skill in this social cognitive area was shown to be positively correlated with Rorschach developmental level (Feffer, 1959), with operational thinking (Feffer and Gurevitch, 1960), and with communicative ability (Feffer and Suchotliff, 1966). On the basis of these findings, Feffer (1970) argues that "the [cognitive] processes involved in the organization of interpersonal events are isomorphic to those involved in the organization of impersonal events" (p. 197). In impersonal cognition, physical dimensions of objects (height, width, etc.) must be kept in a decentered balance for generalized abstractions to be made. Similarly, in social cognition, role attributes must be kept in a relation of reciprocity for mature interpersonal behavior to occur. Thus, in both arenas, mature cognition is a function of the ability to balance reciprocally and simultaneously the complementary polarities of an event.

Feffer's work is the first prolonged and systematic attempt to relate a Piagetian equilibration model to interpersonal cognition. Another important series of investigations in social cognition has been carried out by Flavell and his associates. Flavell's central construct is "role-taking" or "the general ability and disposition to 'take the role of' another person in the cognitive sense, that is, to assess his response capacities and tendencies in a given situation" (Flavell et al., 1968, p. 1).

Perspective-taking, in a literal (perceptual) sense, has been studied by Piaget and Inhelder (1948) and by Lovell (1959), who found clear-cut developmental stages from age four to age eleven. Flavell et al. (1968), however, found a gradual skill increase, rather than clear stages, over the school-age years. Clear developmental stages across middle childhood were found by Flavell et al. on cognitive role-taking tasks, involving ability to think about what other people might be thinking, or ability to suppress one's own point of view while telling a story from another's perspective.

Flavell's work has been followed by some studies which attempt to delineate more clearly certain aspects of role-taking ability, and by others which begin to enter the realm of causal analysis. As an example of the former, Selman (1971b) has delineated stages of perceptual and conceptual role-taking among preschoolers.

From a causal point of view, deficiencies in role-taking ability have been implicated in studies of delinquent behavior (Gough, 1948; Martin, 1968). Chandler (1973) has shown that with delinquents training in role-taking ability can lead to improved ability, and that such training can be based on role-playing, social interaction, and interpersonal feedback.

A fascinating study of direct relevance to the etiology of role-taking ability is that of Hollós and Cowan (1973). Their results indicate that social interaction has a significant effect on the development of role-taking ability, but not on the development of concrete logical operations. Rubin (1973) found only one factor underlying measures of concrete operations and role-taking, but his subjects did not come from varied social settings, as did those of Hollós and Cowan.

A third construct proposed as central to social cognition is that of empathy. Borke (1971) and Chandler and Greenspan (1972), in their debate over the empathic capacities of young children, have generated useful data and clarified the distinction between empathy and non-egocentric thought. Of related interest, Cooper (1970) has provided clarification of the construct of empathy from a psychoanalytic and developmental framework. Cooper's goal is to show the relationship of different stages of empathic capacity to other cognitive and affective functions.

In general, developments in the realm of social cognition promise to extend Piaget's model in a direction that will bring it into more direct, fruitful contact with psychoanalysis. The major limitation of the field from a psychoanalytic point of view is that it deals mainly with a genetic model and has not yet begun to integrate the dynamic perspective.

MORAL DEVELOPMENT

Psychoanalysts, Piaget, and, following him, Kohlberg (1969) have made contributions to a theory of moral development which may eventually lead toward a synthesis of viewpoints. Nass's (1966) review of recent theoretical developments in the psychoanalytic construct of the superego is pertinent here.

As Lustman (1968) and Hoffman (1970) have pointed out, psychoanalysis attempts to relate moral development to drive states, while cognitive theory is concerned primarily with moral judgment. Consequently, the scope of cognitive theory is narrower than that of psychoanalysis. Hoffman (1970) presents a comprehensive review of moral development theory and research. He sets the psychoanalytic and Piagetian theories of moral development in a broader philosophical perspective, relating the former to the notion of original sin and the latter to Rousseau's belief in the innate goodness of the child. From these different perspectives have flowed different research focuses and different central explanatory constructs. Psychoanalytic research has focused on the socialization process and the internalization of standards which hold in check potentially destructive drives. On the other hand, Piagetian research on morality has focused on the role of higher mental processes in moral judgment.

Hoffman's review of research findings is rich and deserving of perusal in its own right, so we shall not attempt to review it here. For our purposes, the major synthetic thrust of his article is to highlight the importance of inductive methods of parental discipline in the development of an adaptive conscience. He argues that the conflict model of traditional psychoanalysis should be complemented by a conflict-free model of moral development, according to which the superego would consist of learned standards which are the rational derivatives of the child's developing capacity for empathy.

The implications of this suggestion for the relationship between Piagetian and psychoanalytic theories of moral development are evident. Kohlberg (1969) and Selman (1971a), 1971b), among others, have argued that role-taking ability is a necessary, but not sufficient condition for the attainment of higher levels of moral judgment. There is thus a convergence of both analytic and cognitive theorists on the centrality of social cognitive-affective processes such as role-taking or empathy.

Still missing, however, are the structural principles that would explain the relationship of these cognitive and affective variables to one another and to moral behavior. Synthetic structures will emerge only from higher-order model building and from observations using the strategic advantages of both psychoanalytic and developmental descriptive methods.

2

INTEGRATION AS A THEORETICALLY ACCEPTABLE GOAL

Some Theoretical Issues

The review of the literature has shown that attempts at integration and synthesis of Piaget's cognitive psychology and psychoanalytic psychology have fallen into one or another of three categories. Many comparisons have been restricted to isolated topics or to areas common to both theories without offering a general synthesis. Of the attempts at general synthesis and integration, some have consisted simply of a cross-translation of terms, an effort with a certain, but limited, value. Finally, there have been attempts to set up parallel systems, best illustrated by Wolff's (1960) comprehensive effort. Even in the latter case, however, the transformational bridges needed to relate the two systems are not adequately articulated.

As has been noted, Wolff postulates that for the organism in a state of low drive tension, Piaget's theory of development may best explain how development occurs, while for the organism in a state of high drive tension, psychoanalytic concepts may offer the best explanation. Although Wolff's detailed analysis of the two systems is commendable, his proposal of level of drive tension as an integrating principle falls far short of an acceptable integration of the two models. Organisms do not function simply at low or very high drive states. The extremes are useful only as ideal types or as simplified models approximated in varying degress by reality. In addition, Wolff limits himself to the sensorimotor stage and does not consider either the preoperational or the operational stage of development.

What is necessary for true integration of the two systems is a model that accounts for the various shadings and gradations between the extremes during the course of development. Since the gradations in question are those of drive states, it follows that a true integration of Piaget's cognitive developmental theory with psychoanalytic theory requires a model that considers the development and functioning of the psychological system under varying conditions of drive states throughout the course of development.

One needs to ask whether drive development influences the very development of cognition. That is, can Piaget's model of cognitive development take into account the input of the drives? At the same time, it is crucial to see if psychoanalytic developmental psychology, which already incorporates the influence of the drives, can admit the variables conceptualized by Piaget. One cannot hold one set of variables constant by suggesting a model of low or high drive state and then say that only one set of propositions or only one group of variables is operative. This essentially begs the issue. In real life all systems are always "go."

Although we may anticipate that the crucial issue in integrating Piaget's developmental psychology with psychoanalytic developmental psychology is the role of the drives, we should begin by stepping back and looking more broadly at the conditions necessary for a true synthesis and integration of the two models.

First, the basic assumptions or concepts of both models must be examined to see if they are compatible. Where they are not, the theoretical reworking necessary to achieve compatibility must be clearly delineated. Ideally, this theoretical reworking will lead to a theoretical reorganization and integration of both models.

The second step is to show that the theoretical reworking leads to an integrated system of personality development, or at least a more comprehensive system than our current one. It is not necessary to propose a total integration, but to offer a system of personality development that includes, at a minimum, the lines of personality development already taken into account by Piaget's cognitive psychology and by psychoanalytic psychology. The proposed system should thus have a scope at least as broad as that of its component parts, along with a new, higher level of integration.

The next condition necessary for a true synthesis of the two models is that within the integrated system of personality all the elements, variables, or parts be functionally related to one another. In line with this, Rapaport (1959) has stipulated the minimal conditions necessary for an integrated system. It is interesting and important to note that Piaget (1968b), approaching the same issue from a different starting point, and using different terms, seems to agree with Rapaport on this.

Rapaport states that since "all behavior is that of the integral and indivisible personality," its explanation must "fit into the theory of the workings of the total personality" (p. 42).

> [It] is not that each behavior is a microcosm which reflects the macrocosm of the personality, but rather that an explanation of behavior, in order to have any claim to completeness, must specify its place within the functional and structural framework of the total personality and, therefore, must include statements about the *degree* and *kind* of involvement, in the behavior in question, of all the relevant conceptualized aspects of personality [p. 43].

Rapaport then outlines the various psychoanalytic perspectives, including the genetic, structural, adaptive, dynamic, and economic points of view, all of which, in essence, conceptualize groups of variables. His basic point is that all of these points of view are functionally related to one another. He illustrates this by showing how all of them can be dependent, independent, or intervening variables in a system. They are all interrelated, can be partially derived from one another, and together form a working system. Any change in a set of genetic variables, for example, implies structural, adaptive, dynamic, and economic changes.

The belief that parts of an integrated system must be functionally interrelated is also held by Piaget, but in a somewhat different context. Piaget's model is based on structuralist concepts, and the integrated systems to which he refers are primarily cognitive structures. For Piaget, the essential properties of structure are *wholeness*, *transformation*, and *self-regulation*. According to Piaget (1968b), in a general sense "a structure is a system of transformations. Inasmuch as it is a system and not a mere collection of elements and their properties, these transformations involve laws: the structure is preserved or enriched by the interplay of its transformation laws, which never yield results external to the system nor employ elements that are external to it" (p. 5).

Piaget differentiates *structures* from *aggregates*. He states that although structures have elements, "these elements are subordinated to laws, and it is in terms of these laws that the structure *qua* whole or system is defined" (p. 7). These "laws of composition" take precedence over the elements and over the whole itself, "which is consequent on [these] laws" (p. 9).

The transformations are those rules or laws that relate the elements of a structure to one another in such a way that the structure forms a self-regulating system. In this sense, the transformations in a structure "always engender elements that belong to [the structure] and preserve its laws" (p. 14). Thus the structure is "closed." This statement does not imply that a structure cannot take into account new sets of variables, but to the degree that it does so, it becomes an evolving, or new, structure that may then become self-regulating and closed at a new level. For Piaget, such a new structure, with an increased range of mobility, exists at a higher level of *equilibrium*.

Thus, Piaget, from a structuralist perspective, and Rapaport, from a psychoanalytic perspective, have posited similar criteria for an acceptable explanatory model of an integrated psychological system. The structuralist hope that explanatory models can be constructed that do not make reference to variables extraneous to the structure itself corresponds well with the criterion Rapaport (1959) outlines for a psychoanalytic exploratory model: that there may be many sets of variables, but they must be related to one another functionally and operate as a totality. Although Rapaport's approach is less precise than Piaget's and is not based on the logico-mathematical foundation of structuralism, as is Piaget's, his criterion also implies a self-regulating quality. His concept of functional relationships between variables is analogous to Piaget's notion of transformational laws.

As we have seen, in both psychoanalytic psychology and Piagetian psychology, the models are potentially open to development and change through the conceptualization of new variables. Both, however, demand that any proposed new variable meet the same criterion, that is, advancement into a new structure. The new sets of variables must be functioning in relation to the existing sets of variables through transformational principles. The system then remains a whole, self-regulating system, governed by the transformational principles, or, put another way, governed by the psychological processes that relate the different subsystems to one another.

It is important to mention here that Piaget's ideas are often equated with an attempt to cast structures into mathematical terms and to quantify things that other systems of psychology currently recognize as nonquantifiable. This characterization is misleading. Although Piaget has attempted to understand aspects of cognitive development in terms of their parallels to logico-mathematical formulas and thus bring his structures to a certain precision, he does not hold this as a general goal for a structuralist understanding of personality development or see these formulas as applicable to all sets of variables pertaining to human personality. In fact, he has stated that "there is, of course, an immense class of structures which are not strictly logical or mathematical, that is, whose transformations unfold in time: linguistic structures, sociological structures, psychological structures, and so on" (1968b, p. 15). For Piaget, the mathematical model fits nicely when one limits oneself to studying cognitive development since, at its higher levels of equilibrium, cognition is characterized by sets of operations that are fully reversible and integrated into holistic systems.

To return to our original point: a theoretical reworking of the discordant elements in psychoanalytic psychology and Piagetian cognitive developmental psychology will, we hope, lead to an integrated system of personality. We have just reviewed the criteria for an integrated system of personality. There must be an essential compatibility between the component subsystems at the level of basic assumptions. The new system must offer a higher level of integration than do its components considered separately; to put it another way, it must have an explanatory scope at least equal to the sum of the scopes of its component subsystems. Finally, the two sets of variables derived from the subsystems must be functionally related to one another within the new system; that is, the transformational bridges must be clear.

Steps Toward Integration

It should be mentioned at the outset that successful integration of the two systems does not require that they be compatible in all ways. The two systems must, however, fit together in such a way that functional relationships between the sets of variables they consider can be established. For example, that Piaget does not consider the dynamic unconscious or the effect of the drives on cognition in no way makes his system of reasoning incompatible with or not useful for psychoanalysis.

In other words, ideally compatible theories do not cover the same phenomena. The most useful models to integrate are those that attempt to account for different sets of variables, different lines of development, and different aspects of human functioning.

Piaget's theory of cognitive development and the psychoanalytic theory of development present models that focus on essentially different aspects of human development. In line with the above, we need not be concerned with whether there are differences in their views of the same behavior; we need be concerned only with differences in theoretical approach that prevent the establishment of functional relationships between the two models' variables. It is not useful to argue whether behavior is motivated by drives, as suggested by psychoanalysis, or by natural tendencies toward achieving equilibrium (the system of *assimilation* and *accommodation*), as suggested by Piaget. Both assumptions may be compatible, but each may be relevant to a different aspect of development: one for emotional development, one for impersonal cognition. Each may help explain a different aspect of behavior.

It is necessary, however, to relate these different assumptions and explanations functionally rather than leave them as parallel but unrelated constructs. The notion of binding and neutralization, for example, may be one way to relate the drives to the functions at the disposal of the ego for the process of assimilation and accommodation. But this is only one example. We must first specifically identify these different assumptions, and then provide the theoretical reworking needed to form the transformational link.

Our goal is to create a more comprehensive psychoanalytic system by including within it, as a subsystem, Piaget's cognitive psychology. We shall thus ignore those elements of Piaget's theory that are extraneous to his major findings. While our goal is to enlarge the psychoanalytic explanatory framework, no assumption is made that the reverse process might not yield fruitful results. It will be seen, in fact, that Piaget's basic concepts, such as level of equilibrium, are central to an integrated approach. The reworking of these concepts to make them applicable to "psychodynamic" variables will prove central to our effort.

3

THE TWO BASIC MODELS AND THEIR SETS OF VARIABLES: AN OVERVIEW

The psychoanalytic model can best be understood in the context of its various metapsychological points of view—genetic, dynamic, structural, adaptive, and economic. Each of these points of view helps us to understand different but related aspects of psychological functioning. Together, they attempt to formulate a cohesive, integrated picture of the multiple determinants of behavior. The psychoanalytic model postulates that behavior results from multiple determinants, and that one cannot understand behavior by looking at any single variable for explanation. Each psychoanalytic perspective, therefore, conceptualizes a group of variables that, among other groups of variables, determines human behavior and human experience.

Briefly, the *genetic* point of view attempts to understand how past experience—in particular, the interaction of innate givens, maturation, and experience with significant others and the environment—forms the basis for human behavior. The *dynamic* point of view, on the other hand, focuses on the drives as determinants of behavior and studies the relationships between drives, defenses, and certain substructures of the ego and superego. The *structural* perspective views behavior as the result of interaction between the different structures of the mind: the id, ego, and superego, as well as the substructures of the ego and superego. More specifically, it sees behavior as a result of the ego's synthetic and integrating function operating on the conflicts generated by drive-affect constellations arising from the id, with prohibitions based on superego structures and the demands of external reality. The *adaptive* point of view attempts to understand behavior in terms of the relationship between the ego and the environment inasmuch as the ego exercises a reality-adaptive function. Finally, the *economic* point of view looks at behavior in terms of its energic determinants and examines its quantitative dimensions. While this point of view has been a point of controversy within psychoanalysis, its potential utility stems from its effort to come to grips with certain issues untouched by the other four points of view.

In a broad sense, the psychoanalytic model attempts to conceptualize human experience and behavior by taking into account both unconscious and conscious determinants. Behavior is seen in the context of a developing human being who enters the world with certain innate givens and evolves as a result of the interaction of these givens with early experiences of the environment. Aspects of relationships with important others become internalized and further develop the nucleus of the ego and superego organizations. Developing drive-affect organizations also are related to these internalized self- and object representations, and these entities form the basis of substructures of the ego and superego. The developing structural organization continuously synthesizes elements of itself, drive-affect expressions, experiential factors, and maturational factors.

The psychodynamic model deals with cognition, in part, in its conceptualization of secondary-process thinking and in concepts such as the *conflict-free sphere of the ego* and the *autonomous ego apparatuses.* These concepts permit some understanding of the relationships among unconscious phenomena, dynamic process, and cognition, but they do not provide a complete theory of cognitive development and organization.

In contrast to the psychoanalytic model, Piaget does not consider to any degree certain realms of experience. His primary study has been of the way the ego *acts on* the external environment to develop cognitive structures. Unconcerned with the vicissitudes of internal experience, such as those generated by alterations in drive or affect states, tensions, and relationships between internal self- and object representations and their derivative structures, Piaget has focused his attention on external stimuli pertaining to the impersonal world in order to understand how the organism interacts with the environment and develops specific internal cognitive structures.

Piaget's narrower focus derives not so much from a theoretical divergence with psychoanalysis, but from the external environments each model has been designed to study. In contrast to psychoanalysis, which studies the human, affect-laden environment (in all its variation and unpredictability), Piaget studies the non-affect-laden, often nonhuman environment. His concepts of conservation, for example, are not demonstrated in terms of relationships with or properties of human beings, but in terms of properties of water, clay, and other inanimate objects. This narrower field of study has permitted Piaget to generate a highly precise model of cognition.

The Psychoanalytic and Piagetian Models of Thought and Intelligence

The limitations of psychoanalytic understanding of cognition are especially clear if we consider how thought is used in the psychoanalytic model and in the Piagetian model. The ego structure in the psychoanalytic model is a system of operations similar in some structural respects to what Piaget would describe as the system at the foundation of *intelligent behavior.*

In psychoanalytic psychology, however, thought is simply the capacity for representation. While the process of thinking or thought in a dynamic sense involves complex mental activities, such as trial action, anticipation, and memory, a thought or, perhaps more appropriately, an idea is, in its most elementary form, a representation. This is what Piaget calls the *semiotic function.* In the psychoanalytic model, thought evolves early in infancy when the drive object is not available at a time of heightened drive state. Freud (1911) held that in the absence of gratification from the drive object, the infant creates a hallucinatory image of wish fulfillment, which is the precursor or the foundation of thought.

Whether or not the very young infant is capable of this hallucinatory image, and what the relationship between forming such an image and drive tension is, are questions not yet resolved by research. With regard to the former, as Fraiberg (1959) has noted, the infant's inability to construct a mental representation by evocative memory does not preclude the possibility of some less differentiated, less actively constructed mental imagery such as *recognition memory*. Similarly, the notion of hallucinatory images does not demand Piaget's constructive *evocative memory*, since the hallucination is not an active construction, but a response to internal stimulation.[1] Without identifying Freud's comments on hallucinatory wish fulfillment with the capacity for a well-organized internal image, we may consider that for psychoanalysis the infant's capacity to represent some undifferentiated experience of pleasure in the absence of the drive object marks the beginning of thought. Such thinking becomes organized as the infant or young child becomes capable of organized mental representation.

In the psychoanalytic model, then, the drives may be discharged through experiences of gratification with the drive object or, in the absence of the drive object, through affect channels into the body. Or, through the process of delay and detour, they may become related to mental representations or thoughts. The concept of mental representation, of course, broadens during the course of development. Thought may be considered one subspecies of mental representation. Initially thought represents the wish and is heavily invested with drive derivatives.

It must be emphasized that thought in psychoanalytic theory is conceptualized as an aspect of representation. The psychoanalytic model does *not* consider thought as an organized system of intelligent behavior. It does, however, consider aspects of intelligent behavior in a variety of other contexts. Hartmann's (1939) consideration of the adaptational aspects of ego functions in terms of the ego's relationships to the environment addresses aspects of secondary-process thinking, including the ego's capacity for means-ends relationships. The concept of secondary-process thinking itself implies the capacity for logical

[1] It should be pointed out that the relationship between internal stimulation and the formation of an image is far from clear.

processes in accord with *the reality principle.* In addition, the idea of an organizing and integrating ego function suggests certain capacities to synthesize discrepant inputs and in this sense implies a kind of "intelligent" functioning. Psychoanalysis thus does consider aspects of what Piaget would call intelligent behavior.

To consider further the difference in focus of the psychoanalytic orientation toward thinking from that of Piaget, a more detailed consideration of psychoanalytic contributions is in order. Rapaport, in his well-known work on the pathology of thought (1951b), presents the building blocks for a theory of thinking. He outlines the primary model of thought, in which delay of gratification by motor action "becomes the cradle of 'conscious experience' " (p. 690). Consciousness is conceptualized as a cathecting of the memory traces of an experience. In addition to object-directed discharge into action, there is also affective discharge into the body's motor and secretory systems. Ideas are the qualitative aspects and affective charge is the quantitative aspect of the drive representation. The representation of both affects and ideas implies the beginning of psychic structure. Rapaport also observes that aspects of structures that channel affective discharge and the structural precursors of memory and ideas are in part related to constitutionally given individual differences. These *inborn structures* do not necessarily enter into conflict and form the nucleus of what is conceptualized as the *conflict-free ego sphere.* These structures are also referred to as *ego apparatuses* (p. 693).

In the primary process, when there is delay of discharge due to structural or environmental conditions, drive cathexes investing early representations are freely mobile and shift from one to another. *Free mobility* is characteristic of the primary process and makes for the displacements or condensations that contribute to the vividness necessary for the hallucinatory images of dreams or other psychic processes.

In addition to the displacements or condensations that make shifts of energy possible along the memories invested with similar drive cathexes, as experience develops and drives differentiate into partial drives, a broader network of potential interrelationships is possible. An experiential system of more differentiated and discrete ideas becomes superimposed on the earlier, more drive-determined system. Experience thus becomes more important. Organization of memory becomes connected by reality experiences—experiences in "space, time, contiguity, similarity" (p. 697). The drive cathexes investing this new system are relatively more bound in comparison with the more free-floating, mobile cathexes characterizing primary-process, drive-oriented thinking. This form of thinking is referred to as a secondary process.

Rapaport, however, has not, nor has psychoanalysis in general, developed a theory to delineate the steps between the early drive determination of the organization of ideas (*primary process*) and the reality-experience organization of ideas informing the *secondary process*. Although aspects of the relationship between the drives and thinking have been delineated, the steps in the structural differentiation from primary-process to secondary-process thinking have not been delineated. Nor does secondary-process thinking remain a stable entity. It develops from premature forms to more advanced thought.

Piaget's theory of intelligent behavior does delineate in a stepped progression the continuum of thinking from primitive to more advanced forms. His model, however, does not consider those primitive forms of thinking in which drives and affects determine the organization of ideas. Our integration will therefore occur around the psychoanalytic model of the drives and Piaget's model of structural differentiation of intelligent behavior.

As indicated above, Rapaport (1951b) considers the vicissitudes of consciousness in terms of attention-cathexes, the relationship between the capacity for delay and the development of affects, and the more general relationships between the capacity for controlling the drives and the development of the differentiated affects, drive derivatives, and energy distributions that make possible the ego's eventual relative autonomy. He points out that "thought-organization . . . cannot be understood unless we assume that the process here described repeats itself in a hierarchic series, controlling organizations thus being layered over each other" (p. 701). He develops the idea that this hierarchical series, as it relates more and more to reality demands, is invested with greater amounts of neutralized energy; as it relates more to drive derivatives and the mobile primary process, it is invested more with unneutralized or drive cathexes.[2]

According to Rapaport, "In [the] reality-testing function, consciousness—that is the distribution of attention-cathexes—reached a remarkable refinement, much of which is still little understood theoretically" (p. 702). It is with such refinements that a more complete theory of cognitive development must concern itself and where Piaget's findings may make important contributions. In this regard, it is of interest that Rapaport describes intellectualization as thinking using drive energy in a relatively unconflicted manner; he thus sees it as contributing to the autonomy of the ego in relationship to the drives. In contrast, rationalization occurs when secondary-process thought is used for compromise and prohibited drive goals are pursued together with superego and reality demands. Rapaport observes, however, that we know only a little about the process of intellectualization, again indirectly highlighting the need for a complete theory of cognition.

Rapaport himself presents some specifics of a general model:

> The thought-organization of the secondary process . . . crystallizes in the conflict between reality- and drive-demands. . . . it is built also on constitutional equipments, such as memory-capacity, perceptual systems, stimulus-barriers, and general endowment. By apperceiving external and internal stimuli, it subserves the ego's internalizing of the conflict between reality and drives. . . . The development of the ego's motivational and defensive dynamics shapes the development of thought-organization. We have assumed that the organization of cathectic energies is a hierarchy in which the forces of the basic energy-distribution are controlled by a superimposed one arising from it, which in turn gives rise to another set of forces which are then similarly controlled, and so on; we assume that thought-organization also follows this hierarchic lay-

[2] Because the value of the economic point of view and the energy concepts are debatable, it is important to point out that although Rapaport used the concept of neutralized energy, his idea of a hierarchical series of structures involving greater degrees of binding and greater capacity for delay does not rest on the idea of energy transformations and, in fact, is in some respects an alternative model.

> ering. It should be noted, however, that these controls are by no means a one-way affair. The "controlled" motivations closer to the base of the hierarchy are still at work, and may trigger and activate the "controlling" motivations. Thus the control is mutual, and no total autonomy exists.
>
> This is also true of thought-organization. We know empirically that it may be repressive, that is, tend to exclude memories and relationships, thus keeping energy-distributions at an equilibrium; or it may be intellectualizing, that is, acquisitive, thus keeping an equilibrium by overextending itself in binding cathectic-energies. We also know that the symbols, displacements, and condensations in dreams are forms of thought-organization corresponding to drive motivations; though ego-motivations also may be represented, particularly in the secondary elaboration of the manifest dream-content [1951b, pp. 703-704].

Rapaport's general model shows the relationship between primitive drive-oriented thought and later secondary-process thought. There is a hierarchy that at one end is closely connected with reality and at the other works according to the rules of the primary process. Thought must be understood from both the reality-adapted component and those components that play a role in motivational and defensive dynamics. Psychoanalysis, as we know, has heavily emphasized certain features of thought processes, particularly motivational and defensive dynamics, and has outlined some of the characteristics of the secondary process and some of the variables that must be taken into account for a full understanding of it. What remains to be developed is a fuller model of cognition, or secondary-process thinking, that is consistent with what is already known about the drive and drive-defense aspects of thought.

In his discussion of concepts, Rapaport indicates a direction for the development of such a model. He even refers to Piaget to help conceptualize the reality-adaptive characteristics of thought. He does not, however, offer a theoretical framework to tie Piaget's reality adaptiveness to the drive organization of thinking.

In discussing memory, anticipation, attention, and concentration, as well as daydreaming, preconscious mental processes, and creative thinking, Rapaport continually highlights the multiple determinants of these processes—the drive determinants—and the need for further understanding the reality-adaptive determinants. He comments, for instance, that in creative thinking energic considerations alone do not provide a complete explanation and that structural factors must be taken into account.

In regard to communications, Rapaport's formulations are worth repeating:

> (1) Communication enriches the store of experiences and thereby counteracts ego-limitation. (2) Psychic life is not a one-way avenue in which defenses limit communications: communications may also combat the deleterious effects of defenses. . . . (3) The enrichment by experiences—originating, in the course of communication, in external perceptions and introspective observations—furthers the differentiation of ego-interests (strivings, feelings, attitudes, and other such motivations) and thereby contributes to the process of "binding" drive-energies. (4) This increased variability of ego-motivations renders memories more easily cathected, and thus more available for use in solving problems and reaching gratification. (5) All defenses—though we know this definitely only about repression—tend to encroach upon the thought-content at its weakest point. . . . Communication, by creating ever-new relations between ideas and casting light on relationships between relationships, combats the spread of the ego-limiting defenses. (6) It provides new percepts and resuscitates old ones; thus it also makes for an integration of isolated experiences, and further integration into broader or new units. In this process considerable cathectic saving is usually achieved, accompanied by relief, insight or discovery. Communication enhances the "synthetic function of the ego" [1951b, pp. 727-728].

Rapaport's statement on communication dramatically presents the balance he emphasizes in his hierarchical concept of psychic structure and thinking. Reality-adaptive communication, he shows, can have a positive effect and interact with dynamic defensive forces. His comments on communication, while having obvious implications for psychotherapy, also have important implications for our discussion of the development of a psychoanalytic theory of cognition. External experience will be seen, as outlined by Rapaport, to be constantly interacting with and providing impetus for further differentiation of existing structures.

In summary, Rapaport presents a general model that at its

base has the drives and in its middle has detours in which drive energies are controlled, modulated, and eventually transformed into neutralized energy. This neutralized energy can then represent the interest of the ego in its reality-adapted matrix. Rapaport focuses on the dynamic aspects of this general model. The dimensions of thought, such as awareness, consciousness, memory, creativity, pathology, and concept formation, are viewed in the context of their dynamic relationships. Yet Rapaport continually reminds us of our need to understand better the process of "binding," as well as aspects of certain substructures of the ego that relate directly to the reality-adapted aspects of the environment. Rapaport thus highlights the need for further development of our understanding of the ego's relationship to the environment through careful consideration of constitutional givens and the structural differentiations underlying the development of those ego substructures that are related to secondary-process thinking.

Rapaport, like Piaget, believes that thought develops independently as an autonomous ego structure as well as in relation to the drives, and that independent and drive-related aspects of thinking need to be seen on a continuum.[3] Rapaport's hierarchical model does not permit an artificial dichotomy from one level to another, but implies a continuous, gradually changing relationship between multiple determinants of any given behavioral phenomenon. Different sets of rules of thinking can be useful only in the abstract to present the extremes of a hypothetical model. In reality, there are always drives, affects, and ego-adapted aspects to any given process. A model must be developed that can show how these different forces interact throughout development.

Two additional works that merit discussion in considering the history of the psychoanalytic approach to thinking are Nunberg's consideration of "The Synthetic Function of the Ego"

[3] It should be pointed out, however, that in considering Piaget's ideas, Rapaport (1951a), like Wolff (1960), indicates that not only does he see drive-determined thought at the bottom of the hierarchy, and autonomous, deductive, reality-adapted thought at the top, but he would set up a dichotomy, with different rules for thought depending on where in the hierarchy the thought processes are.

(1931) and Hartmann's *Ego Psychology and the Problem of Adaptation* (1939). Both Nunberg and Hartmann consider aspects of the ego's relationship to the environment in terms of its capacities for synthesis and for adaptation. Their discussions, like Rapaport's, indicate a direction for psychoanalytic reasoning in constructing a model of cognition. Although these two works are not concerned purely with cognition, their considerations do create a bridge to Piaget's interest in intelligent behavior.

Nunberg, for example, comments on the ego's synthetic function in "assimilating" alien elements from within and without (p. 123). Nunberg relates this tendency to assimilate to a basic human tendency, which Freud referred to as Eros: the tendency to unite, or bind. The tendency for assimilation is interesting, since it relates to one of Piaget's key concepts in the development of cognitive structure: assimilation, or taking in. Interestingly, Nunberg refers to the *need for causality* as a sublimated version of the child's reproductive instinct, and, more generally, of what Freud referred to as Eros. Thus, early in the development of psychoanalytic theory a basic process of assimilation was hypothesized, similar to the process of assimilation hypothesized by Piaget to be at the core of the development of cognitive structures. It will be observed, however, that while Nunberg uses the same word as Piaget does, he talks about the process of assimilation in a broad context as being an aspect of the synthetic function of the ego. He thereby lays a foundation for relating Piaget's observations to psychoanalytic observations, but does not carefully spell out the synthetic processes, particularly the assimilatory processes, of the ego. Again, the developmental psychology of Piaget may provide fruitful additions to a more specific delineation of how certain substructures and basic processes of the ego develop and function.

The similarity of this basic process in both models—assimilation—is also important from another perspective. Later we shall show that the concept of *multiple function* (see Waelder, 1936) is extremely important in integrating Piaget's cognitive psychology with psychoanalytic psychology. Just as Nunberg elaborates the idea that assimilation is the basic process of the ego that functions at all boundaries—that is, in relation to contents arriving from the soma as well as from the external environment—it will likewise be hypothesized that the assimilatory processes considered by Piaget, which he discusses in relation to external stimuli only, may also be assumed to function in relation to aliments from the interior of the body. Thus, this ego process functions in multiple ways, at a variety of boundaries, in the context of a variety of stimulus inputs.

In his discussion of the synthetic function, Nunberg suggests that it is involved in more than assimilating: its role is also "to create from this union a new living being" (p. 129). That is, once stimuli have been taken in, a new organization is formed. To illustrate this, he shows how defenses work in, for example, phobias and obsessional neuroses. This aspect of synthesis goes beyond the process of assimilation (taking in) and the process of reorganization (attempting the best adaptation to what is taken in) and comes close to Piaget's concept of accommodation: the accommodation of cognitive structures to new, assimilated aliments.

Nunberg further points out that "where the instinct has undergone repression the ego also remains fixated" (p. 130) and a special type of accommodation may occur. In all symptom formation, therefore, a part of the ego regresses to a lower stage of development consistent with the fixation point of the instincts. "This procedure causes . . . a part of the ego itself to become 'foreign to the ego.' This unconscious portion of the ego then goes on to develop magical qualities. The magic of the more or less unconscious ego and its unconscious morality uphold the symptoms from the ego's side, allying themselves with the repressed impulses of the id. Thus the symptom becomes the vehicle of instinctual demands that are not ego-syntonic and therefore are repressed, and also of a part of the ego that is not adapted to reality" (p. 130). Undergoing repression and being maintained at some distance from the conscious portion of the ego, certain aspects of the ego do not have the opportunity to become adapted to reality.

This point will be seen to be important later, when we integrate Piaget's cognitive psychology with psychoanalytic ego psychology. To anticipate: cognitive structures develop in a maturational sequence that is in part dependent on biological maturation, but is also in part dependent on continuous interaction of the external environmental aliments that represent reality with already-existing cognitive structures. In the case of repression, aspects of the ego and instincts—that is, functions and stimulus inputs—may not be exposed to certain reality-adapted ego substructures and therefore may have a pattern of assimilation and accommodation somewhat different from, or relatively walled off from, reality-adapted processes. As will be seen, this does not interfere with the development of cognitive substructures, but it does make for a different kind of cognition related to what we shall term *the internal boundary of the ego.*

It is interesting to note also that in a secondary elaboration of symptoms following repression, what is available to consciousness through compromise formation becomes elaborated through a certain secondary-process reasoning. It is as if the cognitive substructures of the ego have, through the development of compromise formation, some stimulus nutriment available that they take advantage of in forming the secondary elaborations. These often are not reality-adapted, or "logical" in the sense of being adapted to reality, because the ego's cognitive substructures are dealing, in a sense, with "faulty" information. What are available to the conscious portions of the ego are not accurate perceptions of the environment, but perceptions of the environment heavily invested with drive derivatives as part of the compromise formation, or perceptions colored through processes of projection.

Nunberg (1931) goes on to point out that when repression is lifted in psychoanalytic treatment, the links between the unconscious and conscious ideas are re-established. The synthetic function is thus enhanced. In this context he states, "In the light of what has already been said about psychic productivity we shall view the final act of conscious thinking, the comprehension of general relations, the forming of concept, etc., as a synthetic act" (p. 133). He then shows how in the various neuroses and psychoses there is some compromise in optimal synthesis, although at the same time they represent attempts at synthetic activity. In speaking about comprehension of general relations and formation of concepts as a synthetic act, Nunberg comes very close to relating the process of synthesis to what Piaget talks about more generally in terms of intelligent behavior.

The foundation for an integration of psychoanalysis with Piaget's cognitive psychology has been laid by Nunberg. The concept of the synthetic function, however, is only a preliminary step. Although the synthetic function is close to aspects of what Piaget calls intelligent behavior, Nunberg does not fully elaborate on the developmental steps of the synthetic function, its organization at different ages, and its relationship to constitutional variables, environmental experience, and other issues involved in the development of psychic structure. As Nunberg himself hints, a more specific theory of reality adaptation is necessary.

In *Ego Psychology and the Problem of Adaptation* (1939), Hartmann also provides a basis for the integration of Piaget's cognitive psychology with psychoanalysis. Hartmann points out:

> Not every adaptation to the environment, or every learning and maturation process, is a conflict. I refer to the development *outside of conflict* of perception, intention, object comprehension, thinking, language, recall-phenomena, productivity, to the well-known phases of motor development, grasping, crawling, walking, and to the maturation and learning processes implicit in all these, and many others. . . . I propose that we adopt the provisional term *conflict-free ego sphere* for that ensemble of functions which at any given time exert their effects outside the region of mental conflicts [pp. 8-9].

Although he admits a lack of systematic knowledge about such matters, Hartmann assumes an autonomous intelligence factor that, "as an independent variable, codetermines the choice and success of the defensive process. . . . Learning to think and learning in general are independent biological functions which exist alongside, and in part independent of, instinctual drives and defenses. Ordered thinking is always directly or indirectly reality-oriented" (p. 14).

Hartmann further elaborates:

> In our clinical work we observe daily how differences in intellectual development, in motor development, and so on, affect the child's coping with conflicts and how this in turn influences intel-

> lectual and motor development. Such observations establish descriptively the interaction of the conflict-sphere with other ego functions. This is an *actual interaction*—that is to say, this too is an instance of the overdetermination of a mental process. Yet . . . we may also speak about two *aspects* of the ego process, since, for instance, it is often one and the same process which we study first in its relation to the internal conflict and then in its dependence and effect on the apparatuses of reality mastery. . . . Our vantage point determines which aspect of the process will assume importance: the two relationships pertain to two different points of view [p. 16].

Like Nunberg, Hartmann establishes a basis for considering aspects of the ego that deal with reality and adaptation as well as with instinctual demands and defense. He and Nunberg both point out that the very same processes deal with different stimulus inputs. What is missing from Hartmann's and Nunberg's considerations, however, is a more detailed examination of how the ego's reality-adapted processes develop over time and are organized at different hierarchical levels. Also missing are the specific ways in which the same functions serve defense and reality adaptation. Although Hartmann begins to elaborate a general model for understanding reality adaptation, it is from Piaget's model of intelligent behavior that we shall extrapolate the very specific hierarchy of the functions Hartmann refers to and demonstrate their developmental sequence.

Hartmann (1939) goes on to indicate why thinking is important in relation not only to reality adaptation but to dealing with the instincts. He points out that "the more differentiated an organism is, the more independent from immediate environmental stimulation it becomes" (p. 59).

> Causal thinking (in relation to perception of space and time), the creation and use of means-end relations, and particularly the turning of thinking back upon the self, liberate the individual from being compelled to react to the immediate stimulus. The intellect understands and invents, and perhaps its function is even more to pose than to solve problems . . . ; it decides whether the individual will accept an event as it is, or will change it by his intervention . . . ; it seeks to control and steer the repetitive character of instincts and instinctual drives; it creates derivative needs, it turns means into ends and ends into means. Here we cannot always separate the various functions of the intellect (understanding, judgment, reasoning, etc.) . . . nor can we discuss their development, their re-

lation to perception (as in reality testing), to language, and so on [p. 60].

Hartmann further discusses intelligent behavior in relation to its multiple functions, and particularly in relation to enhancing the flexibility of the personality to deal with the instincts. He proclaims, as Nunberg did, that "Defenses (typically) not only keep thoughts, images, and instinctual drives out of consciousness, but also prevent their assimilation by means of thinking" (p. 63). He then describes how the interpretative process in psychoanalysis re-establishes these links and permits causal relationships to be reconstituted, thus permitting thinking or reality adaptation to occur.

Hartmann considers the concept of "rationality" as an organizing function (p. 71). Rationality in this sense takes into account irrationality and highlights how knowledge can include insight into its own functioning. The *superordinate organizing function of intelligence* is presented by Hartmann as an important regulating function of the ego that takes into account all the boundaries at which the ego operates—external reality, instinctual demands, etc. As we shall see, Piaget may offer a specific model of developmental processes that can delineate aspects of this superordinate organizing function of intelligence.

In his final chapter on "Ego Apparatuses [and] Autonomous Ego Development," Hartmann further underscores the necessity for a complete model of how the ego's substructures that deal with reality adaptation are developed and hierarchically organized. "This maturation," he states, "must be recognized as an independent factor in addition to learning by experience, by memory, by exercise, by automatization, by identification, and by other mechanisms" (p. 103). He then suggests, "It might be useful to distinguish three kinds of developmental processes: those which occur without any essential and specific influence of the external world; those which are coordinated to typical experiences (that is, which are triggered by average expectable environmental situations, as already discussed); and finally, those which depend upon atypical experiences" (pp. 103-104).

Hartmann points out that the choice of defense mechanisms is in part constitutionally determined and in part influenced by the maturation and exercise of the apparatuses of the conflict-free sphere. "It is possible that the developmental rhythm of these apparatuses is one of the determinants of the sequence in which defense methods arise" (p. 106). In relation to this, he stresses that "no satisfactory definition of the concepts of ego strength and ego weakness is feasible without taking into account the nature and maturational stage of the ego apparatuses which underlie intelligence, will, and action" (p. 107).

Here, in the concluding chapter of his book, is Hartmann's most forceful statement of the need for a more complete model of intelligent behavior. We may, as he indicates, come closer to solving the problem that Freud originally raised about choice of defense by conceptualizing defense in a more general context that takes into account the maturation of ego apparatuses. A complete model of reality adaptation would thus involve a complete model of development and organization of defenses, intelligence, will, and action—in other words, a model of ego adaptability or flexibility.

4

PRINCIPLES OF INTEGRATION: AN OVERVIEW

In attempting to integrate Piaget's theory of intelligent behavior with the psychoanalytic model of personality organization, it will be interesting to observe if Piaget's model is applicable not only to the ego's boundary with the environment, but also to the ego's boundaries with the id and the superego. Do the principles of intelligent behavior help us to understand ego differentiation, not only in relation to environmental adaptation, but also in relation to the internal world of drives, affects, and internalized self- and object representations?

The elucidation of organizing principles may enhance our understanding of the multiple ways in which the ego functions. Although admittedly speculative, it is nonetheless possible that principles evinced in studying the ego's relationships to reality will help us understand the ego's relationship to inner stimuli and to the other structures comprising the mental apparatus. The concept of *multiple function* postulates that the ego's substructures have several simultaneous functions. Thus, a substructure dealing with external reality, which is organized along certain principles, may well deal, along the lines of these same principles, with the unconscious world of drives and affects, the world of internalized representations, and other substructures of the ego and superego.

We could view Piaget's model in a number of different ways in our attempt to integrate it with psychoanalytic psychology. On the one hand, we could view cognition as described by Piaget as a relatively autonomous ego function or as one of the apparatuses of primary autonomy. In this conceptualization cognition would be similar to memory or to other areas with a strong biological-maturational thrust to them and a certain degree of primary autonomy from the drives. Cognition, as an apparatus of primary autonomy, could then become secondarily involved in conflict and be influenced by the various drive-affect defensive substructures or other internal experiences. Our task would then be to see how this relatively autonomous structure becomes involved in conflict.

At the other extreme, we could view cognition as an ego function derived from conflict. As with all aspects of ego functioning, while there would be a certain independent biological or maturational base, this would be related from the start to the vicissitudes of the drives, affects, and internal object relations.

As a third option, we could take a position somewhere in between, viewing cognition, like other substructures of the ego, both as having a certain biological base and a certain maturational sequence, and as being affected by certain nonaffective drive-related aspects of the environment. At the same time, we could view this substructure of the ego as deriving certain characteristic and functional properties from drive-affect defensive substructures throughout development. Its relationship to conflict and internalized object relations would then be essential.

In taking this position, we would differ from Piaget, who views cognition as evolving from inborn maturational factors in interaction with the environment. The activity of the organism on the environment is central to his thinking. Thus, to oversimplify, Piaget sees biological or maturational factors and external stimuli from the impersonal and social environment as forming the basis of internal structures. Through the activity of the maturing organism these structures continue to reach higher and higher levels of organization. In a sense, Piaget considers only one kind of stimulus nutriment, whereas the ego substructure dealing with cognition may arise from multiple types of stimulus nutriments. We would expand his model and say that in addition to what are essentially nonaffective stimuli from the external environment, there are two other sets of stimuli: unconscious and partly conscious drive-affect stimuli (internal stimuli) and drive-colored, affect-laden external stimuli (interpersonal relationships in the outside world). Although

Piaget posits social interaction as a factor in cognitive development, he has not considered to a sufficient degree the affect-laden aspects of social interaction as they relate to structure building.

Our model would thus view cognition as developing in the same manner that any substructure of the ego develops: in relation to a certain biological-maturational unfolding, vis-à-vis the input of stimuli from drives and affects, internalized object relation, the non-affect-laden environment, and the affect-laden drive-colored environment. It is this relationship to the various stimuli that needs to be charted for a full integration of Piaget's cognitive psychology with psychoanalytic psychology.

The task, then, is to show how Piaget's theory of cognitive development can offer further understanding of the multiple determination of behavior. Genetic, dynamic, structural, adaptative, and economic perspectives focus attention on certain variables that may in a relative sense determine behavior. While a cognitive perspective would have certain things in common with the genetic, structural, and adaptative perspectives, we postulate the cognitive perspective presented here to be a potentially separate psychoanalytic perspective in that it would offer a unique focus and would complement the existing perspectives in understanding the multiple determination of behavior.

To add another perspective to psychoanalytic theory, we must satisfy two criteria specified by Rapaport (1959). The first is that any new perspective must be capable of being related to each existing perspective in the same way that the existing perspectives are related to each other. The functional relationship between all the perspectives must be clear. The second criterion is that to be justified a new perspective must create a unique focus and add another dimension to the understanding of the multiple determination of behavior.

In this section we have indicated in a preliminary way the potential uniqueness of a cognitive perspective in psychoanalysis. This follows from the fact that psychoanalysis presently lacks a full theory of cognition as intelligent behavior or a method of explaining the organization and development of the kinds of thinking that involve mental representations.

To satisfy Rapaport's first criterion—that our cognitive perspective can be related to the existing perspectives of psychoanalysis—we shall first consider Piaget's cognitive model in more detail to show its major assumptions and principles and to show in a broad sense that they are compatible with psychoanalytic postulates. We shall then do the same for the psychoanalytic model. With the psychoanalytic model, however, we shall tease out those areas where incompatibilities exist and underscore them as the reasons why the two models have not been integrated more fully in the past. Piaget's model cannot at the current time take into account dynamic considerations—that is, considerations that deal with derivatives of the drives and affects and internalized object relations. Subsequent sections will therefore focus on integrating Piaget's theory of cognitive development with the dynamic perspective of psychoanalysis.

5

PIAGET'S PSYCHOLOGY AND EPISTEMOLOGY AND THEIR RELATIONSHIP TO THE PSYCHOANALYTIC MODEL

AN INTERACTIONIST VIEW

Piaget, widely renowned as a child or developmental psychologist, considers himself primarily a genetic epistemologist (Flavell, 1963). His goal is to account for the progressive development of human knowledge. Piaget differs from someone like Gesell, who may be considered a prototype of the child psychologist who describes behavior characteristics of children at various developmental ages (Hunt, 1969). Although Piaget also does this to a limited extent, his goal is not to describe age-appropriate norms, but to show that despite variability in children's abilities at given ages, there is a predictable developmental sequence. For Piaget, the maturation of genetically determined abilities is only one of the causal factors in development. One must also take into account the interaction between the organism and the environment. These subject-object interactions shape the course of adaptation, which in the human subject, takes the form of intelligence, a term equivalent to intelligent behavior (Furth, 1969). Flavell (1963) notes that Piaget considers the study of ontogenetic development a valuable field in its own right and an essential prerequisitie for an understanding of adult behavior. But, above all, his developmental approach makes possible certain types of explanations of and solutions to fundamental epistemological problems.

Piaget sees intelligence as adaptation, and his genetic epistemology is an investigation of the progressive development of knowledge, conceptualized as a relationship between the organism and the environment. In terms of philosophical epistemology Piaget stands between Plato's conception of the acquisition of knowledge as a process of recollection of innate "pure ideas" and Aristotle's view, shared by the empiricists, that all knowledge is obtained through the senses. While Piaget does not involve himself in the metaphysical aspects of epistemology—that is, he does not inquire into the essence of knowledge—he does take up the issue of nativism versus empiricism. Piaget does not consider himself either a nativist or an empiricist; nor as a psychologist, does he see himself as a Gestalt theorist or an associationist (behaviorist). As he points out, the empiricists assume that objectivity is a given and that the only function of intelligence is to copy it: "But this passive interpretation of the act of knowledge is in fact contradicted at all levels of development and, particularly, at the sensorimotor and prelinguistic levels of cognitive adaptation and intelligence. Actually, in order to know objects, the subject must act upon them, and therefore transform them: he must displace, connect, combine, take apart, and reassemble them" (1970, p. 704).

Similarly unsatisfactory to Piaget is the nativist position held by certain Gestalt psychologists and by certain linguists and psycholinguists (see Chomsky, 1957). Gestalt theorists attribute the origin of knowledge to the "extension, to wider and wider areas, of the 'forms' initially governing the world of perceptions" (Piaget and Inhelder, 1966, p. 49). According to them, the regulatory laws discovered in perceptual functioning, such as the laws of closure, proximity, and figure-ground, also serve as the basis of conceptual intellectual functioning. Piaget (1961), however, has conducted extensive studies of perceptual processes, in addition to his investigations of intellectual development. He has concluded, as we shall see in more detail below, that the concepts characteristic of intellectual functioning are based on a process of abstraction, not from perceptual data, but from actions performed on objects. In addition, perceptual activities function in a less precisely controlled manner than do intellectual operations; in fact, at about the age of seven perception undergoes an increase in the accuracy of its functioning by coming under the control of the intellect.

In contemporary linguistics and psycholinguistics, nativism is represented by Chomsky (1957) and his followers, who attribute all knowledge of linquistic forms and transformational rules to an innate grammar. Some cognitive psychologists have been influenced by this type of thinking to the point that they posit as innate ideas what Piaget considers a construct of the developmental process. Mehler and Bever (1968), for example, argue in favor of an innate notion of quantification, although they admit that children pass through a developmental phase when this relatively weak idea is overwhelmed by inadequate perceptual strategies. In response, Piaget (1968a) agrees that there is an innate, intelligent functioning, but not an innate conceptual structure. Following the lead of biology, he takes the position that a specific innate structure would have to be programmed with the genetic message of DNA and "sufficiently resistant to conquer the perturbing effects of environment" (p. 978).

As stated above, Piaget believes that the concepts characteristic of intellectual functioning are based on a process of abstraction, not from perceptual data but from action performed on objects. In his midway position between the nativist and empiricist schools, Piaget believes in some innate given or functioning capacity that shapes the interaction of the organism with the environment. He thus has an interactionist approach, which he calls constructivist structuralism (Piaget and Inhelder, 1968). According to this approach, the origin of mental structure is to be sought in the subject's actions, not in the object, as the subject strives to adapt to his environment. Structures are then constructed within the subject as a consequence of interactions between the subject and objects.

This concept is illustrated in the way the child changes his sense of space. The child learns about space from an abstraction, not of one physical property or quality from many objects, but from actions themselves. In other words, as the child operates on auditory, visual, and tactile space, he begins to integrate the different spaces by abstracting a commonality from actions in these several domains (see Piaget and Inhelder, 1966).

Throughout his investigations, whatever the age of his subjects, Piaget maintains what he refers to as the principle of genetic epistemology: "in order to resolve the problem of what is knowledge (or its diversity of forms) it is necessary to formulate it in the following terms: How does knowledge grow? By what process does one pass from knowledge judged to be ultimately insufficient to knowledge judged to be better (considered from the point of view of science)?" (1970, p. 731).

Psychoanalytic psychology also believes in the fundamental of human interaction leading to the formation of internal structures, which in turn become the vehicle for human experience and later development. According to psychoanalytic psychology the human being comes into the world with a certain innate potential and a predetermined, inborn maturational sequence. One presupposition here is the development of the drives through oral, anal, phallic, and genital stages, given an average expectable environment.

Similarly, there are certain inborn ego apparatuses with the potential for contributing to the development of ego structure. While there have been many disagreements about when ego functions begin in the life of the child, current views tend to agree with Hartmann's (1939) postulate that there is at first an undifferentiated matrix from which the ego evolves. The development of capacities for responding in infants seems to support this hypothesis (Brazelton, Koslowski, and Main, 1974). The structures that come to facilitate the further development of the process of dealing with human experience are determined largely by the interaction of this innate potential and its maturational sequence with the environment.

Psychoanalytic psychology views the relationship between infant and mother, for example, as in part the vehicle by which certain ego functions are formed. It is through this relationship that the young child eventually internalizes the representations of himself and the significant other—the beginning of internalized self- and object representations. These self- and object representations form the nucleus of the ego structure, leading to the capacity for ego functions that regulate the impulses and test reality. These ego functions in turn form the nucleus of further ego structures, which continue to deal with the environment and, in so doing, contribute to the internalization and formation of additional structures, for example, the superego.

While psychoanalytic psychology in its early formative stages placed heavy emphasis on associations as the process through which access to unconscious contents is gained, it cannot be said that contemporary psychoanalytic psychology is strictly an associationist psychology in the empirical tradition. Psychoanalysis does not believe that the mind is blank and that learning occurs only through experience. It posits three factors that are compatible with Piaget's views: an innate potential, a maturational sequence of development, and an interactionist model of the relationship between the developing ego and the environment in the process of structure building.

Nor, in positing an innate potential and a certain predetermined maturational sequence, can psychoanalysis be designated a nativist school similar to Gestalt psychology, which holds that a determined set of structures is merely channeled and teased out by environmental experience. Although Freud did make statements about the collective unconscious and had some ideas similar to those of Jung about the passing of experience from one generation to another, these ideas are not central to current psychoanalytic theory.

Psychoanalytic psychology therefore locates itself, like Piaget, in the middle of the continuum between nativism and empiricism and believes that human structures evolve through the interaction of innate givens and environmental experience. There is an important difference, however, between Piaget's genetic epistemology and the psychoanalytic view of human development. Piaget relies heavily on the concept of *reflective abstraction;* that is, internal structure develops not only out of the *interaction* between the organism and the environment, but, most important, out of the *action of the organism* on the environment. Psychoanalytic psychology has a somewhat broader view. While it respects the importance of the organism's action on the environment, it holds equal respect for the importance of the environment's action on the organism.

In fact, early in the history of psychoanalysis the importance of the environment's action on the organism was in some respects considered more crucial (see Freud's [1893-1895] early traumatic theory of neurosis). Later, the significance of the young child's own fantasies and distortions about *seductions* became prominent. Thus, the way the human being acted on his environment either in reality or in fancy became important.

In current psychoanalytic psychology, actions in both directions are considered crucial. This broader conception of interaction, however, does not make the psychoanalytic view of development incompatible with that of Piaget. As stated earlier, psychoanalysis surveys a larger spectrum of behavior, considering unconscious behavior and conscious behavior in the realm of wishes, emotions, and internal object relations, as well as in the domain of cognition. In focusing strictly on the development of knowledge as an adaptative process, Piaget is concentrating on a narrower question in the development of human experience. Partly as a corrective to psychological empiricism, he stresses the more specific hypothesis of the importance of the organism's action on the environment. Psychoanalytic thinking *a priori* would have no argument with this point of view, nor is it incompatible with the broader-based interactionist model of psychoanalysis.

Intelligence as Adaptation

As indicated earlier, Piaget postulates that interaction with objects provides the basis of knowledge as adaptive behavior. Piaget's concept of adaptation should be distinguished from the type of adaptation specific to new situations, for example, trial-and-error search for adequate responses. For Piaget, intelligence as adaptation is not equivalent, for example, to insight, the moment of solution. Piaget (1962a) cites the formulations of E. Claparède and Karl Bühler as examples of such narrow definitions of intelligence. Piaget similarly rejects intelligence as being directly comparable to empirical abilities—for example, that intelligence is whatever intelligence tests measure (Elkind, 1970).

Piaget's main interest is not in individual differences in general intellectual ability, but in the development of individuals within relatively restricted fields of intelligent behavior, especially that of logico-mathematical knowledge. From the viewpoint of genetic psychology, intelligence concerns the organism's progressive adaptation to the environment. Intelligence (or intelligent behavior) structures this adaptation, not by repeated trials and errors, but through the organization of a more comprehensive system. Piaget's interest, then, is not in the specific abilities related to general intellectual functioning in a clinical sense, such as verbal fluency, attention span, and memory for design, but in the underlying organization of actions and intellectual operations that marks the particular level of ontogenetic development and makes possible the characterististic pattern of responses. Intelligence functions at its highest or most adaptive level when the rules governing cognition have developed into a system so internally consistent that a conclusion is experienced as logically necessary (Furth, 1969, p. 170).

For Piaget, the rules of logic characteristic of adult thought are not given *a priori,* but are constructed in the course of development. Intelligence cannot be defined by any status criteria: adaptation to novel situations, insight, or discrete abilities considered as indicators (psychometric intelligence). If the highest level of intelligent behavior is linked genetically to organized systems of action that begin in earliest infancy, intelligence must be defined "by the direction that intelligence follows in its evolution" (Piaget, 1962a, p. 158). On the one hand, intelligent behavior occurs at every level of development, and on the other, the optimal adult is in every sense more intelligent than the child.

The general criterion for intelligent functioning stipulated by Piaget is *equilibration,* briefly defined as "a compensation for external disturbance" (1962a, p. 158). Furth describes equilibration as "the factor that internally structures the developing intelligence. It provides the self-regulation by which intelligence develops in adapting to external and internal changes" (1969, p. 206). At every level of development, the mechanism of equilibration is operative in furthering adaptation, but as development proceeds toward the highest level of cognitive functioning, the equilibration process becomes progressively more adequate in enabling the organism to adapt to a wider range of internal and external disturbances.

Piaget's equilibration model is based on his concepts of assimilation and accommodation. These two processes are taken to be "functional invariants" of all intelligent behavior (Flavell, 1963). At every level of intellectual development, from infancy to adulthood, they are operative in the overall process of adaptation.

The assimilation-accommodation account of development stresses the interaction between organism and environment. Furth (1969) refers to assimilation as "an inward-directed tendency of a structure to draw environmental events towards itself" (p. 14). In Piaget's words: "When we say an organism or a subject is sensitized to a stimulus and able to make a response to it, we imply it already possesses a scheme or a structure to which this stimulus is assimilated (in the sense of incorporated or integrated . . .)" (1970, p. 707).

As a functional invariant, assimilation characterizes the behavior of the human organism at every level of intellectual development. However, the stimuli assimilated by the organism vary as development unfolds. For the infant, relatively undifferentiated behavior patterns, which are perceptual and motor in nature, are assimilated to the earliest structures of intelligence. The process of sucking-the-brown-nipple, for example, remains undifferentiated, as the infant cannot yet make a clear distinction between self and objects; it is assimilated to only a generalized sucking scheme. At the other extreme of development, the adult can assimilate such hypothetical possibilities as alternative strategic moves in a chess game. Whatever is capable of being assimilated to an organism's mental structures is termed *aliment* for those structures (Tuddenham, 1966). The variation in appropriate aliment for intellectual structures is a function of the stages of development.

Assimilation is the conservative side of intellectual development. It assures continuity and coherence by incorporating new aliments into the mental structures. But it alone cannot account for growth or change within these structures. Here the notion of accommodation comes into play.

Furth refers to accommodation as "an organism-outward tendency of the inner structure to adapt itself to a particular environmental event" (1969, p. 14). According to Piaget (1970): "in the field of behavior . . . accommodation [is] any modification of an assimilatory scheme or structure by the elements it assimilates. For example, the infant who assimilates his thumb to the sucking schema will, when sucking his thumb, make different movements from those he uses in suckling his mother's breast" (p. 708).

Tuddenham (1966) points out the variations in accommodation relative to levels of intellectual development: "At the lowest psychological level, accommodation refers to the gradual adaptation of the reflexes to new stimulus conditions—what others have called conditioning or stimulus generalization. At higher levels it refers to the coordination of thought patterns to one another and to external reality" (p. 91). Accommodation occurs at points during the developmental periods when new data cannot be wholly assimilated to existing structures, and yet are not so entirely foreign to those structures that their existence can be ignored.

It is the *dynamic* balance between assimilation and accommodation that constitutes equilibrium. "Stated most simply the equilibration process is the process of bringing assimilation and accommodation into balance coordination" (Flavell, 1963, p. 239). Assimilation is the taking-in aspect of intelligence by which appropriate cognitive stimuli are drawn into or incorporated within a structure, and accommodation is the change of a structure itself, which enables it to process a given stimulus.

The equilibration process, which is the essence of intelligent functioning, leads to a sequence of equilibrium states which may be ordered teleologically (Flavell, 1963). To the degree that the equilibrium characteristic of adolescent thought is a higher system than that characteristic of infancy, the adolescent is more intelligent; that is, he is more fully adapted to his environment than is the infant. To specify how the adolescent is more intelligent than the infant, one must look at the four characteristics Piaget defines for equilibrium states: field of application, mobility, permanence, and stability.

The *field of application* refers to "the ensemble of objects or object-properties which the equilibrated action system accommodates to and assimilates" (Flavell, 1963, p. 242). The adolescent, for instance, can deal with hypothetical propositions, or view the concrete as one instance of the possible, while the younger child is restricted to dealing with specific objects.

The *mobility* of an equilibrium state refers to the distance covered by the actions, which exist in time and space. The infant is restricted to an immediate present in both dimensions. He can act on or within only his immediate surrounding and deal only in the present. Later in his development, with the acquisition of the symbolic function and the capacities for thinking, the child can deal with objects that are not in his immediate surrounding but distant from him in space, just as he can deal with instances that occurred in the past. There is greater mobility along these two dimensions.

Permanence refers to the consistency with which the subject actively maintains the value of elements or objects introduced into this system. Early cognitive equilibrium states show a dramatic lack of permanence. The four-year-old may make contradictory predictions about two identical objects, depending on the context and on egocentric needs. In one situation, even the five-year-old may assert that objects that float will be heavy; under the influence of an experimental procedure, however, the child may completely reverse this position and claim that the object that did in fact sink was heavy. Only later does this contradiction become apparent to the child as he coordinates the different dimensions of weight and space and volume to account for the law of floating bodies.

The final characteristic of any equilibrium state is that of *stability*; that is, the ability of the system "to compensate or cancel perturbations which tend to alter the existing state of equilibrium" (Flavell, 1963, p. 243). The young child who is shown two identical glasses of liquid, one of which is then poured into a third, taller but narrower glass, may claim that the taller glass contains more liquid. In later childhood, the subject will recognize that the taller glass has the same quantity of liquid as the original, shorter one. In terms of stability, the younger child may not be able to compensate for the increase in height by considering a decrease in width. Though similar to the concept of permanence, stability refers to the ability of the cognitive organization to function smoothly when discrepant input is introduced, while permanence refers to its ability to conserve appropriate values in the face of perceptual transformations.

In the history of psychology, development has been generally attributed to three factors: maturation, experiences of the physical environment, and the influence of the social environment. Piaget considers each of these classical factors necessary but not sufficient. He introduces the concept of equilibration as a way to account for the interaction between maturation and experiential factors. Equilibration does not replace maturation, physical experience, or social influences. Rather, it complements them and organizes them into a coherent explanation demonstrating how they act at different levels of development and in an ontogenetic scheme from the lowest order of intelligence to the highest. At the highest level of equilibrium, where the field of application, mobility, permanence, and stability are greatest, cognitive structures can assimilate a wide variety of "cognitive experience" without alterations in structure or without forming new accommodations.

We have reviewed certain key notions relevant to Piaget's concept of intelligence as adaptation. These are quite consistent with psychoanalytic psychology. That intelligence is not a static property, but a progressive development in the adaptation of the organism to the environment, corresponds to the psychoanalytic model of the adaptive functions of the ego. Like Piaget, psychoanalysts consider structures that develop in successively higher order and more complicated relationships to both the external and internal environment. More specifically, psychoanalytic ego psychology considers the development of the ego under optimal conditions to advance to higher and higher states of synthetic functioning.[1]

The concept of ego flexibility as an indicator of the ego's ability to experience a broad range of thoughts, wishes, feelings, etc., without pathological defensive operations resulting in major constructions, relates a flexible ego to a high-order equilibrium state. Just as the highest equilibrium state can assimilate new aliments without major accommodations—that is, the existing laws of transformation can deal with most "cognitive events"—a flexible ego at its highest synthetic capacity can deal with a variety of stimulus inputs (e.g., human interactions, drive

[1] Here we should note that while the highest cognitive equilibrium state may be reached in adolescence, it is not yet clear when the relatively highest state of adaptation occurs for other components of psychological life.

derivatives) within its existing structural organization. Existing regulations and defenses are both flexible and stable enough to protect the ego's basic functions without resorting to accommodations that compromise the range of events dealt with (e.g., an ego constriction characterized by massive denial).

Piaget's concept of equilibrium is also consistent with the idea of integration of a progressively more complex sense of self over time. The concept of identity represents the integration of different self- and object representations from different stages of childhood and adolescence with the real perceptions of the external social environment, as well as with ideals, values, and expectations for the future. The fully integrated identity synthesizes all of these and can take into account new experiences in the context of an evolving, consolidated sense of self. Similarly, in Piaget's equilibrated system the organism becomes able to adapt to a range of external disturbances.

Although there are no direct parallels in psychoanalytic psychology to Piaget's concepts of assimilation and accommodation, its consideration of ego functions may imply these concepts in a more general manner. In any event, the concepts of psychoanalytic psychology are in no way inconsistent or incompatible with them. In fact, the processes of assimilation and accommodation offer a rather specific hypothesis for the way in which certain aspects of external experiences become organized in terms of internal structure. The way in which internal structures are formed through the interaction of the organism and the environment has remained vague in psychoanalytic ego psychology.

In terms of the formation of internal structure, it is not completely clear in psychoanalytic psychology how wishes and feelings interact with the regulating ego or how the latter deals with the environment and internalizes in part through the process of identification, certain experiences to form additional structures. While this type of structuralization obviously involves a broader realm than the more narrowly defined formation of cognitive sturctures, the specificity of Piaget's model may hold some utility for psychoanalytic psychology. There is no *a priori* reason that the concepts of assimilation and accommodation could not be used at least as a partial explanation for certain aspects of structure formation.

At present we have no adequate understanding of the gradual evolution or change in the structures, such as the superego structure, after their initial formation. Yet we know that slowly, over time, such internal structures are modified and substructures are differentiated from them. Increased clarification of the processes of internalization, differentiation, and modification of structures would be useful to psychoanalysis. Although it has not yet been demonstrated that the concepts of assimilation and accommodation will enhance the explanation of what goes on at the boundary between the ego and the world of wishes, affects, and emotionally colored human relationships, these concepts and their derivative ideas should be kept in mind as we struggle for further understanding of the processes that lead to internal structure formation and its subsequent modification.

It is interesting to speculate on Piaget's idea that assimilations are possible only to the extent that they occur in the context of age-appropriate capacities and lead to a new accommodation only when they are close enough to age-appropriate capacities to tax the system and force it to alter itself. This idea is consistent and compatible with psychoanalytic views and could be applied to the various boundaries of the ego. The notions of assimilation and accommodation may therefore provide a useful point of departure for a broader consideration of learning in psychoanalysis. As has often been repeated, there is as yet no adequate and complete learning theory in psychoanalysis. Let us consider one example of a learning process in psychoanalysis that may be clarified by Piaget's concepts of assimilation and accommodation.

The working-through process in psychoanalysis shares certain similarities with Piaget's description of the dynamic relationship between assimilation and accommodation in the child's gradual development of the ability to coordinate two dimensions. Initially, the child focuses on only one dimension of a stimulus, for example, the length of a clay "sausage." But if the sausage is made longer and longer, the probability is increased that the child will begin to fluctuate—to focus on one dimension, then on the other. Such fluctuation increases the probability that the child will notice the interrelation between length and width. When this occurs, the child is no longer tied to static perceptual configurations, but is able to understand the transformation involved in changing the shape while retaining the quantity. A major accommodation in intellectual structures has thus been achieved through the equilibration process.

In the working through of an insight in therapy a similar process occurs. Current and past experience, experience of the transference and of reality outside therapy, and fantasy and reality perceptions are the bipolar sets of dimensions equivalent to *static configurations* in Piaget's model. The task of working through is one of coordinating such bipolarities. The juxtaposition of different dimensions and its repeated working through in different aspects of the person's life in the phases of the analytic work may facilitate the formation of new ego substructures similar to Piaget's structure building in the non-affect-laden world of cognition. In both cases the capacity of structures to be modified is a function of the degree of fit between present structure and proposed aliment. If the juxtapositions are composed of aliments that appear totally unrelated to the analysand because of the operation of defense mechanisms, coordination of dimensions cannot yet occur. As the working-through process continues and defensiveness lessens, however, coordination of dimensions becomes more probable.

Piaget's is a specific model of development that describes the alteration of the internal structures through action on the external environment; through this experience, a new internal structure is gradually formed. Once this structure is formed, the organism is able to tie together different dimensions of the system. This process is also what we observe in our psychoanalytic work, although with a different set of stimuli, or aliments. Once the patient integrates an insight that enables him to synthesize a number of dimensions, there is a spreading of the range of internal experience available to him and a generalization of the conceptual base of the insight to other areas of his life. Thus, in a broad sense, we can say that a now internal structure is formed in a manner very similar to the way a person accommodates to new intellectual aliments. There is a generalization of the basic ability to many areas of intelligent functioning.

To compare more closely the concept of equilibrium in the two models, consider the following. Piaget has pointed out that the adolescent's intellectual structures are of a higher order than those of earlier developmental levels and he specifies in what way: field of application, mobility, permanence, and stability. The adolescent has a wider field of application for intelligent behavior; that is, he can consider many variables in many dimensions of his external world. He can deal with hypothetical propositions, whereas the younger child can deal only with concrete examples. With the capacity for combinatorial thinking, the adolescent can consider the many possible interrelationships between variables; he can thus take in most aspects of his environment without causing a disturbance in his cognitive system. In other words, his system can assimilate highly varied aliments without needing to make new accommodations.

As indicated earlier, this explanation is dramatically similar to that offered by concepts of ego flexibility, flexibility of defenses, and level of synthetic capacity. Throughout development the ego structure is continually integrating the disturbances from the external environment, the id, and the superego at progressively higher levels of synthetic organization. To the degree that the adolescent achieves a stable sense of self that, at a high level of organization, integrates superego prohibitions, aspirations of the ego ideal, various drive derivatives from different development stages, and a range of affects, along with the demands of external reality, he has achieved a rather high-level equilibrium state. In contrast, the younger child must either deny new feelings that arise or deny external events that do not fit his picture of himself. A specific parallel to the concept of field of application, therefore, would be the psychologically mature person's ability to take in and deal with a wide variety of wishes, feelings, and the like within the context of a range of external relationships and experience.

The mobility of the equilibrium state refers to the distance covered by the actions of the system in time and space. As Piaget points out, the fully mature cognitive person has much greater mobility. This is true from a psychoanalytic perspective, too. The ideal well-analyzed person is one who integrates past and present successfully and has the capacity for dealing with both the internal (psychological) and external worlds of time and space. Just as Piaget's "formal operational" adult has greater mobility in time and space in terms of the cognitively oriented external environment, the emotionally mature person has greater awareness and acceptance of affect-laden experience across temporal and spatial boundaries.

The qualities of permanence and stability of an equilibrium state are also commensurate with psychoanalytic notions about the flexibility of ego structures. The psychologically mature person can maintain the permanence and stability of his internal representations in the face of disturbances that might offset the existing state of equilibrium. In this sense, the psychologically mature person does not change his internal representation of another person simply because he is happy with or angry at him; he can experience a transformation of feelings while conserving the basic internalized representation. The older child is cognitively able to compensate for increases in height by corresponding decreases in width and can thus maintain the stability of the system. Similarly, in the emotionally mature person, the stability of the ego and its internal object relations is not altered by changes in feeling states even when extreme anger, sadness, envy, or competition are experienced. The system can compensate for strong feelings. The psychologically mature person need not affirm at the moment that he is hating that he must also intensely love the same person. He may have a sense of ongoing regard that can for a few moments tolerate the experience of hatred and feel "nonloving." He does not need to regress to a state of split objects, where the "bad," hated person is separate from the "good," loved person.

As we have seen, Piaget's concept of equilibrium of cognitive structures may be a useful beginning point for psychoanalysis in further refining its concepts of ego flexibility and optimal psychological health. As has been said, equilibration does not replace maturation, physical experience, or social influence as causal factors in the developmental process; rather, it complements them and organizes them into a coherent explanation by demonstrating how they interact. This concept may help psychoanalytic ego psychology in understanding how maturation and experience interact in determining the "optimal flexibility" of the ego.

STRUCTURALISM

Central to Piaget's theory is the concept of structure. This concept and several related concepts can be considered in relation to psychoanalytic constructs, with an eye toward assessing the level of compatibility between the two explanatory systems.

Piaget designates structures in early development by the term *scheme*.[2] "A scheme is the structure or organization of actions as they are transferred or generalized by repetition in similar or analogous circumstances" (Piaget and Inhelder, 1966, p. 4). Schemes exist in the infant in the form of perceptual-motor behavior patterns, e.g., the grasping reflex. They also exist in mature intelligence, although as Furth (1969) points out, *scheme* is more commonly used to refer to early structures, and the general schemes of higher intelligence are referred to as *operations*.

The fact that schemes are generalizations from specific action patterns suggests a type of abstraction process at work in their genesis and development. The abstraction process that leads to the formation of cognitive structures is called *reflective* or *formal abstraction*. It is an abstraction from actions, according to which the similarities inherent in various behavioral acts are dissociated from their particularized contexts.

Piaget makes an important distinction between simple and reflective abstraction in the process of structure building. The former is the abstraction of a common quality from numerous concrete objects; the latter is the abstraction of a common pattern from a variety of actions. "More precisely, reflective abstractions are an enriching feedback into the structures of the

[2] The French *schème* has been translated in some English works as *schema* (e.g., Flavell, 1963). However, following Furth (1969) and Gellerier and Langer (see Piaget, 1970), we shall accept its translation as *scheme*, to differentiate it from schema, designated as the figurative image which may or may not accompany an intellectual operation.

organism from the most general coordinations of actions" (Furth, Youniss, and Ross, 1970, p. 54).

Reflective abstraction concerns ordering. The infant is capable of primitive types of ordering actions, such as pulling a rug on which a toy is placed to obtain the toy. Abstracted out of their original context, these action patterns can yield schemes of *ordering,* which can then be applied at higher cognitive levels. In middle childhood, for example, the youngster is eventually able to order correctly a series of sticks differing very slightly in length—indicating the capacity for seriation (Piaget and Inhelder, 1966).

Piaget's emphasis on the development of cognitive structures places him within the French school of structuralism. It is beyond the scope of the present work to deal extensively with structuralism as an interdisciplinary movement, involving linguistics, mathematics, and anthropology, as well as the physical sciences and psychology. It is, however, pertinent to show why Piaget is indeed a structuralist. He has addressed himself to the question of structuralism in a small volume (1968b), and I will draw upon that as well as his work on logic (1953) to clarify his position.

Piaget views all forms of structuralism as united by a common ideal, "an ideal (perhaps a hope) of intrinsic intelligibility supported by the postulate that structures are self-sufficient and that, to grasp them, we do not have to make references to all sorts of extraneous elements" (Piaget, 1968b, pp. 4-5). A structuralist explanatory system, then, is complete in itself, and does not use elements from other explanatory systems; *a fortiori* it does not view reduction to a different level of abstraction as a goal of scientific exploration. With regard to psychology, this position implies that psychological structures are a legitimate and sufficient type of explanation of human functioning, and need not be reduced to biological or biochemical factors in order to constitute a scientific paradigm.

As discussed earlier, Piaget uses three ideas to define the term *structure*: wholeness, transformation, and self-regulation. The idea of wholeness implies that structures are not composed of independent elements, but rather that the elements of a structure are interrelated and subordinate to a system of laws.

Wholeness then precludes any notion of atomism, which claims that larger entities are composed of smaller entities which have a priority in existence, and that the larger can be effectively reduced to the smaller for purposes of explanation.

The second essential idea associated with structures is transformation. "Were it not for the idea of transformation, structures would lose all explanatory import, since they would collapse into static forms" (1968b, p. 12). Transformations account for change within the system that constitutes the structure, thus permitting a process of movement which yet remains within the boundaries of the system. In anthropological terms, for example, a kinship system undergoes change by the transformation of marriage. In linguistics, Chomsky (1957) has demonstrated the rules of transformation that account for changes in syntactical forms, e.g., from "The dog bit the postman" to "The postman was bitten by the dog."

Piaget, however, objects to Chomsky's tenet that the transformational rules of the grammatical system are innate. Instead, he holds that in a general theory of structure, and especially in a structuralism that seeks to come to terms with the empirical facts of psychology, the historical course of the construction of transformational rules must be taken into account, along with genetic development of the elements within those structures.

The third defining aspect of structures is that they are self-regulating, which implies that input introduced into the system can be processed by the structure, on the basis of transformational rules, without dependence on any regulatory agency beyond the confines of the structure. Furthermore, the new element generated by this transformation will itself be a part of the structure. Piaget gives a mathematical example of this property: "In adding or subtracting any two whole numbers, another whole number is obtained, and one which satisfies the laws of the 'additive group' of whole numbers. It is in this sense that a structure is 'closed' " (1968b, p. 14).

The idea of self-regulation is, of course, closely related to the notion of equilibrium states characterized by permanence and stability. The permanent, stable state is one capable of maintaining itself as a system while processing a wide variety of input. In fact, advanced equilibrium states exemplify the most adequate and complex structures in psychological development.

Mathematical structures may be perfectly self-regulating, according to Piaget, because their regulating rules consist of a set of operations, each of which contains its own inverse (1968b, p. 15). Subtraction, for example, is the inverse of addition. Any operation can be reversed entirely by some other operation in the system. In psychological development, however, cognitive structures do not achieve such a level of complete reversibility until middle childhood, and even then the range of reversible operations is restricted to the realm of the concrete.

In the earliest stages of life cognitive activity is regulated by rhythmic mechanisms. Reflexes, for example, follow a sequential order, from an initial state to a final state, and then begin the same sequence again. Such a simple form of self-regulation is characteristic of sucking behavior and early patterns of locomotion (Piaget and Inhelder, 1966).

As the child begins to form his first sensorimotor habits (Piaget terms these "circular reactions"), his groping activity undergoes a process of gradual correction. To reach his goal, the child must modify his groping in accord with feedback from previous action. Piaget considers the type of self-regulation operative here to be semi-reversible; the action cannot be fully reversed by other actions within the behavioral system, but feedback can lead to further actions which have the effect of correcting the earlier behavior retroactively (Piaget and Inhelder, 1966).

The temporal delay inherent in feedback regulation is overcome when the cognitive structures come under the self-regulating process of *operations*, a term we shall discuss in more detail in considering the stages of intellectual development. The beginnings of the reversibility that will supersede feedback regulation can be seen in the young child's formation of a concept of space in which a displacement $A-B$ can be reversed by an equal and opposite displacement $B-A$ (Piaget and Inhelder, 1966). The reversibility here is still bound to action sequences, however, and the child does not yet have the capacity for symbolic or abstract thought. As he develops higher cognitive abilities, his intellectual structures, considered as self-regulating systems, come more and more under the control of full reversibility. For Piaget, reversibility replaces feedback regulation, just as the latter replaces rhythm, as cognitive development proceeds toward a more adequate adaptation of the knowing organism to the environment.

We have mentioned that reflective abstraction is the mechanism through which higher-order structures are built from lower-order schemes. Before leaving the topic of structuralism, it would be helpful to note the mechanism involved in the solidification and limitation of sensorimotor schemes at their original level of generation. This mechanism is the functional invariant of assimilation, but Piaget denotes four types of assimilation to account for the structuring of schemes.

To begin with, schemes tend to repeat the action patterns that generate them. It is as if they need a certain amount of stimulation from the action of the developing organism in the environment. As Furth puts it, "Every knowing scheme wants to function" (1969, p. 228). Piaget (1936) terms the type of assimilation that satisfies this fundamental need to function *reproductive assimilation.*

In the course of reproductive assimilation, schemes extend "their field of application so as to assimilate new and different objects" (Flavell, 1963, p. 56). Piaget designates this process *generalizing assimilation.* It is analogous to the law of generalization in learning theory; accordingly, schemes do not generalize *ad infinitum.* Parallel to the law of discrimination in learning theory is the Piagetian concept of *recognitory assimilation,* by which the developing organism differentiates appropriate and inappropriate objects for its schemes.

Finally, the interrelation of two schemes, e.g., grasping and seeing, is accomplished by *reciprocal assimilation.* This process represents a type of across-scheme abstraction, so that the bottle-for-grasping and the bottle-for-seeing are assimilated to one another. At a sufficient level of development such reciprocal assimilation will yield an objective concept of bottle, independent of particular action schemes.

One final point needs to be made in reference to structures in general, whether they be sensorimotor schemes or later operations. In the structuralist school of thought, structures are often expressed in formal language (Piaget, 1968b, p. 5). In Piaget's case, this means that organized systems of cognitive processes are expressed in logico-mathematical terms. Piaget does not use logic or mathematics to deduce hypotheses from his theoretical constructs, as did Hull, for example (see Piaget, 1953, p. xvii). Rather, he uses logical techniques to describe empirical psychological data. "Piaget aims at formalizing his findings in the language of logic but not so as to impose an arbitrary logical system on human thinking; rather he is trying to make explicit the forms of logic that spontaneously and in an initially implicit manner arise in the human child" (Furth, 1969, pp. 18-19).

Piaget, then, is not claiming a complete isomorphism between the structures of thought and the structures of logic elucidated by professional logicians. The logical models, which are in part borrowed by Piaget and in part devised by him, should be considered *post facto* constructions designed to account for the progress of cognition as it attains higher forms of equilibrium. As Furth (1969) points out, a logical system, if fully equilibrated (so that intelligence is a progressive march toward equilibration), approximates ever more closely the formal model of logic. And where intelligence is still lacking in equilibration, limited logical structures can be devised to model formally the imperfectly developed cognitive system (Piaget, 1953).

Given these preliminary points, let us now examine their compatibility with psychoanalytic constructs. The definition of structure as an organization of actions generalized across analogous circumstances is compatible with the psychoanalytic concept of structure. According to Rapaport (1959), structures are a stable, relatively slowly changing feature of the mental apparatus, with a certain degree of independence from the effects of the drives (or, for that matter, external stimulation) and from the input of other internal structures. An organization, to constitute a substructure of the ego, would therefore be an ordering of action patterns; it could be a pattern of regulation that is relatively inflexible to change, at least in the short run.

Piaget's idea that schemes and structures are formed from reflective or formal abstraction, rather than from simple abstraction, is also consistent with psychoanalytic psychology. Psychoanalytic psychology, however, considers formation of structures in a broader context. As we have indicated, formation results not only from reflective abstraction—that is, abstraction from actions on the environment—but also from the action of the environment on the organism.

The different points of emphasis here are highly significant. Piaget is concerned with the relatively non-affect-laden external environment. The environment provides the aliment, or the opportunity, for cognitive tasks. The major actor in the sequence is the organism, which acts on this environment. The environment is less active in a relative sense: it needs to be there and available, but its vicissitudes clearly are less important than the acting organism. The external environment is thus considered a relatively constant, stable factor, unless it is an extremely impoverished environment, with a paucity of available aliments. Barring a deficient environment, each person—as an infant, growing child, and then young adult—has the opportunity to act on the environment and thus construct appropriate schemes. It is clear, however, that the external environment includes drive-colored human objects, and that their vicissitudes—the way they act on the organism—have an import, together with what the organism brings to the situation. Although the Piagetian model considers the action of the environment in determining the character of thinking, the formal properties of intelligence, which are generalizable across individuals, are seen to be more dependent on the individual's action on the environment.

In the psychoanalytic model internal structures, such as the internal representations of self and object, result from the *interaction* of the growing infant with his environment. The child's representation of himself, as well as of the significant other, evolves from encounters involving *both* persons' actions. While perceptions or meanings of events are certainly always determined in part by factors generated by the individual, the actions of the environment play a role in determining aspects of both the structure and intent of these perceptions. The relative impact of both internal and external factors must be considered, with the full realization that in some instances one or another may dominate. Thus, Piaget's concept of reflective, formal abstraction may be considered a specific instance of the kind of interactive abstraction from which psychoanalytic theory would postulate that structures are derived. (This distinction will be seen to be important later, when we discuss the differences between the pure cognitive structures described by Piaget and what will be termed emotional structures at the internal boundary of the ego.)

It will be recalled that Piaget's emphasis on structure places him in the broader structuralist tradition. To review briefly: Piaget posits that a structural explanatory system is complete; it does not make use of the elements of other explanatory psychological systems, nor does it need to be reduced further to biological or biochemical factors in order to constitute a scientific paradigm. This idea is wholly compatible with the psychoanalytic notion of structure, and is in fact a restatement of it. Psychoanalysis, in terms of current ego psychology, has become a representational psychology; that is, it considers how the representations of different aspects of the internal and external worlds relate to one another in terms of an organized system of psychological experience. Although there is still interest in relating the organic substrata of behavior (neurophysiological mechanisms) to the psychological systems, most post-ego-psychology psychoanalysts recognize psychoanalytic psychology as a complete explanation. Somatic events become represented as a psychological experience.

Simple one-to-one relationships between organic or neurophysiological events and psychological events are no longer the object of investigation. If in the future, however, complex transformations explaining the relationships between somatic or physiological events and the organization and vicissitudes of mental representations were to be clarified, we would have an enlarged structuralist system. To use Piaget's terms, we presently have a structure at a certain level of equilibration. If we learned the transformations that account for the relationships between neurophysiological or somatic events and psychological experiences, we would have a more highly equilibrated structure—one that would take into account both biological and psychological sets of variables. As it is now, however, even though psychoanalytic psychology is an imperfect system, it meets the structuralist criteria for a system.

As stated earlier, the three central characteristics of Piaget's structures are wholeness, transformation, and self-regulation. In psychoanalytic psychology the characteristic of wholeness pertains to the entire psychic structure or to any separate substructure. Rapaport (1959) demonstrates that the different psychoanalytic perspectives together constitute a "whole" system.

The idea of transformation is highly compatible with psychoanalytic psychology, although the transformational principles that relate different aspects of the structures of psychoanalytic psychology to one another are not as clear as they are in the realm of cognitive structures. Nonetheless, such concepts as defense mechanisms and neutralization deal with transformation. The ego, in essence, comprises executive regulatory agencies, all of which must operate according to certain transformational laws. When drive derivatives become altered—for example, through the mechanism of displacement or reaction formation—we are essentially witnessing a law of transformation.

Self-regulation, the third characteristic of structures, is also compatible with psychoanalytic psychology. The psychoanalytic model is one of gradual internalization and structure formation throughout development. Early in life, input introduced into the system is not wholly processed by the system. Dependence of the young infant on the external environment remains great. As internal structures are built, however, the human being becomes more of a self-regulating entity. While he is always in some relative relationship to the environment—in this sense, there is never a perfect self-regulating structure—the concept can be held as an ideal within which certain studies of human functioning can be viewed. To the degree to which behavior is progressively internalized in the course of development, the adult achieves relatively greater self-regulation than does the young child or infant. The ideal of self-regulation is more closely reached in the cognitive sphere than in that of wishes, affects, and internalized object relations.

Piaget's sequence of self-regulating mechanisms from rhythm to feedback to reversibility has a parallel in psychoanalytic psychology in terms of the development of structures that deal with ever broader realms of internal experience. Observers have certainly documented the infant's rhythmic behavior patterns. It has been recognized that initial rhythmic patterns, particularly those related to state alteration (e.g., sleep patterns) and those involving the object, are important for initial attachment and later internalization (Sander, 1962). They are the primary building blocks of structures, in relation to an even broader realm of human experience than that conceptualized by Piaget.

The concept of feedback is also important in psychoanalytic psychology. Through feedback, the child gets a preliminary sense of his own boundaries. Later, through a different kind of feedback from the environment, he begins his first imitative movements, which provide the foundation for internalization and structure formation.

Although, to date, the concept of reversibility has not been important in psychoanalytic psychology, it is in no way incompatible with it. Examination of the process of reversibility in relation to the world of wishes, affects, aand internal and external relations leads to some interesting parallels to Piaget's construct. In fact, we may find the concept of reversibility in self-regulation the most useful for psychoanalytic inquiry.

In Piaget's system, reversibility implies that the movement *AB* can be totally reversed by the movement *BA*. In a conservation experiment with a glass of water, a displacement of water in one direction can be inverted by a displacement of water in the opposite direction. In the more highly developed system characteristic of adolescent thought, reversibility is used at the level of abstract ideas so that an idea can have its inverse.

Piaget himself does not apply the concept of reversibility in any detailed manner to the world of wishes, feelings and fantasy. Nevertheless, as indicated above, such an application may prove useful. The adolescent, for instance, does not need to "try out" opposing wishes in action patterns as the young child does by doing and undoing. Instead, he can experience them simultaneously in thought, which affords a greatly enhanced freedom and psychic mobility. The adolescent's and adult's capacity for fantasy is thus much greater than that of the latency child, as are the range and flexibility of his psychological system in its capacity for internal experience. By implication, a healthy adult can experience a wide range of feelings, fantasies, and the like, and thus "be in touch with himself" without being overly anxious or frightened about this range of internal fantasy and feelings or even the different intensities of positive and negative feelings toward important people. The latency child, in contrast, must maintain a barrier against certain fantasies and emotions and therefore often adopts a rather rigid obsessive style.

A crucial difference between these age groups is the level of reversibility of which each is capable. (Another difference—the capacity for hypothetical thought—will be more fully discussed later.) The young adult is capable of reversibility by inversion and reciprocity. For example, he can consider anger and the wish to hurt and, at the same time, their undoing or opposites—love and the wish not to hurt. Since he is able to consider both of these as part of one system, he can integrate both his angry and loving feelings toward the same person. That actions can be reversed simultaneously in thought makes these wishes less dangerous to the young adult than to the latency child, who may consider them sequentially and concretely.

With the capacity for combinatorial thinking, the young adult can scan the whole range of possible feelings and, in this manner, determine what is real. The real here does not mean the actively real or what will necessarily happen. It simply means that an internal experience becomes one of many possible action patterns or sequences. The ability to consider a possible action pattern sequence and at the same time be aware of its opposite—that is, the existence of a reversible system—affords vast flexibility. As stated above, a particular action pattern sequence is not so frightening because its opposite is also possible; the two can cancel each other out. The concept of reversibility at the highest level of self-regulation, then, is not incompatible with psychoanalytic psychology. In this rather specific way, it may have a certain value for psychoanalytic ego psychology in understanding the greater emotional flexibility of the "optimal" adult compared with that of the younger child.

In concluding this discussion of structuralism, we should note that Piaget's various forms of assimilation may be useful to psychoanalysis as specific constructs in a model of ego development. They may be seen to pertain to the formation of structures not only vis-à-vis the impersonal external environment, but also vis-à-vis the affect-laden inner world. However, as exemplified by the concept of reproductive assimilation, agreement between psychoanalysis and Piaget would seem blocked because of the latter's position that the motivation for repetition is inherent in the schema itself, without reference to drive constructs. Wolff (1960) and others have commented on this problem. In a subsequent section we shall consider more fully the role of the drives in relation to the type of cognition studied by Piaget.

Piaget's Theory of Perception

Although Piaget is most widely known as a theorist and researcher concerned with the development of intelligence, he has also constructed a theory of perception, related to his theory of intelligence. In *The Mechanisms of Perception* (1961), Piaget provides the fullest account of his own view of perceptual processes, by attempting "to resolve two general problems to which most specialists in perception . . . have paid little attention" (p. xv): the relationship of perception to intelligence and the epistemological status of perception. Only a few aspects of his work will be summarized here.

Piaget's general theoretical position has been outlined in the preceding section. In this regard, Piaget's relative de-emphasis on perception is an essential aspect of his general theory of genetic epistemology. A direct examination of perceptual processes is an appendage to his cognitive theory, but an appendage that is necessary to substantiate the claims of his cognitive theory.

The Mechanisms of Perception is a work of both empirical and theoretical significance. Empirically, it contains, in a well-ordered format, results of over 50 experiments on perception conducted by Piaget and his colleagues, in particular, Lumbercier. The book relates the results of these studies to a general theory of perception, and, in turn, to Piaget's genetic epistemology.

In the first two parts, Piaget presents the empirical evidence for the existence of two types of perceptual errors: primary and secondary illusions. The implications of this work invalidate both Gestaltist and associationist views of the relationship between perception and intelligence. With regard to the "naïve realism" of associationist epistemology, Piaget shows that the immediate evidence of the senses, as received and processed by perceptual processes, leads not to awareness of reality, but to certain systematic distortions. In opposition to Gestalt psychologists, Piaget shows that perceptual structures themselves undergo a process of development, and that they are of a somewhat inferior status compared with intellectual structures, as they are products of a probabilistic process of encounters and couplings rather than a logically necessary and closed system of operations.

Piaget takes an "interactionist" interpretation, holding that at all levels of cognitive development both operative and figurative structures are functioning, but with the figurative structures, including perception, in the subordinate position. In arguing for an interactionist position, Piaget begins by noting fourteen differences between perception and intelligence, each of which points toward a relative superiority of intellectual structures. For example, perception is always bound to the concrete, present object, while intelligence can evoke absent objects; primary perception does not include any process of abstraction from the given datum, whereas intelligence separates out the essential from the nonessential; perceptions are not logically reversible, while operations of intelligence are. Piaget uses perception as a synonym for field effects (primary effects) and thus exaggerates the differences between perceptual and intellectual processes.

The relationship Piaget points out between intelligence and perception, then, is that between two aspects of knowledge, the figurative and the operative. Operative aspects of knowledge pertain to actions performed on objects, whether external or internalized. Figurative aspects of knowledge pertain to static depictions of known object states, as in perception or mental images of an object. In Piaget's genetic epistemology, actions performed on objects lead to the building of cognitive structures on the basis of reflective abstraction. Experience itself, including perception, determines the adequacy of fit of a given framework. Both induction and deduction are thus essential aspects of the knowing process. The immediate data of primary-field effects contain certain systematic distortions which must be corrected by multiple encounters and complete couplings. Essentially, this process represents for Piaget a decentration in the perceptual realm comparable to that which occurs in the realm of cognitive development.

There have been several extensions and criticisms of Piaget's theory of perception.[3] Of importance to this work, however, is not a review of these critiques, but the observation that Piaget's more recent research is an extension of his basic model. In this sense, the compatibility of a Piagetian construct with psychoanalytic ones is retained. It is interesting to note, however, that the postulated relationship between figurative (lower order —open to distortion) and operative knowledge is consistent with early psychoanalytic ideas about the relationship between the perceptual activities activated in dreams and the secondary process. These issues will be returned to later when we consider aspects of primary and secondary process. Piaget's research on perception may eventually help us understand more systematically the developmental aspects of perception not only of the external world, but also of the internal world, particularly the characteristic phase-specific mechanisms of distortion.

Piaget's Concept of Developmental Stages

The concept of developmental stages has a technical meaning in Piaget's system which differentiates it from other psychologies (Pinard and Laurendeau, 1969). For our purposes it is most important to outline the fundamental criteria used to establish the existence of stages in Piaget's thought, and to compare his stages to those postulated in psychoanalysis.

Piaget states: "The Freudian stages . . . are only distinct from each other in that they differ in one dominant character (oral,

[3] See Begelman and Steinfeld (1972); Bever et al. (1975); Elkind (1971); Fellows and Thorn (1973); Girgus, Coren, and Fraenkel (1975); Pollack (1969); and Weintraub and Cooper (1972).

anal, etc.) but this character is also present in the previous—or following—stages, so that its 'dominance' may well remain arbitrary" (1970, p. 710). Piaget sees the Freudian notion of stages as too loose a construct; it "opens the door to arbitrary thinking" (1967, p. 17). The stages of cognitive development he and his associates have delineated on the basis of research are not defined merely by the dominance of some aspect which remains present in a less dominant manner throughout development. Rather, they constitute structured wholes and can be defined by reference to a set of criteria.

In a series of discussions on child development, Piaget (1960) articulates this set of criteria in ascending order of rigor:

1. There is a constant order of succession, irrespective of absolute chronological age. Children in different cultures may attain a given stage at different age levels, but all children, from whatever culture, must pass through the same sequence of stages.

2. Lower-stage elements are integrated into the higher stage. We have already noted that the mechanism of reflective abstraction facilitates the transition from lower-order schemes to higher-order operations in Piaget's system. More specifically, in reviewing Piaget's major periods it will become clear that "the initial sensorimotor structures are integrated into the structures of concrete operations and the latter into formal structures" (Piaget, 1960, p. 13).

3. Each stage contains an element of preparation for the following stage and represents an achievement over the preceding stage.

4. According to this most stringent criterion, all the processes leading up to a given stage, and all the achievements characteristic of that stage, are indicative of a general structure, a whole system of operations and rules of transformation, which is self-regulating, or closed.

Since the structural criterion of developmental stages is probably not applicable to all aspects of human development, and may be peculiar to the type of cognitive development Piaget has studied, a less stringent criterion is proposed to complete the set of criteria applicable in a general theory of developmental stages. This criterion, which Piaget (1960) hopes will be relevant to affective development, is the process of progressively more adequate equilibrium states, i.e., states marked by greater mobility, field of application, permanence, and stability. We have already seen how the progressive stages of intelligence can be understood as improved equilibrium states. Stages of emotional growth or moral development may also fit this equilibrium paradigm, without being so tightly organized as to meet the criteria of a general structure.

While Piaget regards Freud's oral, anal, and phallic constructs as less than stages since they represent shifts in libidinal cathexis, rather than progressively integrating wholes, he is quite sympathetic to Erikson's extension of Freudian theory into psychosocial modes. According to Piaget, "The great merit of Erikson's stages . . . is precisely that he attempted, by situating the Freudian mechanisms within more general types of conduct (walking, exploring, etc.) to postulate continual integration of previous acquisitions at subsequent levels" (1960, p. 13). Aside from Erikson's psychosocial modes, can contemporary psychoanalytic ego psychology meet Piaget's criteria for a developmental-stage psychology? Certainly all psychoanalytic writers adhere to Piaget's first criterion, as did Freud. Therefore the debate centers around criteria two, three, and four.

Piaget's second criterion, that of integration of lower-stage elements into higher stages, seems amply met by certain models within ego psychology. His criticism of Freudian theory on this second criterion is not relevant to current psychoanalytic psychology, in which provision is made for a concept of integration of earlier-stage elements into higher-stage structures. For example, in *The First Year of Life,* Spitz (1965) describes certain organizers that integrate infant behavior. Nagera (1966) has studied the organizational function of the infantile neurosis, showing that not only are elements from the oral, anal, and phallic stages integrated under this more tightly knit psychic structure but that the processes of earlier stages (e.g., developmental and neurotic conflicts) are organized in a higher-order structure.

Of course, if one were to take this second criterion to mean that every aspect of lower-order functioning must be subsumed under a unified higher-order structure, then it is doubtful that psychoanalysis could meet the criterion. In psychoanalytic thought certain elements of prior stages are subsumed under a higher-order structure, but the lower structure as a whole is not incorporated completely. Piaget's cognitive stages, in their operative dimension, do have this holistic quality, but this seems more relevant to criterion four regarding a whole self-regulating system. Moreover, it could be claimed that the figurative aspects of cognition may not follow as organized a path as do the operative aspects.

Piaget's third criterion—that each stage contain an element of preparation for the following stage and represent an achievement over the preceding stage—is also consistent with current psychoanalytic psychology. In contemporary theory, each developmental stage is conceptualized in a broad matrix of psychological functioning and not simply around the vicissitudes and organization of the drives. There are concomitant steps in the development of drives, internalized object relations, and aspects of ego and superego functioning. Each step in these various lines of development emerges from a prior step and in optimal development represents progress over preceding steps. The concept of genitality, which represents not only a focus and organization of the drives, but also a level of object relations and ego functioning, is illustrative.

Piaget's fourth criterion is that of the structural whole. Certain qualifications must be introduced when this criterion is applied even to his own theory. As noted above, it may pertain to operative thinking without pertaining to the figurative dimensions of thought, relatively underdeveloped examples of which can be found even in adults. In addition, Piaget's notion of vertical *décalage* implies that holistic integration, even in the operative realm, is a time-consuming developmental process that is completed only after long preparation.

Certain organizing structures in the psychoanalytic model approach the criterion of a holistic system without attaining it completely. Consider, for example, certain nodal points in childhood development—attachment, separation, attainment of object constancy, attainment of the infantile neurosis, and formation of an organized superego structure—all of which culminate in the adolescent's separation from parents and consolidation of identity. These latter achievements represent the incorporation of earlier achievements into more organized wholes. In other words, separation at the end of adolescence and the consolidation of identity incorporate achievements of preoedipal separation-individuation and of the processes of superego and ego-ideal formation. As Kaplan (1972) has noted, the Piagetian construct of vertical *décalage* is useful to psychoanalysis here in describing the kinds of developmental recapitulations that occur as the personality moves toward higher levels of integration.

While psychoanalytic stages cannot strictly be said to meet the holistic fourth criterion, it can be claimed that within the analytic model, elements of preceding stages are fully incorporated into later stages as adaptive structures, characterological inhibitions, neurotic structures, or relatively conflict-free structures. Transformational rules linking these varied structures have not been elucidated in psychoanalysis, nor has it been demonstrated that they could be. Nevertheless, general compatibility can be seen to exist between the stage concept of psychoanalytic ego psychology and that of Piaget.

6

FURTHER CONSIDERATIONS OF PIAGET'S MODEL: AREAS OF INCOMPATIBILITY— UNCONSCIOUS PHENOMENA AND VICISSITUDES OF DRIVES AND AFFECTS

In the preceding sections we have shown a striking compatibility between the general psychology offered by Piaget and the parallel constructs within psychoanalytic psychology. What has not been addressed is the major area of incompatibility: Piaget's nonconsideration of drive-determined wishes and affective life, and particularly of the concept of the dynamic unconscious.

We shall now specifically consider Piaget's comments on affectivity, his dialogue with Freud, and his critique of psychoanalysis to show further the basic compatibility of the two models. By reviewing what Piaget has said in the light of current psychoanalytic psychology, we shall mitigate many of his criticisms. Piaget's critique is the result, in certain instances, of a misinterpretation of psychoanalysis, and in others, of his focus on an early version of psychoanalytic thinking.

We shall then shift gears and view the structure of psychoanalytic theory, addressing the issue of compatibility from the psychoanalytic perspective. We shall consider the five metapsychological points of view and examine their relative compatibility or incompatibility with Piaget's basic theoretical model.

Piaget's Comments on Affectivity

Compared with his considerations of cognitive development, Piaget's notions about affective development are quite scanty and are not based on substantial empirical data. A number of primary sources contain elements of Piaget's views on affectivity. The most extensive of these consists of a series of lectures delivered at the Sorbonne in 1954. Since this source remains untranslated, and since other, shorter sources are available in English, we shall rely on the latter. They include one of Piaget's addresses during a visiting professorship at the Menninger Foundation (1962b), certain sections of Piaget and Inhelder's *The Psychology of the Child* (1966), and an essay from *Six Psychological Studies* (1964).

It should be pointed out that Piaget has not developed a full theory of affective life. Consequently, we need not attempt to criticize systematically his model of affectivity. We need only look at those parallels to cognitive development that he has posited to evaluate their compatibility with psychoanalytic thought.

Piaget basically holds that intelligence and affectivity develop parallel to each other. He has stated that affectivity may retard or accelerate cognitive development. We accept this. Piaget, however, believes that affectivity cannot be considered the cause of the progressive structuralization that marks cognitive growth. We would go further than Piaget by stating that affective factors can have an impact both on the structuring and on the functioning of cognition. This point will be elaborated on later.

Piaget postulates that the first two years of life (the sensorimotor period) are marked by parallel processes in the transition from undifferentiation to differentiation in both cognitive and affective life. Again, we accept this. It is of interest, however, that although Piaget more or less accepts the idea of development from primary narcissism to object relations, he points out that the initial stage can be more adequately described as *adualism,* a lack of differentiation, with concurrent lack of awareness of either pole of the self-object field. The terminology "narcissism to object relations" focuses more on the drive aspects of psychoanalytic theory, with which Piaget is less familiar, whereas "differentiation" focuses more on the developing ego structure and hence is closer to his interest in pure cognition.

Moving into the preoperational subperiod, Piaget comments that as the child's social and cognitive world expands with the acquisition of the semiotic function and the beginnings of linguistic communication, the parallel in affective development is the growth of interpersonal emotions and interrelated feelings. The child can now maintain mental imagery in the absence of the cognitive object. This ability allows him to maintain a constant stance toward significant others and toward himself.

Obviously there is a correspondence here to the evolving capacity of the child for object constancy. As we indicated in our review of the literature, numerous authors have attempted to integrate Piaget's theory of object permanence with the psychoanalytic theory of object constancy. Some, including Fraiberg (1959), have attempted to account for apparent discrepancies in the two theories by holding that only a minimal form of object permanence, that based on recognition memory rather than evocative memory, is a prerequisite to object constancy. From the point of view of this monograph, that affective factors can affect the structuring and functioning of cognitive schemes, Mahler's comments are most appropriate (Mahler, Pine, and Bergman, 1975). She holds that *libidinal object constancy* occurs later than object permanence in Piaget's sense, because the representation of the internal object is subject to the vicissitudes of external stress and upheaval from the drives.

It is important that Piaget notes a parallel between affective life and cognitive development, but does not offer an integration of the two realms. Such an integration would have to deal with the effects of drives, affectivity, and internalization of human object relations on cognition and vice versa. In other words, to attempt an integration, Piaget would need to postulate something with more explanatory power than parallel features. To use his own language, he would need to postulate "transformational rules" relating affectivity to cognition.

Piaget rejects, as an explanation of the permanence of certain affects and the generalization of identification, the notion that feelings are attached to unconscious representations. Instead,

Piaget (1962b) posits that parallel to cognitive schemes, schemes of reaction or affective schemes are developed in relation to parents and significant persons (e.g., patterns of submission, obedience, or revolt). The infantile feelings connected with these schemes are then aroused whenever a social situation occurs similar to the ones that initially generated the schemes. Piaget's model thus has certain elements similar to those of a learning model of generalization.

Piaget's idea that the stability of certain affects has to do with the construction of schemes of reaction or affective schemes may have some value for psychoanalytic thinking, particularly if these schemes are seen in their interaction with other schemes that may be derived from the unconscious mental representation of the self and important objects. But Piaget's notion of affective schemes is limited and overly narrow. He does not take into account the dynamic determinants of behavior central to psychoanalytic thinking and, as stated above, dismisses unconscious mental representation.

In Piaget's discussion of affectivity he points out concomitant interpersonal aspects of the preoperational period, the period of concrete operations (latency) and the period of formal operations (adolescence). With reference to children's games, he draws a parallel between the ability of the concrete operational child to deal with rules in an interpersonal sense of give-and-take and his cognitive capacity. He contrasts this development with the preoperational child's inability for reciprocal cooperation becaise of cognitive limitation. Similarly, he compares the lack of mutuality, reciprocity, and cooperation in the preoperational child's moral feelings with their presence in the concrete operational child's morality.

The concrete operational child's ability to *conserve* in the cognitive realm makes it possible for him to make judgments based not on perceptual configurations alone, but on transformations that account for change in configurations. Just as the concrete operational child can coordinate two dimensions for a container of water, its width and its length, thus conserving the quantity of the whole even when transformations occur, so can he coordinate the impulse of the moment with the values that orient his life. This ability enables the child to make judgments based on a system of relative values, including past learning and some limited future goals. Also during this time, morality shifts its basis from obedience and unilateral respect to mutual respect. The concrete operational child can comprehend a system of rules and can understand, to some extent, the viewpoint of his peers. Piaget considers the organization of a system of values to be the moral parallel to the organization of cognitive concepts.

Piaget discusses the adolescent's ability for thinking about thinking and his consequent concern with ideological issues. In his thought the adolescent can transform the world, viewing the perceived world as only one among many possible worlds. The adolescent's new ability thus gives rise to an emotional investment in desires to change his world, with a focus on ideals.

As can be readily seen, in his consideration of the behavior of preoperational, concrete operational, and formal operational children from a cognitive standpoint, Piaget makes interesting observations about the nature of interpersonal relationships. His descriptions of the child's ability to understand rules and the adolescent's interest in ideals, for instance, are consistent with the clinical observations of psychoanalysis and in fact enrich these observations. To make Piaget's observations about interpersonal feelings, morality, and adolescent thinking more useful to psychoanalysts, however, it is necessary to integrate these observations with a fuller, more comprehensive theory of behavior that takes into account the importance of unconscious factors, the derivatives of the drives and their concomitant affects, and internalized self- and object representations.

PIAGET'S MOTIVATIONAL CONSTRUCTS

In relation to Piaget's comments on affects, it is important to discuss his motivational constructs. As Flavell (1963) puts it, "His position is simply that there is an intrinsic need for cognitive organs or structures, once generated by functioning, to perpetuate themselves by more functioning" (p. 78). We noted that Piaget postulates reproductive, generalizing, recognitory, and reciprocal assimilatory processes to account for the progressive structuring of schemes. These processes explain and describe the construction of differentiated schemes but do not refer to a motivational system underlying this construction. For Piaget, cognitive structures are self-motivating.

Again, Piaget's lack of a complete motivational theory does not necessarily pose a problem for psychoanalytic psychology. One might take the position that he comes into conflict with the psychoanalytic theory of motivation. To the contrary, if Piaget posed a complex theory of motivation, integration would be a challenging task; it would be necessary to see how the two theories of motivation related to one another. That Piaget essentially has no theory of motivation makes the larger integration somewhat easier.

At this point, we can simply say that his account of how the cognitive sphere of the ego evolves is compatible with the idea that both ego and id develop out of an undifferentiated matrix. Early in life there appears to be primitive ego mechanisms that have a relative autonomy in their involvement with the environment. This view is consistent with that of current developmental ego psychology, as well as many child development researchers. Interestingly, Freud also comments on a basic pleasure in cognitive activity separated from specific drives.

Piaget's Dialogue with Psychoanalysis

We shall now consider Piaget's specific critique of psychoanalytic psychology in order to clarify further the areas of compatibility, areas Piaget may have considered incompatible that in the light of contemporary ego psychology are in fact compatible, and certain areas of important differences that require further reworking and elaboration.

Piaget's most detailed consideration of psychoanalysis and his most elaborate criticism of Freudian theory appear in *Play, Dreams and Imitation in Childhood* (1945). As Cobliner (1967) points out, Piaget lost touch with developments in psychoanalysis in the thirties. Be that as it may, the 1945 critique of Freud's theory of symbolism still articulates major differences between genetic epistemology and psychoanalysis.

The first issue to be considered is the difference between psychoanalysis and Piaget in their respective models of thinking. The psychoanalytic model of thinking is usually referred to in relation to Freud's (1915) early postulate that when the object of gratification is missing and instinctual discharges are delayed, the first affects and cognitions arise. Freud sees the emergence of the hallucinatory image of the need-satisfying object as an effect of delayed gratification. This hallucinatory image is the archetype of thought.

On the surface, Piaget's genetic epistemology disagrees with this model on two points. Piaget holds that cognitive structures are self-motivated, that there is a certain *need to function* implicit in these structures as a means of adaptation. The equilibration process, by which the human organism adapts to internal and external disturbances through assimilation and accommodation, is sufficient to account for intellectual development. Thus, Piaget rejects the notion of the absence of the need-satisfying object as the primary determinant of early thinking. Similarly, he rejects the concept of frustration as the drive behind precursory thought.[1]

The second point of disagreement involves the implication that a figurative dimension of thinking is within the infant's capacity as early in life as originally postulated by Freud (in terms of the hallucinatory image). Piaget posits the beginnings of the semiotic function around the middle of the second year of life. He has referred to a lack of a genetic perspective in classical psychoanalysis—the tendency to attribute to the infant properties characteristic of adult development (1945, p. 185). This important general criticism underscores many of Piaget's more specific criticisms of psychoanalytic constructs, particularly those of memory and consciousness.

To return to the first point in Piaget's critique: the need to function as a means of adaptation is well within the bounds of current psychoanalytic psychology. Contemporary ego psy-

[1] Kessen (1971) has clearly pointed out this difference. He designates psychoanalysis a "hot" theory of cognitive motivation, since, for Freud, thought develops as a result of the frustration of the drives. Piaget's theory of cognitive motivation, however, is a "cold" theory, one which makes no reference to the drive state of the organism.

chology, which holds that the ego and id develop out of an orginally undifferentiated matrix, posits the possibility, even in early infancy, of ego functions capable of dealing with the environment in an adaptive relationship. In energic terms, one might say that neutralized energy is at the disposal of the ego for its relationship to the environment even in early infancy. Because of the broadening of psychoanalysis by ego psychology, it is no longer necessary for analysts to postulate frustration as the drive underlying the first thoughts. Psychoanalytic and Piagetian models are now compatible on the point of the possibility of the ego's interacting with the environment in an adaptive relationship, with no need to consider drive energies or drive-motivating forces as crucial or essential to this early relationship. If we consider the differences among aspects of ego functioning, and focus on those aspects that relate to the non-affect-laden dimensions of the environment, we may even more easily postulate that this aspect of the ego can function in a relatively autonomous adaptive manner.

Moreover, Piaget's formulations regarding assimilation and accommodation are not wholly inconsistent with Freud's early psychoanalytic notions, which were based largely on reconstructions rather than on direct observations of infancy. Piaget does posit that the early tendency for accommodation results from disturbance in a beginning assimilatory scheme. The aspect of disturbance is common to his model and to Freud's early ideas. Freud talks about this disturbance in the context of frustration (the absence of a need-satisfying object in the presence of a need or activated drive state). Piaget speaks of this disturbance in terms of something new from the environment being presented to the infant, who lacks the necessary accommodatory capacity. In a broader sense, however, both theories invoke an equilibrium model such that disturbances in equilibrium lead the organism to make internal changes resulting eventually in internal structures.

Unconcerned with the vicissitudes of internal experiences generated by alterations in drive states, tensions, and their related affect states, however, Piaget views disturbance to equilibrium only in a limited dimension. He is concerned with *one* aspect of the external boundary of the ego: the way the ego deals with the impersonal environment to form its cognitive structures. The psychoanalytic model attempts to understand the process of equilibrium in a broader context, looking at stimuli from multiple directions impinging on the ego, even on the initial ego structure of the infant. Not only must the infant deal with new stimuli of the external environment and attempt to adapt to them, but he must do this in the face of altering states of drive tensions and related affect charges.

In this sense, the psychoanalytic model looks at a different experience than does Piaget and attempts to encompass a wider range of human experience (e.g., conscious, unconscious, logical, illogical, emotional). If we see Piaget's model of cognitive development as a subsystem of the psychoanalytic model, we can state that Piaget is trying to account for only a certain aspect of ego structure. Nevertheless, in order to integrate fully Piaget's cognitive model as a subsystem, it will be important to see how drives do relate to the types of equilibrium Piaget posits. Then we can consider not only the disturbances caused by external stimuli, but also the effects of drive derivatives and affect charges on the development of the cognitive sector of the personality. At this point, however, it is important chiefly to point out that the Piagetian and psychoanalytic models of thought are compatible in the broadened context of ego psychology.

As noted above, the second point of Piaget's critique concerns the stage at which the infant has the capacity for figurative thinking. The concept of a hallucinatory image as the first thought, with the young infant necessarily capable of this, is too literal an interpretation of the psychoanalytic view. The infant is not necessarily capable of a very specific image of the object; rather, the infant is capable of experiencing some internal state of drive-affect activation that has attached to it some relatedness to the experience of satisfaction with the external object world. According to this model, at some point the infant no longer simply experiences a state of drive activation, but, in the absence of satisfaction, he experiences a sense of activation attached to some vague, undifferentiated experience of earlier satisfaction. Contemporary psychoanalysis does not conceive this as necessarily at the level of visual imagery or evocative memory. It may be, for example, an extremely undifferentiated tactile experience. The important point is that at present it is impossible to know what kind of undifferentiated drive-affect states and concomitant states of prior satisfaction the infant is capable of, since there is no research to show when such experiences are possible. We only know that in the second year of life, the infant is capable of internal visual mental imagery as *tested* in an experimental situation; for example, the infant is capable, in Piaget's sense, of searching for a hidden object. A continuing capacity to organize and integrate imagery from the different senses is probably developing throughout the first years of life. We tend to posit particular milestones when we can experimentally verify certain of these achievements.

It is also worth noting that within experimental and developmental psychology the debate continues over when the infant achieves object permanence. Bower (1967), for example, has used tracking experiments rather than search experiments and argues in favor of a type of object permanence prior to that postulated by Piaget. This debate has been very well reviewed by Harris (1975), who has shown that Piaget's timetable appears to be substantiated with regard to the ability to evoke a mental representation of an absent object. As Fraiberg (1969) has pointed out, the capacity to experience hallucinatory imagery under internal stimulation may require a lower level of object permanence.

In sum, the question of in what way and to what degree the infant is capable of Freud's "hallucinatory image" is unresolved by current experimental data. Complete synthesis of Piagetian and psychoanalytic theories of object permanence and internal mental representation must await further empirical findings.

Piaget (1945) also criticizes the Freudian concept of symbols in their conscious and unconscious contexts. However, since his critique is based on early prestructural psychoanalytic psychology, it does not really challenge the assumptions of current psychoanalytic ego psychology and the structural model. It should be mentioned, though, that Piaget has objected strenuously to the early topographical theory and the idea of a region of the mind that contains unconscious symbols and feelings. Piaget has instead suggested that what are unconscious are the action schemes and that they become conscious only when they are stimulated by an external event that causes them and their associated affects to come into action.

In connection with this point, Piaget posits such a relationship between what is conscious and unconscious not only in the realm of symbolism, but throughout all thought:

> We must observe at this point, to avoid losing ourselves in a mythology of the unconscious, that what has just been said is true of all thought, rational as well as symbolic, and that while the result of all mental work is conscious, its mechanism remains hidden. The unconscious is not a separate region of the mind, since in every psychic process there is a continual and continuous coming and going from the unconscious to consciousness. While accommodation of thought is generally conscious, because external or internal obstacles call forth consciousness, assimilation, even when rational, is usually unconscious (1945, p. 172).

According to Piaget, the subject's lack of consciousness of the feelings attached to reaction schemes is a function of the fact that they come into existence only when the scheme is activated. As Piaget puts it, "It is much more difficult to become conscious of a scheme of reaction and its intricate implications than of feelings which are already formed and ready to emerge" (1945, p. 187).

In many respects, Piaget's view of symbols is consistent with that of current ego psychology and the structural point of view, which do not posit separate regions of the mind for the collection of instincts, affects, and ideas, but rather describe the relationships between different structures organized according to their functions. The idea that affects are associated with patterns of reaction, in fact, provides a useful direction for better understanding the development of affects.

Again, it is important to point out a crucial difference: Piaget clearly has not accepted the dynamic point of view of psychoanalysis. Although he would probably agree with the notion that the ego and id differentiate out of a common matrix and thus that aspects of secondary-process and primary-process thought[2] develop simultaneously, he does not have a drive-re-

[2] Thought is used here in its broadest sense, meaning any type of configuration of mental representations. To the degree that the primary process involves not only drive-discharge processes, but the organization of mental representations (e.g., condensations) in the context of these processes, it is possible to speak of primary-process thought.

lated model of primary-process thinking or of the relationship between primary-process and secondary-process thinking as it evolves after the institution of a repressive barrier. In this sense, Piaget does not accept the notion of the dynamic unconscious, although he might accept the concept of a structural unconscious. The dynamic unconscious, however, is as crucial to current psychoanalytic psychology as it was to earlier psychoanalytic psychology.

Piaget has also criticized the Freudian model of memory. But here, too, he has relied on prestructural theory, before the development of ego psychology. Piaget (1945) designates the Freudian model an extraction model in that all memories from the past are preserved in the unconscious and that consciousness reaches into this vault to retrieve a memory. In contrast, Piaget posits a reconstruction model of memory, in which remembrance is constituted when intelligence organizes and reorganizes the data retained in the mental apparatus according to their relationship to schemes. In this sense, memories are deduced rather than extracted holistically. For example, the absence of memories from the earliest years of life is not a function of repression but of the lack of adequate cognitive structures in the sensorimotor period. According to Piaget, the child's first memories are simple recognition memories. A child remembers a significant person in the sense that he reacts to that person in the same way that he has reacted previously. Only later, with the beginning of mental representation during the preoperational period, does the child become capable of evocative memory. It is the ability to construct a mental image of a remembered object in the absence of that object that constitutes evocative memory. Thus, memory itself develops along with the rest of the cognitive processes, and as intelligence develops, memory becomes better organized and more powerful.

It is interesting to view Piaget's critique of Freud in the context of current ego psychology, because Piaget's comments actually agree with and reinforce certain views of contemporary psychoanalysis. Most psychoanalysts do not currently believe that memories in the sense of clear, organized patterns of mental imagery can be evoked from earliest infancy. It is well known in current psychoanalytic work that one attempts to reconstruct early memories through a process that corresponds to Piaget's reconstruction. In the transference the patient experiences certain repetitive patterns of relating (or as Piaget puts it, of reacting) to the analyst. From this the analyst and the patient attempt to deduce some preverbal or prefigurative aspects of the patient's experience—that is, what life may have been like during the stage prior to the patient's capability for mental imagery. Often very primitive affects may be experienced in the context of reliving early interaction patterns in the analytic setting. Through these primitive affects, a sense of conviction may occur about the deduction of events in the first year or two of life. Piaget's theory thus parallels very well what current psychoanalytic practice posits as the way in which the very earliest memories are reconstructed.

Psychoanalysts agree with Piaget that memory in the evocative sense is possible only later in life. In fact, the memories that psychoanalysts refer to in terms of retrieval into consciousness are really those that are secondarily repressed at the end of the oedipal phase. During early development a child may attend to only limited aspects of what is available to him regarding his internal experience. Some of this internal experience is organized in visual imagery, some may be in imagery relating to other sense systems, some may be in terms of schemes or action patterns. The earliest aspects of memory become an important part of psychological structure. This is what Piaget means when he talks about assimilation. His notion is highly compatible with psychoanalytic psychology, particularly when we consider that it is the internalization of early object relations that forms the nucleus of certain ego substructures.

Although early experience is not conscious in a structural sense and is not available to the evocative process, these earliest memories can be deduced and aspects of them can be experienced, particularly through their reliving in the nonverbal transference. The kinds of memories most available to evocation in the psychoanalytic sense, however, are those that are secondarily repressed at the oedipal phase of development. These later memories are affect-laden. There seems to be general agreement between Piaget and Freud that anxiety-provoking and potentially noxious or frightening feelings or memories are relegated to a state of unawareness.

The Piagetian idea that memory itself develops alongside the rest of the cognitive process and becomes better organized and more powerful, as does cognition, is not inconsistent with psychoanalytic ideas. From the psychoanalytic perspective, memory, like other aspects of the ego apparatus, is related to the dynamic process. Psychoanalysis is interested in those forces, unconscious and conscious, that influence memory. It has not been as interested in the development of memory itself as an aspect of the ego apparatus. Just as psychoanalysis does not have a developmental model of impersonal cognition, it lacks a complete developmental model of memory.

Piaget (1945) attacks the Freudian model of consciousness as a "lighting up" or an "internal sense organ." But this is only one aspect of thinking posited by Freud. Also, current ego psychology would separate the "lighting up" function of consciousness from other aspects of consciousness and certainly would distinguish it from thinking in a broader sense. When Piaget (1945) says that consciousness is conscious activity whose function is not to reveal existing concepts but to construct these concepts, he is referring to an aspect of thinking; he readily admits that he is talking about accommodation. Thus he is focusing on a different aspect of consciousness than did Freud. Certainly Piaget's idea of conscious activity would be in accord with certain aspects of secondary-process thinking within modern ego psychology (Hartmann, 1939; Rapaport, 1959).

Piaget ignores an important phenomenon, however. He does not consider accommodation as a characteristic of unconscious thinking. To him, accommodations are always conscious because by definition accommodation is the way intelligence adapts in a structural sense to new assimilations. We know from clinical experience, however, that there are unconscious accommodations. For instance, drive-affect constellations in the context of internalized object relations may evoke unconscious accommodations in drive defense structures. Piaget's formulation is extremely narrow. He is looking at only one boundary of the ego, that which relates to certain aspects of the external world in terms of impersonal cognition.

Piaget's identification of accommodation with conscious comprehension is obvious in his statement that whenever assimilation far outweighs accommodation, whenever reality is incorporated into cognitive structures without a concomitant adaptation of those structures, the subject's level of consciousness is reduced. Only as accommodation comes into reciprocity with assimilation does the subject's awareness reach the full level of consciousness. According to Piaget (1945), this step represents the transition from symbolic play to intelligent behavior.

Since he is concerned with intelligent thought only in the sense of pure or impersonal cognition, it is understandable why Piaget has constructed his model in this fashion. He has not been interested in understanding the "intelligence" of the unconscious. Aspects of primary-process thinking are seen by Piaget only in terms of the development from primitive to more advanced forms of intelligence.

As we have emphasized, Piaget lacks the principles of a dynamic unconscious and of a dynamic relationship between conscious intellectual activity in the secondary process and the gradations of unconscious mental activity involving other types of processes (e.g., condensation, displacement). To utilize Piagetian constructs to describe the construction of unconscious substructures, we must use the assimilation-accommodation model in a way somewhat different from the way Piaget uses it. As a first step, we might speak of the accommodation of structures as not being identical with conscious adaptation. In other words, adaptation can occur outside awareness.

Another point of contention for Piaget is the psychoanalytic notion of free associations, particularly the idea that free associations come to the fore during the course of an analysis from a place in the unconscious. In contrast, Piaget sees the associative process as involving active constructions by the subject. Associations are formed as the analysand relates suggestive material such as dreams, symbols, slips of the tongue, and vague transference experiences to his system of schemes. Free associations, then, are constructs resulting from judgments or acts of assimilation. Piaget here sees a continuity between unconscious association and intelligent activity and calls for a "more functional, less topographical" interpretation of the relationship between the conscious and the unconscious.

This criticism of Freud is again less relevant to current psychoanalytic ego psychology. Free associations provide access to certain dynamic processes, although it is no longer believed free associations lead to a distinct realm of the mind in the topographical sense. In the context of structural theory, the associative process can be seen as highly compatible with a process of active constructions and assimilations. In fact, the success of the free-association technique is a function of the proper balance between free associations and active construction. In the current psychoanalytic model the ideal analysand moves between free association, in which he reduces cognitive control and lets his mind "go," and the intelligent activity of reconstruction. In the reconstruction phase the patient integrates his associations and creates the kind of continuum between conscious and unconscious, past and present, that leads to an integrated understanding of his inner world.

The process of assimilation is essentially the process of letting the intelligent activity take in from the external world what it will. In other words, what it assimilates is what is developmentally appropriate and interesting in the environment. Applying the process of assimilation to the world of drive derivatives and their accompanying affects and of internal representations, the ego takes in certain aspects of this rich internal world just as it does of the rich external world. The degree to which it can assimilate internal stimuli depends on the ego's readiness and on the lack of strong resistances. This ego-directed process of taking in stimuli, essentially a process of assimilation, occurs in the free-association phase of the analytic work.

The corresponding accommodation process occurs when intelligent activity is directed toward relating free associations to existing schemes, or more properly, to expanding existing structures to encompass the new material. Without this balancing process, free association would represent a preponderance of assimilation over accommodation and, in Piagetian terms, would be reduced to play.

Working through an insight can also be viewed within Piaget's model. Take, for example, an infant's development of "pulling" schemes. Here an action applied to one setting is generalized to others; for example, the infant learns that pulling a string leads to a noise in one setting, so he applies the same rule to other settings. In this generalization process new aliment (the elements of the new setting) is assimilated to the action pattern, and, conversely, the pattern is modified to accommodate slightly different stimulus characteristics in the new setting.

A parallel process occurs in working through, as an insight is applied across situations. A patient, after having allowed a preponderance of assimilation over accommodation in the free-association process, begins to put together past experiences with current experiences. In this way available structures are expanded to accommodate new data or new structures are formed. Thus, in formalistic terms, one might describe the result of working through as accommodation to the data of free association, resulting in the formation of a new or more expanded ego structure.[3]

At the end of his 1945 discourse, Piaget offers two general criticisms of Freudian theory. The first of these is that the notion of censorship is self-contradictory. Piaget believes that Freudian psychoanalytic psychology claims that since consciousness censors, consciousness can therefore cause unconsciousness, a paradoxical and essentially illogical state of affairs. It should be pointed out that repression and the notion of censorship in the context of the dynamic relationships between structures of the personality are functions of unconscious ego mechanisms. No assumption is currently made that the conscious ego screens input from the internal or external world and then decides voluntarily which data should be kept out of further awareness. Rather, much of the process of screening and blocking input occurs at an unconscious level.

The other general criticism Piaget makes concerns the psychoanalytic theory of symbolic thought. He feels that his own theory of symbol formation and usage is more universal than Freud's, because the latter's theory is based solely on unconscious, repressed content expressed in disguised form. Piaget's theory of symbol formation is based on the functional invariants

[3] It should be pointed out that the above examples from the psychoanalytic process are to illustrate the compatibility of the theoretical models. It is not being suggested that the psychoanalytic situation per se is synonymous with the psychoanalytic model.

of assimilation and accommodation and thus is directly continuous with all adaptive thinking. Symbolic thinking is unlike adaptive thought, however, in that it occurs as a first attempt to balance assimilation with accommodation, and it differs from operative thought in its figurative quality based on the semiotic function.

Piaget's criticism of the Freudian notion of symbol formation will not be repeated here. Anthony (1957) reviews much of Piaget's 1945 critique of Freud, and responds from a psychoanalytic perspective to some of Piaget's points. He argues that Piaget's idea of an unconscious in continuity with consciousness corresponds to the psychoanalytic notion of the preconscious. What analysts refer to as a dynamic unconscious is so foreign to Piaget's thinking, according to Anthony, that Piaget's use of the terms *dynamic* and *unconscious* leads only to distortions of meaning. In addition, Anthony claims that the dynamic aspect of Piaget's affective schemes is a dynamism without conflict, and thus his dynamic theory of the transfer of feelings from one situation to other analogous situations is too simple to account for a sizable portion of human experience.

It is possible that Piaget's assimilation-accommodation model may help psychoanalysts to explain the actual process of symbol formation, although it adds little to the understanding of specific symbolic content. Piaget has pointed out, appropriately, that there is a continuum of symbolic thought ranging from the conscious to the unconscious; in this respect he offers a corrective by broadening the scope of psychoanalysis.

For Piaget, however, unconscious symbols are not dynamically unconscious. While he admits that the meaning of certain symbols would be anxiety-provoking if revealed to awareness, no conflict model is constructed to explain this process. In attempting to stress the continuity between conscious and unconscious symbols by citing a direct relationship between consciousness and accommodation, and an inverse relationship between consciousness and assimilation, Piaget has offered only a description, not an explanation. It does not enhance understanding to state simply that symbols remain unconscious because assimilation far outweighs accommodation. In effect, this is a tautology.

In its modern structural form, psychoanalysis can largely accept Piaget's criticism of the Freudian theory of symbolic thought. As an explanatory theory, however, it must go beyond the equation of unconscious material with a preponderance of assimilation over accommodation to ask why certain content is kept out of accommodative awareness. The psychoanalytic constructs of defense mechanisms and the dynamic unconscious attempt to answer this question. For all their limitations, and despite their origins in a substantialist psychology, these constructs seem more useful in understanding selective lack of awareness of certain content than do the more general constructs of assimilation and accommodation.

Finally, in discussing Piaget's dialogue with psychoanalysis, Piaget's more recent exchanges with several analytic thinkers, including Erikson and Bowlby (see Tanner and Inhelder, 1960), should be briefly described. One discrepancy, highlighted again, is Piaget's rejection of a dynamic unconscious that might contain active memories. Rather, Piaget holds that what is unconscious are action patterns, tendencies to react continually in a certain way. These action patterns are stimulated in situations reminiscent of the situations in which they were formed, and they carry certain affective charges. Piaget would not agree with the idea that unconscious memories are related to these action patterns or with the position that as unconscious memories are remembered and integrated, the repetition of certain action patterns is no longer necessary.

The question arises whether Piaget's assertions in this respect can be proved or disproved on the basis of psychoanalytic evidence. In a successful psychoanalysis the re-experiencing of certain action patterns through the transference often makes possible the discovery of prior memories. Such a temporal relationship does not necessarily indicate a causal relationship, that the memories are causing the action patterns. In a sense, we can take Piaget's controversial statement about psychoanalysis as useful provocation for opening up an area of further inquiry. While psychoanalytic experience is quite convincing about the existence of a relationship between memories and the repetition of certain action patterns and a relationship in treatment between re-experiencing, reworking, and remembering, the causal nature of these relationships is not clear. Certainly many aspects of current psychoanalytic ego psychology are consistent with Piaget's basic thrust that remembering is an active process involving construction. Psychoanalysis has moved in this direction, but at the same time it has not left behind its body of discovery about the dynamic unconscious.

Psychoanalysis has only little to say about the development of pure cognition. Piaget has evolved a refined, delineated system to explain the development of pure cognition. Psychoanalytic psychology, however, goes far beyond Piaget's very preliminary notions about the dynamic unconscious and related phenomena. It is interesting as a sidelight that were Piaget to see a well-analyzed patient, he might say, "Ah, ha! This person now has the accommodations within the conscious ego necessary for integrating or actively deducing unconscious symbols." His theory would not be able to delineate in any specific manner how this had occurred, however.

7

THE PSYCHOANALYTIC MODEL AND PIAGET'S COGNITIVE PSYCHOLOGY: POINTS OF COMPATIBILITY

We shall now reverse the process of the preceding chapter and view psychoanalytic theory in terms of its compatibility with Piaget's cognitive psychology. As noted earlier, both systems have in common a criterion of explanation that holds that structures may be understood as wholes linked by transformational processes. Piaget's theory is a formal structuralist one, but without attaining the level of formalization possible for a theory of impersonal cognition, psychoanalysis shares many attributes of a structuralist system, including the "constructivism" characteristic of Piaget's epistemology. This constructivist position claims that the gradual process of interaction between organism and environment leads to the process of structuralization. The resultant internal structures, in turn, determine certain types of behavior.

The psychoanalytic belief in multiple determination, by which each determinant relates to every other one, can be viewed in the context of structuralism. The multiple determinants are elements of a system that constitutes a whole and undergoes certain transformations according to the principles that relate its components to one another. The system tends toward self-regulation, since the multiple determinants are all determinants of behavior and the behavior itself is within the confines of the system. Thus, when Rapaport (1959) states that "an explanation of behavior, in order to have any claim to completeness, must specify its place within the functional and structural framework of the total personality" (p. 43), he takes a structuralist position highly compatible with Piaget's.

The Metapsychological Points of View

The Genetic Perspective

The genetic perspective in the psychoanalytic model implies that every behavior must be studied in its historical development in order to be fully explained. Rapaport (1959) points out that the notion of an epigenetic course includes the regulatory influence of organismic laws and the influence of experience. He demonstrates the breadth of the genetic viewpoint in relating it to all aspects of a given behavior, that is, to the history of the relevant drive processes, structures, and situational variables:

> The genetic character of the psychoanalytic theory is ubiquitous in the literature. The concept of "complementary series" is probably the clearest expression of it: each behavior is part of a historical sequence shaped both by epigenetic laws and experience . . . ; each step in this sequence contributed to the shaping of the behavior and has dynamic, economic, structural, and contextual-adaptive relationships to it [p. 45].

The genetic perspective also includes statements about the relative autonomy of certain behaviors from genetic determinants.

> Certain behaviors do . . . cease to be shaped further by their recurrence: they become automatized . . . and relatively autonomous from their genetic roots; they take on a tool- or means-character and attain a high degree of stability. However, automatization and autonomy make not only for stability, but also for the availability of the behavior as a means of adaptation [p. 45].

While these automatized behaviors can be studied genetically, they are stimulated into action not by factors from their past, such as drives, but by the present context. Thus, the genetic perspective highlights the importance of both epigenetic laws and experience in interaction with the environment. While the history of behavior often exerts a powerful determining force on current behavior, some behavior becomes relatively autonomous from its historical context, so that its occurrence depends primarily on the present situational variables.

The genetic perspective not only is highly compatible with Piagetian psychology, but is directly comparable to Piaget's own view of how development occurs in the purely cognitive sphere. As indicated earlier, he views behavior as a result not of innate factors alone nor of experiential factors alone, but of an interaction between organism and environment. He believes that cognitive behavior unfolds in a fixed developmental sequence that results from the organism's actions upon the environment and that there are characteristic functional capacities at each level of development.

Psychoanalysis also postulates that an epigenetic sequence unfolds in an organized pattern as a series of "developmental stages," each with certain characteristic aspects. Piaget has claimed that his model of developmental stages is more rigorous than the psychoanalytic model because it is marked not only by a fixed sequence but by an organized structure at each stage that incorporates the elements of earlier stages. He criticizes the psychoanalytic stages because they are highlighted only by characteristic behaviors or drive-determined patterns and do not meet the criterion of incorporating in a complete way the behavior of the preceding stages. As we have argued, however, the psychoanalytic model does postulate a characteristic organized, integrated structure at each stage. In terms of drive development, the organization of the drives at the oral, anal, and phallic stages is such that the higher level of organization incorporates elements of the preceding stages. With the expansion of psychoanalytic theory into object relations theory, each stage can now be seen as involving the coordination and organization not only of the drives but also of certain internalized object relations and certain ego structures.

Thus, Piaget and psychoanalysis are conceptually very similar from the genetic perspective. One important difference, however, is that the psychoanalytic genetic perspective includes the unfolding of the drives and unconscious processes. The concept of the dynamic unconscious is not one that Piaget accepts, as we stated earlier.

The Structural Perspective

The structural perspective in the psychoanalytic model was posited when "It was observed that drives do not unequivocally determine behavior in general, nor symptom formation in particular. In contrast to the drive processes, whose rate of change is fast and whose course is paroxysmal, the factors which conflict with them and codetermine behavior appeared to be invariant, or at least of a slower rate of change" (Rapaport, 1959, p. 53). In other words, the structural perspective became important when it was seen that there were relatively invariant factors acting as determinants of behavior.

The best example of a structure is the ego. According to Rapaport (1959, p. 54), "the ego was defined as a cohesive organization, whose function was to synthesize the demands of id, superego, and reality (Freud, 1923)." Rapaport, however, notes that the ego is so complex a structure that its exploration remains at a beginning stage.

The psychoanalytic concept of structure contains two points of particular relevance to our discussion. One is that some structures are present at birth; the second is that all psychologically relevant structures have a developmental sequence. Initially, there are some preliminary structures, such as the constitutionally given apparatuses of motility, the perceptual system, the memory system, and thresholds. (Rapaport, 1959). Through the interaction of these innate givens with the environment further substructures develop and differentiate.

In addition, Rapaport notes that although originally all structures were considered to be related to conflict, it is now assumed that certain inborn apparatuses are not dependent on the drives. These apparatuses are only relatively free from the drives, but their relative autonomy implies that they can function even when they do not serve drive gratification. There are also structures that may originally be determined by the drives and then become secondarily autonomous. Their autonomy, too, is only relative.

In summary, according to Rapaport (1959), the structural position in psychoanalysis holds that there are determinants of behavior that are relatively permanent and that certain of these are inborn and certain acquired. Structure building transforms stimuli from within the body—that is, motivations—into new structures, and certain of these may become relatively autonomous determinants of behavior.

The psychoanalytic concept of structures as relatively invariant determinants of behavior that may be relatively autonomous from the drives is compatible with Piaget's model of cognitive behavior. For Piaget, structures are internalized action patterns that in the course of cognitive development become organized into closed systems that process input from the environment in such a way as to yield logically necessary results. Within the cognitive domain, then, Piaget posits structures that once formed are invariant unless some extraordinary disturbance in thinking occurs.[1] In general, the process of cognitive structure building is unidirectional: toward systems of greater field of application, mobility, permanence, and stability (see Dudek and Dyer, 1972).

Thus, in both theoretical systems structures are seen to result in an ordered sequence from the organism's interaction with environmental stimuli. In analytic theory, however, innate factors are also termed *structures* in themselves, while Piaget posits only certain very simple reflexes, as well as the functional invariants of assimilation and accommodation, to be present at birth.

In both systems structures, once formed, become the psychological organizations that process additional stimuli. Psychoanalysis, however, does not have a specific model of the formation of such structures vis-à-vis inner stimuli. In this regard, it may prove useful to see if the constructs of Piaget's assimilation-accommodation model of structure building can be generalized to relationships with the internal environment.

In order to construct a general, more integrated theory, we might postulate that a structure has an internal and an external boundary. The external boundary comes into contact with non-affective, non-drive-colored aspects of the environment, while the internal boundary relates to the drives, their derivative wishes, and affect-laden aspects of external reality. It should be pointed out that the concept of boundary is employed here as an explanatory abstraction and does not indicate the existence of a real entity. A person relates to mental representations

[1] Anthony (1956b, 1958) has in fact found regressions in cognitive structure building among psychotic infants.

which convey meanings to experience. Organizations of these representations deal with and convey meanings in different spheres of experence, more or less. The term *internal boundary* is intended to convey one such sphere of experience, and the term *external boundary* another. The boundary concepts are obviously simplifications to facilitate discussion about phenomena which differ more in degree rather than in absolute terms.

Just as Rapaport (1959) claims that every behavior has a peremptory or wish-affect aspect to it as well as a purely ego-autonomous or relatively conflict-free aspect to it, we shall consider certain structures of the personality as having these two boundaries. We shall later postulate that laws that hold for the external boundary may hold for aspects of development at the internal boundary (principle of multiple function). In discussing the dynamic perspective and Piaget's cognitive psychology, we shall present a detailed examination of how the internal and external boundaries relate to each other cross-sectionally and during the course of development.

The Adaptive Perspective

The adaptive perspective focuses on the relationship between the ego and reality. The concept of reality in psychoanalytic theory has grown in a number of steps, which Rapaport (1959) reviews. Originally, Rapaport points out, reality was considered a target of defense—the memory of a real event was defended against. In a second conception of reality (Freud, 1900), the drive object and the secondary process were related to reality. Reality was that which made available the object of the drives and which was accurately reflected in secondary-process thinking.

It was not until the third conception of reality, which appeared in Freud's ego psychology of the 1923-1938 period, that reality became conceptualized as the internalized regulator of behavior in terms of internal structures, or constituents of the ego and the superego. The ego was still seen in a limited capacity as an internal structure that integrated the demands of external reality, the id, and the superego. Yet the initial ideas of the capacity for structural differentiation and structure building were beginning to emerge: "The identifications with the objects of social reality imply that reality has not only a defensive-conflictful role, but also an ego-structure-forming role" (Rapaport, 1959, p. 60). Thus, the concept of the ego's relative independence from drives and a concomitant objectivity vis-à-vis reality was in ascendance.

It was not, however, until Hartmann (1939) presented a fourth conception of reality that the adaptive point of view became an important independent perspective in psychoanalysis. In Hartmann's conception, through the process of evolution, man is from birth potentially adapted to reality through the ego apparatuses of primary autonomy. As Rapaport (1959) puts it:

> In [Hartmann's] conception reality and adaptedness . . . are the matrix of all behavior. Hartmann's concepts of *relative autonomy, secondary autonomy, automatization, and neutralization* for the first time provide a framework for understanding the development and the function of the secondary process as one of man's major adaptative means. But Hartmann goes even further and conceives of the reality to which man adapts as one created by him and his predecessors [pp. 60-61].

The fifth conception of reality is Erikson's (1950, 1956) psychosocial extension of the adaptive point of view suggested by Freud's third conception and by Hartmann's ideas. In this conception, "Man is potentially preadapted, not only to one average expectable environment, but to a whole evolving series of such environments. These environments to which man adapts are not 'objective,' but rather social environments which meet his maturation and development halfway" (Rapaport, 1959, p. 61).

The adaptative point of view is probably the least difficult to integrate with Piaget's theory. It is strikingly compatible with the major thrust of his genetic epistemology, which views intellectual development as a process of adaptation. At the level of impersonal cognition, Piaget's discoveries further delineate Freud's (1900) conception that the secondary process accurately perceives reality throughout life. Piaget's findings demonstrate that the child constructs the major categories in which he comes to comprehend reality. Wolff (1967a) has already pointed this out in connection with his psychoanalytic view of learning and language.

At the level of psychosocial cognition, Piaget's interactionism accords quite well with Erikson's notion of a mutual regulation between organism and environment. Moreover, as we have seen, Piaget finds Erikson's modes of behavior sufficiently general constructs, once abstracted from their biological origins, to contribute to an understanding of the lifelong process of adaptation.

Genetic epistemology itself studies the process of knowing as a process of adaptation. The psychoanalytic notion of adaptation is broader and views intelligent behavior as one aspect of adaptation. Piaget would no doubt agree; he does not attempt to construct a general model of adaptation, but he has suggested that such a model, of which genetic epistemology would constitute a part, could be constructed in the economic language of loss and gain.

The major difficulty in integrating Piagetian and psychoanalytic views on adaptation, then, is in reconciling the analytic emphasis on the drives and unconscious forces with Piaget's model of epistemological adaptations, which makes no reference to these factors. The difficulty reduces to one pertaining to the economic and dynamic points of view. Within the adaptive point of view itself, no essential barriers to integration of the models are apparent.

Perhaps one important difference between the structural and adaptive points of view of psychoanalysis and Piaget's theory should be stressed. Piaget emphasizes the importance of the organism's acting on the environment in the formation of internal structures that facilitate adaptation rather than the environment's action, even though he posits an interactionist model. The psychoanalytic model does not focus as specifically on the action of the organism. Also, it respects what the organism brings to this interaction in terms of biological givens and drive tendencies. It thus depicts the interactive processes more broadly in terms of an acting organism and an acting environment together forming an integrated matrix.

This difference derives not from a basic theoretical divergence, but from the environments each model has been designed to conceptualize. Psychoanalysis studies the human, affect-laden environment—the interaction of the organism with other human beings, all of whom are active and capable of a wide variety of predictable or unpredictable behaviors. Thus, there is an active evolving organism within an equally active evolving family or social environment. Piaget focuses on the non-affect-laden, often nonhuman environment. His concepts of conservation, for example, are not demonstrated in terms of relationships with human beings, but in terms of properties of water, clay, and other inanimate objects. This is not to criticize Piaget. On the contrary, the study of such domains has provided a suitable form of experimental control. However, this point may explain why he has been concerned more with the organism's action on the environment than with the reciprocal process. For him, the environment must include the available stimulus nutriment to be assimilated into shemes and to create the circumstances necessary for accommodations to take place, thus leading to further structure building. In the psychoanalytic model, which deals more with the human, affect-laden environment, we see a sequence of more balanced or mutual interaction.

The Dynamic and Economic Perspectives

We shall examine the dynamic and economic perspectives of psychoanalysis together because they are so closely tied to one another.

The dynamic point of view studies the relationship between the drives and behavior. Rapaport (1959) sees the principle of drive determination as having both an empirical and a conceptual basis.

> The empirical discovery embodies . . . two familiar observations: (1) behavior is not always triggered by external stimulation but often occurs without it, as though spontaneously; (2) behavior . . . evinces a goal-directedness, a purposive, teleological character. The conceptual discovery, which took the form of the definition of the drive concept, was the first large-scale attempt to cope with both of these observations simultaneously. The drive is defined as a causal agent inherent in the organism . . . and thus it can account for the apparent "spontaneity" of behavior. Moreover, since the definition makes the effectiveness of the drive dependent on an environmental condition, namely, the presence of the drive object, it can also account for the purposiveness of be-

> havior. This coordination of drive and drive object—which is assumed to be guaranteed by evolution—at first tolerates little if any means-activity and demands immediate consummation (pleasure principle). In the course of development, it becomes more flexible, and permits delay and interpolation of means-activities, though it selects and organizes these in the service of consummation. Later on it permits substitute goals and a variety of means- and consummatory-activities, until finally it prescribes only the consummatory behavior, and provides no more than the motivational framework for instrumental behavior. This conception of motivation accounts not only for the spontaneity and teleology of behavior, but also for behavior elicited by external stimulations, since the latter may be conceived of as drive objects, or substitutes for them [Rapaport, 1959, p. 48].

The drives are no longer thought of as the ultimate or only determinants of behavior, but as one set of determinants in interaction with other sets. Freud (1915) postulated that the drives have a variety of effects on behavior as a result of interactions with defenses, controls, substructures, reality, etc. Thus, the concepts of drive fusion, drive differentiation, and partial drives have all become part of the dynamic point of view.

When we take into account economic considerations that derive specifically from the dynamic point of view, we see the transformation of the drives not only through change of direction, detour, or secondary motivation, but also through *neutralization,* which changes the very quality of the drive, making energy available to the ego for relatively conflict-free, autonomous activities. Although there has been much controversy as to whether the economic point of view is a necessary construct in the psychoanalytic system of multiple determination, it seems useful in its concern with emphasis, degree, or intensity. While the energic concept may be a poor construct, with many liabilities, no equally useful construct has taken its place to account for this aspect of behavior.

Rapaport (1959) reviews the history of this point of view. As he notes, the first phase of energy theory was in the context of therapeutic experiences of abreaction. The postulated model depicted a system containing a set quantity of energy that needed to be discharged. "In the second phase (1900 to 1926), psychological energy was conceptualized as drive energy, and the methods used in discharging it as the primary process. It was recognized that other (secondary) processes, using minute quantities of energy, have a regulative function. . . . In this phase, however, little attention was paid to the nature and origin of the secondary process" (p. 50). In the third phase the ontogenetic development from primary- to secondary-process functioning was taken into account.

According to Rapaport, all behavior has primary-process and secondary-process aspects. While the primary process is associated with drive energies and is regulated by the pleasure principle, seeking tension reduction, the secondary process uses the principle of least action and is directed toward objective reality. The primary process uses mechanisms of displacement, condensation, and substitute formation. In contrast, the secondary process operates through delays, detours, and trial action to plot the safest course toward the desired object. The secondary process can thus suspend the discharge of drive energies until the object is found.

Rapaport (1959) uses the metaphor of a system of dikes to describe the hierarchy of defenses and controls that develop to delay discharge or to diminish the tendency of the drives toward immediate gratification.

> Their effect of diminishing the drives' tendency toward immediate discharge is conceptualized as "neutralization," special instances of which are referred to as delibidinization, deaggressivization, or sublimation. . . . These processes of binding and neutralization make cathexes (hypercathexes, attention cathexes) available to the secondary process, to be used in small quantities for experimental action in thought . . . , as signals in the form of affects . . . , and as countercathexes (against drives) for building new and for reinforcing existing defensive structures [p. 51].

Of major significance here is Rapaport's observation that the process of neutralization changes the relationship between primary- and secondary-process functioning. Earlier psychoanalytic models viewed this relationship as a dichotomy; with neutralization, however, it is viewed as a hierarchy with two extremes. It should be pointed out that Rapaport's use of the concept of neutralization does not necessarily imply transformations of energy. Rather, it suggests a structural differentiation which permits greater degrees of binding, detour, and delay. "The energies of lesser degrees of neutralization (drive derivatives) show characteristics of their drive origin, whereas those of higher degrees do not, and are at the disposal of the ego" (p. 51).

The dynamic and economic points of view conceptualize the drives as evolving in a series of steps from initially undifferentiated forms pushing for expression, to forms organized at first around certain libidinal and aggressive issues. On the libidinal side are the characteristic oral, anal, phallic, latency, and genital organizations of drives and their derivatives. The aggressive drives have no known sequence of this sort, but are seen as organized along with the libidinal drives in a developmental sequence related to the more broadly defined developmental stages. In energic language, energy becomes successively neutralized at stages of development, making more energy available for relatively autonomous functions of the ego.

It should be pointed out here that dynamic determinants are often unconscious, and the derivatives of the drives are often unconscious ideas and wishes. The unconscious determinants of behavior have played an important role in the history of the psychoanalytic model, and it is only the psychoanalytic model that takes them into account. The original topographical model, which consisted of the systems *Ucs.*, *Pcs.*, and *Cs.*, has been superseded by the structural model, which recognizes that aspects of ego functions as well as derivatives of the drives and affects can be unconscious. Thus, the unconscious should no longer be thought of as a region of the mind distinct from that of the preconscious and conscious. Rather, in current psychoanalysis the term *unconscious* is a referent for phenomena that are not in awareness and not readily accessible to awareness. These phenomena can pertain to functions of the ego, id, or superego, or to elements of external reality that are assimilated by the ego but unrecognized.

In essence, then, psychoanalysis conceptualizes dynamic unconscious events as determinants of behavior. Again, we should point out that the utility of the energic concept lies in its adequacy as a description of the vicissitudes of the drives. It is not essential to the integrity of the psychoanalytic model, however, and should not be a point of maximum focus for integration with Piaget's cognitive psychology. What, however, is the minimum we must use from dynamic, economic, and unconscious constructs to integrate psychoanalytic theory adequately with Piaget's cognitive psychology? The following set of propositions summarizing the dynamic and economic points of view will serve as this necessary minimum.

The construct *drives* refers to stimuli that arise from within the organism. These stimuli become expressed, in the context of drive derivatives, as wishes and their vicissitudes. In conjunction with other sets of determinants, drives and their derivatives have a determining effect on behavior. Often these internal stimuli are relatively unconscious; that is, their determining effect on behavior does not imply subjective awareness or ready accessibility to subjective awareness. It is at the internal boundary that the ego structure makes contact with these inner stimuli. Just as it processes external stimuli, the ego can process internal stimuli through its various substructures.

In the light of this, since certain ego substructures involve the processes of thought, or cognition, at times these processes may be in the service of the drives. Cognition, then, can be utilized to fulfill certain needs and wishes just as it can be utilized in the process of adjustment to impersonal external aspects of reality. To repeat our analogy with Rapaport's (1959) formulation, just as every structure has its peremptory drive-related component and its adaptive component, so cognitive structures may have capabilities for processing impersonal external stimuli and drive-related internal stimuli. After a brief summary of the psychoanalytic model, our task will be to delineate this relationship between the development of cognitive structures and the realm of internal stimuli. Only in this way can the potential compatibility of Piaget's theory and psychoanalysis be demonstrated.

One further point: in considering the dynamic point of view, we must also consider the relationship of the drives to early object relations. When drives and affects are experienced in relation to early objects, the nuclei of early object relations are formed. Eventually these relationships and their specific coloring by the original drive-affect dispositions become internalized. As these internalized object relations become organized at the level of mental representation, they are secondarily invested with drive-affect expressions.

For an understanding of the relationship of the dynamic perspective to cognition, it is important to note that early object relations, which in a sense are "external" and are not yet structurally internalized, are highly varied and far different from the basically inanimate or non-drive-colored environment the infant confronts. The stimulus nutriments Piaget discusses arise from nonaffective aspects of the environment. Other stimulus nutriments, also affecting intelligent behavior or early cognitive capacities, may arise from very complex and somewhat unpredictable relationships in which the action of early (human) objects on the infant is as important as his action on them. Because the vicissitudes of these early object relations and their secondary investments with certain drive-affect discharge expressions are so different from the relatively stable, predictable inanimate environment, it will later be postulated that the internal boundary of the cognitive structures of the ego is different from the external boundary. The internal boundary, it will be shown, may be relatively more flexible and less logically fixed, and may exist at levels of development very different from the level of development of the external boundary.

Summary of the Psychoanalytic Model

As indicated above, both the psychoanalytic and the cognitive models are basically processing models of personality; that is, both have stimuli impinging on or entering the mental apparatus. The mental apparatus processes these stimuli, which become internalized or coordinated with prior structures, thus leading to further structure formation. Together with maturational processes, the stimuli coming into the mental apparatus continually contribute to the development of the apparatus; at the same time, in a broad sense, their processing leads to behavioral output.

In Piaget's theory of cognitive processes the stimuli impinging on the mental apparatus are aliments from the relatively non-affect-laden environment. In the psychoanalytic model the stimuli are more complex. There are external stimuli similar to those Piaget conceptualizes; stimuli arising from within the organism, conceptualized as the drives and/or affects; and environmental stimuli that are colored by affects and drives—that is, those aspects of the environment that are experienced in an emotional way. Within the psychoanalytic model all relevant conceptualized stimuli play a role in the development and differentiation of structures. Piaget deals with a very narrowly defined range of stimulus input and therefore with only certain aspects of intrapsychic structure—those dealing with cognition.

In the psychoanalytic model development occurs from immediate drive discharge onto the drive object, to hallucinatory wish fulfillment in the absence of the drive object, and eventually to the formation of internal structures that mediate between the drives and the final behavior patterns. These internal structures form as a result of the three above-mentioned kinds of stimuli impinging on the mental apparatus in interaction with maturational processes. Initially, according to the psychoanalytic model, logical thinking is in the service of obtaining gratification and then satisfaction. Eventually, detour structures permit logical thought to become relatively autonomous, that is, to establish its own relationship to the environment relatively exclusive of drive influences. It then comes into an adaptational relationship with the environment. In this sense, logical structures evolve from detour mechanisms and further develop and differentiate.

As both Rapaport (1959) and Hartmann (1939) have pointed out, the substructures of secondary autonomy, as well as those of primary autonomy, are always only relatively free from the influence of the drives. Rapaport indicates that even substructures dealing strictly with logical thought exist in a hierarchical relationship with other structures, although they may have a relatively conflict-free existence. In other words, there are substructures closer to the input of the drives, and substructures closer to the boundary with the environment.

Within this psychoanalytic model we can place Piaget's model of pure cognition. The psychoanalytic model offers only very general consideration of how these structures dealing with intelligent behavior evolve and develop and what the principles, rules, and laws that govern them are. Certain characteristics of primary-process and secondary-process thinking have been elaborated. What is missing from the psychoanalytic developmental model, however, is an understanding of exactly how intelligent behavior develops. That is, what is the specific sequence from early infantile action patterns to secondary-process thinking? What are the specific characteristics of secondary-process thinking, and what is the sequence from lower forms of secondary-process thinking to higher forms of secondary-process thinking? It is with such questions of how knowledge develops and what rules govern it in lower and higher forms that Piaget concerns himself. Piaget offers psychoanalysis a rather specific developmental model of the particular substructure of the ego that constructs, by secondary-process thinking, an adaptational relationship with the environment. Piaget has studied what analysts would consider an ego capacity to deal with the environment in an intelligent way, without positing a superstructure similar to the ego.

What has been missing from Piaget's conceptualization, however, is the influence of the drives and the unconscious phenomena on the development of intelligent behavior. For this reason, psychoanalysis has so far made use of Piaget's findings and conceptualizations only in a very general way. As pointed out, in the psychoanalytic model substructures of the ego may initially have or later attain relative autonomy from the drives. In most instances they are tied to the drives at their deepest level. Using Rapaport's model of a hierarchically layered structure, which at the bottom is tied to the drives and at the top may be in an adaptational relationship to the environment, it is incumbent upon any who would attempt an integration of cognitive and analytic models to delineate the relationship between the drives and the development of intelligent behavior.

If we are successful at integrating Piaget's model of cognition with psychoanalysis, we shall have a determinant of behavior that represents an extension of the adaptative perspective and facilitates a fuller understanding of "intelligent functioning." We shall be able to see how the logical substructures of the ego can act as a determinant of behavior alongside all the other determinants. In addition, we shall be able to see how the development of these cognitive substructures of the ego relates not only to the environment in terms of logical operations, but also to the internal milieu, that of drive derivatives, affects, and the affect-laden relationships in the external world.

Take, as a hypothetical example, a young latency child who has unconscious murderous wishes toward his father but who becomes overly concerned with being good. From the point of view of the drives, oedipal derivatives might be observed, while from the point of view of defenses, a reaction formation in the service of superego prohibitions against rage and killing might be noted. Viewing this phenomenon from the perspective of Piagetian cognitive psychology suggests yet another interpretation. In latency the youngster for the first time has the capacity to organize his cognitive operations in systems whose transformational laws depend on reversibility by inversion. Thus, the child can see both a direct and an inverse relationship between two variables; for example, *A* may hate *B*, or *A* may not hate *B*. It will be hypothesized later that this new cognitive capacity leads to differences between the latency and the prelatency child in handling concerns with angry feelings. The latency child can change a wish into its opposite (the inverse relationship), while the prelatency child does not have this cognitive capacity and may therefore be limited to denial of the wish.

This simple example, which will be elaborated on later, demonstrates that an understanding of cognitive structures may facilitate understanding of the ego's defensive operations against drive derivatives. In this way, the cognitive aspects of the adaptive point of view may give us a further understanding of the determination of behavior. It will later be shown that understanding cognitive substructures of the ego will significantly expand the adaptive perspective into a psychoanalytic developmental model of intelligent behavior.

8

INTEGRATION OF THE DYNAMIC POINT OF VIEW AND PIAGET'S COGNITIVE PSYCHOLOGY

In relating the dynamic point of view to cognitive psychology, two distinct but interrelated topics must be taken into account. One is the construct of drives; the other is the construct of the dynamic unconscious. We have seen above in numerous instances that Piaget's theory and his experimental methodology do not include conceptualizations of internal stimuli, such as drive derivatives, or their effects on behavior. Thus, to integrate psychoanalytic and cognitive constructs, the transformational links between internal stimuli and cognitive structures must be delineated, at least in a preliminary and largely speculative fashion.

As reviewed earlier, Piaget's functional unconscious refers to the organizing principles or processes of mental events and is therefore quite different from the psychoanalytic notion of the dynamic unconscious, which refers to ideas that are potentially available to consciousness but are kept out of awareness by repression and other auxiliary defenses. The key to the concept of the dynamic unconscious is that the material is unconscious because psychic operations maintain the phenomenon at an unconscious level. A certain amount of activity is involved in keeping the material from consciousness.

Our consideration of cognitive and dynamic development will not be comprehensive, but will attempt, through touching on key points in development, to evolve a general model. In the discussion below, we shall see that the cognitive laws central to Piaget's system are, in fact, compatible with clinical observations and inferences about events ordinarily conceptualized within the psychoanalytic model. Organizations of experience from a Piagetian cognitive perspective and a psychoanalytic perspective, in fact, follow similar principles and sequences when studied in the context of process and structure.

It will be suggested that cognitive and drive-affect structures differentiate from a common matrix and are influenced over time by similar and different experiences. They are interrelated in a hierarchical structure and always exist in some relative relationship to one another. Their greater or lesser autonomy from one another is hypothesized to depend on a number of variables, including the strength of the drives; the structure or definition of the cognitive task; the integrity of cognitive, defensive, and adaptive structures; the situational context; and the degree of mutual enhancement between these two lines of development.

In the remainder of this work the concept of an internal and external boundary is used to indicate organizations of experience. Again, it should be kept in mind that the concept of boundaries, internal and external, is a simplification and is not to be taken literally. It is a shorthand to indicate those organizations of experience which relate more (or less) to the stimulus world connected to drives, wishes, feelings, internal representations, and affectively colored human relationships and those which relate more (or less) to the impersonal, often inanimate world. The human organism throughout development deals with a variety of stimulus worlds. Once the organism begins to develop, it is difficult to separate our genetic and constitutional proclivities, the unfolding of certain internally derived maturational sequences, and experience which more or less has to do with wishes and feelings, the affect-laden external personal world, and the impersonal or inanimate world. After development begins all human experience becomes a multiply determined integration of various factors.

In thinking about the way in which experience is organized psychologically, it is important to note that there is no completely impersonal experience.[1] Whatever a human experi-

[1] That Piaget has never fully considered the interpersonal aspects of his experimental procedures (e.g., the effect of the experimenter on the child's behavior in carrying out the cognitive tasks) should not go unrecognized.

ences, even if it has to do with the inanimate environment, is a human or personal experience. Similarly, no experience is strictly or solely derived from drives or wishes, because derivatives of drives and wishes have internal and/or external objects which play a role in the way they are perceived and organized.

The concept of internal and external boundaries and stimulus worlds is useful, however, as a metaphor and as an oversimplification to set up two polarities ("straw men") which can later be broken down. It will then be possible to observe how what are referred to as the internal and external boundaries are part of the same basic psychological structure and follow the same principles of learning and development. These organizations of experience, as is true for other psychological organizations, differ in degree rather than in structure, and the degree pertains to the level and character of the psychological organization achieved. Thus, the types of organization of human experience that Piaget has studied and the types that psychoanalysis has studied can be considered in the same conceptual framework. Particularly useful in demonstrating this is the articulation of the transformational and organizing principles that relate and govern the specific levels and character of psychological organization that contribute to the total personality.

Cognitive and drive-affect structures will be observed to have relatively different patterns of development, in part related to the nature of the stimulus worlds each assimilates. Patterns of interaction with the environment, for example, may be quite different for cognitive structures and for drive-affect structures.

Of particular importance will be to show that discordant development—a differentiation of cognitive and affective structures—is attributable to the greater variability of the human as opposed to the inanimate stimulus world.

The principles that connect the two organizations will be developed and other variables that influence them will be stated, leading to the principles of an integrated model of development.

Developmental Considerations of the Dynamic Perspective

In this section we shall observe how dynamic issues at each stage of development relate to cognitive structures. Our basic hypothesis here is that a relatively undifferentiated structure exists at birth or shortly thereafter. This structure develops an internal and an external boundary. The external boundary, in an oversimplified sense, relates to the inanimate and impersonal world, the world not colored to a significant degree by feelings. The internal boundary relates to the inner world of drives and affects and the external affect-laden human environment. While the outer boundary also relates to this external human environment, to the degree that feeling states, through mechanisms of projection, influence the experience of the human, outside world, or to the degree that the outside world influences affective life, it is the internal boundary to which we refer. When dynamic issues come to color even the inanimate world, the inanimate world, too, will be considered to relate to the internal boundary. This, in fact, is a crossover point between cognitive and affective development. In the proposed model there are not two completely distinct boundaries, but rather a gradient between two extremes.

The initial structure, however, is relatively undifferentiated in terms of internal and external boundaries. In early development, in fact, there is relatively little difference between the infant's experience of the animate and of the impersonal world. The schemes the infant uses to relate to one or the other are the same, beginning with simple reflexes and primitive reaction patterns. This is not to say that the infant does not experience the human world as in some way "different." For example, the sensitive mother who rocks rhythmically to comfort her baby undoubtedly provides an experience of some basic core pleasure very different from what the infant experiences simply by moving his body against his crib. What is being stated here, however, is that the infant's initial structural processing of these two experiences is relatively similar (even if distinctions at the level of experience are made).

Starting with this assumption that the internal and external boundaries are at first undifferentiated, we can posit a progressive differentiation in the course of development between Piaget's impersonal cognition and what we shall call drive-affect and object-relations cognition, that is, cognition as it relates to the internal milieu. For example, between the third and fourth periods of sensorimotor development, means-ends relationships are developed at the external boundary. Simultaneously, the infant develops a clearer notion of himself as separate from the primary mothering figure. We may at this time begin to see differentiation along cognitive lines in that the infant may become capable of manipulating inanimate objects to gain an end, but may be at a different level in his capacity to use means-ends distinctions with human objects.

Not all the reasons for this differentiation are clear, but some features of the inanimate and the animate environment may play a role. The human objects—mother and father—may be very active in their involvement with the infant. Each human object and each object relationship has individual differences, making for an *interactive* relationship. To some degree this interactive relationship will have a strong determining effect on the evolution of initial human means-ends relationships and on subsequent development along these lines. Inanimate objects, while at times intensely cathected, have a lesser role as interactive elements. Inanimate objects are relatively more stable in configuration and do not alter their phenomenological stimulus character as do animate objects. A major variable in the inanimate world is the richness and availability of objects provided for the infant. Even given this variability, it is far less than that provided by the relative input of human objects. As a general principle, we see the inanimate world as relatively more constant, and in some ways more structured, than the highly variable, somewhat unpredictable, individualized world of human relationships.

If the infant has some noise-making toys, for example, he can begin to experiment with means-ends relationships to produce noise. The infant with a depressed mother who rarely responds to him, however, may find it very difficult to test out means-ends relationships with her. The overanxious, overidentifying mother, on the other hand, may overwhelm her infant and provide inconsistent responses (ends) to the infant's reactions (means). In either case, the infant's concept of means-ends relationships may have a relatively different pattern of development in the animate and the inanimate worlds.

Once differentiation between the internal and external boundaries of the ego occurs, relative advances along one line of development may occur out of concert with the advances along the other. Nevertheless, relationships between these two aspects of development exist, as is suggested by clinical experience and by some limited research. Blatt, Allison, and Baker (1965), for example, found some correlational evidence that persons with unresolved conflicts over body integrity or with a poor body image have difficulty on cognitive tasks demanding the ability to assemble wholes from parts presented visually (the Wechsler Object Assembly Subtest).

Basic Principle of the Integrated Model

We shall now examine the relationship between the internal and external boundaries of the ego from a developmental perspective, using Piaget's stages as an organizing construct. Aspects of each cognitive developmental stage will be considered. We shall show that the processes described for "pure cognition," or cognition at the external boundary, are consistent with clinical observations of processes at the internal boundary. The demonstration of this basic structural symmetry forms a most important aspect of the integrated model. *If it is shown that the basic processes that organize these different stimulus worlds are the same, the basis for an integration of the dynamic and cognitive aspects of development will have been established.*

It will then be possible to observe how the different characteristics of each stimulus world can lead to relatively different developments at each boundary of this postulated structure. For each stage of development, we shall illustrate how the vicissitudes of development at the internal boundary may exert a determining influence at the external boundary. Later, some of the variables mediating the degree and character of this influence will be considered. It will therefore be seen that a single structure can be postulated to function in relation to the external and internal stimulus worlds; that the processes that organize one group of stimuli are the same as those that organize a very different group of stimuli; that the difference in the stimuli accounts for the differences in the structural development at each boundary; and that the events at one boundary influence the structure and character of the other boundary.

The level of discourse in what follows is partially speculative. However, heavy reliance is placed on clinical observations and inferences. We hope that in this way the process of theory building will, in preliminary fashion, be advanced. Controlled studies may then be designed to test the theoretical model constructed in this effort.

Before discussing each developmental stage, it should be mentioned that Piaget is not entirely consistent in naming or enumerating his own stages of cognitive development. His descriptions, however, are consistent, and the only possible source of confusion in relatively recent writings is whether the so-called preoperational period is to be considered apart from the period of concrete operations in which it culminates. Following Flavell (1963) and a recent article by Piaget (1970), we shall delineate three major periods and one subperiod of intellectual development. Within these periods are found subdivisions referred to as stages. The major periods are:

1. The sensorimotor period, which extends from birth until approximately two years of age. This period is divided into six stages, which will be described in general here, and again later, with reference to the development of the concept of the permanent object.

2. A period of preparation for and acquisition of concrete operations. This period is initiated by the appearance of the symbolic or semiotic function and ends with the beginning of higher mental operations applied to concrete objects.

3. The period of formal operations, which begins at approximately eleven years of age. During this period full adult intelligence develops as the operations are extended to apply to propositional or hypothetical thinking.

THE SENSORIMOTOR PERIOD

The Piagetian View

The sensorimotor period of intelligence is so named because the construction of mental structures or schemes is in no way aided by representations, symbols, or thoughts. Hence the schemes are totally dependent on perceptions and body movements (Piaget and Inhelder, 1966). The first stage of sensorimotor development is marked by relatively few reflexes, which stand out against the background of the spontaneous general activity of the neonate. Among these early reflexes are the sucking reflex and the palmar reflex. By reproductive, generalizing, and recognitory assimilation, these primitive reflexes take on the nature of the first scheme.

The second stage of sensorimotor intelligence is that of the first habits and the primary circular reaction. The first habits develop out of the original schemes as these are applied to objects in the environment or to parts of the infant's body, but without any differentiation between means and end. In a primitive state of consciousness, the infant is aware only of action sequences, and not even aware of self. "The end in question is attained only by a necessary succession of movements which lead to it, without one's being able to distinguish either an end pursued from the start or means chosen from among various possible schemes" (Piaget and Inhelder, 1966, p. 9).

The primary circular reactions of stage 2 are due to reproductive or functional assimilation. After the child makes a new response with novel results, he tends to repeat the response numerous times. At the primary level of circular reactions the infant's behavior is directed principally at his own body.

Stage-3 behavior includes circular reactions at a secondary level, i.e., the repetition of motor actions designed to create interesting effects in the environment. To cite an example from Piaget and Inhelder (1966, p. 10): when the child pulls a cord which shakes a rattle over his crib, he repeats the action as in primary circular reactions. Such a secondary circular reaction may then be applied in totally inappropriate circumstances, whenever the child wants to reproduce an interesting effect.

This "magical" application of a scheme is evidence of the still primitive nature of the developing intelligence, but it gives evidence of some differentiation between means and ends.

Stage 4 of the sensorimotor period is marked by the coordination of the secondary circular reactions, and by the completion of the differentiation of means from ends. The remaining limitation of stage 4 is that only known means are utilized in striving for an end. Flavell (1963) calls attention to two behavior patterns characteristic of stage 4: (1) "setting aside an obstacle to obtain a desired object" and (2) utilizing "objects as instruments in attaining the goal" (pp. 109-110).

The fifth stage of sensorimotor development is marked by a search for new means based on further differentiations of already-known schemes, and by the tertiary circular reaction. The latter differs from the secondary circular reaction in that the child no longer uses schemes that were effective in one situation to produce magically efficacious results in every situation. Instead, he relies on real exploration and variation to test for effectiveness. Discovery is a hallmark of stage 5.

> An example of this is what we call the "behavior pattern of the support." An object has been placed on a rug out of the child's reach. The child, after trying in vain to reach the object directly, may eventually grasp one corner of the rug (by chance or as a substitute), and then, observing a relationship between the movements of the rug and those of the object, gradually comes to pull the rug in order to reach the object [Piaget and Inhelder, 1966, p. 11].

The sixth and final sensorimotor stage is actually a transition into the preoperational subperiod. Now the child becomes capable of inventing new means, not by direct actions on object, but by mental combination. Where discovery marked stage 5, insight is characteristic of stage 6.

> For example, a child confronted by a slightly open matchbox containing a thimble first tries to open the box by physical groping (reaction of the fifth stage), but upon failing, he presents an altogether new reaction: he stops the action and attentively examines the situation (in the course of this he slowly opens and closes his mouth, or, as another subject did, his hand, as if an imitation of the result to be attained, that is, the enlargement of the opening), after which he suddenly slips his finger into the crack and thus

succeeds in opening the box [Piaget and Inhelder, 1966, p. 12].

During the sensorimotor period a number of extremely significant concepts are developed. These include the child's concepts of space, time, and causality. These categorical concepts develop in a parallel process according to the sequence of six stages outlined above. Above all, during the sensorimotor phase the child develops the scheme of the permanent objects, the first major victory of conservation and the foundation of all future knowledge. (This concept will be discussed more extensively later.)

THE CONCEPT OF SPACE

During the six stages of the sensorimotor period the child moves from a concept of space as a disparate collection of independent spaces to a concept of a unified space containing his body and other entities as objects within it. During stages 1 and 2, no unified space concept develops. Rather, the child, unable yet to differentiate his own bodily actions from the objects on which they are performed, experiences a separate space for each major bodily realm of activity. It is as if objects in his field of vision were in a visual space, objects emitting sounds in an auditory space, etc. As yet these objects are not coordinated among themselves, nor are they differentiated from the "object" of the infant's body. Likewise, their spatial "containers" are as yet uncoordinated.

The appearance of secondary circular reactions in stage 3 implies that independent action schemes are beginning to be coordinated, and a primitive differentiation is arising between means and ends. In connection with this development, the child experiences objects across schemes, as it were, seeing and grasping the same object, for example. In terms of the development of the space concept, this coordination of action schemes implies a coordination of spatial locations. The object located in visual space is coordinated with the object located in grasping space. In addition, the child "begins to perceive himself acting on things; or more accurately, he perceives his hands and arms interacting with objects" (Flavell, 1963, p. 138). This marks the start of the differentiation of self from objects, but it is as yet only a very crude beginning.

The fourth stage of the sensorimotor period brings a significant advance in the concept of space. Space becomes objectified as objects and actions are differentiated from the child's body. Flavell (1963) calls particular attention to the child's new behavior pattern of hiding and finding an object behind some sort of screen (p. 139). This behavior implies a coordination of the two objects (the hidden object and the screen) within a unified space.

Flavell mentions additional signs characteristic of this stage which signify the advent of an objective concept of space. Among these is the child's fascination with the problem of size and shape constancy, i.e., the apparent changes in the size and shape of the same object as it is displaced through space. Piaget (1937) observes:

> OBS. 87. As early as 0;9 (6) Laurent, during the exploration of new objects, seems to study the object's shape as a function of its position. He slowly displaces in space the toys he is holding, either perpendicular to his glance or in depth. . . .
>
> At 0;10 (11) he moves away and brings close to himself a box of matches while looking at it as though it were an entirely new object, whereas he knows it well. This time there is surely involved a systematic study of the apparent shape of the displaced object [p. 156].

Such behavior gives evidence of an increasing effort to coordinate disparate appearances, and in this sense, to unify the series of spaces extending away from the child's immediate body boundaries. In fact, it is also during stage 4 that the child's concept of space begins to extend further away from his body. In earlier stages, the child appeared to be aware of relative displacements only when they occurred close to his body. Now, however, the range of his spatial comprehension is extended. The space away from the body, which had been perceived as a single plane, is now ordered in depth.

> At 0;11 (7) Jacqueline is seated on a sofa. I make an object disappear under the sofa; she bends over to see it. This action shows that for her the vanished object is located on a plane deeper than that of the edge of the sofa, the latter plane itself belonging to distant space (inaccessible to prehension) [Piaget, 1937, p. 172; quoted in Flavell, 1963, p. 140].

The fifth stage is characterized by the child's intensified interest in the spatial displacements of objects, apart from the fascination with his own body actions which was so marked in earlier stages. The differentiation of self from objects is attained to such an extent that consecutive displacements of objects can be a source of fascination and wonder in their own right. Behavior patterns characteristic of this stage include: "stacking a series of objects on top of each other; putting objects into containers and then removing them; rotating and reversing objects, no longer simply in relation to the self and its perspective, but in relation to other objects" (Flavell, 1963, p. 141).

The general ability of the stage-6 child to master mental combinations by internally representing them has its specific applications to the development of the concept of space. The child can now represent internally his own spatial movements and can do the same for the "invisible" (not perceptible) displacements of objects. Piaget (1937) gives an example of the first achievement: After having walked about a kilometer from the house, Jacqueline, when asked where the house is, "turns around and points in the right direction" (p. 207). Later, when asked the same question on the return trip, she at first points behind herself but then corrects this to point in front. Since she cannot yet see the house, this answer must come from a recognition that she is on her way home, moving toward the house.

In terms of the second achievement—in relation to external objects—Flavell (1963) notes that the "best examples . . . are those involving detour behavior" (p. 141). Piaget (1937) offers this observation:

> OBS. 124. Lucienne also reveals the behavior pattern of detours from about 1;6. We have already noted . . . how, playing with a doll carriage for the first time, she has pushed it against the wall of her room and is unable to pull it back; she releases the handle of the carriage and goes to the other side, between the wall and the forward end, and begins pushing in the new position. The detour is here all the more distinct since it is accompanied by a reversal of direction in the traction of the object [p. 205].

THE CONCEPT OF TIME

Another major concept developed during the sensorimotor period is that of time. As Flavell (1963) points out, Piaget relies on a hypothesized parallel with the concept of space in articulating the stages of the temporal concept (see Piaget, 1937, pp. 325-326). We have seen how the concept of space develops from the infant's coordination of his own body movements. Similarly, the infant in stages 1 and 2 begins with "a vague feeling of duration immanent in his own actions" (Flavell, 1963, p. 147). Gradually, over the course of sensorimotor development, this vague duration is replaced by a real sense of sequence. Piaget here employs a formal analogy between the spatial concepts *in-front-of* and *behind* and the temporal concepts *before* and *after*.

It is probably during sensorimotor stage 3, the stage of secondary circular reactions, that the child first becomes aware of a before and after sequence in his actions, e.g., pulling a string in order to shake a rattle, or pulling a string before shaking a rattle. However, the lack of self-object differentiation characteristic of this stage implies that temporal sequence is perceived only with regard to actions in which the child himself takes part.

As in the case of the spatial concept, stage 4 is the point of significant development in the temporal concept. Again, Flavell (1963) calls particular attention to the child's searching behind a screen to find something he has seen another person hide there: "Piaget believes that it is in this behavior pattern that the child for the first time reveals a capacity for retaining a series of events in which his action did not directly intervene" (p. 148).

Stage-5 behavior can best be interpreted as a solidification and extension of stage-4 behavior. Flavell cites the following example from Piaget to indicate the child's increasing capacity to hold events in memory:

> At 1;3 (12) she [Jacqueline] plays with an eyeglass case at the moment when I am putting a book on the other side of the bars of the playpen in which she is seated. As she wants to reach the book she puts behind her the case which is in her way. For at least five minutes she tries unsuccessfully to pass the book through the bars. Each time the book slides out of her hands. Then, tired, she searches unhesitatingly for the case which she no longer sees; turning halfway around she extends her hand behind her back until she touches it [Piaget, 1937, p. 343; quoted in Flavell, 1963, p. 148].

Stage 6 is marked principally by an extension of the power

to evoke events of a relatively more and more distant past, an ability consequent upon the general representational ability which makes its appearance at this stage. At the level of stage 6, this ability involves manipulating and combining events mentally, by interior representation. It thus involves a great new freedom, a breaking with the bonds of the here-and-now—bonds that held as long as the child could only proceed by manipulating and combining concrete objects. Obviously when objects or people can be represented mentally, they need not be physically present to be the objects of the child's cognitive schemes. With regard to the concept of time, then, an awareness of sequences outside the immediate present and the immediate past becomes possible.

THE CONCEPT OF CAUSALITY

A third major concept developed during the sensorimotor period is that of causality. Again, a general trend can be observed throughout the six sensorimotor stages, although it is somewhat more complex than for the temporal and spatial concepts.

The concept of causality begins with two magical notions: efficacy and phenomenalism.

> The first, *efficacy*, . . .refers to a dim sense that the inchoate feelings of effort, longing, etc., which saturate one's actions are somehow responsible for external happenings. Efficacy is therefore a causality of action-at-a-distance (since presence or absence of spatial connection between self as cause and event as effect is irrelevant to it) in which the cause is vaguely sensed as inhering in one's action, without, however, the subject being sufficiently advanced to see self and actions as a separate causal agent in the universe. The second, *phenomenalism,* refers to the feeling that temporal (but not necessarily spatial) contiguity between any two events means that one caused the other [Flavell, 1963, p. 142].

Through the six stages of sensorimotor development these two magical forms of causality become differentiated from one another, applied to different realms (after the distinction between self and objects), and objectified, or purified of magical content. At that point they may be termed psychological causality and physical causality. The first refers to the personal, internal sense of will and self-direction. The second is the awareness that objects independent of the self can stand in causal relation to one another through spatial, as well as temporal, contiguity (Flavell, 1963, p. 142).

Stages 1 and 2 are marked by the lack of differentiation between efficacy and phenomenalism. Piaget hypothesizes that any temporal contiguity between an external event and an internal feeling of need or action generates attribution of causality to the latter. "This hypothesis is in a way a more cautious and toned-down version of the psychoanalytic 'feelings of omnipotence' conception" (Flavell, 1963, p. 143).

The beginnings of subject-object, action-result differentiation occur in stage 3, with the primitive means-end distinction implied in the secondary circular reactions. However, the application of action schemes effective in one situation to other, nonappropriate situations, indicates the severe limitations on the developing concept of causality. "Rather than an objective and spatialized causality, it seems that there is simply a dim sense of power inherent in the action and its concomitant sensations, wishes, etc. (efficacy) which is activated whenever this feeling-action complex co-occurs in time with some interesting external event (phenomenalism)" (Flavell, 1963, p. 144).

The means-ends sequences which begin to appear in stage 4 give evidence of significant development in the concept of causality. Magical procedures are replaced by truly effective means. In the examples of behavior cited for this stage, we can see the beginnings of both psychological and physical causality:

> At 0;9 (0) [Laurent] grasps my hand and places it against his belly which I have just tickled; he thus merely sets my hand in motion and does not strike it as before and as though my activity depended entirely on his. . . .
>
> At 0;9 (13) Laurent is in his baby swing which I shake three or four times by pulling a cord; he grasps my hand and presses it against the cord [Piaget, 1937, p. 261].

Psychological and physical causality are combined in this example since the child's willed action is linked to a belief in the causal efficacy of some event outside his own body. A further differentiation of these two types of causality marks stage 5. This stage is characterized by a growing awareness that objects and people can be causal agents apart from any intervention by the self.

> At 1;0 (0) for example, [Laurent] takes possession of a new ball which he has just received for his birthday and places it on top of a sloping cushion to let it go and roll by itself. He even tries to make it go by merely placing it on the floor, and, as no movement is produced, he limits himself to a gentle push [Piaget, 1937, pp. 274-275].

The final stage of the sensorimotor development of the concept of causality is shaped by the child's new ability to represent things to himself mentally. In the realm of causality, this implies an ability to go beyond the perceptually given, be this cause or effect, and to represent mentally the perceptually absent link in the cause-effect chain.

We have so far reviewed the progress in cognitive development characteristic of the sensorimotor period, with its six well-defined stages. At the end of this period, the child enters upon a new realm of cognitive growth, anticipated by his stage-6 ability to represent events mentally without directly acting upon them. The child's utter cognitive dependence on perceptions and overt motor acts is ended. However, entrance into a period of higher mental functioning is not smooth or immediate. The world the child now enters is much larger and more complex than the one left behind. In order for the structures of sensorimotor intelligence to be uplifted by reflective abstraction into a fully internalized intelligence, several years of preparation and transition are demanded.

Dynamic Considerations and the Sensorimotor Period

As we have seen, in the first stage of the sensorimotor period, the infant possesses some reflex capabilities, such as the sucking reflex and the grasping reflex. There is, however, a general lack of differentiation in the categories of space, time, and causality, and in the construction of the scheme of the permanent object. Similarly, there is a lack of differentiation of self from other in the realm of personal object relations. Thus, there appears to be no meaningful difference between the internal and external boundaries of the ego at this stage. One could anticipate that should difficulties in development occur, they would have an impact on the functioning of this entire undifferentiated structure—that is, on both of what will become two boundaries.

Among the infant's major experiences at this time are rhythmical experiences, interaction with the primary mothering person, and transitions between states of awareness ranging from deep sleep to alertness and irritability. To the degree that these experiences are not optimal or that problems exist in the initial homeostatic mechanisms, a global effect on the internal and external precursors to ego functioning may occur.

During the second sensorimotor stage, Piaget has observed initial habits and primary circular reactions directed toward the external environment or toward the infant's own body. There is still no differentiation between means and ends, and while there is some vague awareness of action sequences, no delineated sense of self as agent is present. The concepts of space and time are not yet abstracted from their occurrence in specific sensory modalities, and the notion of causality remains undifferentiated. In terms of human object relations and the prime effective experience, the infant is in a very primitive stage of pleasure orientation, with the wish for discharge and gratification and the beginnings of human attachment. During these two sensorimotor stages, then, there is not much difference between the internal and external boundaries.

One could ask the question: What would happen in terms of beginning habits and primary circular reactions to the external human object if this object were not available and therefore not able to facilitate an attachment? In a simpler sense, what happens if an infant is frequently left hungry? It is interesting to note that Piaget claims that hunger during the earliest phase of development will serve to increase certain primary circular reactions and even some initial discriminations, as though to cause some precocity (Piaget and Inhelder, 1966). In fact, clinical work with some infants who are emotionally deprived has shown that some of these infants are maturationally advanced in the earliest stages of their cognitive development, particularly if they come into the world with sound constitutional capacities. An example is the emotionally "hungry" infant who is quite active and skillful in using intermediary devices, such as his hands or later on a spoon, to get inanimate objects, such as a marble, into his mouth. Thus, at this stage of development, increased drive tensions can have the effect, so to speak, of driving the organism. Since there does not appear to be a basic differentiation between the infant's knowledge of the inanimate and the animate world at this stage, it is not yet necessary to delineate transformational links between the two ego boundaries beyond the level of this general observation. On the other hand, increased drive tensions in the infant whose basic equipment (thresholds, channeling and organizing of sensation, capacity for rhythmical experiences and relaxation, etc.) is less than optimal may shut down, so to speak, or show beginning patterns of disorganization, withdrawal or apathy.

During the third stage of sensorimotor development secondary circular reactions appear. Action patterns become more complex, habit sequences begin to interact, and it becomes possible for the infant to see that actions create effects, although this awareness remains couched in an egocentric and quasi-magical context. For example, if pulling a rope rings a bell in one setting, the infant will repeat the pulling action in other, inappropriate settings. During this time, the infant also begins to coordinate spatial locations across sensory modalities and to coordinate the sense of before and after in time.

At this stage of development the drives are beginning to differentiate as well. We see the formation of an oral drive organization in relation to a strong and important attachment to a primary object. With appropriate intensity in the initial attachment, there is also the beginning of self-object differentiation. Because of the intensity of the potential for human attachment and interaction during this phase of development, there is also the potential for the beginning deviation of the two lines of development—that is, impersonal or external cognition from what we are calling interpersonal, emotional, or internal cognition.

During this phase of development, if the mother is not available to show the infant that actions can create effects in a human relationship, this may not be learned in the primary human relationships. The infant may be able to pull a string to ring a bell and thus learn cause-effect relationships at the external boundary but may not learn that to smile produces a reciprocal smile in the mother—in essence, the precursor of the concept that at certain times loving produces a loving response in return.

What if the mother does not respond to the infant's demonstration of his hunger through crying or through facial grimaces? The infant may not learn that his actions can lead to satisfaction of a felt need for food. The scheme for tying together somatic impulses from the body with the precursors of a mental representation of those impulses and the expectation of a satisfying end may not come into being. It is interesting to note that Bruch (1966), in studying anorexic individuals, has hypothesized that one of their primary difficulties is that they never learned early in life to experience certain sensations from inside their bodies. Perhaps development at the internal boundary of the ego is adversely affected in such individuals because a cause-effect chain is not established in the context of the primary caretaker relationship.

Another illustration of what can happen at this point in the area of human object relations is the situation in which attachment and responsiveness to needs are present, enabling the infant to learn that actions create effects, but concomitant personal differentiation is absent. The mother's needs may pervade the situation so that she inhibits the beginning differentiation of the infant from herself. In terms of Piaget's scheme, the beginning sense of action-creating effects may be impaired. A mother who initially reads the infant correctly as to his needs, but then uses massive projections to keep the infant from separating and overwhelms the infant with her own symbiotic needs, may begin to misread the infant continually. The infant's attempts to consolidate schemes through reproductive assimilation may thus be impaired by the mother's inability to repeat certain patterns in a predictable manner.

To extend these two simplified illustrations, might such situations affect the beginning cognitive schemes developing in this third stage in the areas of space, time, and causality? As indicated, in connection with the inanimate object world, these schemes can develop independently. However, because at this early stage there is not much differentiation between the internal and external boundaries, sufficiently severe problems at the internal boundary may cause retardation of development at the external boundary. In the most general sense, the infant who is not able to learn that actions have effects in the human object world or that he is separate from the primary mothering figure may not be able to make analogous distinctions in the inanimate world. To define more specific relationships, one would have to look at the criteria we shall develop later (including the strength of the drives, the integrity of the cognitive structures, and the structure and the ambiguity of the task and its relation to dynamic issues).

As we have seen in Piaget's example of the hungry infant, sometimes, at this early stage of development, retardation along the internal boundary may facilitate development along the external boundary. There may be a precocity of impersonal cognitive development in response to lack of development on the internal boundary, particularly if this lack of development is accompanied by a lack of drive satisfaction and an increased intensity of the drives. If the difficulty at the internal boundary results in a reduction of drive activity or in passivity or inhibition, however, it may globally affect the external boundary in terms of exploratory activity.

To summarize: the vulnerability to mutual retardation is greatest at this early stage because of the lack of real differentiation between the two boundaries. Clinically, if difficulties are observed in object relations and in affective and drive development, there are often delays in the development of impersonal external cognition. Décarie's work (1962), showing the parallel course of human and nonhuman object permanence during the first two years of life, is consistent with more subjective clinical impressions.

Sensorimotor stage 4, according to Piaget, involves the coordination of secondary circular reactions with complex action patterns related to one another. The differentiation of means from ends is completed, and the magical quality is no longer prominent. The youngster will not pull unless there is a string, and soon will not pull unless the string has a bell attached to it that makes the desired sound. Also illustrative of the differentiation of means from ends is the infant's setting one object aside to reach another object and the use of intermediary objects to get to an object. Thus, there is not only complete differentiation of means from ends, but also a clear preliminary picture of the relationship between means and ends.

In the development of spatial relationships, space farther away from the body is coordinated, breaking down the egocentrism of earlier stages. Similarly, in the realm of time, before and after become coordinated, even if the infant himself is not the active agent in a sequence occurring across time.

At the inner boundary many significant developments occur. There is a beginning of the full recognition of a separate human object. The differentiation of means from ends and the ability to use detours have implications for stimuli arising from inside the body. There detour mechanisms form the precursors of defenses and coping mechanisms. The infant can now delay and use detours to find alternate modes of obtaining pleasure, discharge, or equilibrium. Thus, just as the infant can get the inanimate object by using an intermediary object, such as his hand, he is more skillful in using intermediary devices to gain pleasure or achieve discharge. Internal tensions no longer demand immediate discharge. The infant shows enhanced capacity to derive satisfaction from his own body, knows better how to woo his parents, and perhaps, most interesting, shows the beginning capacities for imitation (a precursor of identification) as a way to obtain pleasure without immediate gratification from the object.

To facilitate development at the internal boundary, however, the primary human object must respond to these new capacities, permitting delay, facilitating detour, and at the same time consolidating the relationship between means and ends. The mother who forms a comfortable symbiotic attachment may not be capable of the "balanced empathy" necessary for discriminative responses to the infant's varied motor and affective responses. Mothers who tend to overidentify and/or project may not provide clearly discriminated and appropriate feedback to support differentiation. These schemes are still vulnerable to regression. Without going into detail, we can speculate about what will happen if a human object relationship does not support the schemes of the internal boundary. We must not forget that at the external boundary these schemes can be supported simply by reproductive assimilation on the infant's part. However, he is not the sole actor on the stage of human object relations; the mothering figure must be available for his repeated practice and, as indicated, she must provide highly discriminative feedback. The mother also must provide enough general pleasure to maintain the infant's intense attachment and interest in the human object world, lest, because of frustration, he find it so aversive or painful, that he pulls away from this attachment.

At this stage of development, then, if the human object world is not supportive, the infant may regress to the schemes of stage 3. Thus, he may fail to find detours or to use intermediary objects to obtain pleasure. If the infant has developed satisfactorily this far, he may continue to use the inanimate world to develop the external boundary of pure cognition. However, as in stage 3, and depending on a group of transformational variables to be described later, what is going on at the internal boundary may affect the external boundary. In the most general sense, the infant who is not supported in differentiating himself from the object of his primary human attachment may begin to regress and may become unable to differentiate himself from inanimate objects or to differentiate means from ends. There is suggestive, though not yet conclusive, evidence that these parallel regressions in ego functions at the external and at the internal boundaries do occur in certain psychotic children (Anthony, 1956a).

In stage 5 of Piaget's sensorimotor period, the child searches for new means by combining known schemes. The more complex behavior patterns of tertiary circular reactions occur, and a greater flexibility in problem solving is evident as trial-and-error combinations lead to discovery of effective behavior chains. The reduction of egocentrism continues in the realms of space, time, and causality as the child coordinates these concepts at greater distances from his own body or personal agency. Discussing causality, Piaget (1937) notes that the stage-4 child will move an observer's hand to start a causal chain, but the stage-5 child will simply position himself with the observer in such a way that the latter can be effective as a cause on his own initiative. The child does not have to see himself as the prime mover. In terms of time, there is the beginning of memory at this stage of development. We can observe the child picking something up from behind him as needed, indicating that he remembers putting it there.

For the internal boundary, these new schemes and capacities have a corresponding importance. Just as, externally, new means can be searched for from known schemes, internally, there can be new combinations of means for discharge of tension, for achievement of pleasure, and for dealing with the human object world (e.g., greater use of displacement). The child finds possibilities for new methods of coping, styles of defense, and ways of regulating the internal world of drive, affect, and mood, as well as ways of relating to the human object (e.g., greater use of imitation and the beginnings of identification). We thus see greater flexibility along the internal boundary, similar to that along the external boundary.

This flexibility, however, depends on a satisfactory human object relationship. It is important to state that the quality of human object relations at this point in development has special implications for the optimal consolidation of schemes at the internal boundary. The world of human object relations is under the pressure of an already differentiated oral drive organization and is shifting into the more advanced anal drive organization. The child is in a special relationship to his world because of his enhanced motor skills, his greatly enhanced capacities for tertiary circular reactions, and his heightened capacity for movement in space. In short, the child is moving around in a vastly larger, more organized world. Lacking the beginning conceptual ability that initiates stage 6, the child, according to Mahler, is in a stage of omnipotence (Mahler, Pine, and Bergman, 1975). While he can differentiate himself from the primary mothering object emotionally, he is still tied to her and shares an "omnipotence umbrella" with her. Thus, he moves around the house as though she were omnipresent. This sense of security, omnipotence, and trust enhances his explorations and his consolidation of the aforementioned schemes.

What happens if this sense of omnipotence is interfered with or is overly enhanced? If the sense of omnipotence is overly compromised or deflated, the loss of energy, trust, and the capacity for exploration may severely curtail or modify the development of the new cognitive abilities at both boundaries. The curiosity, interest, and activity necessary for consolidation of both impersonal and affective structures through repeated experience may be undermined. On the other hand, if these capacities are overly enhanced, one may not see "the beginning of insight" because the experience of frustration necessary to consolidate a capacity for delay and the use of mental representation is compromised. As in the earlier stages of sensorimotor development, if the growing capacities are not supported by the subtleties of the human object relationship, the development of parallel functions at the internal boundary may be impaired, and the external boundary may be affected as well. However, with the new differentiation between the internal and external boundaries that has occurred by this time, and because of the greater freedom to "act on the environment" as a result of increased motor capacity, compromises along one boundary do not necessarily lead to compromises along the other boundary.

The sixth stage of sensorimotor development is characterized by the child's ability to make new mental combinations and to experience cognitive insight. Combinations of actions are internalized, as in Piaget's (1936) observation of his child examining a matchbox, opening and closing her mouth, and then becoming aware that she can perform a formally similar action with the box (p. 337).

The new capacity for internalized mental combinations has ramifications for the construct of the permanent object and for developments in the concepts of space, time, and causality. In terms of object permanence, the child can deduce the existence of the missing object from the series of actions he has observed in its being moved. In relation to concepts of space, time, and causality, the stage-6 child can represent to himself events in these domains that are not perceptually present.

These new developments have profound importance along both the internal and the external boundaries. New mental combinations provide new ways of dealing with the internal world's wishes, affects, and human relationships. Needs can be met in new and imaginative ways. But at the same time the young child's capacity for experiencing pain is greatly increased, and the capacity for new combinations makes it possible for the young child to develop fears at a conceptual level. We see phobias for the first time at this stage in the child's development.

Perhaps most important at this stage of development, we can see the beginnings or precursors of what may be called the dynamic unconscious. Prior to the capacity for representation, early experience was incorporated in sensorimotor or drive-affect schemes, but not in a figurative sense. Early experience shapes action patterns and prerepresentational feeling states such as those that arise in preverbal transference configurations. With the capacity for memory, new mental combinations, and representation, however, there can be a whole constellation of mental images attached to a variety of wishes and affect states. Since some of these are kept out of awareness, we see the beginning of the dynamic unconscious.

The early defenses used at this time, such as denial, avoidance, displacement, and condensation, are rather primitive in comparison to the postoedipal defenses, which will solidify the existence of the dynamic unconscious. Nevertheless, their presence lends a dynamic quality to any lack of awareness of emotionally charged events. Prior to stage 5 in cognitive development, experiences may have an effect on the affect discharge channels, certain behavioral predispositions, and even certain moods, but now, for the first time, experiences that are not conscious are potentially available to consciousness at the level of representation.

What is happening in the world of human relationships at this time is also quite important. Mahler's (1968) *rapprochement subphase* of separation-individuation begins around this time (18 months). Here the toddler who, at a preconceptual level, was able to experience the new world of discovery under the "omnipotent umbrella" of an emotional fusion with his parents now recognizes, at a beginning conceptual level, his own separateness. He sees his smallness in relation to the universe, and from an emotional point of view, often needs considerable reassurance and reaffirmation of closeness from his parents. He can no longer pretend, so to speak, that his parents are with him all the time and that he can share in their strength as he roams around the house; he thus seeks them out for reassurance and dependency gratification. Sensitive and intuitive parents are available for this additional emotional support and respond well to this greater dependency as the toddler, with his new conceptual abilities, prepares for more separation and individuation. The child subsequently moves toward what Mahler (1968) has called *libidinal object constancy;* that is, the maintenance of the internal representation of the human object even when there are strong feeling states or separations. This capacity develops and consolidates during Mahler's fourth subphase of individuation (around three years).

Thus, it is at stage 6 of the sensorimotor period that we begin to see what will be an ever-increasing separation of developmental lines between the internal boundary and the external boundary. The toddler has achieved object permanence at the level of inanimate objects. He is able to maintain the representation of the human object, but this ability is vulnerable to the vicissitudes of emotional storms and human separations and will not consolidate for yet another year and a half. Stage 6, then, marks the beginning of an increasing differentiation of the internal and external boundaries of ego cognition. From this point on it is no longer as clear how factors along one line of development affect factors along the other.

At this time in development, with the possibility for new mental combinations at the level of representation, the internal boundary takes on special features and characteristics. Human object relations now depend not only on the vicissitudes of the primary human objects—that is, the mother or father or other important caretakers—but also on the vastly increased and immensely flexible fantasy life of the toddler. At the external boundary the task is relatively simpler than at the internal boundary because the inanimate object world the toddler is now able to represent mentally is more stable than the internal world. Earlier in development the lines begin to differentiate because the human partner is more flexible and has more input than the inanimate world. Now the lines separate even more, because the input to the internal boundary involves not only the vicissitudes of human relationships but also internalized object relations and their accompanying drive-affect dispositions.

In relation to the inanimate world, the child's new mental capacities foster cognitive development as that world makes available opportunities for use of new combinations and representations. In relation to the human world, however, the child's new capacities interact with a variable interpersonal world and are in part at the disposal of drive-affect dispositions that are in themselves highly variable. In addition to his vastly improved capacities for dealing with his internal milieu, then, the child has a vastly enhanced capacity for experiencing this internal milieu, including those features of it that may be perceived as frightening and dangerous.

At this stage of development a number of pressures from the internal boundary can affect the external boundary. At the most devastating level, if human object relations become too frightening, the beginnings of human object constancy are not possible. If symbiotic pressures are too great, there may be massive regression toward autistic states, with fragmentation of the external cognitive schemes, as observed in autistic and symbiotic psychosis. If the toddler is not supported during the rapprochement subphase, more subtle regression may be manifest. Cognitively, there may be compromise in representational capacity and the ability for new mental combinations, as indicated by regressions in impersonal object permanence (Décarie, 1962) and in libidinal object constancy.

We have shown that there is a symmetry between the processes and their structural underpinnings posited by Piaget for the external boundary and those processes and structures observation and clinical inference have taught us exist at the internal boundary. In fact, we have observed that if we apply Piaget's concepts to help us understand how the infant and young toddler processes his "inner" drive-related stimuli, we gain increased insight into the early development of aspects of the internal boundary of the ego. We saw, for example, that initially, for the infant, the two boundaries are relatively undifferentiated. At the external boundary simple reflexes slowly coordinate in secondary and tertiary circular reactions and in the establishment and then differentiation of means-ends relationships. Parallel processes occur at the internal boundary as the infant first reaches homeostasis in a simple, undifferentiated manner (e.g., by shutting out stimulation or by direct discharge) and then becomes capable of more complex processes of avoiding pain and seeking pleasure (e.g., through mutual cueing responses with mother). Eventually human means-ends relationships and their differentiation are established in the context of primitive drive-affect states and human relationships.

The differentiation of means from ends at the external boundary by using intermediaries is paralleled at the internal boundary by intermediary steps toward achieving pleasure and satisfaction (e.g., imitative behavior, displacement). The capacity for figurative thinking—that is, the capacity to form an internal representation—is also symmetrical at the two boundaries, as indicated by both experimental and clinical work. This capacity heralds and intensifies the differences in stimuli being processed at the two boundaries and makes greater differentiation possible. We have also shown in a preliminary way how the vicissitudes of the highly variable stimuli at the internal boundary, such as human object relations, may affect the structural development of this boundary and that of the external boundary as well.

The Subperiod of Preoperational Thought

The Piagetian View

The advent of the preoperational subperiod is marked by the appearance of what Piaget calls the semiotic function. This new ability "consists in the ability to represent something (a signified something: object, event, conceptual scheme etc.) by means of a 'signifier' which is differentiated and which serves only a representative purpose: language, mental image, symbolic gesture, and so on" (Piaget and Inhelder, 1966, p. 51).

In the sensorimotor period a thing could be represented in a limited sense by a part of itself, e.g., the mother's voice might "represent" the presence of the mother in the room. Such "signifiers" are indexes undifferentiated from their significants. Symbols and signs, on the other hand, are signifiers that are differentiated from their significants. They become available to the child only with the appearance of the semiotic function.

With the semiotic function, representational thought becomes possible. As Furth (1969) points out, representation has first of all an active meaning in Piaget's theory. The child becomes capable of summoning up a symbol or sign to stand for a given significant. It is important to point out that for Piaget representation is not the essence of thought. Rather, it serves an auxiliary function.

The semiotic function which makes representation possible is heralded by five characteristic behavior patterns in evidence during the second year of life: (1) "*deferred imitation,* that is, imitation which starts after the disappearance of the model"; (2) "*symbolic play* or the game of pretending"; (3) "the *drawing* or graphic image"; (4) "the *mental image* [which] appears as an internalized imitation," and not as a function of perception; (5) "*verbal evocation* of events that are not occurring at the time" (Piaget and Inhelder, 1966, pp. 53-54). Let us examine each of these behavior patterns briefly, in order to understand better the origins of representational thought and the beginning of the preoperational subperiod of cognitive development.

It is possible to trace the development of imitation through the six sensorimotor stages delineated for the concepts of space, time, and causality. Piaget has done this in *Play, Dreams and Imitation in Childhood* (1945). For our purposes, however, it is sufficient to point out that a radically new form of imitation occurs during the second year of life—deferred imitation.

> In a behavior pattern of sensori-motor imitation the child begins by imitating in the presence of the model . . . after which he may continue in the absence of the model, though this does not imply any representation in thought. But in the case of a little girl of sixteen months who sees a playmate become angry, scream, and stamp her foot (new sights for her) and who, an hour or two after the playmate's departure, imitates the scene, laughing, the deferred

> imitation constitutes the beginning of representation, and the imitative gesture the beginning of a differentiated signifier [Piaget and Inhelder, 1966, p. 53].

It should be recalled that intelligence, for Piaget, is seen as an equilibration process in which assimilation and accommodation are in balance. Imitation, on the other hand, is behavior in which accommodation outweighs assimilation, behavior in which "the subject's schemes of action are modified by the external world without his utilizing this external world" (Piaget, 1945, p. 5). In imitation the cognitive structures undergo temporary change without at the same time incorporating new aliment.

A second new behavior pattern appearing at about the same time is symbolic play. In imitation the imbalance between assimilation and accommodation is weighted in favor of accommodation; in play the opposite holds true. Play is a lessening of the demand of the adaptive process.

> Obliged to adapt himself constantly to a social world of elders whose interests and rules remain external to him, and to a physical world which he understands only slightly, the child does not succeed as we adults do in satisfying the affective and even intellectual needs of his personality through these adaptations. It is indispensable to his affective and intellectual equillibrium, therefore, that he have available to him an area of activity whose motivation is not adaptation to reality but, on the contrary, assimilation of reality to the self, without coercions or sanctions. Such an area is play [Piaget and Inhelder, 1966, pp. 57-58.]

Play, too, can be followed in its development through the six stages of sensorimotor intelligence, but the use of symbols in play is found only at the end of the sensorimotor period. This type of play is characterized by games of pretending. A little child will pretend, for instance, that she is asleep, that a box is her pet cat, or that she herself is a church. In each of these cases symbols are generated "in order to express everything in the child's life experience that cannot be formulated and assimilated by means of language alone" (Piaget and Inhelder, 1966, p. 61).

According to Piaget's theory, as we shall see below, these symbols are created by the same process that gives rise to deferred imitation. In fact, Piaget views imitation as the process underlying the development of the entire semotic function. In symbolic play, then, symbols are generated by a process in which accommodation outweighs assimilation. But instead of being used accurately, i.e., to represent that from which they are derived, they are then placed at the service of a process in which a liberating assimilation outweighs accommodation.

A third behavior pattern associated with the rise of the semiotic function is graphic imagery, or drawing. Piaget sees in this activity elements of both play and imitation. In developmental terms, he considers drawing as "halfway between symbolic play and the mental image," which appears at about age two or two and a half (Piaget and Inhelder, 1966, p. 63). It is playful activity in the sense that it is an end in itself, and is characterized by reproductive assimilation. In other words, the child enjoys producing drawings for their own sake. However, this graphic play also has accommodative elements, especially as the child grows older and attempts to draw not just a formless scribble, but some *thing*.

Very closely related to drawing is the mental image itself. Piaget sees the genesis of the mental image as tied to accommodative imitation. He explicitly denies that mental images can be the product of perception itself. His reasoning is based on neurological and genetic evidence. The mental image, then, is not directly given by perceptual input. Rather, it is constructed by the process of accommodation. We shall return to the role of imitation in the production of signs and symbols later.

The fifth behavior pattern associated with the rise of the semiotic function is verbal in nature. It consists of the verbal evocation of events that are not present. Piaget gives the example of a little girl who exclaims, "Anpa, bye-bye [Grandpa went away]," and points to the path he took on leaving (Piaget and Inhelder, 1966, p. 54). The parallel with deferred imitation is obvious, but here the new representational ability is supported by the social system of language.

These five behavior patterns mark the child's initiation into the preoperational subperiod. For Piaget, the semiotic function which serves to enlarge the child's world to such a great extent—liberating him from the bonds of immediate space and time and enabling him to begin to manipulate symbols and to think rather than just to act on immediately present objects—finds its roots in imitation.

Imitation during the sensorimotor period prefigures later representation by "standing for" something else in action (but not in thought). A case in point is the child, mentioned above, who, in her efforts at opening a matchbox to obtain a desired goal, opens her own mouth. Gradually imitation becomes deferred, so that a primitive symbol can be evoked in the absence of any perceptual stimuli related to its significant. The appearance of the mental image marks the point at which imitation is not only deferred but also internalized. Mental imagery, then, provides the foundation for what Piaget terms the figurative aspects of cognitive functions.

Figurative aspects of cognition include those mental activities which do not transform reality, but merely represent it. Chief among these are perception, imitation, and mental imagery (Piaget, 1970). Of these, perception does not, strictly speaking, participate in the semiotic function. It is a figurative element of thought that functions by means of indexes that are not differentiated from the object they represent. Deferred imitation and mental imagery, on the other hand, are figurative aspects of thought that are part of the semiotic function, since the representation of objects they accomplish occurs by way of symbols distinct from the immediate perceptual data yielded by the represented event.

The aspects of thought that transform reality are termed the operative activities of the subject. For Piaget operational cognition is the essence of thought, taking on its full stature only in the periods of concrete and formal operations. In discussing these periods below, we shall point out the characteristics of operational thinking. At this point it needs to be repeated that operational thinking is built up from the general coordinations of actions. It is not a product of the figurative aspects of cognition (Piaget and Inhelder, 1966). In other words, the new mental abilities which develop in the child, enabling him to transform aspects of reality, are not a function of figurative cognition. Even those advanced figurative abilities which appear at about age two, under the rubric of the semiotic function, are not mere extensions of perception. They, too, are based in action, the action of imitation.

Piaget points out experimental evidence to demonstrate his claim that operational thinking is not dependent upon prior figurative properties of cognition. In studying mental images with Inhelder, he has made the distinction between "reproductive" and "anticipatory" images. The former is the image of a known but not immediately perceptible event or object; the latter, the image of some new (unseen) transformation of an event or object. The former is static; the latter, dynamic. Research indicates that anticipatory images do not occur in children younger than age seven. "For example, the subjects experience systematic difficulty in imagining the intermediate positions between the initial vertical and final horizontal position of a falling stick" (Piaget, 1970, p. 718). After the advent of concrete operations, such anticipatory images become possible. Piaget interprets these results to indicate that the mental ability to combine, transform, etc., given with the period of concrete operations, antedates the ability to imagine such actions.

Similarly, Piaget denies that operational thinking is dependent upon language development. Language is one part of the semiotic function, but it is not a figurative aspect of thought, since it makes use of socially shared *signs,* rather than individually constructed *symbols,* to represent events. The difference here is that symbols retain some element of similarity with their significants, while signs are social conventions with an arbitrary connection to their significants (Piaget, 1970). Although language aids operational thinking and makes social communication possible, it is not to be identified with the structure of thought itself.

Again, this position is supported by research. The work of Sinclair, cited by Piaget and Inhelder (1966), has shown that children lacking concrete operations use linguistic descriptions different from those of children already in the period of concrete operations. For instance, in comparing pairs of objects, preoperational children tend to use what linguists term *scalars:* "big–small," "a lot–a little." Concrete operational children use *vectors:* "bigger than–smaller than," "more than—less than." In addition, the younger children compare objects on only one dimension at a time, while the older children will say, "*A* is longer but thinner than *B*."

The important point is that the preoperational children may be trained to use the higher-order linguistic expressions, which they can comprehend. They have difficulty learning them, however, and, once learned, they do not seem to have an appreciable influence on the child's ability to perform concrete operations (Piaget and Inhelder, 1966). Linguistic development thus cannot be considered a sufficient condition for the development of operational thinking.

Even more convincing evidence is yielded by Furth's (1966) studies with deaf subjects. Obviously, this population has been deprived of normal language experience. Even if linguistic development were a necessary condition for the development of operational thinking, one would expect to find significant deficits in operational functioning among the deaf. Furth and his colleagues tested their deaf subjects on tasks that were not verbal in form, and found that "the basic manifestations of logical thinking in linguistically deprived deaf children were present without any important structural deficiencies" (1969, p. 119). Furthermore, while on certain tasks the deaf did show some inferiority due to hearing deficits, there was no consistent relationship between failures and specific logical operations, so that existing deficits, which seemed related to styles of problem solving, might well be attributable to inadequate social experience in a less than challenging intellectual milieu.

Operational thought, then, is constructed from the coordination of actions, and not from a figurative or linguistic base. Although figurative and linguistic aspects of thinking can serve as auxiliaries to operational thought, development toward concrete operations is considerably delayed by the difficulties involved in harnessing some of the new abilities acquired at the end of the sensorimotor period. The appearance of the semiotic function is certainly not to be confused with its mastery. In a certain sense, the child has to learn all over again on the level of representational thought what he has already mastered on the motor level. Piaget (1962a) recounts a test he constructed with Szeminska:

> We took children of four to five years of age who went to school by themselves and came back home by themselves, and asked them if they could trace the way to school and back for us, not in design, which would be too difficult, but like a construction game, with concrete objects. We found that they were not capable of representation; there was a kind of motor-memory but it was not yet a representation of a whole—the group of displacements had not yet been reconstructed on the plane of the representation of thought [p. 162].

It should be noted that the group of displacements had, of course, been mastered by these children on the sensorimotor level, in their construction of the concept of space. Such an apparent "regression" when children pass to a higher stage of development is termed by Piaget a *vertical décalage*. To achieve adequate constructions on the new level of functioning, the child must once again pass from a condition in which the environment is centered on his body to one in which his perspective is simply one among many. Given the new social complexity of his larger world, this type of decentering is quite difficult (Piaget and Inhelder, 1966). Experimental evidence indicates the preoperational child's difficulties with his newly expanded cognitive world.

At the end of the sensorimotor period the child has attained a concept of space as unified and objective, in the sense that it is detached from dependence upon his body activity. However, the objectivity of this spatial concept is severely limited at the start of the preoperational subperiod, as can be seen in the child's inability as yet to incorporate various spatial-geometric properties into his spatial concept. An example of this inability is given in Piaget's well-known experiment on the acquisition of the topological property of order, as summarized by Flavell (1970):

> *E* slides three different-colored wooden balls into, say, the left-hand opening of a tunnel in a particular order (*A*, then *B*, then *C*), and then asks *S* a series of questions. In what order will the three balls exit at the right hand end of the tunnel *(ABC)?* In what order would they reemerge on the left side *(CBA)?* What will be the order of appearance on the right side when the whole tunnel is rotated 180° *(CBA)*, or 360° *(ABC)*, etc.? Preoperational children tend to have problems with all but the first question, and occasionally even pre-

> dict that the middle ball *(B)* will emerge first under one or another of the experimental conditions. Above all, they seem to lack any sense of a rule system governing the occurrence of direct versus inverse orders under the various rotations and directions of exit [p. 1016].

It should be noted here that the child's lack of consistency when changing directions in representational thought is characteristic of the lack of true operations. Reversibility has not yet been established.

Other studies related to spatial properties involve the child's ability to assume the perspective of another person. "In the best known of these studies [Piaget and Inhelder, 1948], the child sits facing a scale model of three mountains and is tested for his ability to predict their appearance from various other perspectives (from the right of where he is seated, from the opposite side, etc.). The most interesting finding was that a number of the younger children kept confusing their own perspective with the others" (Flavell, 1970, p. 1026). This experiment clearly illustrates the problem of decentering in representational thought. The preoperational child, in constructing a mental image of a scene from another's perspective, is a captive of his own perspective. He has difficulty dissociating thought from the psychological center of his own body.

A final example of preoperational difficulties with the concept of space involves Euclidean properties. Piaget's concern here is with the child's growing ability to construct an objective measurement of spatial dimension, i.e., one independent of his bodily perspective.

> In one study the child is presented with a tower of blocks which stands on a table. His job is to build a second tower the same height, but with the following restricting conditions. His building blocks are of a size different from the model's; his tower stands on a lower table than that of the model; and a screen prevents him from actually seeing the model as he builds, although he can at any time go around it to look [Flavell, 1963, p. 335].

Results of this study indicate a progressive development in the child's ability to measure space, a development which continues into the middle of the concrete operational period. As Flavell (1963) reports, the youngest children merely measure by visual inspection, often failing to take any account of the discrepancy in height of the two tables. Later, measurement is introduced, but only with reference to points on the child's body; he measures by holding his hands apart, or by designating the end points of the model by reference to a distance along his body. When the child finally begins to measure with an instrument independent of his body, at first the measuring stick must be exactly the same length as the model. Later, it can be longer, with the excess appropriately marked off. Only in the midst of the concrete operational period, can the child utilize a standard shorter than the model.

Turning to the concept of time, we see a development roughly analogous to the reconstruction of objective space. At the start of the preoperational subperiod the child's concept of time is confounded with his concept of space (Flavell, 1970, p. 1020). His task is to separate the two categories and to construct what Piaget (1946) terms a "homogeneous time," within which all movements proceed in common and can thus be ordered and compared on a common temporal basis. One example will demonstrate the original confusion of space and time which must be overcome:

> The child is shown two series of pictures representing the year-by-year growth of two fruit trees. One of the trees is planted a year after the other but, growing at a faster rate, eventually outstrips the first in size, quantity of fruit, etc. Young children tend to judge this tree to be the older of the two, disregarding their knowledge that it was planted later [Flavell, 1970, p. 1021].

In our consideration of the sensorimotor period we saw the transition from an undifferentiated magical-phenomenalist conception of causality to a relatively more objective conception, distinguishing effects of the child's internal feelings of effort (psychological causality) from effects of causal agents or causal relations between objects exterior to the child (physical causality). On the representational level of thought, a similar development must be undergone in the child's concept of causality. At the beginning of the preoperational subperiod the physical-psychological confusion of the early sensorimotor period is recapitulated on the higher level. Psychic phenomena are given physical, substantial existence, while physical substances are endowed with psychic attributes. An example of the first tendency, which Piaget terms *realism,* occurs when the young child conceives of dreams as "external, palpable realities, potentially visible to others" (Flavell, 1970, p. 1023).

An example of the second tendency is *animism,* in which "everything that is in movement is alive and conscious, the wind knows that it blows, the sun that it moves, etc." (Piaget and Inhelder, 1969, p. 110). Other examples include "*finalism* [in which] explanations [are] couched in terms of anthropocentric functional purpose (boats float so that people can ride on them)" and "*artificialism*—the positing of a human or (human-like) divine architect to account for the origin of natural objects and events (. . . lakes are thought to be dug *by* men . . .)" (Flavell, 1970, p. 1023).

Piaget's early work on children's concepts of causality has been the subject of heavy criticism, and follow-up studies have resulted in contradictory evidence. Flavell (1970) notes, however, that Laurendeau and Pinard (1962) have reviewed these data and conducted an extensive study which gives general support to Piaget's theoretical account. On the other hand, in a comprehensive review of the literature on animism, Looft and Bartz (1969) point out numerous methodological and semantic difficulties in the research stimulated by Piaget. They note that Piaget himself considers his work on animism as preliminary and methodologically inferior to his later structural investigations of cognition. Since studies of animism have yielded contradictory results, these authors suggest that firm, scientific conclusions concerning the existence of animistic causal thinking cannot be drawn until new studies have been conducted, in which more advanced methodologies are employed.

It is of interest, in this connection, that Anthony (1957) speculates that Piaget's account of animism may have been responsible for his growing distance from psychoanalytic theory (after 1922). Where Freud explains animism on basically emotional grounds, as an instance of the mechanism of projection, Piaget explains it on cognitive grounds, as a result of the lack of differentiation between self and objects characteristic of the recently entered preoperational subperiod.

Dynamic Considerations and the Preoperational Subperiod

The preoperational subperiod begins with the emergence of the capacity for deferred imitation and mental representation and ends with the achievement of conservation concepts characteristic of concrete operational thinking. As reviewed above, symbolic play, the use of symbols in drawings, and the first use of words are also cognitive achievements of this subperiod. In general, then, the preoperational child has the ability to form symbols through representation, that is, to utilize the semiotic function.

Movement from the appearance of the semiotic function to the beginnings of concrete operations constitutes a type of relearning on a higher plane of what has already been learned in a sensorimotor fashion. In the realm of causality, the "regression" to a magical type of thinking at the beginning of the preoperational subperiod is most pronounced. As we noted earlier, the child's concept of causality at this time in development is poorly differentiated. Through what Piaget terms finalism and artificialism, anthropocentric qualities are inappropriately attributed to inanimate environmental events. Similarly, life is attributed to everything that moves (animism), and the boundary between fantasy and reality is blurred (realism).

It is important to re-emphasize that just as the baby develops means-ends relationships at the level of action patterns, the preoperational child learns means-ends relationships at the level of figurative capacities or at the level of representation. The gains made in terms of sensorimotor intelligence are not lost. They remain an important foundation for a certain level of adaptation to the world (a basic level of reality testing to be described later). Sensorimotor intelligence is not transferable to the representational system, however, and the steps in means-ends differentiation must occur again at this new level.

The preoperational subperiod is one in which the distinct aspects of development studied by Piaget and by psychoanalytic observers are very similar. It is interesting that the English translation of *La formation du symbole chez l'enfant* (1945)—Piaget's major work on the preoperational subperiod—is *Play, Dreams and Imitation in Childhood.* One could hardly designate three topics in childhood development of more immediate interest to psychoanalysts. Thus, we are faced with a time period for which the major observer of *impersonal cognition,* or what we have called cognition at the external boundary of the ego, has studied the same aspects as have many analytic observers of cognition at the internal boundary.

The implications of this fact for the present integrative task are clear. The preoperational subperiod is one lacking in operational thinking as such; that is, thinking that transforms reality in accordance with coherent systems of interrelated and reversible interiorized actions. Just as Piaget pinpoints a vertical *décalage* during this time, psychoanalytic psychologists note a regression in what had been an increasing differentiation between ego functioning at the internal boundary and at the external boundary. In other words, the boundary of cognition dealing with drive- or affect-related objects is poorly differentiated from that dealing with impersonal external objects. Even though the boundaries are relatively undifferentiated and the process at each boundary is therefore, by definition, symmetrical, it will prove useful to examine the events at the internal boundary to further document this symmetry and, more important, to show how the events at the internal boundary influence the external boundary.

Psychoanalytic observers have noted the rich and complex development during this phase of life. In terms of drive development, the young child moves from orality to anality and eventually to the oedipal period. The process of drive energy neutralization permits him greater flexibility in delay and detour mechanisms. In terms of object relations, dyadic attachments predominate. Chronologically, the time period for the appearance of Piaget's semiotic function roughly corresponds to that of Mahler's rapprochement subphase of separation-individuation. Mahler has noted that cognitive capacities are one determinant of the subphases she has observed (Mahler, Pine, and Bergman, 1975). Certainly, the capacity for mental representation and symbol formation can lead the child to a new experience of smallness vis-à-vis the universe around him. In consequence, there is a re-establishment of dependency and a demanding type of egocentrism, as Mahler has described in some detail in terms of the rapprochement subphase. Thus, from both a cognitive and an emotional point of view, the capacity for figurative thinking puts a new burden on the growing youngster, to which he responds initially by an increased egocentrism.

While there is a certain parallel between Piaget's observations and those of psychoanalytically oriented observers, there is a relative lack of differentiation of the realms under study, with a consequent limitation in the potential for mutually enriching integration, though each model adds to and delineates more specifically certain aspects of development included in the other. For example, Piaget's concepts of animism, finalism, realism, and artificialism describe aspects of magical thinking in a more specific way. His observations have shown analysts that certain phenomena observed in children may be a function of structural cognitive limitations and not necessarily only a consequence of drive derivatives. Clinical observations, however, suggest strongly that the content of children's play, fantasy, and imitation is often related to emotional issues. Its expression in certain forms may be a function of the cognitive structures available, but its full richness is missed unless drive-related and object-relations determinants are considered. If, as Anthony (1957) suggests, the initial split between Piaget and psychoanalysis occurred over the issue of animistic thinking in children, that split may be reversed by consideration of a more general model in which a developmentally determined set of cognitive structures interacts with external and internal stimuli. We have suggested that at the preoperational stage the resulting differentiation between internal and external ego boundaries is quite limited. Magical thinking may thus be seen in relation to both emotionally charged issues, such as parental omnipotence, and external reality factors, such as the child's very particular understanding of principles of physics.

Only one special case need be discussed at this point concerning integration of the internal and external boundaries of ego structures as they progressively differentiate. Drive-related object relations can affect development of impersonal cognition by interfering with the slow progression away from egocentrism and magical thinking. If emotional factors lead to a compromise in the maintenance of figurative capacities, or if these capacities become so bound to need-satisfying object relations that they cannot attend to the external, non-affect-laden world, the development of impersonal cognition may be delayed.

The steps in the process of separation and individuation, which begin in the prerepresentational stage, in part repeat themselves in the context of the representational capacity. The development of means-ends relationships from simple to more complex configurations described so clearly for the sensorimotor period of development may have a parallel course of development in terms of internal representation at the internal boundary.

Clinical observation and reconstructive data support the impression that there is differentiation in the development of the drives (oral to anal to phallic). Internalized self- and object representations become progressively more integrated (e.g., integration of the good and bad object) and differentiated from one another (e.g., less projection). The foundations of such basic ego functions as defense and reality testing are laid, with increasing development of detours and progressive neutralization of drive energies. The consolidation of self- and object representations, which reach their pinnacle in the establishment of libidinal object constancy, sets the foundation for the structuralization of basic ego functions related to secondary-process thinking. Internalized means-ends relationships, in the realm of internalized self- and object representations and their drive-affect dispositions, become progressively differentiated, just as external means-ends relationships did in the sensorimotor period.

In the sensorimotor phase of development, the relationship between the primary mothering figure and the developing infant is central in terms of providing an "average expectable" interpersonal nutriment. So, too, in the preoperational phase, the determination of the character and integrity of psychic structures underlying ego functions related to secondary-process thinking is in part dependent on the primary nurturing figure's interaction with the growing toddler. The subtleties of this period have been well described by Mahler (see Mahler, Pine, and Bergman, 1975). If, for example, the primary nurturing figure is not available for the extra emotional support needed by the toddler during the rapprochement subphase, when the toddler sees himself as realistically small and needy in relation to a huge and at times frightening world, a regression to the prefigurative or prerepresentational level may occur. Thus, the consolidation of the initial components of object permanence may be lost if the affective aliment is insufficient. As the toddler establishes the schemes for means-ends relationships at the level of representation (which he did earlier in sensorimotor action), if he experiences frightening separations from his primary human objects or highly inconsistent, unpredictable responses from them, the differentiation of means from ends and the establishment of libidinal object constancy may be compromised. Children who have been exposed to traumatic separations or to highly inconsistent patterns of response, particularly around heightened emotional states of neediness or anger, often have difficulty maintaining a consolidated and differentiated representation of their primary nurturing figures and the world they represent. Extreme separation anxiety, manifested by a refusal to go to school and accompanied by stubborn clinging and negativistic behavior patterns, is not infrequently observed in such cases. Equally important, however, is that such children maintain magical patterns of thinking, not only in relation to their internal world but often at the external boundary, and thus have difficulties at school. Under emotional pressure, logical thought (concrete operations) may be compromised.

More subtle and less marked is the influence of certain types of parental patterns in relation to the toddler's drive-affect states. In the case of the mother who is depressed and withdraws when her child is angry, the toddler may feel that his anger and "badness" hurt mother and caused her to leave. A later depressive tendency, "I cause people to withdraw with my badness," may be based on magical thinking consolidated by this pattern. Such a depressive scheme at the internal boundary may only indirectly affect the external boundary. It may not affect the ability to solve mathematical problems, but may affect logical decision making in business—for example, a person may tend to overweigh his own causal role in a negative outcome.

The Concrete Operational Period

The Piagetian View

Having observed the manifestations of preoperational thought in the realms of space, time, and causality, we shall turn now to the development of logical operations. A crucial difference between preoperational and concrete operational thought is the presence within operational thinking of concepts of conservation. When concrete operations have been organized into a system they enable the child to conserve, i.e., "to discover what values do and do not remain invariant . . . in the course of any given kind of change or transformation" (Flavell, 1963, p. 415). Hence, the clearest sign that a child remains in the preoperational subperiod is the absence of the concept of conservation. Piaget (1962a) gives the following example: If a child pours some liquid from a short, wide glass into a tall, narrow one, he believes it has changed in quantity. "This absence of conservation indicates essentially that at this stage the child reasons from the configuration. Confronted with a transformation, he does not reason from the transformation itself; he starts from the initial configuration, then sees the final configuration, compares the two but forgets the transformation, because he does not know how to reason about it" (p. 163).

At the level of concrete operations, however, the child is no longer overwhelmed by the perceptual discrepancy between the two configurations. He begins to reason about the transformation, and his correct judgments regarding the conservation of quantity are accompanied by explorations grounded in logical properties. Of course, the child is not assumed to be aware of the logic he utilizes. In the following example from Piaget, the children's responses are in quotation marks, and the logical properties they imply are set off in parentheses.

> . . . at the level of concrete operations, after seven or eight, the child says: "It is the same water," "It has only been poured," "Nothing has been taken away or added" (simple or additive identities); "You can put the water in *B* back into *A* where it was before" (reversibility by inversion); or, particularly, "The water is higher, but the glass is narrower, so it's the same amount" (compensation

or reversibility by reciprocal relationship) [Piaget and Inhelder, 1966, p. 98].

In beginning to solve problems of conservation, the child passes from the preoperational subperiod into the period of concrete operations, for which the former was a long time of transition and preparation. The progressive and continual structure building that takes place in the concrete operational period is evident in the increase, with development and age, in the scope of such concepts of conservation.

At the age (on the average) of about seven or eight, the child can solve the conservation of quantity problem mentioned above, and make similar judgments about the conservation of substance of a lump of clay following a transformation in its shape. Between the ages of nine and ten, the child discovers that the weight of a given object is also conserved even if its shape is transformed. However, it is not until approximately age eleven or twelve that children have a logical comprehension that the volume displayed by a given object is conserved even after transformation of the object's shape. There are many such examples of the development of conservation concepts in the concrete operational period. In each case, conservation entails logical certainty that one characteristic of an object remains invariant while the object itself undergoes some type of perceived transformation.

To take one more brief example, the concept of cardinal numbers develops from an initially nonconserving to a conserving stage. Preoperational children can be presented with two rows of dots in one-to-one correspondence (Flavell, 1963). Let us say there is a row of six blue dots with a row of six red dots directly beneath it and in optical correspondence, i.e., imaginary vertical lines could be constructed between each blue dot and its corresponding red dot. If the experimenter destroys this optical correspondence by spreading out one of the rows of dots, the preoperational child will think the longer row now contains more dots. Only after conservation of cardinal number has been established as a logical necessity does the child maintain the numerical equivalence of the "spread-out" row. Obviously, preoperational concepts of number would provide an inadequate basis for arithmetic skills. Thus, a lag in the development of number conservation may underlie certain arithmetic-related learning disabilities.

We have seen that notions of conservation are the mark of well-established concrete operational thinking. It is appropriate at this point to delve further into the examination of the concrete operations themselves. As the name indicates, they are operations concerned with concrete objects, in contradistinction to formal operations, which act upon propositions and hypothetical statements. Despite this limiting characteristic, concrete operations represent a very significant development over the types of thinking evident at preoperational levels because they are systematically organized and have the properties of true operations.

At this point it is essential to discuss the meaning of *operation* in Piaget's thought. Operations themselves constitute essential thinking (Furth, 1969). For Piaget, an operation is an action that is (1) interiorized, (2) reversible, and (3) part of an organized system of such actions. The operations forming this system are, first of all, interiorized actions. In the sensorimotor period external behavior patterns gave rise, through a process of abstraction, to the construction of sensorimotor schemes. In similar fashion, internal thinking patterns now give rise to operations. It is the generalizable aspects of actions, "those which can be found in any coordinating of particular actions," that enter into the construction of operations (Furth, 1969, p. 58). To say that the crucial aspect of actions in this regard is their generalizability is to explain the importance of interiorization in the construction of operations. Interiorization refers to "an increasing dissociation of general form from particular content" (Furth, 1969, p. 60). In other words, the notions of generalizability and interiorization merely point to the process of abstraction at work. For example, a child adds 2 apples and 3 apples to obtain 5 apples. In another instance he adds seven blocks and 1 block to obtain 8 blocks. In a third instance he combines the category of fathers with that of mothers to obtain the category of parents. The operation abstracted from these three mental actions is that of addition or combining, without reference to the particular content of numbers, objects, or categories.

Not only must an operation be interiorized action; it must

also be reversible. The action of combining (addition) is not an operation until its relationship to the action of separating (subtraction) is comprehended. To understand reversibility is to understand the third criterion of an operation, its inclusion in a system. "A given operation, put into concrete effect in the here and now, always presupposes a structured system which includes other, related operations, for the moment latent and inactive but always potentially actualizable themselves" (Flavell, 1963, p. 167).

The reversibility essential to operatory thought may be of two types: inversion or reciprocity. In reversibility by inversion an action $+ A$ is reversed by $- A$. Thus, in our conservation of quantity example, the pouring of liquid into the second container ($+ A$) may be mentally reversed, i.e., mentally poured back into the first container ($- A$). In reversibility by reciprocity, a relation $A < B$ is reversed by the relation $B < A$. Referring again to the conservation of quantity example, let A stand for the first container and B stand for the second container. Then, the rising height of liquid in the second container ($A < B$) is offset by its narrower width ($B < A$).

Corresponding to these two types of reversibility are the two major categories of concrete operations: those pertaining to classes and those pertaining to relations. In the system of operations performed on classes, reversibility is by way of inversion; in those performed on relations, it is by way of reciprocity. These two categories of concrete operations can be discussed at two levels: the level of logico-mathematical models and the level of observable, testable performance in a particular sphere. Flavell (1963) delineates the logico-mathematical models and then describes the connections between these models and the observable cognitive behavior of children.

The logico-mathematical models of concrete operations are termed "groupings" by Piaget and consist of structures composed of a set of elements and rules governing their interaction. Nine such groupings are proposed, four whose elements are classes, four whose elements are relations, and one, the grouping of equalities, which pertains both to classes and to relations. In what follows, based on Flavell (1963), we shall briefly describe these groupings and, where possible, show their direct relevance to cognitive behavior or observable performance.

Groupings I to IV have as their elements classes of objects. As an example, consider the class of robins and its supraordinate class, birds. The class of all birds other than robins would be a complement to the class of robins, such that addition of these complementing classes would yield as a product the supraordinate class. If A = class of robins, A' = class of all birds except robins, and B = class of all birds, then $A + A' = B$.

Grouping I, whose elements are class additions, similar to the above example, has a set of properties governing such additions. These properties—composition, associativity, general identity, reversibility, and special identity—are properties derived from mathematical theories of groups and lattices.[2] They are present in all nine groupings and, in fact, are the defining characteristics of a grouping from the logico-mathematical point of view. One might consider them the unifying characteristic of the grouping structure which enables it to function as a closed system.

For our purposes, it is most relevant to discuss indications of the presence of grouping I in the cognitive behavior of the concrete operational child. The major task used to test for this level of development is the class inclusion task. In a typical class inclusion experiment, a child is presented with pictures of, say, six dogs and two cats, and is then asked, "Are there more dogs or more pets?" The preoperational child will answer "more dogs." This response does not arise from verbal confusion, but from the child's inability to view the array simultaneously from the point of view of subordinate classes and from the point of view of the supraordinate class. The proof is that the child will correctly count dogs, cats, and pets, yet still give the incorrect answer. He is unable to include the subordinate classes within the supraordinate class, maintaining both levels of classification in mind while forming his answer. "He is unable to respond according to the inclusion $A < B$, because if he thinks of the part A, the whole B ceases to be conserved as a unit, and the part A is henceforth comparable only to its complementary A'"

[2] Descriptions of these properties are given in Flavell (1963) and will not be repeated here.

(Piaget and Inhelder, 1966, p. 103). Only when a system of classifications has been established, such that $A + A' = B$, $B + B' = C$, etc., can problems of class inclusion be correctly solved. Such a system, or structure, is marked by reversibility and mobility of thought between successive nestings of classes.

Grouping II again contains as elements the additions of classes. However, the addition equations in this grouping are not simply those of one subclass and its complement. Rather, they are those of the many possible subclasses of a supraordinate class, plus the complement of each. Put more simply, the supraordinate class, birds, can be constituted from numerous subclass additions. Robins and birds that are non-robins equal birds; likewise owls and birds that are non-owls equal birds. Thus $A + A' = B$, but so also $A_2 + A_2' = B$. This grouping is evidenced by the concrete operational child's ability to classify a set of objects in more than one way. For example, given a set of objects varying both in color and in geometric shape, the child could classify them by one criterion and then by the other.

The third grouping pertains not to addition and subtraction of classes, but to their multiplication and division. To take a simple example, consider humans as subdivided by sex $(A_1 + B_1)$ and by age $(A_2 + B_2 + C_2 + D_2)$ where A_1 = males, B_1 = females, A_2 = children, B_2 = adolescents, C_2 = adults, and D_2 = senior citizens. Multiplication of these classes yields a 2×4 matrix:

$$
\begin{matrix}
(A_1A_2 & A_1B_2 & A_1C_2 & A_1D_2) \\
(B_1A_2 & B_1B_2 & B_1C_2 & B_1D_2)
\end{matrix}
$$

Two types of observable cognitive behavior are dependent upon development of this operational structure. One of these is the simple one-to-one correspondence evident, for example, in the child's ability to align a row of six white buttons in one-to-one relationship with a row of six red buttons and to realize the numerical equivalence even when the optical array is transformed (Flavell, 1963). A more complex task dependent on grouping III is that of direct multiplication of classes. Flavell (1963) describes an experiment in which "the subject is presented with a horizontal row of pictures of different colored leaves (class of leaves) which meets to form a right angle with a vertical row of pictures of green-colored objects of different kinds (class of green objects). The subject's problem is to determine what picture should be placed at the intersect of these two rows" (pp. 192-193).

Grouping IV is not shown by Flavell to be relevant to specific observable cognitive tasks and will not be discussed here. In brief, it assumes a form nearly identical to that of grouping III, but pertinent to correspondences that are not reciprocally one-to-one, but rather one-to-many.

The next four groupings have as their elements relations between objects rather than classes of subjects. For grouping V, the relevant elements are asymmetrical relations and the pertinent operations are those of addition. Let us consider $A < B$ as an asymmetrical relation in which one object is greater than another. Given $B < C$, it follows with logical necessity that $A < C$, and that, in this sense, the differences between *A, B,* and *C* are ordered in a given direction. The ability to form an ordered series of asymmetrical relations between nonequivalent elements, and, following from this, to perform logical judgments of transitive inference (if $A < B$ and $B < C$, then $A < C$) are the criteria of concrete operational thinking in this realm of cognitive behavior.

Seriation refers to the ability to order an array of objects according to one dimension, e.g., length. Presented with a number of sticks of varying length, the preoperational child may "seriate" them in pairs or subgroups, but he has difficulty ordering all the sticks consecutively, as his older counterpart can do. The concrete operational child of about age seven will systematically line up the smallest stick, then the smallest of the remaining sticks, etc. A logic of relations underlies this ability, for the older child is capable of understanding that stick *C* may be larger than *B*, but smaller than *D* ($C > B, A$; but $C < D, E, F$, etc.). The reversibility inherent in this structure is one of reciprocity (Piaget and Inhelder, 1966, p. 102).

The structure underlying seriation enables the child to infer with logical necessity the relation between two unequal objects given the relation of each to a third intermediary object. Failures in transitive inference occur in preoperational subjects, who may decide that $B < C$ because $A < C$ and $A < B$ or, conversely, that it is impossible, without an empirical test, to conclude $A < C$ from $A < B$ and $B < C$ (Flavell, 1963, p. 193).

Grouping V concerns addition of asymmetrical relations; grouping VI pertains to symmetrical relations. Flavell (1963) notes that Piaget's favorite example here is that of relations within a family, such as *x* is the brother of *y*. While few links have been established between the logico-mathematical model of addition of symmetrical relations and observable cognitive behavior, Piaget's early work demonstrates that the preoperational child lacks a comprehension of the symmetry involved in common family relations. Thus, "he will affirm that *x* is his brother but deny that *x* himself has a brother" (Flavell, 1963, p. 194).

The seventh grouping entails multiplication of relational series in a one-to-one manner. One such series might be one of increasing length and the other of increasing width. Schematically, this could be represented by a matrix in which increasing length corresponds to placement further to the right on the horizontal axis (⟶), while increasing width corresponds to placement higher up the vertical axis (↑).

A number of cognitive behaviors have been demonstrated in concrete operational children which derive from the operations based on grouping VII. Two will be mentioned here. First, the concrete operational child can order two sets of asymmetrical relations in one-to-one correspondence. Flavell (1963) gives the example of a child who is presented with ten dolls, differing in height, and ten "walking sticks for the dolls" also differing in height (p. 194). The child is able to match each doll with the appropriate stick. Second, the concrete operational child can construct two-way matrices with objects varying in two qualities. Here Flavell (1963, p. 194) cites Piaget's experiment in which the child is asked to arrange 49 cut-out pictures of leaves. These can be ordered both according to seven different sizes and seven different shades of color.

Groupings VIII and IX are of interest primarily to the logician and mathematician and have little demonstrated relevance to specific cognitive behaviors. Thus, they will not be discussed to any extent here. Grouping VIII is the parallel, for relations, of grouping IV, for classes. The ninth grouping, common to classes and relations, concerns equalities and thus, as Flavell (1963) notes, is a special case closely related to grouping VI, addition to symmetrical relations.

The nine groupings of concrete operations mentioned above pertain to classes of and relations between discrete objects abstracted from the constraints of spatial or temporal proximity. To perform the operations based on these groupings, the subject need not be concerned with spatial or temporal contiguity or distance between the objects of the operation. In contrast to these groupings, Piaget posits another set of groupings relevant to continuous objects which, of course, are bound in proximity both spatially and temporally. He terms these groupings *infralogical* (Flavell, 1963, p. 196). We shall discuss one area of cognitive development dependent upon the construction of infralogical structures: the concept of space.

Piaget is fond of noting that the order of development of fundamental spatial concepts in children is the opposite of the historical development of mathematical geometry in science, but the same as in proper theoretical derivation. Developmentally, the child's first spatial concepts are topological. In early preoperational years (about age four), the child can discriminate objects on the basis of such topological characteristics as openness–closedness, enclosure, or proximity. At about age seven or eight, such topological concepts are superseded by projective and eventually Euclidean concepts. Thus, the concrete operational child can distinguish a circle from a square, even though both are topologically closed figures, on the basis of projective properties such as straight versus curved lines. Eventually, the capacity for real measurement and for comprehension of Euclidean properties demanding measurement, such as angularity and length, makes its appearance.

An experiment recounted by Flavell (1963), and mentioned earlier, depicts these stages in the development of measurement. A tower of blocks is placed on a table and the child is instructed to build another tower of the same height on a table which is lower. Certain potential measuring instruments (sticks) are available for use but no further instructions are given. A screen is placed between the child's table and the model tower to prevent him from seeing the model while he builds. He is allowed, however, to go around the screen for a look at any point.

Four stages of development are noted. The youngest, preoperational children merely compare the towers visually from top to floor, without taking the differential table heights into account. In the second stage, children use parts of their bodies as measurement points, e.g., a length along the torso, or the distance between hands held apart. The third stage is characterized by use of a measuring stick longer than the model and appropriately marked off. Only in the final stage can the children use a stick shorter than the model as an iterative unit of measurement (Flavell, 1963, p. 336).

Dynamic Considerations and the Concrete Operational Period

Logical operations first appear in the concrete operational period and are initially applied to concrete, or real, not hypothetical objects. Operational thinking is marked by concepts of conservation that enable the child to discover what value or values are invariant through a process of transformation.

As described earlier, an operation is an action that is interiorized, reversible, and part of an organized system. The concrete operations are subdivided into those that deal with classes of objects and those that pertain to relations among objects. In the former category, every operation has an inverse as its form of reversibility; in the latter category, every operation has a reciprocal. For example, if the subclass A is added to A' to construct the supraordinate class B, the process can be reversed by subtracting A' from B (inversion). If the relationship between P and R is such that in the dimension of length $P > R$, any difference in area can be nullified if the dimension of width $P < R$ (reciprocity).

The concrete operations are not yet performed on hypothetical statements or propositions; that ability must await the formal operational period. There is a cognitive realism in the child that limits his ability to understand transformations in the realm of the possible. Nevertheless, the advances of the concrete operational period over those of earlier periods are very significant. As the operations become interiorized, the child no longer needs to perform actions in an empirical fashion on concrete objects. He can deduce certain conclusions about classes and relations with logical certitude. In general, as transformations lead to certain changes, he can understand relationships among objects and elements.

The new capacity to understand transformations, particularly as they relate to relationships between elements within a system, has significant implications for the child's impersonal cognitive abilities, or what we are referring to as cognition at the external boundary of the ego. What has been described as concrete operational thinking at the external boundary will be shown to have its parallel process at the internal boundary.

It is perhaps easiest to see the symmetry between impersonal cognitive abilities and those at the internal boundary by looking at the phase-specific defensive operations of the ego, which enable repression to be reinforced by latency defenses. The defense of reaction formation is very similar to the concept of reversibility espoused by Piaget. In reaction formation the ego at the internal boundary replaces an accurate cognition, "*A* hates *B*," with an inaccurate, defensive one,"*A* loves *B*." This appears to be a type of reversibility by reciprocity, as if the equilibrium state of the ego can be maintained only by compensation for a powerful negative affect.

The understanding of serial ordering and of transitive relationships may be related to rationalization as a defense, which makes its preliminary appearance during latency and is used more fully in adolescence. Rationalizations may take the form of attenuation by placement of feelings, wishes, and fears in a serial order; for example, "I may have bad wishes, but they are not as bad as *X's* wishes." This implies an ordering of degrees of badness, with an eventual understanding of transitive relationships among the ordered elements. If $<$ stands for "is not as bad as," then the notion $A < B < C$, etc., may underlie such rationalizations.

If we take just a few of the ideas that Piaget has used to help us understand logical thought in this phase of development, we can see some of the similarities between cognition at the external boundary and at the internal boundary. In the most general sense, the capacity to see what values remain invariant (are conserved) in the course of a given transformation is a useful way to look at the enhanced flexibility of the ego's defensive operations during this period. Whereas to the younger child, black is black and white is white and there are no subtle gradations between them, the latency child has the capacity to see such gradations. Compared with his preoperational counterpart, one would expect him to have a more established concept of conservation in terms of the maintenance of stable object representations across the stresses and strains of interpersonal life. Extrapolating this principle in regard to his dealing with peers, we would expect him to feel stable, in the sense of having a more constant sense of identity across various peer relationships and across situations of peer and familial stress and separation.

The concrete operational child's ability to perform operations on classes of objects not only helps him in school with addition, subtraction, multiplication, and division, but also has its parallels in his ability to deal with a wide variety of wishes and ideas. His ability to classify is involved in his capacity to separate his feelings within the family from his feelings outside the family. He can both generalize and discriminate certain feelings. If he is angry at mother and angry at father, then maybe he is angry at his parents. If he is angry at mother, father, and siblings, then he is angry at the whole family. This classification excludes his teacher and other categories of people. If his anger toward mother has not destroyed her and his anger toward father has not destroyed him, perhaps his anger toward his siblings will not destroy them, and his anger toward his friends will not destroy them. This conclusion is in contrast to the global, overly generalized effects of feelings seen in preoperational children and illustrated by phobias.

The concept of reversibility in an operational system implies that for every action in the present there is a latent, potential action in the future that can reverse it. In the emotional sphere, again to use a simple example, being angry at somebody and wanting to kill him does not mean that you cannot love him in the future. All feelings can be reversed by their opposites: love by hate, or hate by love. Thus, it is not so frightening to dislike someone; it does not necessarily mean that this will be forever and ever. Not everybody has this capacity for reversibility in the realm of affects. Some people feel, even as adults, that to hate means to hate forever. At least in optimal development, the cognitive capacity for reversibility is there and can be applied to the vicissitudes of feelings. The same may be true for more conflict-laden ideas and wishes.

The idea of reversibility implies not simply that an action can be reversed by another action, that *A* can be reversed by *B*. Reversibility within an organized whole encompasses relationships among varied elements: *A* is related to *B* in one way, *B* to *C* in another way, and *C* is related to A. This understanding allows for gradations between different relations and feeling states. Thus, in the context of one object relationship, the set of emotional states directed toward the other may include a degree of love, partly reversed by a degree of hatred, and interrelated in an idiosyncratic equilibrium with feelings of envy, admiration, etc.

The idea of a system with an equilibrium established by the basic law of reversibility is quite important. It gives a sense of constancy to the universe. Just as the structure or system applied to the amount of water poured into and out of different-sized pots or glasses lends constancy to quantity, a similar sense of constancy about human relationships and feelings is now possible.

Libidinal object constancy is tremendously reinforced by the cognitive capacities of this period, which exert their effects at both boundaries. Prior to libidinal object constancy, intense feeling states are dealt with by splitting the object or self-representations (e.g., into good and bad parts of whole objects). Kernberg (1975) discusses ego splitting as a central mechanism in certain borderline and narcissistic conditions. With increased capacities for equilibrium, extreme feeling states can be "conserved" within one integrated system and splitting is not necessary.

The cognitive abilities to classify and seriate may underlie or be the external boundary concomitants of the internal boundary capacities for increasing sophistication of coping and defensive maneuvers. Classification enables one to see the relationship between subordinate and supraordinate classes.

Thus, again, the latency child can have a basically good tie to a family unit, yet within that supraordinate class, he can love, hate, and experience many other subordinate feeling states and subrelationships. He can, for the first time, hate his sibling, wish to murder him, and yet picture that sibling as a member of the family and feel solidly bound to that family, since there is a basic feeling of security not only with the parents but with the entire family unit.

In terms of seriation, the child can see the relativity among relationships, at least along one dimension, and can infer relationships from other relationships. This capacity enhances the ability to understand feelings and affects in the context of relationships among people. For example, if a child is jealous of his brother and if someone at school is acting like his brother, he may be jealous of that person at school. Schematically, if $<$ stands for "is jealous of," then this state of affairs could be represented as: $A < B, B = C, \therefore A < C$. This would represent a transitive inference at the inner boundary, and self-awareness here would constitute insight. The capacity for seriation, which enhances the ego's integrative and synthetic as well as its defensive functioning, is utilized often in treatment, during which its evolution can be observed. It is interesting to see, for example, when one begins working with a five-year-old, that this capacity does not come into play until the child is seven, eight, or nine. The capacity is only partially related to the interpretive process; it is also related to the child's maturation and growth. In fact, the analyst helps free those forces which are constricting the development of this kind of internal inferential capacity.

A useful exercise at this point would be to study each of the nine variations on concrete operations and to see their potential application to understanding not only operations on impersonal external stimuli, such as clay or sticks, but on personal internal stimuli (wishes, affects, internalized self- and object representations, and human relationships).

In grouping I, the formation of sub- and supraordinate classes—$A + A' = B$—makes possible the organization of wishes, affects, and feeling states into classes that can then be more readily conserved. Thus, love and hate directed at mother can be seen as "feelings toward mother."

In grouping II, classes can be maintained by subclasses with more than one characteristic. The concept of "mother" can encompass not only feelings A_1 and A_1', but also wishes, A_2 and A_2'; and her behaviors, A_3 and A_3'. The concept of "mother" can therefore be conserved along a number of dimensions.

In grouping III, the range of variables conserved in a system is increased by the principles of multiplication and division. A series of variables are conserved in a matrix, in which, for example, different variables may be delineated in the vertical and horizontal directions and the task is to relate them. Complex feelings, wishes, fears, and expectations can be more flexibly conserved in a system in which division and multiplication are possible.

In grouping IV, the correspondences of one to many make it possible for "condensations," in the psychoanalytic sense, to have a stable relationship in a logical configuration (e.g., the infantile neurosis).

Grouping V involves the ability for seriation, seeing the gradations or relationships between different variables. For example: "Anger is less than hate, which is less than a wish to murder," and "If I hate *A* more than I hate *B* and I hate *C* more than I like *A*, therefore I hate *C* more than I hate *B*." Feelings are no longer global and undifferentiated but graded, and are experienced in relation to, at a minimum, triangular patterns. Also, if *A* loves *B* a little and hates *B* a little, the reciprocal changes in loving and hating feelings can be conserved with a system—for example, a little more hate makes for a little less love—thus increasing the flexibility of feelings toward a single person within the internalized representational system.

Grouping VI involves symmetrical relationships, such as the recognition that "If *A* is *B's* brother, *B* is *A's* brother" or "If she is my mother, I am her son." A number of dimensions of a relationship can now be conserved. At the internal boundary the ability to see that "If I hate him and I am his son, he is still my father" may facilitate resolution of family-romance fantasies. Similarly, one might ask whether the recognition of symmetrical relationships—"If I can love and hate him, he can love and hate me"—marks the beginning of empathy.

Grouping VII involves multiplication and relative relationships. A two-variable matrix can be constructed in which symmetrical and asymmetrical relationships are explored; for example, leaves can be ordered by size and shape. Similarly, relationships to important family members may be ordered and characterized by loving feelings, rivalrous feelings, and fears. To put it more generally, internalized object representations may be conserved both despite and with variations in affect dispositions, wishes, limits, and fears. This ability expands flexibility, or tolerance of ambiguity, in the internal world while maintaining, or conserving, constancy.

The brief examples above have focused on conserving stable self- and object representations through the ego's increasingly flexible capacity to deal with wishes, affects, and fears without regression to preoedipal states of ego splitting. The operations of the concrete operational period also carry implications for many other aspects of personality development. They may be useful, for example, in understanding the development of individual defenses, such as the enhanced flexibility of reaction formation, rationalization, identification; the development of new affects, such as empathy; and the further development of the superego. While many of these implications are suggested here, their detailed study requires further clinical and experimental observation, and is beyond the scope of the current work.

To show that Piaget's purely cognitive theory is compatible with psychoanalytic views of latency and, in fact, may enhance the specificity with which we can describe certain ego mechanisms is only part of our task. The next step is to see how drive activity during this phase of development relates to these external cognitive tasks.

A slight digression is necessary first. Some of the psychological changes that occur during this period of the child's life should be summarized. During latency proper, before the upheaval of adolescence, the drives are generally thought to be in a period of quiescence. However, this is thought to be true only where a reasonable amount of oedipal resolution has occurred. It should also be mentioned that this is an area of inquiry in which there are differing opinions. Latency may not be so latent and more needs to be known about the drive organization at this stage of development.

The oedipal stage of development occurs near the beginning of the period of concrete operations, and the full attainment of the latency period may be dependent on oedipal resolution. In the oedipal stage phallic drive derivatives are in ascendance in relation to complex patterns of object relations (triangular relationship patterns). These patterns take two forms and occur in different steps for the boy and the girl. To simplify matters, we shall not review the postulated sex differences but shall consider only the different triangular configurations in the boy.

In the positive oedipal configuration, the object of the young boy's libidinal phallic drive derivatives is his mother, and he perceives his father as his rival for her. He feels jealousy, competitiveness, and rage toward his father and wants to dispense with him in order to have his mother to himself. If the oedipal situation is successfully resolved, the youngster gives up aspects of these strivings, repressing his longings for his mother, as he realizes that his father is bigger and stronger. He settles for two secondary prizes, so to speak: the establishment of a warm, supportive relationship with his father and the possibility of identifying with him, and the future possibility of having a mother-type figure for himself when he is big and strong like father. From a strictly dynamic perspective, the angry rage toward father gets resolved via the process of identification. The aggressive drive energies toward father become internalized in relation to the internalized object relationship, thus forming a nucleus of the superego and the future value system. To the degree that neutralization also occurs, because of the loving feelings toward father and the positive gains from this resolution, the superego structure becomes a flexible one.

In the negative oedipal situation the triangle is reversed. Here the father is the libidinal object of the young boy and the mother is seen as the competitor. All the issues of the triangle mentioned earlier are reversed. The resolution here involves similar processes and forms the basis of certain aspects of the superego, particularly the basis of later components of the ego ideal.[3]

During this period the affects of rage, jealousy, envy, and

[3] For the young girl both of these triangular configurations occur, but they occur in a two-step process. There are, then, four oedipal configurations.

lust give way to greater capacities for empathy and, during middle latency, to interpersonal affects related to such things as fair play. The complex, rich object relations of the oedipal situation, when resolved, give way to a quieting of the relationships within the family system and to a movement toward relationships with peers. Here again, latency sexuality may be far from quiescent and aspects of sexual curiosity, a prelude to adolescence, may be actively present.

Successful resolution of the oedipal situation demonstrates the ego's new flexibility in dealing with complicated relationship patterns and with a variety of affects and emotions without being overwhelmed. The resolution of the oedipal situation is crucial for further ego development in (1) the consolidation and internalization of the superego structure and (2) the institution of a barrier repressing oedipal and preoedipal drive derivatives. Latency and adolescence can then be experienced without compromises caused by unsublimated drive derivatives. With a reasonable amount of oedipal resolution, we see the oedipal repression fostered by new and sturdy defenses: for example, reaction formation, isolation of affect, beginning rationalizations, and more sublimated identifications.

It is especially important at this time to look at the relationships between the impersonal cognitive tasks of latency and the drive-affect, object-relation tasks at the internal boundary. Certain transformational links may enable progress along one boundary to facilitate progress along the other. To speculate on this, let us consider for a moment what is involved in a successful oedipal resolution.

A youngster comes into the oedipal phase with strong narcissistic, egocentric investment. His initial stance in the oedipal situation, with all its complexities and intrigues, is to try to win, to remain in the narcissistic, omnipotent position. If earlier development has been successful enough, the youngster has the confidence to take this initial point of view. As a first task, he must be capable of seeing that if he wants mother, he has to deal with father—that is, in a three-person system. Earlier his interpersonal system was dyadic, he and another. Thus, he has to have some capacity to understand a system of three parties in which there are relationships of inequality and equality.

Initially, he may understand this from the point of view of inversion: "It's either him or me. He has her, or he doesn't (and I do)." In order to resolve the oedipal situation, he must be able to see that father is larger and more powerful and that he is fighting a losing battle. He must also be able to see some of the potential benefits of aligning with father and giving up equality with mother.

At this point he may reverse his initial position by a form of reciprocity. In that case, instead of a frontal conflict with father, the boy accepts father's superiority and his type of relationship with mother, but reciprocates by identifying with father and settling for a different type of relationship with mother. Thus, where $A > C$ in one type of relationship with B, $C > A$ in a second type.

Essentially we are dealing here with the kind of general economic language of gains and losses that Piaget himself (1960) has suggested as a language to integrate cognitive and affective models. The oedipal situation, a triangular rivalry, can readily be described in terms of the child's maximization of gains and minimization of losses. Elementary, preliminary forms of classification and seriation may be operating at this point along the internal boundary. To maximize gains and minimize losses, the child subordinates an immediate desire to have what he wants to a more general need to ensure survival in the face of a strong rival. This precursor of classification facilitates identification with father and the formation of the superego. A similar precursor of seriation is the child's ability to let go of his omnipotent, narcissistic position and to see himself as smaller and weaker than his rival. Thus, in a schematic way, we can speculate on the need for the oedipal child to possess certain preliminary concrete operational skills in order to enter and resolve successfully the triangular conflict that envelops him.

Let us suppose the child does not, or chooses not to, resolve the oedipal conflict. How might this affect his capacity for concrete operations in latency, even in relation to the inanimate world? Failure to resolve the triangular conflict may reflect a certain magical thinking in the realm of interpersonal relationships such that the child believes he can, without fear of father's aggression, have mother as father does. No attempt is made, then, to form a new type of relationship with mother that effectively reverses father's relationship by reciprocity. In the same manner, no realistic precursor of seriation appears in the realm of the father-son relationship. In addition, with regard to wishes at the internal ego boundary, no subordination of immediate wishes to more fundamental needs occurs. From the point of view of internal cognition, this situation may indicate a defect in the precursors of classification, while from the point of view of the drives and defenses, it may represent a failure of oedipal object relations to facilitate identification, neutralization, and sublimation.

In a simplified form, in order to resolve the Oedipus complex, the child must be able to see that he can't have his cake and eat it too, so to speak. In a three-person system he cannot have mother and also expect father's love and support (in an "average expectable family," that is). If, because of certain innate drive potentials, family interaction patterns (e.g., one that supports a youngster's impression that he can win without any losses), or cognitive delay or limitation, a youngster holds on to the view that he can have his cake and eat it too, he may subsequently need to limit his impersonal cognitive abilities for classification and seriation to support his preoperational thinking at the internal boundary.

In other words, the cognitive properties involved in concrete operational thinking—the capacity for constructing the inverse and the reciprocal—are intimately tied to the oedipal triangular patterns. Unless there is a capacity for constructing the inverse and the reciprocal, a three-person system is not possible. A three-person system, we must remember, involves not just three persons, but three persons in a series of all possible relationships around certain emotional issues. True triangular oedipal fantasies amply demonstrate this point. The various positive and negative oedipal configurations and their relationships to the libidinal and aggressive drive organizations accompanying them are highly complex and involve alliances between two against one; that is, they involve both a classification scheme based on the capacity for constructing the inverse and a seriation scheme employing comparisons among the three based on the capacity for constructing the reciprocal. To have a system in which you can be either "with them" or "against them" (the inverse and classification) and in which a feeling can have more than its opposite and equal return feeling (reciprocal relationships) demands certain cognitive capacities.

To enter a true triangular oedipal situation, therefore, demands the existence of internal boundary cognition. We see many pseudo-oedipal situations in which seeming phallic strivings are really disguised dependency strivings representing preoedipal concerns. These oedipal-like preoedipal configurations lack the complex interrelationships of a three-person system and are invariably based on the simpler dyadic system with its concomitant preoperational (magical) thinking.

As we have seen, to resolve the oedipal situation, once attained, demands some consolidation of the cognitive schemes mentioned in order to be convinced that one cannot win without losing. This consolidation is at the internal cognitive boundary and involves both the developing maturational capacities for constructing the inverse and the reciprocal and the types of familial relationships that will foster an oedipal resolution. The not-too-seductive opposite-sex parent and the loving but firm same-sex parent, who foster oedipal resolution, may be considered the appropriate aliment necessary to the full development of cognition at the internal boundary.

Although in external boundary cognition the child may develop the capacities for the inverse and the reciprocal in the inanimate world, these capacities are consolidated only after their counterparts are established at the internal boundary and clearly rest on this internal, more emotional foundation. This point will be pursued later as we look more closely at how the internal boundary exerts a regressive pull on the external boundary. It should be emphasized here, however, that innate constitutional factors and a variety of environmental factors influence both boundaries during the course of development. At this point we wish only to stress the parallel development in terms of structural schemes for both boundaries.

Where the lack of oedipal resolution is severe and the drive-affect structures are intense, we should see at least some reverberation into the external boundary, where cognitive tasks relate to the inanimate world. If the oedipal situation remains unresolved, the construction of mutually exclusive classes, such as being father's rival and having his support, is not accomplished. This failure at the internal boundary may then affect the construction of classes at the external boundary. Doing addition and subtraction, for example, depends on constructing the schemes for the inverse and the classification schemes that evolve from them. Cooperative classroom behavior depends in part on understanding the reciprocal and the seriation schemes that evolve from them, as in seeing one's own needs and feelings in relation to and relative to other persons' needs and feelings. Whether lack of resolution at the internal boundary will affect these functions at the external boundary, or in what specific area or under what circumstances the external boundary will be affected, depends on additional variables, such as strength of the drives, symbolization of the external boundary task, and structure or ambiguity of the task. These variables will be discussed in more detail later.

In considering the relationship between the internal and external boundaries, it is also important to consider that if a partial oedipal resolution involves the formation of a neurotic structure, that structure involves a component of magical thinking. There is always a delineated and limited ego regression together with the drive regression. The capacities for concrete operations at the internal boundary are therefore compromised in a specific sector and will exert a regressive pull on aspects of the external cognitive boundary related to the neurotic configuration.

It would be interesting to study very bright children with severe oedipal difficulties to see to what degree they have attained their cognitive potentials. It would be especially interesting to look at children in latency with learning problems who do not have clear perceptual-motor problems, but have functional emotional disorders. Do they lack full capacity for reversibility in terms of inversion or reciprocity? Do they lack full capacity for classification or seriation? With what kinds of stimuli do such limitations appear?

In concluding this section, we should also consider that while there appears to be great distance between the drives and purely cognitive tasks during latency, there is also a great need to keep the drive-activated structures relatively unconscious during this period. This repression is not only because of the drive content, but also because of the cognitive limitations of this period. As we reported earlier, during this period there is a capacity for operational and figurative thinking and for understanding the transformations of relationships through the use of logic. The focus, however, is still on the real world; that is, the child cannot yet apply these schemes to hypothetical possibilities as can adolescents. Since the latency child is tied to the real and cannot yet consider it as simply one instance of the possible, awareness of inner feelings is correspondingly concrete and they are experienced as real and possible. This cognitive limitation may help to explain why the strength of repression is so great during the latency period proper and why latency children are generally resistant to introspection. Wishes and feelings are, in a sense, real and probable and are therefore difficult to even consider. The adolescent, in comparison, may be willing to consider almost anything.

During the course of latency, the capacities for constructing the inverse and the reciprocal expand to more complex systems—for example, from two variables to multiple variables—and the sophistication of reaction formations—turning feelings into their opposites—and beginning rationalizations also increases. The further development of defensive constellations, or "internal cognitive schemes," makes it possible in the later stages of latency for the child to tolerate somewhat greater experiences of affects and drive derivatives.

It was interesting to observe during the psychoanalysis of a youngster with a severe childhood neurosis that at age five (when she began analysis) feelings and drive-related thoughts were either denied or displaced onto inanimate objects. From age six and a half to seven, feelings and thoughts were acknowledged in their defensive forms, often by use of the inverse or the reciprocal—for example, "I'm not angry with my sister, I like her," or "It's not me who's angry at her," or "I didn't miss you while you were on vacation, you missed me." By age eight and a half she was able to make "connections" and observe, "I don't think my mother loves me; it's connected with my being angry at her," and "Sometimes when I'm angry at my mother or teacher, it's really you [the analyst] I'm mad at." The development of an observing ego that could look at how she dealt with wishes and feelings was based not only on the analytic work, which facilitated access to formerly repressed and defended material, but also on developing cognitive capacities for constructing the inverse and more complicated classifications and for constructing the reciprocal and more complex seriations. At age eight she played a "doctor" game in which she was the doctor and I the patient and in which important feelings and wishes were discussed and related to genetic material. After the game had stopped, she would readily attribute the feelings that had emerged to herself. It was only later in the analysis that she no longer "needed" the doctor game.

At age eight this child could classify sufficiently to develop a game in which there was an experiencing and an observing ego. From a dynamic perspective, the doctor game represented in part an identification with the observing functions of the analyst and, as later discovered, an identification with the aggressor (both the analyst and her father, who was a surgeon). From a cognitive perspective, it demonstrated new abilities to classify based on the construction of the inverse. She could use reciprocal relationships, with herself as the doctor, to facilitate exploration. Sometimes the two of us talked about a third person, whom she later acknowledged as herself, showing how a three-variable reciprocal and/or classification scheme afforded her enough distance from the "real" consequences of her wishes (characteristic of concrete operational thought) to permit associative and integrative analytic work.

As latency proceeds and there is an increase in the number of variables that concrete operations can be applied to, a corresponding increase is seen in the child's ability to make connections. This ability is more easily observed along the external boundary, in impersonal cognition. Here the child can, in the latter part of latency, construct a multiple classification table. In an experiment involving the use of weights to bend different kinds of rods into a basin of water,[4] the late latency child can see relationships between the length of the rod and its bending, the thickness of the rod and its bending, etc. The late latency child can also see some interrelationships—for example, between the weight on the end, the thickness, and its bending. He cannot, however, construct a scheme in which all the variables are seen in relation to each other and thus solve a problem involving the total system. In other words, he can experiment and see some relationships. To achieve a more nearly total capacity to do the equivalent of a multivariant analysis, he must await the period of formal operations.

The capacity to construct a multiple classification table and observe some interrelationships, however, has important implications at the internal boundary. Psychological life exists in the context of past, present, and future and in the face of multiple wishes, feelings, and concerns. The capacity to construct causal relationships has by now become increasingly reality-oriented, after the vertical *décalage* (e.g., magical thinking) that occurs with the beginning capacity for representation. This capacity is gradually enhanced so that a number of variables can be seen in interaction within and across time and space. Thus, at the internal boundary the latency child shows an increased ability to observe connections between past events and current behaviors and between different wishes and feelings, both past and present. Future concerns, however, rely in part on hypothetical thinking, which will emerge in adolescence.

To give another case example: a five-year-old child in analysis was able to put feelings into words and say "I want to bite you," but could not show me this by acting it out with a puppet. Although magical thinking was present in play and fantasy, the ability for reflection on the play and fantasy in terms of secondary-process thinking was not yet present. By age six and a half this same child was able to connect "feeling mad" with "not getting my way." By age seven and a half he was able to connect "feeling mad" and "not getting my way" with a general feeling of "I want everything—all the time." Subsequently, "sad feel-

[4] This experiment is described in detail in the next section.

ings" were seen as preceding angry demands and as being related to the demandingness. Only by age eight and a half was he able to integrate past experience—particularly his separation at age two from a caretaker and, shortly thereafter, the birth of a sister—with his sadness, demandingness, anger, and some phobic symptoms connected to retaliatory fantasies developed in the course of the analysis. While the work followed a progression in interpretation and exposure of new wishes, feelings, and fears, the ability to "connect things," a term he began to use at age seven and a half, was dependent in part on emerging cognitive abilities.

Analytic work with children is not dependent on such secondary-process integration, but it does provide useful illustration of the development of the internal cognitive boundary, which may play more of a role than we have thought in the nature of analytic work and outcome with young children. With adolescence, there is an even greater ability to deal with the internal life because of the capacity for hypothetical reasoning. An increased awareness of the many possibilities for emotional change and development may be one subset of the general adolescent awareness of the possible.

The Period of Formal Operations

The Piagetian View

Following Flavell (1963) and Inhelder and Piaget (1955), we shall discuss the basic characteristics of this final period, the period of formal operations. As Flavell points out, the key principle of formal operations involves the *real* versus the *possible.* "Unlike the concrete-operational child, the adolescent begins his consideration of the problem at hand by trying to envisage all the possible relations which could hold true in the data and then attempts, through a combination of experimentation and logical analysis, to find out which of these possible relations in fact do hold true" (p. 204).

The relationship between the real and the possible characteristic of adolescent thinking represents a reversal of concrete operational thinking. For the concrete operational child, Inhelder and Piaget (1955) note, the real has priority, and possibility is conceived of as merely a prolongation or extension of real operations, "as, for example, when, after having ordered several objects in a series, the subject knows that he could do the same with others" (p. 249). For the adolescent, however, the possible occupies the place of priority and the real is seen as a particular instance of it. The adolescent perceives "the given facts as that sector of a set of possible transformation that has actually come about" (p. 251). This immediately presupposes that the adolescent can take a given empirical event, such as "the long, thin rod bends," and categorize it within a system of possible combinations of events: long rods–short rods, thin rods–thick rods, bending–not bending.

Three characteristics follow from this fundamental reorientation in thought: (1) adolescent thought is hypothetico-deductive in nature; (2) it deals in propositions rather than in concrete events; (3) it is capable of isolating variables and of examining all possible combinations of variables (Flavell, 1963).

As a hypothetico-deductive form of thought, formal operational intelligence proceeds from the possible to the real. In this sense, it mirrors scientific reasoning. The implications of a propositional statement are drawn and then tested against reality. Rather than building by induction from disparate concrete examples to a loose generalization, it operates systematically from general statement to particular instance via testable hypotheses. "To try to discover the real among the possible implies that one first entertains the possible as a set of hypotheses to be successively confirmed or infirmed. Hypotheses which the facts infirm can then be discarded; those which the data confirm then go to join the reality sector" (Flavell, 1963, p. 205).

When it is said that formal operations deal in propositions rather than in concrete events, an increased freedom from immediate content is implied, with a correspondingly greater intellectual mobility. At one level this freedom implies the ability to manipulate abstractions that have never been tied to concrete examples or events. The adolescent, for example, can perform a transitive inference ($A < B$, $B < C$, $\therefore$ $A < C$) without any empirical demonstration of the referents for the terms A and

B. At another level this freedom implies that, having performed a concrete operation, the adolescent can abstract the results of that operation and perform further operations upon them. Thus, an adolescent can perform the concrete operation of combining two liquids to observe the color of the resultant mix, and can then take the result and systematically relate it to results of all other combinations of available liquids.

This example helps to explain the third characteristic of adolescent thought mentioned by Flavell: the isolation of variables and the examination of all possible combinations. Instead of dealing with disparate concrete experiments, the hypothetico-deductive adolescent can organize his investigations into a coherent pattern *a priori* and then perform all relevant combinations of variables to test his hypotheses, in this way isolating causal factors. It should be quite obvious from this brief description that Piaget's theory of formal operational cognition has focused on scientific thinking. In fact, Piaget's model of adolescent thought has been found to explain well the results of Inhelder's experiments on the discovery of scientific principles (Inhelder and Piaget, 1955). Since the qualitative differences between concrete and formal operations are best illustrated by reference to these experiments, we shall cite one such investigation here.

> The experimental technique is as follows: The experimenter presents the subject with a large basin of water and a set of rods differing in composition (steel, brass, etc.), length, thickness, and cross-section form (round, square, rectangular). Three different weights can be screwed to the ends of the rods. In addition, the rods can be attached to the edge of the basin in a horizontal position, in which case the weights exert a force perpendicular to the surface of the water. The subject is asked to determine whether or not the rod is flexible enough to reach the water level. His methods are observed and his comments on the variables he believes influence flexibility are noted; and finally, proof is demanded for the assertions he makes [Inhelder and Piaget, 1955, pp. 46-47n.].

The point of this procedure, then, is to determine how the subject goes about the process of identifying and separating out the relevant variables that will cause the rods to bend. The task was administered to preoperational, concrete operational, and formal operational age groups. The results clearly illustrate the differences among these groups.

Preoperational children "explain" by describing what they perceive. Such causal statements as they venture are marked by the finalism, animism, or moral causality characteristic of precausal thought.

> HUC (5 ; 5) after a number of trials puts 100 grams on a rod and waits as if it were going to descend in a moment. "Why don't all the sticks go down the same way?"—*"Because the weight has to go in the water."*—Then he places 200 grams on a thick rod and 100 grams on a fine one: "Which one bends the most?"—*"That one"* [the fine rod].—"Why?"—*"The weight is bigger here* [he points out 200 grams on the other one]; *it ought to go into the water."*—[We put 200 grams on the thin one, which then touches the water. He laughs.] "Why does it touch now?"—*"Because it has to"* [Inhelder and Piaget, 1955, p. 48].

Children at the period of concrete operations go about their search for relevant causal variables by using the structures of classification and seriation available to them. Thus, mere observation is replaced by ordered classification. However, the system of all possible combinations of variables remains unavailable to concrete operational subjects, and their consideration of variable interaction effects is only rudimentary. Inhelder and Piaget distinguish two substances within this period. During the first substage, simple comparisons are made which are accurate within the confines of single factors. Interaction effects, however, are ignored, resulting in completely confusing results.

> MOR (7; 10), after having put the weight on a narrow rod which reaches the water, says: *"It won't fall the same way with this one* [thick] *because the other one is thinner."* Then he changes the weight: *"This one isn't so heavy as the other one";* he places the heavy weight on a short rod and the light one on a long rod, predicting that the curve will be sharper *"because the other weight is lighter than this one."* The experiment does not confirm his prediction, and then he lengthens the short rod; *"Oh! with this* [thick] *one you have to do that . . .?"* etc.—The subject is asked to summarize what he has discovered up to that point by ordering the rods serially according to flexibility: "Which one bends the most?"—*"This one because it is the thinnest."*—"Next?"—*"That one"* [long and thin, metal]. —"Next?"—*"That one"* [short, wood].—"Next?"—*"This one* [thicker];

> *it goes with the weight"* [heavy].—"Next?"—*That one* [heavy, metal]; *it didn't go in the water because I had to do that"* [lengthen it] [Inhelder and Piaget, 1955, pp. 49-50].

This example shows the beginning of classificatory operations, as raw data are interpreted in terms of categories corresponding to causal variables (weight, length, etc.). Similarly, seriation of rods along a one-variable dimension begins. Only at the second substage of concrete operations does the child begin to consider variables in interaction. In terms of a logico-mathematical structural model, he then begins to multiply relations and classes.

> OT (9 ; 3) begins by referring to length: *"You see that because the bar is longer it can go down better."*—"And if you take two bars of the same length?" [he is given a thick and a thin one].—*"There it goes down further, because it is thinner than the other which is fat, and that one isn't."* Next he determines the influence of weight and predicts for a short rod: *"That won't work: the rod is too short and the weight is too light for the rod"* [Inhelder and Piaget, 1955, p. 52].

A multiplication of classes yields a logical product consisting of elements that are members of both classes. Such multiplications can be expanded beyond two factors to include any number of factors. In a two-factor logical multiplication, for example, different values of length and different values of weight can be seen in interaction, along with their possible results. In the experiment under consideration the possible results are only two: the rod touches the water or it does not.

Following Inhelder and Piaget (1955, p. 53), let X stand for the class of rods touching the water, and X' stand for those not touching. Let A_1 stand for rods 50 millimeters or more in length, A_1' stand for shorter rods. And let A_2 stand for the class of weights equaling or exceeding 300 grams, and A_2' for lighter weights. The logical multiplication of these two factors and the two possible results yield the following possibilities:

$$A_1 A_2 X + A_1 A_2 X' + A_1 A_2' X + A_1 A_2' X' + A_1' A_2 X + A_1' A_2' X + A_1' A_2' X$$

($A_1 A_2 X$ = rods of 50 millimeters or more with attached weights of 300 grams or more that touch the water, and other multiplied classes are similarly symbolized.)

Inhelder and Piaget hold that such a multiple classification table can indeed be constructed by the concrete operational child, even for more than two variables and their results. Such a table, however, yields static products which remain essentially isolated once they have been generated. One might discover for example that the class product $A_1'A_2'X$ is falsified, $A_1'A_2X$ is verified, etc. Up to this point, the process is insufficient to tease out the causal influence of each variable. To accomplish this goal, a complete combinatorial system must be accessible to the subject. In such a system isolated multiplicative products such as those yielded above would in turn be combined one-by-one, two-by-two, etc.

> In other words, if the substage II-B subjects do not yet isolate the variables but simply establish the empirically given correspondences, it is because they have not acquired the combinatorial system which constitutes propositional logic. The result is, on the one hand, that they do not know how to combine empirical results in such a way as to demonstrate which among the possible associations of variables actually occurs, and, on the other, that they do not know how to reason by implication, etc., in such a way as to combine the various factual data that they observe in a form that is both necessary and conclusive [Inhelder and Piaget, 1955, p. 55].

The combinatorial system will yield necessary conclusions by implication. Combining these three empirical associations, $A_1X + A_1'X + A_1'X'$, yields the conclusion that the presence of A_1 leads necessarily to result X (given no further variables), since the absence of A_1 (A_1') may be associated either with the presence or absence of X, but the presence of A_1 is associated only with the presence of X (Inhelder and Piaget, 1955, p. 56).

Such a complete combinatorial system only makes its appearance during the period of formal operations. Instead of focusing on empirical givens, as the concrete operational child does, the formal operational adolescent constructs a hypothetical system, of which the empirical givens are members. Where the younger child is capable of classifying events according to the various categories of length, width, weight, etc., his adolescent counterpart uses this classification as a basis for abstracting all possible combinations of variables. Having done this, he can then test hypotheses derived from the combinatorial system. In the problem at hand, the end result of this new ability is the adolescent's capacity to test the causal significance of each individual factor in succession by holding all other factors constant.

At the start of formal operations the structure of the combinatorial system is only imperfectly formed.

> PEY (12 ; 9) speculates that if the rod is to touch the water it must be "long and thin." After several trials, he concludes: "*The larger and thicker it is, the more it resists.*"—"What did you observe?"—"*This one* [brass, square, 50 cm long, 16 mm.[2] cross-section with 300 gram weight] *bends more than that one* [steel; otherwise the same conditions which he has selected to be equal]: *it's another metal. And this one* [brass, round] *more than that one*" [brass, square; same conditions for weight and length, but 10 and 16 mm.[2] cross-section].—"If you wanted to buy a rod which bends the most possible?"—*would choose it round, thin, long, and made of a soft metal*" [Inhelder and Piaget, 1955, pp. 56-57].

It can be seen in this protocol that the subject, instead of limiting himself to discrete empirical observations on any two given rods, is systematically combining certain empirical observations, and attempting to ascertain the influence of one variable holding all others equal. In this particular case, however, the twelve-year-old errs once, in his last comparison, when he varies two factors at once, cross-section shape and thickness. At a later point in formal operational thinking the combinatorial system is more firmly established and such errors do not occur.

As we have stated, the combinatorial system enables the adolescent subject to examine the effects of a given causal factor, while holding all other factors equal. This means that every combination of potential causal factors can itself be juxtaposed and compared with every other combination of factors, with an eye to ascertaining which combinations lead to the result of interest. Where the concrete operational child could combine objects into classes or order them in relations, the formal operational adolescent can go further and combine those very classes and/or relations into higher-order categories.

Berlyne's (1965) formulation of this difference between concrete operational and formal operation thinking is useful here. In terms of the concrete operational groupings (discussed above), recall that grouping III enabled the school-aged child to multiply classes. Given two dimensions of two values each (Berlyne's example is of vertebrate and flying animals), this grouping underlies the concrete operational ability to form a two-way classification matrix or 2 × 2 table. But the concrete operational child cannot proceed beyond a correct pigeon-holing of particular animals into one of the resulting four categories. Only with formal operational freedom from embeddedness in the concrete can the adolescent take each of these four categories and combine them in every possible way with every other category. "In every possible way" means in every possible dyad, triad, null, and complete set. Thus, for two dimensions of two values each, there are sixteen possible combinations. The adolescent realizes, at least implicitly, that any one of these sixteen combinations is a possibility, and that the real is to be selected from this realm of possibility by a process of empirical verification. To cite Berlyne's (1965) example:

> Suppose that we have two ways of dividing up animals—into vertebrates (V) and invertebrates (v) and into flying (F) and non-flying (f). A child at the concrete-operations stage is capable of allotting a particular animal to one of the four possible classes, (VF), (Vf), (vF), and (vf). An adolescent at the formal-operations stage is capable of going further and considering all the sorts of animals that there are in the world or the sorts there conceivably could be. There are now sixteen possibilities: there might be no animals at all, there might be animals of all four classes; there might be (vF) only, there might be (VF), and (Vf), and (vF) animals but no (VF), etc. [pp. 187-188].

Inhelder and Piaget do not claim that a table of all the possibilities is actually constructed mentally by the adolescent in his problem-solving process. "The main point is simply that when he encounters the four cases A_1A_2 + $A_1A'_2$ + A'_1A_1 + $A'_1A'_2$ [or in Berlyne's terminology (VF) + (Vf) + (vF) + (vf)], the potential relationships between A_1 and A_2 are seen as multiple" (Inhelder and Piaget, 1955, p. 277).

As we saw above, in discussing concrete operations, the groupings relevant to classes have inversion as their form of reversibility, while those relevant to relations have reciprocity as their form of reversibility. In the combinatorial system, however, the two forms of reversibility are themselves integrated into a structured whole. Another way of phrasing this is to say that each element in the system has both a reciprocal and an inverse. While during concrete operations the two types of reversibility operate independently of one another, during formal operations both are available simultaneously.

Let us consider first the propositional "translation" of Berlyne's table of sixteen possible combinations. It will then become clearer what is meant by the simultaneous availability of inversion and reciprocity in the structured whole. Any one of the sixteen possible combinations can be stated in propositional language. For example, combination (12): (VF) + (Vf) + (vF) states that one or both of the positively valenced dimensions are true. In Berlyne's terms, this is equivalent to stating that those animals which occur, or are real, are either vertebrate, able to fly, or both. The class of nonvertebrate, nonflying animals is excluded. Let *p* stand for the proposition "The animal is vertebrate" and *q* for "The animal can fly." The relationship between these two propositions *p* and *q*, given by combination (12), is that of disjunction ($p \vee q$). Thus, either *p* is true or *q* is true or both are true.

A similar translation into propositional language can be made for each of the sixteen combinations, yielding sixteen binary operations of propositional logic. Berlyne points out that "each of these sixteen combinations corresponds to one of the sixteen relations between two propositions recognized by modern logic. For example, 'if an animal can fly, it must be a vertebrate,' would correspond to (VF) or (Vf) or (vf), i.e., the (vF) possibility is excluded" (1965, p. 188). Given our definitions of *p* and *q*, this example given by Berlyne represents the translation of combination (13) into a relation of reciprocal implication ($q \supset p$), *q* implies *p*, or, if *q*, then *p*.

To return to the issue of reversibility, it should now become clear in what sense reciprocity and inversion are integrated in the formal combinatorial system. Every element in the system, viewed either as a combination or a proposition, has both an inverse and a reciprocal within the same system of sixteen binary operations. As Berlyne notes, " '*p* implies *q*' has both an inverse ('*p* does not imply *q*') and a reciprocal ('*q* implies *p*')" (p. 107).

The relation between these propositions and their inverses and reciprocals is itself that of a closed group of transformations. In all there are four such transformations, but the product of any one of them, or any combination of them, is always a member of the system of sixteen binary operations. In addition to the identity transformation ($p \supset q$), the inverse, ($p \cdot q$), and the reciprocal ($q \supset p$), there is a fourth transformation termed the correlative ($p \cdot q$). Stated most simply, the correlative means that the effect may be caused by factors other than that which has already been posited as a cause, without denying the efficacy of the latter.

These four transformations are linked in such a way that the inverse of our original binary operation is also the reciprocal of the correlative. That is, if $p \supset q$ is the original operation, its inverse is $p \cdot q$; the correlative of $p \supset q$ is $p \cdot q$; and the reciprocal of $p \cdot q$ is, again, $p \cdot q$. Put more simply, if N symbolizes the inverse (negation), R the reciprocal, and C the correlative, then, as above, $N = RC$. In addition, $R = NC$, $C = NR$, and I(identity) $= NRC$ (Inhelder and Piaget, 1955, p. 134). Thus, the four transformations are synthesized in a closed system which has both reciprocity and inversion available as forms of reversibility.

Having discussed formal operational thinking from the points of view of the sixteen binary operations and the integration of two forms of reversibility, let us recount Piaget's explanation of the origins of such thinking. Naturally, Piaget interprets the rise of formal operational thought in the context of his equilibrium model of cognitive development. Thus, he considers neurological maturation and experience of the object and interpersonal world as necessary but not sufficient conditions to explain this qualitative improvement in thinking.

In essence the equilibration explanation is as follows. During concrete operations a number of qualitatively heterogeneous factors—including quantity, weight, volume, time, length, etc.—are constructed mentally by the child, resulting in the achievement of conservation of the factor in question even in the face of perceptual transformations. Eventually the child discovers that in many concrete instances the operation of these factors is interrelated. Thus, although they have been constructed mentally in relative isolation from one another, their presence in real objects is mixed. The equilibrium achieved by concrete operational structures is disturbed under these conditions of multifactor interactions. Inhelder and Piaget (1955) give the example of a child who discovers that brass bars are almost always flexible, but who also finds instances where bars that are not brass are flexible and even instances where *brass* bars are *not* flexible. In other words, he discovers that "there are exceptions to the rule" (p. 283). The exceptions are attributable to the factors other than kind of metal that can influence flexibility (cross-section, length, etc.). Therefore, the child is faced with the need to separate out the pertinent variables from the complexity of phenomena before him.

In this task of separating out variables, the role of reciprocity is most important. To hold all other factors equal in a complex problem, such as that of the flexible rods, demands utilization of reciprocity. Obviously, to hold the effect of length of the rods equal one cannot resort to total withdrawal of the factor of length (as in inversion). "In this case it is no longer one of the terms (a property or an event) that is negated but the difference between the terms. . . . this is no longer *inversion* but *reciprocity*" (Inhelder and Piaget, 1955, p. 286). The effect of length is controlled by equating the lengths of two or more rods, thus negating any difference.

As the child develops the ability to separate factors by negating their influence through either inversion or reciprocity, Piaget holds that he uses the resulting associations of factors (in double-entry tables or matrices) as a basis from which to choose crucial causal variables. Thus, the move is made from multiplication of classes (concrete grouping III) to generation of the combinatorial system. "In sum, the isolation of variables necessarily leads the subject to combine the base associations among themselves *n*-by-*n* and thus to substitute for the simple multiplication and correspondence operations which gave rise to the base associations the combinatorial system which characterizes the 'structured whole' " (Inhelder and Piaget, 1955, p. 288).

The "structured whole" to which Piaget here refers is the combinatorial system seen as possessing the logico-mathematical properties of a lattice and of a group. Without detailed analysis of these terms, it is sufficient to say that the lattice properties derive from the fact that any two of the sixteen possible combinations in the system can be joined by conjunction or disjunction to yield a product that remains within the system. The group properties derive similarly from the closed system of four transformations which possesses the defining qualities of a mathematical group.

Flavell (1963) has pointed out that Piaget's work on formal operations may be discussed on three levels. As in his work on concrete operations, there is the level of the logico-mathematical model, here represented by the combinatorial system and the integration of inversion and reciprocity. Also similar to his work on concrete operations is the level of more or less specific cognitive behavior. In this case such behavior involves the solving of scientific problems, such as the discovery of the law of floating bodies, or of the crucial factor determining the oscillation of a pendulum (see Inhelder and Piaget, 1955). Unique to formal operational thinking, however, is an intermediary level of generality which Piaget designates as formal structured operational schemes. "These operational schemata consist of concepts or special operations (mathematical and not exclusively logical), the need for which may be felt by the subject when he tries to solve certain problems" (Inhelder and Piaget, 1955, p. 308). These particular schemes are more general than the concepts discovered in particular problems and tend to appear in a variety of specific problem situations. We shall discuss one of these schemes here, that of probability.

The notion of probability arises in the formal operational period as a consequence of development of the child's concept of chance. Piaget and Inhelder published the French edition of their research in this area in 1951, but the English translation was completed only recently (1975). In this book they delimit three stages in the child's development of a concept of chance, corresponding to three major periods of intellectual development.

During the preoperational subperiod, children lack operatory structures based on forms of reversibility. Therefore, deductive necessity is lacking in their judgments. To take one of Piaget's examples, if the child is shown two subclasses and their supraordinate class ($A + A' = B$), he does not conclude with logical necessity that $A = B - A'$. Thus, when asked to take one element from a mixture of two, the child cannot form a proper concept of randomness in his choice. He will demonstrate uncertainty as to whether he will end up with A or A', but this uncertainty does not stand in distinction to the generalized uncertainty that $A = B - A'$.

The notions of determination and chance are not clearly differentiated in the preoperational child's mind. As a result, chance as the opposite of necessity is not present as a concept. In one of Piaget's experiments, children are presented with a line of beads at one end of a rectangular tray. One half of this line consists of red beads, the other half, of white beads. As the tray is tilted back and forth, this original nonrandom distribution becomes increasingly randomized. Preoperational subjects, however, tend to perceive a mysterious lawfulness in the randomization process, some going so far as to predict that the end result will be a re-creation of the original array (Flavell, 1963, p. 343). As Piaget and Inhelder (1951) indicate, "This systematic reaction . . . is really only strange and incomprehensible for those minds already in possession of deductive order, because then the mixture appears to be precisely the contrary of such an order. But for the subject still incapable of what is properly called deduction, it is natural for disorder to be able to mask a hidden semi-order since deductive order itself is a result, as they see it, of such analogous intuitions" (p. 219).

In contrast the concrete operational child does have at hand a series of structures based on forms of reversibility and capable of yielding certain deductive results. As we have seen, he can conclude from $A < B$ and $B < C$, that $A < C$. As a consequence, he can also differentiate the realm of chance from that of necessity. What remains beyond the reach of the concrete operational subject is the notion of probability, i.e., that some things have a higher chance of occurring than do others (Flavell, 1963). To achieve a structure of probability, the subject must create a new synthesis from the antithesis of chance and necessity by applying operatory procedures to the realm of chance.

This is the accomplishment of the formal operational period.

Two abilities underlie the formation of a concept of probability, and both are related to the general structure of formal thinking. The first is the ability to generate the combinatorial system of all possible outcomes. In the case of a distribution of random events, this capacity enables the adolescent to approach the problem from the viewpoint of the whole distribution, and not merely from the viewpoint of isolated events.

> In order to estimate . . . the probability that two or three balls of the same color will be drawn at random from a bag containing fifteen red balls, ten blue balls, eight green balls, etc., the child . . . must be able to apply a combinatorial system that enables him to take into consideration all the possible combinations of the given elements [Piaget and Inhelder, 1966, p. 144].

The second relevant ability is the capacity to understand proportions. Piaget and Inhelder (1966) note that proportions are essential in the understanding of probabilities because they enable the subject to comprehend the equality or inequality of ratios between favored and possible events (2/4 = 4/8, etc.). The achievement of the concept of proportions is itself a characteristic of the formal operational period, because proportions are relations between ratios, and, as such, operations performed on prior operations. An understanding of proportionality is dependent upon the capacity to integrate reciprocity and inversion in a single system of reversibility. Thus, Piaget notes that the discovery of proportionality in the problem of the two-arm balance begins when the subject discovers that the increase in weight on one side of the balance can be reversed either by removing the excess weight (inversion) or by reducing the distance of the weight from the center of the balance (reciprocity). Proportionality here appears in the form: "increasing the weight and reducing the distance . . . is equivalent to . . . decreasing the weight and increasing the distance" (Inhelder and Piaget, 1955, p. 316).

To summarize, the combinatorial system and the group of four transformations generated by the inclusion of inversion and reciprocity in one system are the two major structural developments of the formal operational period. They provide a structured whole which serves as a foundation for generalized intellectual abilities, such as concepts of probability, and for specific problem-solving abilities requiring separation of variables and controlled experimentation. The reversal of priority in adolescence between the real and the possible also constitutes a necessary condition for the adolescent's characteristic emotional involvement with ideals and hypothesized changes in social systems. There is, consequently, a verifiable intellectual foundation interacting with social and other biological factors to cause the patterns of behavioral change associated with adolescence.

Dynamic Considerations and Formal Operations

During adolescence there is a gradual shift over time from the stage of concrete operations, which characterizes latency, to the stage of formal operations. As we have seen, one major difference in the formal operational period of cognitive development is that the adolescent deals with the possible rather than only with the real. During the stage of concrete operations, operations are utilized only on concrete, real objects. The latency child can perform classification and seriation tasks, for example, but only on real things. As we postulated, if the latency child applies these same capacities to the internal boundary of his cognitive structure, he will treat his feelings and wishes in a realistic rather than hypothetical way. In contrast, the adolescent can envision all possible relationships that may be true but are not necessarily so.

Through experimentation and logical analysis, the adolescent in the period of formal operations can find out which of all the possibilities do hold true. He can do this through the process of hypothetico-deductive reasoning, dealing with propositions rather than only concrete events, and isolating and combining variables in all possible ways to see their relationships. This ability affords the adolescent tremendously increased intellectual freedom. In dealing with propositions he can consider certain abstractions never tied to the real. In other words, he can develop propositions from propositions. He can combine different abstractions into higher-order abstractions. An experiment (mentioned earlier) that shows this increased freedom in the ability to abstract from abstractions is the one in which the adolescent mixes two liquids to find out the color they form and then relates this combination to every other combination he has formed with sets of liquids.

In the experiment with rods and weights described earlier, we saw how the adolescent capable of formal operations can conceptualize all the relationships among different variables. In comparison, the latency child in the latter half of the period of concrete operations may figure out only one or two sets of relations. He may be able to see the relationship between the heaviness of the weight and its tendency to make the rod bend, or he may be able to see the relationship between the placement of the weight on the rod and its tendency to make the rod bend into the water. He can observe empirically what happens, but he cannot relate the results of multiple empirical experiments to one another. Thus, the late latency child can construct a multiple classification table along a number of dimensions, but he cannot complete a total combinatorial system; that is, a system in which all the variables are systematically related to one another so that causal relationships are elucidated. The formal operational adolescent, on the other hand, is capable of developing this full combinatorial system of all possible relationships among the different variables.

Earlier we described formal operational thinking from the point of view of reversibility. The formal operational child can use both the inverse and the reciprocal together in one system. In contrast, the latency, or concrete operational, child can use only one or the other at a time: the inverse for operations in classes, and the reciprocal for operations on relations. If both the inverse and the reciprocal are combined in one system, then every proposition can have both its inverse and its reciprocal. In addition, the reciprocal can be inverted to become what Piaget terms the *correlative*. These four transformations together have the properties of a mathematical group and underlie the increased flexibility of adolescent thought. As noted above, the adolescent's ability to use the group of four transformations and to generate the combinatorial system of all possible combinations of events leads to derivative abilities to understand such complex notions as proportions, probabilities, and double systems of reference.

The ability to consider cognitively all possible combinations marks the final equilibrium state in development. The system can take into account all possible events on the external boundary of the ego without altering its structure. Formal operations thus have a high degree of flexibility.

The adolescent's cognitive abilities in dealing with the external world appear, from clinical observation, to be operative at his internal cognitive boundary. In contrast to the latency child, the adolescent shows increased freedom in dealing with wishes, affects, and object relations, as he can consider the possible rather than only the real. He can talk about such affect-laden issues as sex, rage, death, and life in the abstract and can consider the possible aspects of these events. He can talk about hypothetical relationships, feeling states, and wishes. In fact, the adolescent's discussions of his internal life are remarkably full of this hypothetical or "what if" quality. In contrast, the latency child generally does not talk about such matters. If he does, and the topic is closely related to conflict-laden drive-affect structures, his discussion is usually fraught with anxiety and defense.

Thus, during adolescence there is greater awareness, though not always direct, of the internal world of drive derivatives and wishes, affects and emotions, and internalized object relations. There is also a much greater conscious awareness of different subtleties in feeling states, as well as a deepening awareness in the realm of interpersonal relationships. Certainly, biological changes and their psychological representations are partial causes of these changes, but cognitive development is also a factor. It is not just that the events of puberty produce an intense rekindling of oedipal and preoedipal issues; it is also that the new cognitive abilities permit the adolescent the freedom to experience a wider range of internal issues.

The latency child views his internal world as real and therefore potentially frightening. He thus maintains a strict repressive barrier, reinforced by such defenses as reaction formation, denial and isolation of affect. In contrast, the adolescent may need to disguise his internal world but not necessarily to repress it as fully as does the latency child. He can view his internal world in a propositional sense and in a hypothetical sense; thus, it is not necessarily real. Rage does not lead to killing; oedipal feelings do not lead to the act of incest; yearnings do not necessarily lead to fusion. The adolescent, then, can scan his internal boundary with his new cognitive capacities. Although he may, in a defensive way, intellectualize and rationalize about it, he can also experience to a greater degree the vicissitudes of his internal world because his appreciation of possibilities reduces the frightening aspects of internal stimuli. They are not necessarily real and are not limited to simple transformations.

The new capacities of adolescence, as with new capacities earlier in development, make higher-order adaptations possible at the same time that they place new psychological stress and tasks on the growing youth. The semiotic function, as indicated earlier, adds inestimable new adaptive flexibility to the growing child. It gives him added mobility in understanding temporal, spatial, and causal relations. This capacity for representation, however, also makes possible new internalized fears and dangers. Although it is a crucial step in the separation-individuation process, at the same time it creates a major hurdle for this process.

Similarly, the capacity for propositional thinking adds great adaptive potential as well as new developmental hurdles (e.g., greater access to earlier developmental issues, formation of the ego ideal). On the adaptive side, the new cognitive capacities, if applied to "internal stimuli," make possible the bringing together of numerous discordant elements into a "reversible, whole system," in other words, into an integrated system at a high level of synthesis. The capacity for hypothetical thinking may, however, also be accompanied by a vertical *décalage*. The multiple regressions observed in adolescence are crucial to the reworking of earlier issues and provide a foundation for a consolidated identity. The new hypothetical ability makes these regressions both possible—that is, the ego can function at multiple levels—and probable—that is, the new capacities bring together psychic states that had formerly been split off from one another.

The major task of adolescence, in terms of identity formation, is to bring into a cohesive organization the representations of the past along with those of the present and with those structures encompassing aspirations for the future. The new capacity to organize a number of variables into one system, if operating at the internal boundary, may, from a cognitive perspective, be what makes this accomplishment possible. The higher level of equilibrium possible—the increase in field of application, mobility, permanence, and stability—permits the adolescent to conserve more discordant variables than ever before in an interrelated system.

Viewing the synthetic function in the context of internal cognition may give us a precise way to look at some of the increased ego capacities of this stage of development. If every relationship can have, within the same system, its inverse, reciprocal, and correlative, there is vastly increased flexibility over a system in which a relationship can have only an inverse or a reciprocal. Assume the simple relationship, "I am hungry at mother." The inverse is, "I am not angry at mother"; the reciprocal is, "Mother is angry at me"; the correlative is, "Mother is not angry at me." In relation to a single feeling, anger, there are four possibilities. If we consider other variables—loving feelings, competitive feelings, etc.—a system including the above four transformations allows all the variables to exist in an economically sound relationship.

Assume that alongside the relationship, "I am angry at mother," there is the relationship, "I love mother." The transformations would lead to, "I don't love mother," "Mother loves me," and "Mother doesn't love me." Considering only this two-variable relationship system, there are sixteen combinations covering a variety of possibilities. The basic representation of *mother* can therefore be conserved, and relationships can be selected that will synthesize dynamic and realistic considerations. "I am angry at mother" might, from experience, correlate with "Mother still loves me," yet all the other possibilities remain within the system, so that it is possible that "I am angry at mother" *and* "Mother loves me," or "Mother is angry with me," or "Mother loves me, but a little less" (these can be put into a reciprocal relationship of *more* or *less*).

The concrete operational child, in comparison, can use only the inverse or the reciprocal, but not both together. The relationship, "I am angry at mother," can have only its inverse,

"I am not angry at mother," or only its reciprocal, "Mother is angry at me." Similarly, if this child experiences "I love mother," he can within the same system consider either "I don't love mother" *or* "Mother loves me," but not both. If the inverse is the system available to him, he has the possibilities, "I am angry at mother," "I am not angry at mother," and "I love mother," "I don't love mother." Given these two feeling states, there are only four possible combinations that constitute a whole "synthesized" system. This system cannot conserve, or synthesize, many discordant feeling states. To the degree that it does organize discordant elements, it lacks flexibility; nor can it deal with the subtleties possible in a system of formal operations. Thus, in observing that mother is angry with him, the concrete operational child can feel: "I don't love mother," or "I love mother," or he can change it to the inverse, "Mother is not angry with me" (a denial). "I don't love mother" may be too strong a feeling, and "I love mother" too painful, to accept. Within his two-variable system he may have only one possible correlational feeling—the inverse. Constructing the inverse is similar to using the defense of denial and constitutes an inflexible defense system.

In comparison, consider the formal operational youth who observes that mother is angry with him. Within his two-feeling system, he can consider sixteen possibities and select the one that most closely fits both dynamic and adaptive purposes. He can correlate his observation with the reciprocal, "Well, I am angry with her," and at the same time create classes of different levels of love based on his capacity for constructing the inverse. He can have a class with some anger and some love and locate his feelings in that subclass, thereby maintaining a basic loving relationship. His system is a much more flexible one. Denial by use of the inverse is not necessary when this full combinatorial system is operative at the internal boundary.

If we expand our system to three variables, for example, three feelings—love, anger, and envy—the restrictions of the concrete operational system in comparison with the greater flexibility of the formal operational system become even more apparent. The possibilities will not be elaborated here, but it is important to point out that in a system that can synthesize either only the inverse or only the reciprocal, as the numbers of variables presented to the system increase, the more the system is limited to one or sometimes no possibilities to conserve or maintain synthetic harmony at a high level. For instance, in the nine-year-old trying to integrate discordant feelings, wishes, and fears, we can see his use of basic inverses and reciprocals in the defenses of denial, projection, and reaction formation. Adults who are similarly limited in their internal mechanisms demonstrate marked constrictions, severe affect inhibitions, acting-out patterns, ego splitting, or fragmentation in relation to discordant wishes, feelings, or self- and object representations. These disorders are the result of using inflexible mechanisms to maintain synthesis: inverses (denial), reciprocals (reaction formation, projection), or magical thinking.

The full combinatorial system, which makes use of the four transformations noted above, can accommodate an infinite number of variables and conserve them within one system. Wishes, feelings, fears, internalized prohibitions, different self- and object representations, realistic perceptions, anticipations of the future, and memories of the past can thus be conserved within a closed system leading to a relatively stable identity. None of the variables needs to be denied or experienced in an uneconomic relationship to the other variables. New relationships and feelings or wishes can be accommodated by the system.

It is interesting to note that an adolescent's confusion about feeling states and interpersonal relationships may be related to his rapid use of cognitive transformations. In dealing with feelings about anger and concerns about separation, for instance, the adolescent may feel that his anger causes another to separate from him (direct). At the same time he may hypothesize that his anger did not cause a separation (inverse), or that the separation by another resulted in his anger (reciprocal).

It should be made clear at this point that the model of formal operations, even at the external boundary, is an *ideal* one. By necessity, formal operational cognition at the internal boundary falls short of this ideal, as will be seen shortly. The ways in which it falls short make possible an elucidation of pathology and the range of individual differences in the context of optimal adaptation.

The nutriments for the external boundary in adolescence are still relatively predictable and stable: the challenges and tasks of understanding the inanimate world, presented in a structured manner at school. The stimulus nutriments for the internal boundary, however, include the often chaotic familial, peer, and other types of relationships, as well as inputs from the internal world of drives, affects, and self- and object representations, which are making their presence felt with special intensity and from multiple developmental levels. The variability across individuals at this boundary contributes, together with biological and maturational factors, to a highly individualized outcome that is often quite different in level from the outcome at the external boundary.

In addition to different stimuli at the internal and external boundaries, a special aspect of the internal boundary should be considered. This involves a distinction between a true combinatorial capacity and a defensive one. The adolescent who is minimally troubled by conflict-laden, unconscious drive derivatives can achieve a state of comfortable awareness of his internal world and utilize a true combinatorial capacity at the internal boundary. This adolescent can scan his internal ego boundary and use his enhanced cognitive ability to be relatively in touch with his internal world.

Thus, we might view the adolescent's combinatorial capacity as a correlate of a flexible ego structure. Such an ego tolerates internal conflict and anxiety and has a high capacity for synthesis and resolution, with only minimal neurotic structuring or characterological restrictions. Implicit here is the ability to consider a wide range of feelings, to see subtle relationships between them, and to see how certain feelings are evoked in the context of various combinations of relationships with other people. This ego capacity is similar to the adolescent's ability at the external boundary to deal with a wide range of diverse data, form multiple hypotheses, and see the relationships that hold in the real world. What we call the highly developed synthetic function at the internal boundary is the equivalent of the new combinatorial capacity in impersonal cognition at the external boundary.

If we postulate such an equivalence, how, then, do we view the adolescent who uses this combinatorial capacity in a defensive manner? We hypothesize that where this combinatorial capacity is used for purposes of rationalization and intellectualization, the adolescent is scanning a previously distorted or defended-against drive derivative. In other words, his scanning apparatus works appropriately, but it works on faulty information. The faulty information is a product of defense rooted in the failure to resolve oedipal and/or preoedipal issues in the period of latency. If, for example, feelings of anger are defended against by repression supported by reaction formation, the adolescent may experience a wish to be helpful even though, at an unconscious level, he feels hurt and angry. His combinatorial capacity does not have access to the hurt and angry feelings, but only to the "wish to be helpful." The combinatorial capacity, or the capacity for scanning complex relationships and constructing a system in which both the inverse and reciprocal are possible within the same system, may, however, be used in an elaborate defensive system. The wish to be helpful may be altered by its inverse, not to be helpful, or to be belligerent (if, for example, being helpful comes too close to feminine identification in a man). It may then be altered by the reciprocal, "It is he who wants not to help me, or wants to injure me," and possibly further altered by another inverse, "He wants to help me," reinforced with rationalizations, etc.

Whether the capacities for formal operations are used in the service of greater self-awareness or defense depends on the issues raised and the accompanying anxiety. If there is intense anxiety due to the drives or to external stresses in adolescence proper, a regression in internal cognitive ability may occur. The reason for hypothesizing this is that prior to adolescence, particularly in latency, the internal world is viewed as real and frightening, whereas in adolescence it can be viewed as propositional or possible. When the drive-affect structures become very intense and frightening, the hypothetical quality may no longer be possible, and the ability to look at all the possibilities and to determine the real may be lost. What is breaking through appears to be overwhelming and real, and thus there is a regression in internal cognition to the stage of concrete operations or preoperational thinking. This formulation is supported by the clinical observation that almost all neurotic structures use elements of concrete and preoperational thinking, at least in the formation of a particular neurotic structure. Other aspects of the ego may be free for more abstract, logical, and flexible thought, but the neurotic structure seems to be constructed around "stupid" thinking or, as it would appear in the context of adult logic, illogic.

Thus far we have considered some of the ramifications of development at the external cognitive boundary on development at the internal cognitive boundary during the stage of formal operations. We must also consider how developmental changes during adolescence may affect the formation of the internal boundary itself, which is exposed to its own special stage-specific "aliments."

The adolescent's initial reaction to the activation of both oedipal and preoedipal drive-affect states is fear and an attempt to keep the internal world under control while directing greater interest toward external reality. He attempts to exert control and to disguise concerns relating to castration, fusion with the preoedipal mother, masturbation, and emerging genital sexual wishes. Early adolescent patterns may include avoidance of or contempt for the other-sex individual, a search for powerful figures to identify with, idealization of people outside the family, and rapid superficial changes in identifications. As adolescence proceeds, a greater access to both inner and outer experience appears, with greater fluidity of defensive processes, less rigid obsessional defenses, expansion of relationships (at first brief, later more lasting), sexual involvements, and further breaking away from parents. New cognitive abilities, as noted above, can be used defensively or in the context of a greater self-awareness, as well as for investment in abstract ideas and social ideals. During the later stages of adolescence, the dominant issues concern the real separation from the parents and final resolution of preoedipal and oedipal ties. Concurrent with this process is the establishment of a consolidated identity and increasing movement toward relationships of mutuality and intimacy.

Aspects of the above issues determine in part the capacity for forming optimal cognition at the internal boundary. As we have noted, one general cognitive capacity is the ability to use hypothetical reasoning, implying a separation from the real to include the possible. This separation may relate to the crucial real separation from the parental figures during adolescence; that is, a decathecting and a shifting to other adults, with a working through of the earlier representations of the parents. We might postulate that if this decathecting of the parental representations does not occur, it will be impossible for the adolescent to achieve the distance necessary for viewing internal stimuli with appropriate detachment. In other words, if the relationship to the parent is too intense and there can be no distancing, the internal world relating to the parents cannot be viewed in terms of multiple hypothetical possibilities. Instead, the concrete realities of certain stimuli will predominate, as at the level of latency. Thus, although the maturational capacity for hypothetical reasoning, or taking distance from the real, may be in ascendance, if this ability is overwhelmed by a psychological reality that maintains the parents and their earlier representations "too closely," the capacity for hypothetical thinking in terms of internal issues may be compromised.

If this first step of minimal separation cannot be taken, there may then be a compromise along the rest of the adolescent internal cognitive boundary. The ego flexibility dependent on formal operations—for example, considering shades of feeling states and the various possibilities for interpersonal relationships—may be compromised. Thus, cognitive abilities for hypothetical reasoning and combinatorial thinking may emerge along the external boundary but fail to emerge fully along the internal boundary.

It is interesting to observe the difference between the young adolescent who has truly made some separation and can apply his combinatorial capacities to scan his internal world of feelings and the adolescent who has not made this step and is still dealing with the internal world as a latency child would do. In the former case, there is greater awareness of subtle feelings and of complex relationships. In the latter case, there may be the concreteness and rigid defensiveness of latency, faulty logic, circular reasoning, or anxious, illogical intellectualizations based on distorted pictures of internal feeling states.

Another important developmental accomplishment in adolescence is the ability to form, at first, fleeting relationships with same-sex and opposite-sex peers, and then intense relationships with both kinds of peers. In the context of these age-appropriate relationships, it is possible for the adolescent to review and explore age-appropriate concerns, to rework earlier developmental concerns, and to form new structures, such as the ego ideal. In this light, it is also important for the young adolescent to be able to relate to older individuals in a close and admiring manner. Where these relationships do not occur or are not possible, again there may be a limitation in the ability for internal cognition.

These relationships serve, in a sense, as aliment for the internal cognitive system. Deprivation along these lines would have results analogous to stimulus deprivation along the external cognitive boundary. For example, the capacities for formal operations may not fully develop unless the adolescent works on problems of sufficient complexity to tax his newly emerging ability to understand the relationships among a group of variables as part of a system (mathematical or logic problems). Similarly, the capacities for combinatorial thinking at the internal boundary may not develop unless interpersonal aliments are sufficiently complex to facilitate the development of internal cognitive structures. The construction of a relatively stable representational system (identity) that integrates and synthesizes may emerge only when the internal boundary aliments are sufficiently complex to provide the assimilations that will lead to age-appropriate accommodation.

In some cases, because of unresolved earlier conflicts, family interaction patterns, or unique social situations such as isolation, human relationships that stimulate a variety of wishes and feelings, generate interpersonal experiences, and provide restraints and limits are not available. Given such inadequate aliment, the operations characteristic of adolescence may not develop and the flexibility of the ego at the internal boundary (e.g., capacity for complex transformations) may be compromised. One sixteen-year-old boy, for instance, had withdrawn from age-appropriate peer relationships and was associating with younger children and making model airplanes. Although he could do some formal operational tasks in mathematics, his internal world was at the level of concrete operations.

Another youngster, who was stealing from neighbors' homes,

had a covert but prominent fear of separating from his "admiring" mother. There were oedipal and preoedipal levels in his anxious attachment to her. Although he was involved in adolescent peer relationships, his capacity to take distance from his feelings toward his mother and look at his delinquent behavior was compromised. Despite an above-average IQ, he was also having difficulties in school. He had trouble performing logical tasks, and, interestingly, even in his delinquency his ability for hypothetical thinking was impaired.

The internal boundary needs its own type of aliment. As pointed out, opportunities for less-than-optimal development are greater at the internal than at the external boundary. Parents can interfere by holding their adolescents too close to them and not permitting separation, or earlier needs may lead the adolescent to hold on to his parents. Unresolved earlier issues can make it difficult for the adolescent to form growth-facilitating relationships. Familial patterns may undermine the "need for integration of identity" (Wynne and Singer, 1963a, 1963b). All these factors can compromise the development of capacities for internal cognition or for the full use of the combinatorial capacity to scan and experence, in a flexible manner, the internal world.

In summary, the internal cognitive capacity of the adolescent in its ideal state is marked by the ability to scan the internal world of wishes, affects, and relationships, to perceive the many derivatives in terms of ideas and feelings and to experience a wide range of them, to observe the many hypothetical and potential causal relationships within the emotional realm and, through experience, to discriminate real relationships from possible ones. Because of the greater flexibility of issues that contribute to the formation of the internal cognitive structure, however, it is rare that this ideal is reached across the board. Rather, we see it in certain areas, with limitations in others.

As we have seen, the developmental level and integrity of the internal cognitive structure may influence, in part, the external cognitive structure. For example, we may find that in an adolescent who has not made an appropriate separation from parents, drive derivatives and affects appear too concretely realistic for any distancing, propositional capacity at the internal boundary. The same adolescent may be susceptible to regression in certain external tasks that relate too closely to internal boundary issues. In fact, we see this rather frequently when adolescents begin to discuss seemingly external issues that have some link to emotionality in their lives, such as planning for college education. When the adolescent is trying to apply combinatorial capacities to such issues, we often see the reasoning break down and the logical hypothetico-deductive system become inoperable.

We can even see this process in some adolescents' inability to write certain kinds of essays. They may be quite competent in mathematics, but when it comes to reading literature and writing organized essays, which involve principles of hypothetico-deductive reasoning, there may be a regression to preadolescent levels of cognitive ability. This is not just because the literary task is difficult for them, but because the issues raised (romance, rebellion, death, etc.) are closer to their emotional life. As a further example of this, it is amazing to see to what degree, after leaving home and going to college, may late adolescents suffer from serious regression in their cognitive abilities because of the pressure of unresolved family-separation issues. Thus, even when tasks appear to be distant from drive-affect derivatives, there is nonetheless the force of unresolved drive tensions and its effect on the internal boundary, which in turn affects the external boundary either globally or partially, resulting in external cognitive regressions.

The Dynamic Relationship between the Internal and External Boundaries of the Ego: Some General Principles

In the preceding sections we discussed, for each stage of development, the functioning of the ego at its internal and external boundaries. In this way a relationship has been proposed between the kind of structures studied by Piaget and the kinds of internal stimuli considered by the dynamic perspective. We have shown that Piaget's cognitive psychology is generally compatible with the metapsychological points of view of psychoanalysis, including the dynamic point of view. In addition, we have shown, in an admittedly preliminary and speculative fashion, that cognitive considerations may add significantly to a full understanding of behavior.

Since Piaget's cognitive psychology has been generated in the context of a genetic epistemology—that is, within the broader area of the adaptation of the knowing organism to its environment—his major constructs seem to pertain most directly to the psychoanalytic adaptive point of view. Our cognitive perspective, then, would be an extension of the adaptive point of view, which would enhance understanding of the total process of ego adaptation to internal and external stimuli. In this regard, cognitive structures should be seen as only one of the multiple determinants of behavior, and cognition, as one of the multiple perspectives in understanding behavior.

In our preceding discussion of the interrelationships between the external cognitive boundary (that studied by Piaget) and the postulated internal boundary, we attempted to demonstrate that the processes operative at each boundary are symmetrical. In other words, we postulated that a structure with processes that operate according to certain principles relates to events at each boundary. That the structure is the same in terms of process at each boundary and differs only with regard to the stimulus world it encounters is crucial to our integration. It is recognized that this structure can exist at different developmental levels at each boundary and in different relationships to its stimulus world. In fact, it was pointed out that the different factors influencing the development of the internal boundary and the external boundary cause a relative differentiation of these two boundaries throughout development. The way in which these two boundaries are connected, however, provides us with a synthetic link and permits us to make use of Piaget's findings in a psychoanalytic context.

We have already mentioned that means-ends differentiation and the capacity for figurative thinking may be highly dependent on early internal object relations. At the earliest stage, for example, there can be no development of psychic structure without the capacity for attachment. While there may be some development with compromised attachment, it cannot be the rich development that leads to optimal cognitive development, even in the impersonal realm. It is the infant's attachment to a human object that permits him to begin to differentiate means from ends and self from others.

Not only attachment, but the facilitation of the separation-individuation process after attachment is necessary for normal cognitive development. If there are severe limitations in any of these processes, there will be severe interferences in the development of cognition at both boundaries. The consequences of the failure to achieve attachment are well known (Bowlby, 1969; Spitz, 1965). If attachment is formed but separation and individuation are not facilitated, there may be limitations in the capacity for representational thinking (Décarie, 1962; Mahler, Pine, and Bergman, 1975). If enough of the interactive process is present to facilitate the development of this capacity, but separation and individuation are compromised, there may be severe arrests at the level of preoperational thinking, characteristic of many borderline and psychotic syndromes (Kernberg, 1975; Mahler, Pine, and Bergman, 1975).

If things go well during the sensorimotor and preoperational periods and are facilitated by the human relationships of both of these phases of development, there is good potential for the first operational period, the period of concrete operations. As previously discussed, the capacity for certain concrete operations may be dependent on some degree of oedipal resolution. Just as earlier the capacity for attachment was a prime necessity for the development of sensorimotor intelligence, the capacity for an oedipal involvement may be necessary for the development of those cognitive tasks characteristic of the concrete operational period.

The oedipal situation is a three-person system. Prior to this, the young child is in a basically dyadic system; at times it may be triangular but without much investment in the triangular aspects (e.g., rivalry). During his first few years of life, the child relates to a primary mothering figure. He may relate intentionally to father and may even be able to distinguish mother from father, but he does not perceive them in a triangle. Rather, even if he distinguishes them as "different," he perceives them as substitutes for one another. In other words, this system is a two-person system, consisting of the child and one other. The "one other" can be mother, father, uncle, or aunt, but the child's psychic mechanisms are involved in a two-person system. It should be mentioned that this tenet of psychoanalytic developmental psychology is contradicted by the theories of Melanie Klein (1928), who postulates a three-person system beginning much earlier in life than classical psychoanalysts do.

The basic point to be stressed is that for the full development of concrete operations, involvement in the more complex three-person system of the oedipal period may be a necessary aliment. With such involvement, the youngster begins to perceive, not in terms of self and one another, but in terms of a system of relations in interaction. We noted earlier that one of the concrete operational structures pertains to the addition of symmetrical relations (grouping VI) and another to the addition of asymmetrical relations (grouping V). Both of these structures may be stimulated under the influence of the oedipal situation.

In the oedipal involvement the child comes to understand the asymmetry that marks his relationship with each parent, as well as the symmetry that characterizes their relationship with each other. Where the preoperational child lacks comprehension of the symmetry of certain relationships, the concrete operational child understands that if x is the brother of y, y is necessarily the brother of x. In similar fashion, the symmetry of the relationship between his parents (x is the spouse of y) becomes understood in the course of solution of the oedipal conflict. In other words, prior to concrete operations, father may be mother's husband, but that does not mean that mother is father's wife. During the early oedipal phase, such thinking could be quite "economic." Once symmetrical capacities are established, the fact that mother and father are reciprocally attached cannot be denied quite so easily. Similarly, the symmetry between son and father cannot so easily be denied after the advent of concrete operations.

The degree of successful oedipal resolution may influence the freedom of concrete operational structures from drive influences. In other words, since it is likely that considerable aliment for the development of these ego structures, in terms of highly significant object relations, is present at the internal boundary, unless this aliment is successfully assimilated to the structures dealing with relations, it may be difficult for the same structures to be applied to the inanimate world at the external boundary. Thus, just as there may be a regression in emotional development from an oedipal to a preoedipal level if oedipal issues remain unresolved, there may be regression in certain cognitive capacities from a concrete operational to a preoperational level. Other aspects of concrete and formal operational thinking in latency and adolescence were considered above and need not be resummarized.

We shall now turn our attention to some general principles. We shall consider the relation of the drives in a very general sense to the development of the internal and external cognitive structures. First, there is the issue of lack of drive satisfaction; for example, deficiencies in physical contact during infancy. This situation often leads to an increase in activity and in displacement of energy toward other stimuli. The young infant may turn to the inanimate world and, if there are objects available, may increase his involvement with them. Past a point, however, lack of drive satisfaction may lead to decreased activity and withdrawal, a type of giving up. The lack of aliment is accepted, so to speak, and there is withdrawal from the world and also possibly from interest in the self. The infant lies apathetic and listless.

In the first instance, mild lack of drive satisfaction may lead to increased search for displaced aliment (nonorganic or nonhuman). We may see precocious development in certain children, but only in relation to the inanimate world. Although early in life this may appear to be advanced cognitive development, it is vulnerable to later regression because of the lack of development at the internal boundary, where human object relations play a major role. In the second instance, however, lack of drive satisfaction is so complete that even a displaced interest in impersonal stimuli cannot be aroused.

Consider a third situation, in which there is excessive human stimulation at the external boundary and oversatiation. This situation may lead to a pulling away from certain aspects of the outside world and a shifting of interest toward aspects of the internal boundary (e.g., narcissism). Such a shift can occur in a specific area, but if generalized, can lead to decreased intake of external aliment and a lack of development of impersonal cognition. Here we are postulating, in Rapaport's (1958) sense, an equilibrium between external stimulation and internal stimulation necessary to maintain the ego structure. When there is overstimulation from the outside, there may be a shifting of the equilibrium toward the inside. Thus, there may be a lack of interaction with the outside world and a lack of cognitive development.

A fourth situation involves overstimulation at the internal boundary and may shift interest disproportionately toward the outside world. At low intensity, overstimulation from the inside may lead to increased attainment of aliment from the outside. But if intense enough, such overstimulation may overwhelm the schemes at the internal boundary so they cannot be organized and may similarly compromise the schemes at the external boundary (e.g., the very high-energy infant who cannot organize his sensorimotor reactions and other adaptive patterns to the external world).

The influence of the drives depends in part on the stage of development and the structure of the ego, and, in particular, on the relationship between the two boundaries. During early development, particularly during the first few months of life, ego structures are relatively undifferentiated in terms of internal and external boundaries. Precursors of the external boundary are tied to drive-related structures (the precursors of the internal boundary). As development proceeds, there is a progressive differentiation, partly because of the different stimulus inputs or aliments from the internal and external milieus.

This differentiation proceeds hierarchically, however, so that at the base the internal boundary is intimately tied to the external boundary. Further along the developmental hierarchy, relative autonomy prevails between external boundary functioning and internal boundary functioning, but a connection remains that can be called into play under certain conditions.

When both boundaries of the ego structures develop evenly, general personality development is consolidated. However, when impersonal external cognitive development forges ahead normally because of the availability of suitable aliment, but a fixation occurs at the drive or object-relations boundary because of the vicissitudes of the drives or of interpersonal relationships, the fixation at the internal boundary can exert a backward pull on the external boundary. We then have a dyssynchronous or uneven development.

When, for any of a variety of reasons, there is a regression of cognitive functioning at the external boundary, the cognitive structures may take on the characteristics of those cognitive structures appropriate to a correspondingly lower level of drive organization. If, for example, there is regression on the side of the drives from an anal to an oral organization, the level of impersonal cognitive development may regress to the level of cognitive development that ordinarily accompanies an oral drive organization. Thus a two-year-old child who has attained a capacity for representation may exhibit characteristics of pre-representational sensorimotor "intelligence" rather than those of the more advanced level. The regression in impersonal cognition would not be expected to occur broadly along all areas of cognition. Cognitive functioning may at times regress only in relation to certain formal or content areas that bear a symbolic similarity to the underlying drive issues.

A useful model in discussing regression in the cognitive sphere related to the pull from the drives is Rapaport's (1958) model of stimulus nutriment. He claims that the ego, to maintain its equilibrium, must receive at least relatively constant stimulation from the external world as well as the internal world of the drives and affects. If, for example, there is a lack of consistent stimulation from the external milieu, structures such as the superego may undergo regression under the pull from the drives. The effects of sensory deprivation show what happens in a more global way when there is a deprivation in external stimulation. On the other hand, if the drives are extraordinarily weak, the ego may lose important functions related to its ability to perceive the internal body and aspects of the sense of self. Thus, there is a constant need for balance between external and internal stimulation.

If we apply this model to the relationship between the drives and impersonal cognition, we can view cognitive structures as needing a certain kind of enrichment from external boundary nutriments. At the same time, a certain level of drive stimulation is needed to maintain the advanced level of cognition in relation to the internal milieu. When the pull from a regressive drive organization becomes particularly strong, the imbalance between external and internal stimulation leads to a new equilibrium at a regressed cognitive level. As indicated earlier, this will often be in a specific sector of cognition related to the structure evolved around the regressed drive organization. We have also seen, however, that if pressure from the drive becomes more generalized and global, a massive regression in cognition may occur. To understand further how the internal and external boundaries relate to one another leads to a consideration of a number of specific principles.

One of these principles is the idea of a transitional operation—that is, a series of gradients from primitive drive cognition to impersonal cognition. At one end of the spectrum we find primitive drive-colored cognitions, then developmentally more mature drive-colored cognitions, then cognitions only mildly colored by mature drive organizations, and eventually, at the other end of the spectrum, impersonal cognitions only relatively or minutely affected by drive derivatives. What, we must ask, are the transformational variables that relate impersonal cognitive structures to drive-colored cognitive structures?

Discontinuity between the Internal and External Boundaries

It has been shown that the internal and external boundaries may develop to different levels of cognitive operations. The degree of discontinuity—for example, external boundary at formal operations, internal boundary at the preoperational level—has an important influence on the vulnerability to regression of the boundary at the higher level. It is as though a backward pull were exerted by the lowest level of development. With appropriate stress (from the internal drives or external environment), a new equilibrium may be found at the lower level of cognitive operations. We can observe this most clearly in a psychotic reaction in a "latent psychotic." His emotional cognition may have barely reached the concrete operational stage, and he may process much of his internal world in the context of preoperational processes (magical thinking). In the psychotic regression, particularly in response to a minimal stress, aspects of his external boundary, which may, in part, have reached a formal operational capacity, may regress to preoperational and early concrete operational modes of cognition. In a delusion about an "influencing machine," for instance, the machine may be given human qualities (preoperational) and have components that function in the context of concrete operational logic (in the secondary elaboration of the delusion).

To a lesser degree, regressions to the level of development of internal boundary are seen in all neurotic compromise formations, since they all use some preoperational and concrete operational thinking. In some phobias, for example, an inanimate object is experienced unconsciously as alive and dangerous and put through some complex transformations. To the degree that reality testing remains intact, only a small symbolized aspect of cognition is involved and the regression is therefore quite limited.

What is being emphasized here is that the levels of cognition achieved at both boundaries exist in relation to each other and influence the regressive potential. When one boundary is globally significantly lower than the other, there is a backward pull of potentially great magnitude. When one boundary is lower only in certain sectors and/or not significantly lower, the backward potential is less ominous. The way in which this pull is mediated depends on a number of other variables, including the pressure of the drives.

Drive Pressure

Initially, we may consider drive-colored schemes in the context of object relations. We know that early relationships with human objects are colored by the drives, as in relationships during the oral stage of development. The oral stage connotes a certain drive organization around orality, and at this time the infant is beginning to develop a primary attachment to a primary object, usually his mother. As noted above, the earliest relationships are dyadic: whether they be with the mother or father, or others, they occur in a two-person system. As relationships proceed, the drive organization changes to anality. Usually this phase also occurs in the context of dyadic relationship patterns. As movement continues into the triangular oedipal pattern, there is a corresponding movement toward a phallic drive organization. Attending to just these three basic early drive organizations, we may look at the issue of pressure from drive-colored structures.

Consider a young child who is experiencing a conflict related to his early drives and their concomitant object relations and is unable to accept loss. The young child in the dyadic pattern is egocentric, needs to have what he wants, and cannot sufficiently maintain a representation of the external object to accept its loss and feel some sadness. If the object leaves, the child feels as though the world is disintegrating. At the next level, the oedipal level, the youngster who had trouble accepting loss may not be able to get fully into and/or resolve the oedipal situation.

In order for the young boy to enter the oedipal situation fully, he needs to be willing to be competitive with his father, and to some degree this means giving up a certain reliance on his father, at least temporarily. The young girl may experience this problem even more acutely; for her to enter into full oedipal rivalry where she feels competitive with mother means some relinquishing of the early, more dependent orientation to mother, at least temporarily. This letting go, or giving up, of some earlier feeling toward the parent is necessary for progression.

Similarly, in order to resolve the oedipal situation, the youngster who has moved into it by being able to picture in fantasy one of the parents as a rival and take him on, so to speak, needs to be able to see that he "can't have his cake and eat it too." The young girl cannot have the mother as her rival and father as the longed-for object of her desires and at the same time begin to develop a close identification with mother and expect support from mother. If she tries to do both, she gets involved in a series of covert, tricky relationships characteristic of those who have unresolved oedipal patterns. She also often gets involved in defensive neurotic formations. The same thing applies to the boy who is unwilling to relinquish his possessive feelings toward mother and rivalrous feelings toward father at the same time that he wants father to love him and wants to be the center of attention of both parents. He may refuse to resolve the situation, thinking he can have his cake and eat it too, but this will involve him in many defensive patterns.

To take a step away from this and look at it from a cognitive viewpoint, consider just the oedipal situation. In a sense, the child is unable to say "I cannot be a rival to this parent and also be a warm, secure, dependent lover of this parent." Thus, the young girl who stays in the middle of the oedipal situation often wants mother to be her supporter and to have all of mother's attention, while at the same time she wants to get rid of mother, the rival. On an emotional level there is a failure here in simple classification. One person cannot be rival and nonrival at the same time. To wish for this state of affairs is to engage in egocentric, magical thinking that disregards logical classifications or categories.

However, the youngster with unresolved drive pressures, who never learned to give things up at the early dyadic level, has tremendous yearning and hunger to try to get some needs met in an oedipal configuration. He therefore has trouble resolving his oedipal difficulties and gets stuck in the middle of the oedipal triangle. He may, then, because of the pressure of his drives, be unable to perform the simple cognitive task of forming mutually exclusive categories in human relationships, particularly with primary important objects that are closely connected to the drives. This inability may appear in impersonal relationships as well. On the other hand, if these drive pressures are not too great with, for example, nonfamily relationships, the child may be able to perform the task of mutual exclusivity in nonfamily settings. Thus, with peers the youngster may be able to understand that he cannot love and hate the same friend at the same moment.

Drive pressure may, however, affect not only the primary objects but also secondary objects, such as friends or peers, and yet not affect the inanimate world. In terms of manipulating blocks, the drives, since they are primarily placed on human objects, may not affect cognitive efficiency. There may be a progression from the primary objects, which are closer to the drives, to inanimate objects, which may be relatively removed from drive pressures. Nevertheless, if the drive pressures are intense enough, we may speculate that they would affect even the inanimate world. A general inability for classification, and therefore mathematics, may result from an internal boundary limitation in this area or from a severe-enough fixation at the internal boundary. Drive pressure is therefore an important variable affecting cognition.

Degree of Structure or Definition of Cognitive Task

A third variable relating drive-colored and impersonal cognition is the degree of structure or the definition of the cognitive task. Where the inanimate external environment is highly delineated (e.g., round versus square pegs) and the cognitive task is also clearly delineated (e.g., classification), a high degree of structure is present. Such an instance is higher in structure than, for example, labeling human beings with different facial expressions. The degree of structure or definition of the task or of external reality reminds one again of Rapaport's (1958) concept of a certain amount of stimulus nutriment being necessary to maintain the tie to external reality. Rapaport points out that there is always a balance of forces operating on the ego: external reality and the force of drive tensions.

If a person is removed from external stimuli, such as reminders of the moral codes, often the superego system may regress and, in a sense, be overly influenced by unconscious drive derivatives. In other words, there will be a process of destructuralization. Rapaport points out that to maintain structures, a certain degree of minimal continual external stimulation is required, at least on an intermittent basis. Thus Rapaport, too, considers the valence of the external properties of the stimulus configurations as determinants of behavior.

If we want to look at the two extremes, a task such as classifying the round and the square pieces of wood is relatively clear, whereas a task involving classifying human relationships and emotions is much more ambiguous. The general rule here is that the less clear or the more ambiguous the external configuration involved in the cognitive task, the more likely that the influence of drive pressures or derivatives will be felt. In regard to this, we may speculate why Piaget, in his original experiments, did not study or learn about the effects of the drives in determining cognitive behavior. It may have been because he studied cognitive behavior in the most extreme sense as it applied to well-delineated or well-structured inanimate objects. He did not study the same conceptual or cognitive abilities, such as categorizing, or later abilities, such as hypothetical reasoning, in relation to more ambiguous aspects of human beings. While choosing inanimate objects gave him a clearer or simpler experimental field, it also limited the breadth of his conclusions. He has studied cognition only insofar as it refers to the nonhuman world. There have been later studies of empathy,[5] and Piaget himself did study moral development (1932, 1947), but as we know, these are relatively minor excursions compared to the major data base of his theory.

The Development of Internal Structure

The fourth variable to be considered is the organism's history of interaction among innate givens, maturational forces, and environmental influences. This variable includes the innate and developmental strengths of the cognitive structures and of the drive- and affect-modulating structures. If a person has basically intact innate equipment and good opportunities to act on his environment to develop psychological structures, and if there are no major early emotional insults to compromise them, one may assume very strong structures in relation both to inanimate objects and to tasks relating to human objects. Such structures are relatively resilient in the face of pressures from drives. They have a great deal of integrity and strength based on the original genetic and constitutional factors from which they evolved and on the environmental experiences that served to consolidate them.

The drive- and affect-modulating structures, the defensive

[5] See Chapter 1 for a review of these studies.

and synthetic structures of the ego, are included in considering this group of variables. Where they operate effectively, they tend to free the organism for age-appropriate cognitive tasks, at least in the areas of cognition not related to compromise formations due to neuroses. Where these structures are weak, where neurotic formations fail to contain conflict and there is pervasive diffusion of the drive derivatives, there may be regressive movements in the functioning of cognitive structures. Thus, we have to consider both the degree of consolidation of the drive- and affect-modulating structures and the degree of strength or integrity of the cognitive structures themselves, which as indicated, are based on innate as well as experiential factors.

Situational Context

A fifth variable is the situational context, which is partially related to the strengths of the drives and their related affects. In some situational contexts drive derivatives and affects are very active and tend to pervade cognition; in other contexts drive derivatives may be relatively inactive. For example, one could study a person's performance on certain cognitive tasks under situations varying in cues related to hunger, dependency, sex, or aggression, and observe their impact on cognition in relation to the personality organization.

Mutual Enhancement

A sixth variable is the degree of mutual enhancement between cognitive and drive-affect development. Mutual enhancement occurs when the development of the drives, object relations, and cognition is at the same level—for instance, when there is oedipal resolution and, at the same time, the cognitive capacity for concrete operations. Out of this enhancement and mutual consolidation there may be a resistance to regression.

If, however, there is a split between these two lines of development—for example, the youngster develops cognitively in relation to his inanimate world but cognitive development is compromised in relation to his internal world—we may see greater vulnerability to regression. It is likely that Piaget, who studied normal children, looked at subjects in whom both lines of development were roughly equally advanced. If splits in the two lines of development occur, however, youngsters with compromises at the internal boundary may be vulnerable to regression at the external ego boundary. Dudek (1972), it will be recalled, found a preponderance of constrictive, obsessional defenses among subjects who showed stage regression on Piagetian tasks.

Meaning of External Stimulus Configuration

The symbolization of a cognitive task involves images that have a relationship to each other because of continuity along dimensions determined by drive investment. During the course of development experiences become attached to initial drive-determined organizations, providing a secondary associative-experiential organization to memories or images. At one extreme of this hierarchy is the external configuration of reality, which may have features independent of a relationship to drives.

The degree to which an external boundary task is similar in stimulus configuration to issues at the internal boundary, however, may be another variable mediating the influence between the two boundaries. Classification tasks in arithmetic, for example, may be connected to real experiences involving "arithmetic" with parents. In consequence, there may be anxiety and regression of the external boundary in relation to arithmetic problems at school because they are so similar to emotion-laden issues at home. Another, more process-oriented example would be a task involving the use of the reciprocal by a youngster in whom the internal construct of reciprocal relationships was either newly organized or laden with conflict and anxiety. Still another example would be where arithmetic came to have a sexual meaning because of an unconscious association with early experiences. A teenager whose father was a mathematician had a "math block" due to sexual fantasies tied to his father as a "doer of math."

The Variables as Part of a System

None of the above variables ever acts in isolation; rather, they are part of a dynamic interrelated system. This point perhaps needs no elaboration. The fact that even under high drive pressure and with a fragile cognitive structure a person may carry out a highly structured cognitive task is not surprising, as can be observed with many psychotic patients. These variables are in a relative relationship to one another and are weighted in their influence in a manner specific to each person.

Degree and Manner of Influence of Drive Derivatives on Cognition

We have outlined thus far some variables that determine the influence of dynamic factors in cognitive functioning: the discontinuity between the boundaries, the pressure of the drives, the degree of structure or definition of the cognitive task, the integrity and strength of the cognitive and the defensive and adaptive structures, the situational context, the degree of mutual enhancement between cognitive and affective development, and the external stimulus configuration. As these variables influence the cognitive system, their force may lead to a greater or lesser incapacitation in cognitive functioning. In other words, the drives may affect cognition in a series of steps increasing in intensity.

First, the drives may influence the selection of cognitive content. In this situation the cognitive processes or operations remain intact, but the selection of what one cogitates about is partially determined by dynamic considerations. Thus, the latency child with the ability for concrete operations chooses to use those operations in certain types of games or with certain types of inanimate objects which are in part determined by dynamic considerations. Some children may apply cognition to war games, while others apply it to house cleaning.

A second, more pervasive influence of drive derivatives on cognitive capacity is the symbolization or deneutralization of a limited number of cognitive tasks. We may see a latency child who has difficulty in learning simple mathematical procedures that are within the range of what appears to be his cognitive developmental stage. The mathematical tasks demand no more than simply initial concrete operations, yet this youngster appears to have a learning problem because for some reason he has symbolized math. It may be a substitute for a human object or a symbol of some sexual or aggressive issue. The reason for this symbolization, as we are calling it, of a certain area may be multiply determined. Math may be perceived in a competitive context as "getting ahead of others." The child may be involved in rivalry with another child, and there math touches on a type of competition and raises oedipal anxiety. Or math, because of a parent's interest in it, may be associated with a specific identification.

The third level of influence of the drives on cognitive tasks is that in which the capacity for cognition is more generally compromised by unresolved dynamic concerns. This level is similar to the second one except that its scope is broader. For example, if the child is competitive in class and does well in math, he outdistances a rival and therefore experiences oedipal anxiety. In this case, however, there is not just an inhibition in the area of math but a general cognitive regression to the level of development attained in relation to dynamic concerns. The child who has not resolved oedipal issues denies himself the use of the classificatory capacity (since he does not use classifications to resolve his oedipal situation), and therefore has a pervasive learning problem.

The fourth level in this hierarchy is a fixation or arrest in the development of drive-related aspects of ego structure severe enough to cause arrest in the development of cognitive structures. An example would be a seven-year-old who has an inability to perform even beginning concrete operational tasks and is fixated at a preoedipal level of development, without signs of neurological problems or generalized retardation.

The Special Case of Impaired or Delayed Maturation

Organic impairment or delay, as illustrated by biologically based mental retardation, raises some special issues. Where the cognitive structure does not develop, except in a rudimentary form, the capacities at both the external and internal boundaries will be severely affected. Consider, for example, a retarded youngster who can develop cognitive structure only to the early phase of concrete operations. The limitations on his general intellectual functions are well known. It is also well accepted clinically that many such youngsters develop emotional problems. While many reasons can be suggested for the development of emotional problems (e.g., a defective self-image), the model being developed here would offer a rather specific hypothesis.

The limitations in cognitive development restrict the flexibility of operations available to deal with stimuli at the internal boundary. The mildly retarded youngster has only the relatively simple mechanisms of early concrete operational cognition to deal with a developing internal milieu. As illustrated earlier, the early latency child, in contrast to his adolescent counterpart, has only a few cognitive operations and, in parallel, only a few defensive operations.

It is not surprising that retarded youngsters often develop or demonstrate emotional and/or behavioral difficulties in adolescence. Their internal milieu is becoming more intense and complex due to the biological and related psychological changes (e.g., drive-affect dispositions) of this period. Yet they have only the cognitive or, at the internal boundary, the parallel defensive and adaptive ego functions of early latency. The equipment, in a sense, cannot handle the stimulus input. Complex human relationships and their related drive-affect states, as well as the independent psychological changes of adolescence, are too much for the relatively inflexible system characteristic of the early concrete operational stage to cope with.

It should be pointed out that while retardation is often diagnosed by IQ scores, a more useful assessment of intelligence would be to observe the cognitive level attained. Marked biologically based limitations in cognition may restrict the development of the internal boundary as well as that of the external boundary. This hypothesis raises many interesting questions about treatment for such youngsters. Take, for example, the youngster with limited cognitive capacity who is relatively successfully using denials and reaction formations. Should these be interpreted or supported? What is the role of external boundary intelligence in treatment? Some of these issues will be taken up in a later chapter.

Testing the Model with a Diagnostic Tool

Along the lines discussed, we might develop a diagnostic tool to pick up difficulties in cognition. Since one central hypothesis is that some problems in cognition are related to unresolved issues in the internal world of drives and affects, we might develop a series of verbal and manual tasks to test such operations as classification and seriation and, later in adolescence, combinatorial and hypothetico-deductive logic. These tasks would first be tested with the most innocuous or drive-distant media. Varied blocks could be used to test classification, other non-drive- or affect-invested kinds of stimuli to test seriation, and very abstract impersonal issues to test combinatorial and hypothetico-deductive logic. These skills could then be tested with a series of drive-related issues. We might set up a gradient from purely impersonal cognitive tasks to tasks that come progressively closer to drive-affect concerns. On a classification task, we would start out with blocks, then move to human beings, then to particular human relationships, and then to the world of feelings within human relationships. We might attempt to come closer and closer to those issues we know are dynamically laden for the individual being tested.

The tool would show how close we have to get to the drives and affects before they cause a cognitive regression, and we could observe to what degree and to what developmental level this regression occurs. Such a diagnostic tool, if validated and found reliable, would support the present model of the internal and external ego boundaries. In addition, it would delineate the character of the cognitive structures. In other words, it would show at what point the regression occurs, in what areas it occurs, how resistant it is to drive pressures, how truly autonomous it is, and in what specific ways dynamic issues color it.

A validated psychodiagnostic test might also yield information on how to develop remedial programs when we do find difficulties in cognition. In testing a latency child, for example, if severe cognitive regression occurred as soon as oedipal material loomed and then also occurred in association with human relationships and even with certain purely cognitive tasks when the issue of competition was involved, we would realize that we needed to rework these internal drive-related issues with this youngster to free up his purely cognitive abilities.

At the same time a youngster was being helped in a psychotherapeutic setting, the purely educational approach might involve helping him distance his internal concerns from his external cognitive tasks. Thus, the youngster might practice impersonal cognition with a teacher who understood how dynamic issues color these tasks and could help him separate this out by using a variety of educational approaches.

In the broader question of development in general, as we reach back into the first three years of life and try to facilitate ability to deal with the world, the present model of cognitive-affective interaction may prove useful. Those who are concerned with cognition cannot offer programs of cognitive stimulation without considering the underpinnings of human object relations and their drive-affect investments. A program of cognitive stimulation must take into account the child's capacity to reach a state of equilibrium, to attach to a human object, to develop a process of complex reciprocal interaction, to work through the separation-individuation process, to move on to form an oedipal attachment, to rework the oedipal situation, and to move into latency issues. There may be ways to facilitate the cognitive aspects of these processes, but they would have to take into account early and later object relations and their associated drives and affects. No longer can we be limited to seeing one line of development in isolation from the other.

9

AN INTEGRATED MODEL OF INTELLIGENT LEARNING

Thus far we have shown how the principles Piaget developed to explain the relationship between the development of internal structures and impersonal aspects of the external world may also apply to a broader range of stimuli than simply impersonal ones. They may be able to take into account stimuli arising from the interpersonal world and the internal world of drives, affects, self- and object representations with their specific drive-affect dispositions, and aspects of the ego and superego.

From a consideration of each stage of development, we developed a model encompassing the relationship between certain internal psychological structures and both the internal and external environments. The model presented both external and internal ego boundaries, connected through a set of transformational principles. We proposed that not only do internal psychological structures have a simultaneous relationship with impersonal, interpersonal, and drive-affect stimulus organizations, but that the principles governing these relationships are symmetrical and can be conceptualized within a single frame of reference. We also suggested, however, that because the vicissitudes of the external and internal worlds differ, development at the internal and external boundaries may occur with varying degrees of symmetry or asymmetry. In any case, as we indicated, development at one boundary will affect the other through the set of transformational principles.

In this section we shall further consider an integrated model of intelligent learning. The principles to be elucidated are those of a general model of intelligent learning and functioning; that is, psychological intelligence and cognitive intelligence are seen as essentially one and the same. Our model is an adaptive one, within which the human organism adapts to complex stimulus inputs from varying sources in a developmental sequence of increasing complexity and higher-order equilibrium states.

Before presenting this integrated model of intelligent learning and functioning, we shall first briefly review the different components contributing to it. At the first level, we have already suggested how understanding the internal world—the drives, feelings, and the like—helps us to understand the development of cognition. From this perspective we have hypothesized that certain learning disorders may be understood in part by a fixation at the internal boundary in terms of the resolution of certain emotional issues.

The ability to learn arithmetic, for example, requires the development of certain concrete operations (inverse and reciprocal relationships). At the internal boundary, just prior to the development of the capacities for constructing inverse and reciprocal relationships at the external boundary, is the Oedipus complex. It was hypothesized that in order to resolve the Oedipus complex successfully, the youngster must be able to construct inverse and reciprocal relationships at the internal boundary. The youngster who cannot see that he cannot have his father's love and respect and at the same time view his father as his competitor for his mother will have difficulty resolving the oedipal situation. In terms of his internal cognitive boundary, he has not achieved the ability for constructing inverse relationships. Similarly, if he cannot see his smallness in relation to father's largeness—suggesting that he has not achieved the ability for the seriation task derived from reciprocal relationships—he will also have a difficult time resolving the oedipal situation.

If, for a variety of reasons indicated earlier—overstimulation by parents, covert support of oedipal and preoedipal fantasies, heightened drive tensions—the youngster does not develop these cognitive schemes at the internal boundary and therefore does not resolve the important elements of his oedipal situation, these deficits may generalize and interfere with the construction of these schemes at the external boundary. Whether or not this happens depends on a number of other forces, such as the symbolization of certain external boundary tasks. Nevertheless, we have suggested that if the lack of resolution of the oedipal issues is so dramatic as to prevent the formation of certain internal cognitive schemes, there may be a general vulnerability of external cognitive schemes.

At the second level, we observed for each stage of development how understanding impersonal cognition—cognition at the external boundary—helps us understand what goes on at the internal boundary. It was seen that the model of impersonal cognition, if applied to the internal boundary, helps us understand the differentiation of self and object, the development of crucial ego functions, the development of defenses, and the development of ego flexibility. We observed, for example, that in the first year of life the development of means-ends relationships from initial primary and secondary circular reactions helps us understand more clearly the differentiation of internal means-ends relationships—that is, relationships between internal feelings and their consequences in the world—and thereby the differentiation of self from nonself. This, as we all know, lays the foundation for certain crucial ego functions dealing with causality and reality testing, not only in terms of impersonal external world functions, but also with the internal world of drives and affect.

We also saw how one could trace the development of defenses in terms of a more general model of internal cognition. For example, the typical defenses of latency, such as reaction formations, can be seen to be based on a cognitive scheme for constructing the inverse relationship. Similarly, the capacity for certain rationalizations is paralleled by the cognitive ability for reciprocal relationships. The developmental model of cognition allows us to examine the development of defensive functions based on the evolving capacities of the youngster to process and accommodate varying stimuli.

At a third level, we shall examine not just how the internal world and impersonal cognition relate to each other, but how an integrated model can help us understand the development and organization of structures that are foundations for intelligent learning at different levels of development and in the context of multiple stimulus inputs. We are proposing a general model of both emotional and impersonal learning, a model of adaptation that takes into account a variety of stimulus situations confronting the human organism. This model is built on the model already suggested by Hartmann (1939) and Nunberg (1931) in their considerations of the adaptive functions of the ego. The ego is seen as the differentiating structure that deals with a variety of kinds of stimulus nutriments. In developing this model more fully, the concepts of assimilation, accommodation, and equilibrium states developed by Piaget will prove useful. By combining these concepts with those of ego flexibility and the integrative functions of the ego, we shall have a more unified model of human learning, or human intelligence.

In order to develop this integrated model of human learning, we need to consider it from a number of perspectives. First, we have to consider the unique structural properties of what we are proposing here as a psychological structure. What are the principles of its organization that will help us understand how it processes and integrates stimuli from a variety of inputs? How can it help us comprehend the development of a hierarchically organized structure that differentiates itself over time and that, in some optimal state, approaches what we call intelligent functioning? We also need to consider the range or definition of the stimulus world that this "developing intelligent structure" can accommodate to or process and how it develops relative resistance to stress. In addition, we need to understand how this structure develops in the context of constitutional, maturational, and experiential factors.

Level of Equilibrium and Intelligence

Let us first consider what we mean by intelligence in an integrated sense. What we mean by cognitive intelligence, at least in Piaget's sense, is clear. Its epitome is a cognitive structure characterized by an equilibrium state of a higher order than that of former structures. Piaget characterizes an equilibrium state by its field of application, mobility, permanence, and stability.

If we look at the adolescent, we see that, in terms of field application, he is capable of applying his intelligence to a wider variety of stimulus inputs than can younger children. The adolescent can consider hypothetical situations as well as real here-and-now situations. He can deal not only with what he can "concretely" observe and touch, but also with what he can imagine to be possible. In contrast, the latency child does not have the ability to think or use intelligence in terms of hypothetical possibilities and can only process what he can concretely observe.

In a similar way the preoperational, or prelatency, child is more advanced than the sensorimotor child. The sensorimotor child's field of application is restricted to things he can manipulate and act upon. Later, with the advent of the semiotic function, the child can represent things mentally and therefore can conduct operations on stimulus organizations that are not actually in front of him. Thus, the field of application widens from the sensorimotor period to the preoperational subperiod to the stage of concrete operations and, finally, to the period of formal operations.

Similarly, the adolescent has greater mobility in his cognitive capacities than he had in earlier developmental stages. Mobility in this sense is mobility in terms of time and space. Perhaps the greatest advance in mobility occurs at the time of the development of the semiotic function and the movement from the sensorimotor period to the preoperational subperiod. Once the youngster can represent things figuratively, he can perform cognitive operations on things that are not tangibly in the here-and-now and thus has greater mobility in terms of space; things do not have to be in front of him. There is also greater mobility in time in that things or events from the past can be remembered. The adolescent's mobility is enhanced even more in that he is not limited to past representations, but can also consider future representations and a wide range of probable possibilities. Thus, we can also see a hierarchy in terms of mobility.

Permanence and stability refer to the ability to maintain the permanence of particular stimuli or stimulus organizations and the stability of a particular system. This is best illustrated in Piaget's experiment with floating bodies. A young child will say a body sinks because it is light, but, if the experimental situation changes, he will turn around and say it sinks because it is heavy. There is no permanence to his perception of the qualities of weight in terms of sinking or floating. Similarly, when water is poured from a tall, narrow container into a short, wide container, the young child will claim that the quantity of water is less; that is, he cannot conserve the concept of quantity across the dimensions of height and width in terms of the concept of volume. When a youngster becomes capable of doing so, his capacity for conservation is greatly enhanced. As indicated earlier, these capacities are most highly developed in the formal operational period. A number of properties can then be varied simultaneously, yet the permanence of any one stimulus and the stability of the entire system can be maintained due to the ability to compensate and to see the multiple interrelationships among all the stimuli, or variables, within a system.

The capacities for permanence and stability grow in a hierarchical manner. In the sensorimotor period, the variables are relatively impermanent or unstable, depending on their presence in space and time. In the preoperational period, permanence and stability can be conserved in a figurative sense; that is, they can be represented, but will be altered as soon as there is any change in the system (magical thinking). In the period of concrete operations, there is some capacity for conserving the permanence of a variable and the stability of a system because of the ability to construct inverse and reciprocal relationships. However, because the inverse and reciprocal cannot both operate within one system during latency, this ability is limited. Thus, in the floating body experiment, the seven-year-old will claim a body floats because it is heavy and then say that it sinks because it is heavy. He will also claim that the volume of water has changed because the container has changed. He will, however, be able to operate in simpler two-variable systems. Dealing with a complex multivariant system, which can conserve both the permanence of a single variable and the interrelatedness of the whole system, must await the formal operational capacities of adolescence.

The period of formal operations is thus a higher-order equilibrium state in that it has advantages, in terms of field of application, mobility, permanence, and stability, over developmentally earlier equilibrium states. Another way to look at this is to view it as a system that is both whole and self-regulating in the context of a hierarchy of regulating principles.

According to Piaget, early in life psychological systems regulate themselves with basic rhythms. New stimuli are dealt with in this way. Later, feedback mechanisms are used; that is, movement in one direction can be corrected by feedback to movement in another direction. This modus operandi affords greater flexibility to deal with new stimuli, but is quite limited because perturbations in the system can be compensated for only over time, and then only over a narrow range. With the ability for concrete operational thinking, conceptual schemes are developed in which movement in one direction can be compensated for automatically and without time delay by movement in another direction (e.g., by addition and subtraction schemes). In other words, there is an integrated system for seeing relationships among variables (though carrying out problem solving based on this scheme may take time). This system reaches its ultimate capacity in formal operational thinking, when operations can be used for what in mathematical terms would be called multivaried analyses; that is, the relationships between a number of variables can be simultaneously conceptualized. Movements and compensations in a number of directions are possible simultaneously.

The highest-order system can conserve its own structure while assimilating the widest variety of stimulus input. In other words, the highest-order cognitive equilibrium level can accommodate to any new stimulus situation from the impersonal world without having to form a new accommodation. The system is whole and self-regulating. It does not need to call on principles external to itself to integrate new variables with existing variables. It does not need to change itself to accommodate to these new variables. The system, in this sense, approximates a perfect structure. Piaget's model is based on and closely related to the model of logical thinking. It is a model of impersonal intelligence.

The question to consider now is: What is the relevance of Piaget's model for intelligences that deals with interpersonal relationships, drives, affects, internalized representations, and psychological substructures? We know, for example, that a person can be brilliant in solving complex mathematical problems. On the other hand, the same person can appear to be "stupid" in dealing with feelings. The clever logician or physicist may appear to be quite dumb in thinking out the simplest problem of interpersonal relationship or in experiencing and knowing how to deal with certain kinds of feeling states. In this regard, it is interesting that Neil Miller, a well-known learning theorist who has attempted to portray neurosis in learning terms, calls neurotic behavior "stupid behavior" (Dollard and Miller, 1950).

The first step in developing a more integrated model of human learning is to see if we can apply the concepts of an equilibrium state, including field of application, mobility, permanence, and stability, to those variables that relate to what we call the internal boundary of the ego. In terms of field of application—that is, the variety of stimulus inputs—a more highly developed structure would be one that can assimilate, or take in, a variety of stimulus inputs from the internal boundary. In other words, a person with the highest-level field of application can assimilate and integrate a wide variety of wishes, prohibition, feelings, and thoughts in the context of age-appropriate interpersonal relationships.

We see restrictions in the field of application in encapsulated neurotic formations in which certain feelings or ideas are repressed and are not available to the synthetic and integrative functions of the ego. We may see, for example, such a restriction around a particular sexual or aggressive fantasy. In severe characterological constrictions we may see aspects of interpersonal relationships or more basic and general feeling states avoided (not assimilated). The schizoid person who avoids interpersonal relationships, for example, has a relatively narrow field of application. The person with a narcissistic character disorder, who cannot experience intimacy or loving feelings in any meaningful sense, may have a severe global constraint in the field of application. At an even more severe level, states of ego splitting, in which self- and object representations cannot be integrated within one system, demonstrate a major limitation in the field of application; the psychological structure cannot assimilate loving and hating feelings in the context of the same interpersonal relationship. A most severe case of restriction in the field of application is seen in total autistic withdrawal, in which all external reality is avoided.

In terms of field of application we can therefore see a certain parallel between Piaget's application of his concept to the impersonal world and how we might apply it to the interpersonal and internal world. The broader, or more encompassing, the field of application in the context of age-appropriate developmental expectations, the higher the level of emotional intelligence. It should be pointed out that an immature, polymorphously perverse person does not have a wide field of application even though he may claim great freedom. Such a person is usually not capable of "genital" sexuality in its broadest meaning (i.e., intimate relationships) and is unable truly to integrate a seemingly wide array of impulses, which are often a cover or defense for a few, basic, developmentally early wishes.

Mobility in time and space is the second dimension Piaget considers. Here, too, there is a parallel with the internal boundary. The emotionally mature or "intelligent" person can assimilate derivatives of conscious and unconscious psychological structures in terms of feelings and thoughts from the past and the present, as well as those anticipating the future. He can consider not only feelings and thoughts derived from experiences close in space, but also representations of those not available in immediate space. This process of mobility in time and space is perhaps best illustrated by the analysand who achieves greater synthetic and integrative capacities through the psychoanalytic process. One of the main achievements of analysis is the development of psychological structures that attain a high degree of integration in the context of continuity over time and space. Through the process of regression and transference, early experiences that may have been repressed or integrated in other ways can be reintegrated with current psychological structures, thereby providing the patient with continuity of self over time. Formerly discrepant aspects of self- and object representations are integrated and afford the patient a broader, deeper range of feelings and interpersonal capacity, which emerge in dealing with both himself and with others. Mobility is limited in certain pathological states—for example, in encapsulated neurotic configurations in which aspects of the past are repressed. Further restrictions are evidenced by the severe repressive barriers in character constrictions and the even more severe walling-off in states of ego splitting and fragmentation or total withdrawal.

The permanence and stability of psychological structures also have dimensions parallel to cognitive structures. If we shift our focus from the weight or volume of an object to the permanence of a feeling such as anger or love, we can see how the psychologically intelligent person can maintain the permanence of a feeling state even when a situation is changed. For example, a feeling of love may still exist even with the introduction of frustration into an interpersonal situation. Although the person feels frustrated and temporarily angry, his more basic state of feeling toward the other person will remain. He will not perceive the other person as having changed and suddenly become a different person, a phenomenon we observe in young children who have not yet integrated the good and bad object and in borderline psychotic patients who have split objects. Thus, in the emotionally mature person, we find a sense of permanence to feelings as they are attached to both internal representations and currently important persons.

The concept of stability is perhaps best exemplified by the psychologically intelligent person's ability to conserve a system of self-representations in the face of new elements that would tend to disturb that system. Just as the cognitively mature person can conserve the integrity of a volume of water even when it is poured into different-sized containers, so the psychologically mature person can maintain his representation of himself even when there are perturbations in the system because of rage, frustration, anger, envy, or "unacceptable" impulses.

Clinically, we may compare the person who suddenly feels derealized or depersonalized when unacceptable impulses become too strong with the person who maintains or conserves a sense of self even under the pressure of strong states of affect or unacceptable impulses. Again, there is a relative hierarchy in the limitations and the abilities to conserve an integrated sense of self, from mild and vague experiences of depersonalization and derealization, to more severe experiences of ego splitting, to extreme experiences of fragmentation. We see persons who maintain or conserve a sense of self in the face of intense frustration or extreme deprivation of need satisfaction. While everyone may have his "breaking point," in some the resilience to stress is much greater than in others.

At times, we see mild, limited alterations in an attempt to maintain a stable system, such as the self system. Here we refer to minor distortions with certain kinds of perturbations. The pressure of certain drive-affect upheavals, for instance, may lead to neurotic encapsulations that distort the continuity of self *over time.* Thus, the system does not conserve itself completely. More major distortions would be the characterological constrictions in which certain aspects of the self are denied, such as anger. Even more major would be cases of ego splitting and fragmentation. We find a continuum from minor alterations in one's picture of one's life history, to more major alterations in one's connection to certain basic feeling states, to major alterations in one's capacity for interpersonal relationships and ability to integrate basic feeling states within oneself and toward others, to total inability for integration, with concomitant fragmentation.

Thus far we have considered some of the structural characteristics of an integrated psychoanalytic model of intelligence or cognition. The construct *equilibrium state,* with its characteristics of field of application, mobility, permanence, and stability, has been used to conceptualize the relationship of internal structures not only to impersonal external stimuli, but also to the internal boundary, or the emotional world. The characteristics of the most advanced equilibrium states have been described, and the similarity, or symmetry, between the most advanced states for emotional intelligence and impersonal intelligence have been characterized. We shall now examine the development of the highest-order equilibrium state, which characterizes the highest-order structures from a developmental perspective.

Structures Characterized by High-Order Equilibrium States in a Developmental Context

During the early stages of development—the sensorimotor period cognitively, pre-object constancy in the affective sphere—a certain type of emotional intelligence gradually evolves. As as postulated earlier, the intelligence developed during this time is similar for both the emotional and the nonemotional, or impersonal, spheres. Initially, the infant is relatively undifferentiated and simple reflexes slowly coordinate into secondary and tertiary circular reactions, followed by the establishment and then differentiation of means-ends relationships. In terms of emotional life, the infant first reaches homeostasis in a relatively undifferentiated manner—by shutting out stimulation or direct discharge. Following this, the infant becomes capable of more complex processes of avoiding pain and seeking pleasure, such as mutual cueing responses with the mother or using substitutes for mother. As human means-ends relationships and their differentiation are established in the context of primitive drive-affect states, there is further growth in the capacity to use intermediary devices. In terms of the external impersonal world, the infant can now pull a rug toward himself to reach something he wants on it. In relation to emotional life, he is now able to use not only substitutes but true intermediaries, internal precursors of what will later be internal representations (e.g., imitative behavior).

In summary, we see a gradual growth from simple reflex actions to perception of means-ends relationships and their differentiation. From an undifferentiated egocentric state, the infant evolves a relationship to both his internal and external worlds and is eventually able to use detours in the context of differentiation of means from ends. Accompanying these developments is a greater capacity to deal with both the impersonal external world and the emotional internal world. The capacity for more organized internal representation finally emerges toward the end of this first stage of development.

During the initial stages of development, the major device the infant has for reaching a state of equilibrium is rhythmical experience and this governs much of his internal life. The basic rhythms that exist during the earliest part of the first year—sleep-wake rhythms, movement patterns, etc.—gradually give way to the use of feedback mechanisms to establish states of homeostasis (to compensate or correct the system). During this early phase of life the infant does not learn in the adult sense. He is protected in terms of his basic rhythms, which guarantee a certain adaptiveness to the environment. This innate rhythmic capacity may be viewed as the most preliminary form of intelligence in both the impersonal and the emotional realms. As he gets on in his first year and into his second year, however, the infant begins to learn, through feedback, what will bring a greater state of pleasurable equilibrium.

Feedback is initially best illustrated by the mutual cueing responses. The infant learns which response on his part elicits the kind of response he finds pleasurable from his mother, and so forth. The use of feedback becomes more complicated as the infant learns to relate to his internal milieu as well as to his interpersonal and impersonal external worlds. While learning by feedback can be understood in operant learning terms (pleasurable consequences tend to increase the responses upon which they are contingent) it should also be seen in terms of the infant's initial schemes for understanding the internal milieu as well as the external impersonal and interpersonal milieus.

Feedback schemes are simple schemes in which movement in one direction can be compensated for by movement in the opposite direction over the same terrain (similar to a thermostat mechanism). Feedback regulation in a simple sense does not permit simultaneous alterations in a system to compensate for perturbations. The system goes first in one direction, then in another. Although a feedback system provides more flexibility than a rhythm-based system, it still cannot accommodate a wide variety of input simultaneously and maintain a constant state of equilibrium.

The clinical parallel is observed in cases of primitive defenses based on ego splitting. One state is experienced and then another, in contrast to more advanced psychological systems which can integrate and compensate for a number of diverse feelings simultaneously. It is as though a person walks down one road, then back, retracing his steps, and only then goes down another road. He does not have an internalized image of the entire terrain. In states of ego splitting, a person experiences one aspect of the self as distinct and separate from other aspects of self. He does not have an organization of self that integrates, via an internalized map, the entire extent of his internal world. Although such schemes are hypothetical constructs, they form the basis for an evolving model of intelligence based on internal structures (which are another way of conceptualizing the transformational principles governing intelligent behavior).

Before considering the next stage of development, it should be clear that in early life the level of equilibrium possible in relation to both the internal emotional world and the interpersonal and impersonal worlds is relatively limited because of the infant's dependence first on basic rhythms, then on basic feedback mechanisms. In other words, the infant's capacity for equilibrium is highly dependent on external conditions. There is little in the way of internal structure, and that little is related to very primitive schemes.

With regard to the four characteristics of an equilibrium state, we have already seen that the infant is very limited. In terms of field of application, he is initially restricted to what he can experience directly with his sensory modalities. Toward the end of the second year of his life, with the capacity for imitation and the beginnings of the capacity for representation, he broadens his field of application to that with which he is not in direct sensory contact. In terms of mobility he is constrained to what is directly tangible; only toward the end of the second year is the capacity for memory and moving back and forth in time possible. Permanence and stability during this period are quite limited and are dependent on repetitive contact in both the interpersonal and impersonal worlds. Gradually, over time, some simple schemes are laid down through repetitive assimilation. The concept of the permanent object is just beginning to be established in the second year of life. While it becomes relatively established in relation to the inanimate world, it is more vulnerable in terms of the inner and interpersonal worlds. The capacity for organized internal representations of the human object begins toward the end of the second year, but remains highly dependent on the continued re-experiencing of the human object. Thus, in terms of the four characteristics—field of application, mobility, permanence, and stability—the equilibrium state of the young infant reflects a very low level of intelligence.

In the next phase of development from approximately age two to age four (the preoperational phase cognitively and the remaining preoedipal and beginning oedipal phases of development in the affective realm), we see the development of what Piaget calls the semiotic function, the capacity for figurative thinking. The capacity for figurative thinking vastly expands the child's universe in terms of the field of application. He now can deal not only with those aspects of his external world that are experienced through his immediate sensory modalities, but also with those that are not present but are represented. In terms of his internal world, he can begin to represent aspects of drives and affects, as well as events in the interpersonal, emotion-laden external world. The capacity for constructing combinations—that is, the ability to combine schemes in new and imaginative ways—which appears at the end of the sensorimotor period, is evident in the rich and complex imagery of the young toddler. Language acquisition, which is in part based on the capacity for representation, further enriches this capacity for figurative thinking. In terms of field of application, the youngster can now deal with a variety of stimuli.

Mobility in time and space is also enhanced. As has been mentioned, the capacity for memory appears during this period. The youngster can not only deal with what is not immediately present to him in terms of figuratively represented stimuli from inside and outside, but can also represent events from the past, and thus can begin to move between past and present.

As for permanence and stability, the ability to represent things is a major advance from the sensorimotor period, when internal events, such as drive derivatives and affects from the interior of the body, were experienced mentally only as transient sensations and could not be represented in any organized, stable manner. Interpersonal relationships were also, relatively speaking, more dependent on their actual presence. The youngster's world is now more permanent and stable in that what is not immediately felt in the present can still be there through the figurative capacity, and events from the past can be partially conserved. Thus, the new capacity for figurative thinking, which develops during the preoperational subperiod, represents a higher-order equilibrium state than that of the sensorimotor period.

It is important, however, to highlight the vertical *décalage* discussed earlier. Piaget uses this term to describe the process that occurs when a child who has achieved a degree of accomplishment in terms of sensorimotor logic—for example, establishing causal relationships in initial means-ends schemes—experiences a regression to magical thinking. In the sensorimotor period, the infant may put a few initial reaction patterns together but then employ them in a "magical" manner—for example, pulling a string when there is no bell attached, or even pulling at the air when there is no string. Similarly, at the level of figurative thinking, the preoperational child shows the capacity for magical thinking. There is no established logic or causal relatedness to the way in which he puts together his internal representations. He maintains his ability for sensorimotor logic; that is, at the level of action patterns, he can deal with his world in a reasonably effective way. Much of the figurative thinking of young children, however, remains on a magical level, as has been described by both Piaget and, in rather similar terms, by psychodynamic observers.

The capacity for testing reality develops slowly during this period; the child must still experiment with the world, as he did during the sensorimotor period. Earlier, however, he dealt with the world through physical action on the environment; now he does so with his new figurative capacities. With these new capacities the child in essence must "learn" all over again how to differentiate means from ends. The means-ends relationship is now developed at the level of internal representations. This process, which we commonly call secondary-process thinking, slowly evolves in a fashion similar to the way in which the child experimented with his world and learned causal relationships in sensorimotor action patterns. The important milestones in logical thinking, however, are reached only in later stages of development: concrete operations and formal operations. Suffice it to say here that during this period there is an increase in the level of intelligence because of the further development of the capacity for figurative thinking and its application to both the internal and external worlds.

Earlier we discussed the integration of dynamic constructs with Piaget's constructs for this period. We covered some of the child's tasks in the emotional realm that lead to libidinal object constancy, and highlighted the importance of the child's internal world and his interpersonal relationships for achieving and integrating his cognitive capacities at the internal boundary. We shall not repeat that discussion here except to present a few examples of the youngster's enhanced intelligence at this stage.

The youngster has greater variability in how he handles drive derivatives. He can now represent them; there are possibilities for new combinations, intermediary symbols, condensations, displacements, etc. The concept of libidinal object constancy perhaps best illustrates the enhanced adaptive potential or the "greater" emotional intelligence of this stage of development, particularly in terms of the permanence and stability of an equilibrium state. Around age three, according to Mahler (Mahler, Pine, and Bergman, 1975) and other observers, the young child can hold a constant representation of himself and of the primary mothering figure. These representations are independent of each other yet constant, even in the context of changing states of internal drives and affects (e.g., hunger, anger) and an altering external world (e.g., short separations or disapproval from important persons).

While the adaptive gains of this period of development are considerable, and therefore constitute an advance in emotional intelligence, there are still considerable limitations in emotional intelligence. The youngster learns to represent things and eventually to differentiate means from ends; he thereby develops an ability to perceive the boundary between his internal self and that which is external to him and thus to perceive things as they actually are in reality. Nevertheless, he is limited in his flexibility in dealing with external and internal sets of stimuli. Although he can maintain his representations even in the face of a storm of impulses or affects or changing external situations, he can maintain the integrity of his figurative capacity only to a certain point. There are no "interiorized" transformational options that give the system the flexibility to handle a wide variety of stimuli past a certain point of intensity and ambiguity. Therefore, in certain situations, the child during this stage of development uses primitive defenses, such as projection, incorporation, denial, and avoidance. At times of pressure these defenses distort his ability to perceive aspects of either internal or external reality. The ability to be in touch with the wide variety of elements of internal reality may be further compromised by such mechanisms as ego splitting, in which whole groupings of internal events are temporarily denied while other groupings are experienced.

As we have seen, regression to more "magical" or less differentiated means-ends thinking also characterizes this stage. The youngster does not have organized internal transformational structures to modulate his internal or external world and thus add flexibility to his structure. In a sense, while new assimilations throughout the course of development lead to new accommodations and therefore to further structure building, in each stage of development the structure of the psychic equipment is such that if the aliments to be assimilated are over a certain quantitative or qualitative threshold in terms of their dynamic meaning, the accommodations that occur will be regressive. That is, there is a change in the structure to deal with the aliments to be assimilated, but the change is a regressive one, as in ego splitting or dedifferentiation of means from ends. The use of the word *accommodation* here may not be appropriate, because although the structure is accommodating to the new aliment, the integrity of the structure is being compromised in order to maintain a state of emotional equilibrium. The structure functions at a "lower level of intelligence" in terms of its field of application, mobility, permanence, and stability.

The reason for the limitation in flexibility of the internal structure, even with the addition of the semiotic function, is that the basic regulatory mechanism is still out of feedback. The youngster, in order to test out relationships, still needs to experiment on the actual environment in order to deduce conclusions about reality. The child in this phase of development will experiment through trial and error or empirical testing to see a relationship between two external variables. In a similar manner, he is still somewhat dependent on feedback to maintain his picture of his internal world in terms of wishes and affects. In other words, in order to compensate for movement in one direction, he must, either through fantasy or real events, move in another direction. If he is angry at a sibling and wants to undo this feeling, he will need to do something nice to the sibling to get back to his starting point. In fact, the defense of "undoing" is prevalent during this period of development, as the youngster is still dependent on feedback loops to maintain an equilibrium state. These feedback loops are not connected by transformational principles, and there is therefore relative isolation, or "splitting," between the states of being that compensate for each other. The phase of concrete operations, the first step in the attainment of formal operational thinking, is yet to come.

An operation, as stated earlier, is an *action* that is interiorized, reversible, and part of an organized system. The capacity for operations adds considerable flexibility to internal structures, thus enhancing their field of application, mobility, permanence, and stability. In what Piaget calls the concrete operational period, logical operations make their first appearance, but during this period they apply only to the concrete or real. (Later, in adolescence, they will apply to hypothetical objects.) Operational thinking is marked by an increased capacity for conservation, which enables a youngster to hold certain values invariant through the process of transformation. Since earlier actions have become interiorized, the child no longer needs to perform actions on concrete objects in an empirical fashion. He can deduce certain conclusions about classes and operations with logical certitude. In general, he can understand relationships among objects and elements as transformations leading to certain changes.

The concrete operations are subdivided into those that deal with classes of objects and those that deal with relationships among objects. In the former category, every operation has an inverse as its form of reversibility. In the latter category, every operation has a reciprocal. Thus, if the subclass *A* is added to *A′* to construct the supraordinate class *B*, the process can be reversed by subtracting *A* from *B* (inversion). If the relationship between *P* and *R* is such that in the dimension of length *P* is greater than *R*, any difference in area can be nullified if in the dimension of width *P* is proportionately less than *R* (reciprocity).

This capacity for conducting concrete operations—that is, for conducting internal mental experiments to understand relationships between sets of variables—is a significant advance over the simple capacity for figurative thinking. The youngster no longer needs to test empirically his hypotheses about the external world through trial and error and therefore is not dependent solely on feedback. He has organized schemes within which he can simultaneously and almost automatically see the relationships between sets of variables.

In an oversimplified, metaphorical sense, we might view the significant difference in the flexibility of the structures the child now has to deal with his impersonal, external world and his internal and interpersonal affect-laden worlds as follows. The child early develops the ability to organize a picture of reality, that is, to represent objects. But to see logical relationships among his pictures of reality—both imaginary or subjective reality and external or objective reality—he has to conduct empirical experiments (trial and error). When he is finished, he does not necessarily retain or generalize the results of his experiments (this depends on the complexity of the relationships). He does, however, have a capacity to combine mental pictures—not according to adult logic, but according to magical, primary-process thinking.

With the capacity for interiorized operations, it is as though he has an internal roadmap on which some logical relationships are constructed. Instead of being the proverbial mouse going through a maze in a trial-and-error fashion, the youngster can now draw a conceptual map, although it is limited to relationships among certain sets of variables—inverse or reciprocal relationships. In any case, the child can now construct relationships based on an interiorized system. If, for example, the child has the interiorized system of the inverse, he does not need to move a car in one direction and then back in the opposite direction to see if he can compensate for movements in one direction by movements in the other. Simply by *seeing* the car and the track, he immediately knows that he can move it in both directions. He has the scheme for understanding the relationship between movements forward and backward and how they compensate for one another. Similarly, in terms of reciprocal relationships, he can see how a change in the length of a rectangle may be compensated for by a change in its width (this occurs a little later in the concrete operational period).

These relationships are perceived because there are interiorized schemes for them as part of a mental structure. In terms of his internal emotional world, a child no longer needs to undo an angry act toward a sibling with a nice act; that is, he does not need to experiment repeatedly and empirically to get back to his beginning point or to re-establish equilibrium. He can fantasize about anger and niceness simultaneously within one system. He has a sense that these two variables can compensate for each other and that they can be part of a complicated system of relationships and feelings.

Similarly, the concrete operational child can perceive slight gradations between feelings in one direction and reciprocal feelings in another direction. This capacity was spelled out in some detail in the section relating cognitive development to the dynamic perspective. We looked at how the schemes, or structures, for classes derived from the capacity for inverse relationships and how the schemes, or structures, for transitive relationships derived from the capacity for reciprocal relationships. The implications of concrete operational capacities for structural flexibility were illustrated in terms of our understanding of defensive and adaptive ego functions: the ability to conserve the integrity of self- and object representations in the face of a variety of wishes and affects as well as changing external states, and to deal with and discriminate various classes and groups of stimuli arising from both the inside and the outside.

The relevance of these new structural capacities to a youngster's immersion in and appreciation and resolution of the oedipal situation has already been discussed. In a most general sense, the capacity for forming inverse and reciprocal relationships and the derivative capacities for doing classification and seriation tasks increase the flexibility of the internal processing structure sufficiently to permit the simultaneous processing of multiple groups of internal and external variables. The ability to perceive and process triangular object relations, in contrast to only dyadic relations, is thus derived from the concrete operational capacity. Similarly, the use of the defense of reaction formation is based on construction of the inverse and beginning rationalizations on construction of reciprocal relationships. The increased capacity for sublimation develops from the ability to construct multiple detours or intermediary steps, facilitating the process of neutralization.

The ego's synthetic and integrative functions are enhanced by the concrete operational capacities. A sense of constancy is facilitated by the capacity to group together self- and object representations as part of the ego structure and the developing superego structure. Putting the emerging sense of self and the beginning formations of large clusters of self- and object representations into an organization that integrates them and provides for a feeling of sameness of self (a precursor of identity formation) is based on these capacities for constructing complex relationships between formerly disparate sets of variables.

While the smooth interworkings of all the pieces of the personality have been described in terms of the synthetic workings of the ego, in this particular phase of development we can see clearly what we earlier referred to as an enhanced synthetic capacity. We can describe it specifically in terms of structural operations based on two delineated capacities: the capacity for constructing the schemes for the inverse and the reciprocal, and the derivative capacities for classification and seriation.

As indicated earlier, throughout the course of latency the capacity to interrelate groups of variables increases. Toward the end of latency we find the capacity to construct a multiple classification table. Since psychological life exists in the context of past, present, and future, and in the face of multiple wishes, feelings, fears, and concerns, the late latency child can begin to relate past and present in the context of dynamically relevant variables (feelings, wishes, internal substructures). The ability of the late latency child to perceive connections between the past and the present and to perceive the multiple interrelationships between the different parts of his personality has already been described. What is important to emphasize is that the operations for the inverse and reciprocal, which make possible the construction of multiple classification tables at the external boundary and the interrelating of groups of variables at the internal boundary, allow the youngster greater emotional flexibility and greater emotional intelligence.

In the formal language of our model of equilibrium states, the capacity for concrete operations provides significant advantages over earlier states in the field of application, mobility, permanence, and stability. The child can conduct various logical experimental actions internally and represent relationships in terms of operations. This capacity enables him to deal with a wide range of external and internal states that are not immediately present. In comparison with the younger child, who needed to use such basic defenses as avoidance, ego splitting, and denial, the latency child can hold in mind opposite polarities (even when he must use defenses such as reaction formation). The feeling states of love and hate are part of one organized system, not split off from one another. Repression supported by reaction formation represents part of an organized system rather than two separate systems, as ego splitting does. The combination of groups of defenses, such as reaction formations with rationalizations, indicates the structural advance of the latency child over the younger child. In terms of mobility, a number of impulses and feeling states can be combined and integrated over time. The capacity to conserve more effectively, illustrated at the external boundary by the ability to conserve quantities of water, is evident at the internal boundary in the ability to conserve self- and object representations. Splitting is not necessary because alterations of impulses and affects by interiorized operations—inverses (reaction formations) and reciprocals (rationalizations)—can protect the ego. More important, however, the permanence and stability of self- and object representations are enhanced because of the capacity for making a greater number of connections between what were earlier perceived as disparate elements (e.g., love and hate).

The superego structure becomes organized at the beginning of latency and achieves further organization throughout latency. It is interesting to note that the infantile neurosis, as described by Nagera (1966), is an organized, integrated structure that, in a highly economic, condensed fashion, brings together experiences from the preoedipal period with phallic-oedipal experiences under the umbrella of triangular object relations. As the initial adaptive neurotic structure of the personality, it is in a sense parallel to our description of the capacity for concrete operations as the first "real" organized structure. The structure providing the basis for the infantile neurosis becomes further elaborated with consolidation of the superego at the end of the oedipal situation in latency and during subsequent developmental stages. We see a similar path in terms of the organization of emotional intelligence.

In a way, we have here a specific explanation of why it becomes possible, from the perspective of equilibrium states, for the child to develop the infantile neurosis and a consolidated superego structure during this period of development. The capacity for organizing inverse and reciprocal relationships and its derivative cognitive capacities provide the structural flexibility to begin integrating various aspects of the personality. Nagera's (1966) description of the infantile neurosis implies a highly complex, tightly integrated neurotic structure, which provides a type of cohesion to the personality and therefore represents a developmental adaptation as well as the foundation for later neurosis. The integration involving the consolidation of the superego structure at the end of the oedipal period, which gets refined during latency, also indicates a highly condensed, tighly woven structure based on, or explained in part by, the evolving concrete operational capacity characterizing this stage of development.

In a general sense, this structure has a wider field of application, greater mobility, and a higher degree of permanence and stability than the earlier structure had, based on the figurative capacity alone. The capacity for internal representation is now enhanced by a capacity for interiorized operations that connect groupings or sets of variables along the dimensions of the inverse and reciprocal—that is, a capacity for synthetic activity. It is important to note, however, that in this phase not only are the variables that can be seen in relation to one another limited (e.g., the construction of a multiple classification table), but also they are real and concrete, in the sense that they represent the real "imagined" world or internal world.

As indicated earlier, not being able to deal with hypothetical situations or possibilities, but only with operations on the real, limits the flexibility of the concrete operational structure. In terms of the internal boundary, certain feelings, when experienced as real, are experienced as immediate and probable. They therefore stimulate anxiety and/or other frightening affects, leading to the strict repression often observed at this stage. Access to unconscious material is limited, and repression is reinforced by simple latency-age defenses, such as reaction formations, simple rationalizations, denials, isolation of affects, and the developmentally earlier defenses of projection and displacement. (These defenses are well within the cognitive capacities to construct the inverse and reciprocal; these capacities, in fact, offer a way to organize our conceptualization of these defenses and explain their existence at this time.)

The lack of capacity for hypothetical thinking makes it difficult to have greater access to a variety of feelings and drive derivatives. If one cannot imagine possibilities, what is experienced seems highly probable and real; therefore, to avoid overwhelming fear and anxiety, continuity with the unconscious and past is sacrificed. Thus, although this structure is flexible and therefore "more intelligent" compared with earlier structures, it still leaves a great deal to be desired.

The next stage of development, described by Piaget as the period of formal operations, includes two important advances: the capacity for hypothetical thinking and the capacity for constructing a system that involves not only the inverse and reciprocal, but the inverse and reciprocal in a system of relationship to one another. The inverse, the reciprocal, and the inverse of the reciprocal create a mathematical set that allows for a system within which a wide-ranging group of variables can be related to one another. Thus, compared with the latency child, who can draw up a table relating only certain variables to one another, the adolescent can solve a problem with many sets of variables. This difference was illustrated earlier with the rod and weight experiment, as well as the one involving the changing color of a fluid.

The adolescent's capacity for hypothetical thinking, his ability to think in terms of the probable, frees him from the frightening nature of feelings, fears, and wishes. A particular feeling or impulse is now one possibility among many, as opposed to the real and only one. The consequences of aggression, sexuality, and other such matters can be thought about in hypothetical ways. The adolescent's capacity for hypothetical thinking is most clearly seen in his consideration of future possibilities, which plays an important role in the consolidation of the ego ideal.

In addition to the increased distance probalistic thinking affords the adolescent from the frightening nature of impulses, the ability to interrelate and solve problems involving a wide range of variables makes it possible for him to integrate and synthesize a variety of discordant elements. In terms of the internal boundary, unconscious wishes, fears, affects, and self- and object representations can be integrated from different developmental levels with substructures of the ego and with the newly emerging ego ideal and aspects of the superego into a cohesive structure (identity formation).

It has been long recognized that during this period of development (mainly toward the end of it), an individual consolidates an integrated and organized representation of himself in relation to his past, present, and future. This organization involves groupings of self- and object representations in the context of past history, present reality, future expectations, and ideals. To repeat: the capacity for complex transformations makes it possible to integrate a wide variety of variables, including many discordant ones—for example, loving and hating feelings toward the same person, different perceptions of self from different developmental levels, widely varying expectations for the future. The degree to which discordant elements can be synthesized is an indication of the flexibility of the system.

Clinically, in patients who have not achieved this highest equilibrium state, we see limitations in their ability to synthesize or integrate discordant elements. Ego splitting and fragmentation indicate the most severe inability for integration (this is different from a shifting but basically integrated identity). Less severe are characterological constrictions in which certain avenues of endeavor are given up. In order to maintain the integrity of identity, certain spheres of feeling and thought or areas of endeavor are relinquished because the issues and conflicts pertaining to them cannot be integrated within a cohesive organization. In the severely narcissistic person, for example, intimacy is foregone. In other cases, certain adult sexual activities may be relinquished. In still others, successful competitive activities are given up. The most subtle examples involve neurotic configurations in which there are encapsulated limitations (e.g., in availability of certain memories and affects) in an otherwise well-synthesized, organized structure, as well as some symptoms that may limit behavioral flexibility (e.g., phobias).

As we have seen, the structural characteristics that make this a higher equilibrium state of emotional intelligence than prior states are the capacities for probablistic or hypothetical thinking and the capacities for including the inverse, reciprocal, and correlative together in a system. It is now possible to integrate within one system, or structure, an infinite number of variables—to conduct a multivaried analysis, so to speak. A system with the inverse, reciprocal, and correlative constitutes a mathematical grouping, or set, which is constructed so that as the number of variables increases the transformational possibilities of the system increase in such a way that the total structure can deal with and integrate an infinite number of variables.

This logico-mathematical model operates to some degree at the external boundary, although there are limitations (the capacity for impersonal cognition has been extended by use of computers). At the internal boundary this ideal capacity obviously is never fully reached, but it is an extreme that provides a measure of the relative potential attainment for this period of development.

The advances of formal operations, which enable, for example, the solution of the floating body problem, suggest that not only can many variables be interrelated, but that variables can be interrelated to solve a problem at the internal boundary.

What is being emphasized here is that the person with formal operations is not simply a computer that can do multiple correlations. The structure can find a human solution. The interacting variables exist in the context of evolving human experience, which sets guidelines and selects answers and solutions that fit the personal history of the individual. Thus, the variables are not simply put in multiple correlation with one another, but are interrelated according to certain "equations," which are the patterns in the individual's life history.

The capacity for combinatorial thinking in an optimal sense makes it possible to bring together into one cohesive system a large variety of discordant elements from past and present, as well as anticipations of the future. The system can assimilate a wide range of changing inputs and states without making major new accommodations; that is, there can be a relatively stable identity. It is worth emphasizing again what makes this identity possible. The system, having the option of an infinite number of multiple correlations, allows for the section of those variables that fit with other variables to constitute a cohesive identity.

Variables do not need to be ignored, but they can be seen in varied relationships to other variables. Thus, it is not a question of simply loving or having a reaction formation against loving, or hating and having a reaction formation against hating, as may be true for a latency child. Rather, the system can accommodate relationships on many levels and include subtle shadings. Derivatives from drives, affects, and self- and object representations can be organized around themes in a hierarchical manner, with varying degrees of consciousness and weighted degrees of relevance to a particular evolving human experience. The optimally developed adolescent, in consolidating his identity, can select from variables (e.g., experiences in terms of drive-affect constellations) attached to early experiences and early self- and object representations, as well as later experiences, and choose those that can be best integrated with his current experience in the light of his anticipation of the future.

The important advantage for "emotional intelligence" in terms of adaptation is that in having an interconnected system, the individual (ideally) has access to all his prior experiences and can now integrate them with his present and future in a way that makes sense. Earlier in development his cognitive structures were more limited; he did not have full access to an infinite number of variables and thus did not have the selective potential he now has for forming this organized system. In other words, when the inverse and reciprocal exist separately, as in latency, there are only sixteen possibilities for dealing with two sets of variables, or, we could say, two feeling states. If three or four feeling states are added, instead of increasing the number of possibilities, they reduce them. There are only a few ways in which four different feeling states can be synthesized. If the feeling states are very different and discordant, the only way to synthesize them is through use of primitive mechanisms; in many cases they cannot be synthesized and thus a lack of integration occurs (defensive distortions, repression, or ego splitting and fragmentation).

Perhaps an analogy is appropriate. Take a talented sculptor who molds a human figure with every conceivable option for shaping the limbs, the head, and the torso as he wishes. He can create an infinite number of lines and curves and shapes moving into other lines and curves and shapes, all of which he integrates into his finished form, representing the best that the infinite variety he is capable of can bring to it. Compare this with the child who can only form triangles and squares. What he is capable of sculpting will be much less rich and varied than the potential product of someone who can use triangles and squares plus all other angles, curves, etc. Similarly, the person with the combinatorial capacity can sculpt a sense of self using an infinite number of possibilities.

As before, we are referring to a hypothetical ideal. In reality, of course, how the finished sculpture is shaped is determined largely by dynamic issues. In a cognitive sense, a person may have access to an infinite number of possibilities, but from an emotional point of view he is limited by dynamic considerations. Although the possibilities open to him are relatively greater during this period because of his cognitive potential, they are limited by the unique dynamic and emotional considerations pertinent to his life history. Similarly, the degree to which he has access to all prior life experiences will be determined largely by dynamic and emotional issues. Obviously, certain sets of early experiences will be dynamically loaded, others more heavily defended, etc. In addition, the options available to him to shape these experiences—the flexibility of his sculpting skill—are also the product of his prior experiences and thus are limited by dynamic considerations. Even with these relative limitations, however, the cognitive capacity of this phase of development yields greater potential under optimal circumstances of development than did earlier capacities.

If we look at our model as an ideal model—one that is not necessarily characteristic of human functioning, yet one within which we can learn about the way to view human functioning—it helps us to assess optimal emotional intelligence. To the degree that this multiple combinatorial capacity is reached, an optimal state of emotional intelligence may be reached. That is, the more mature, more emotionally healthy and intelligent individual has greater access to his sense of person over time. He can shape his sense of self in terms of his identity, by assimilating those aspects of his "self" that have dynamic meaning for him. He has a method and style of sculpting that can integrate elements with a minimum of compromise, constriction, splitting, or fragmenting. This formulation is not dissimilar to the description of infantile neurosis given by Nagera (1966), who refers to a highly economic, condensed structure. However, although for some this structure condenses in an economic and adaptive manner, for others the condensation is economic but not adaptive in the context of a hierarchy of human adaptation.

If we consider the characteristics of an equilibrium state—the field of application, mobility, permanence, and stability—in terms of the capacity for probablistic and combinatorial thinking, we can see that the eqilibrium state of the adolescent is of a higher order than that of the latency child. The field of application of the formal operational or adolescent period is greater, as the adolescent can consider not only real feelings, but also hypothetical ones and anticipations of the future. There is greater access to early experiences and to a wide variety of feeling states because of the ability to put them in a probablistic context. The permanence and stability of structures are greater in the sense that greater conservation is possible when a large number of variables as well as changing conditions can be integrated within one system without making new accommodations. The mathematical grouping or set made possible by including the inverse, reciprocal, and correlative together in one system increases the flexibility to conserve over that provided by the use of only the inverse or only the reciprocal, as was true for latency-type thinking. The system can conserve any element within it (e.g., a particular feeling of love), as well as maintain the integrity of the system even in the face of perturbations (e.g., feelings of hate), because it can assimilate new elements without making new accommodations. The equilibrium state of this level of development is thus of a higher level of intelligence.

As we have seen, the characteristics of an equilibrum state can help us delineate emotional intelligence as well as cognitive intelligence. A system, or structure, is at a higher equilibrium state in terms of emotional intelligence if its field of application is broader, its mobility greater, and its capacity for permanence and stability greater, particularly in the face of a greater variety of potential perturbations in the system.

In the next section we shall discuss a model of general intelligence in relation to internal boundary variables. Before doing so, however, a brief review is in order. At the internal boundary the field of application in the first year of life is limited to what can be experienced in interpersonal affective relationships or in stimuli arising from within the body. These aliments are assimilated, and basic accommodations are made in beginning psychological structures. The field of application is limited, however, because the lack of capacity for differentiation and for representation (figurative capacity) restricts what is actually experienced. Mobility is similarly limited to the here-and-now, and permanence and stability are highly variable; that is, feeling states, the sense of self and of other, and the beginning organizations, or structure, change with changing situations. Nevertheless, through experiences with the interpersonal world and repetitive experiences with internal drive-affect states, beginning psychological structures attain some relative permanence and stability. There is also an increase in the field of application and mobility at the level of repetitive, rhythmic action patterns. However, until the child has the capacity for figurative thinking—the semiotic function—all these advances are quite limited. Simple rhythms and then feedback mechanisms are used to bring the psychological system into states of emotional equilibrium. Such states usually take time to occur, and the infant is not able really to conserve a system in the face of perturbations. Strong feeling states, external stress, frustration, and change are not easily tolerated. Even the more advanced feedback method of attaining equilibrum involves moving in one direction and then returning to the starting point before moving in another direction. In psychoanalytic terms, using feedback is consistent with the splitting of representations (e.g., behaving angrily and then nicely); there are two separate states rather than an integrated system. The defenses of this period support these observations; avoidance, shutting down, denial, splitting of objects, projection, and incorporation. Eventually feedback loops may become established, setting the foundation for an integrated system.

With the development of the semiotic function and the capacity for memory, the sense of sameness and continuity of self and object can begin to exist over time. Derivatives of drives and affects in terms of thoughts and feelings begin to cluster around self- and object representations, and the self and the external world begin to take on predictable qualities. Initially, however, strong surges of affect, such as anger, tend to lead to fragmentation of the sense of self or others, as in the intense separation anxieties seen prior to the stage of libidinal object constancy. In addition, differentiation of feeling states and the capacity for complex interpersonal relationships are limited during this early stage of development. Relationships are organized along anaclitic lines and tend to be viewed in dyadic patterns; only later do they move into more complex triangular patterns and intricate interpersonal configurations. Shadings of interpersonal relationships and varying feeling states begin to be appreciated only toward the beginning of the oedipal phase of development. Thus, although the capacity for figurative thinking greatly enhances the field of application, mobility, permanence, and stability of beginning psychological structures, they are still highly vulnerable to stress during this time, and the sense of self and object, as well as of the representative world, is not well conserved. When it is conserved, it is conserved at the expense of the field of application and mobility. In other words, permanence and stability can be obtained, but with a decrease in the range of the field of application and mobility (e.g., by withdrawal, negativism, or denial).

The next step in cognitive abilities is the acquisition of concrete operations, the capacity for interiorized operations—figurative schemes of the inverse and the reciprocal. This advance has significance for both emotional and impersonal cognition. Now impulses and feelings can have their opposites and can exist in a reciprocal system with one another; that is, there can be various gradations or shadings. Love and hate can both exist within one system. The latency child can love and hate the same person, and that person can be conserved and maintained within one system rather than split into two separate object representations (the good and the bad). Similarly, various gradations of love can exist in a seriated order because of the capacity to construct reciprocal relationships. This capacity allows greater flexibility in processing stimuli from the internal world. Derivatives of the drives and feelings can now be processed—assimilated and accommodated to in the development of new psychological structures—without sacrificing the range of the field of application or mobility of internal events. To take a simple example, the capacity to construct inverse relationships allows the latency child to use reaction formations to deal with feelings of sibling rivalry. The ability, based on inverse and reciprocal relationships, to construct groupings and seriation schemes helps the child to develop a series of rules and regulations within which he can begin to order and categorize thoughts and feelings, thereby achieving a greater degree of comfort. He can thus conserve complex, or relatively complex, internal self- and object representations within these basic but still limited capacities for interiorized operations. Feedback loops, which are more consistent with ego splitting, are no longer necessary.

The limitations of this period are clear. Defenses are still relatively primitive—turning feelings into opposites, reaction formations, simple rationalizations, displacements, isolation of affect, projection, and denial. When the child experiences strong stimulus inputs, such as intense feelings of envy or anger, or a "breakthrough" of forbidden oedipal impulses, he often regresses to more primitive defense mechanisms which limit the field of application and mobility and, at times, even permanence and stability. Repression tends to be strong during this period, with major limitations in the capacity for integrating past and present. Yet the system at this stage functions more flexibly in terms of the four parameters outlined than it did at an earlier age. In adolescence the new capacity for a psychological structure that includes the inverse and reciprocal together, as well as the correlative, and the capacity for hypothetical thinking allow for much greater freedom in the field of application, mobility, permanence, and stability. As we discussed earlier, the capacity for probabilistic thinking and the increased number of variables that can be accommodated in a system in which the inverse and the reciprocal operate together permits conservation of psychological events to occur across a much wider range of feelings and thoughts.

While, according to Piaget, the system of formal operations achieves its highest equilibrium state during adolescence, this is not true for the parallel psychological structures that deal with the internal world. Although all capacities are at a higher level during adolescence than earlier, those relating to the internal world do not achieve their ultimate level in the same way as do those relating to the external world. This difference relates to the different nature of the stimulus inputs. With regard to the external world, there is, in a sense, a limited number of external variables that the system must assimilate and learn to accommodate to. But internal life continually shifts and goes on. Input from the drives arising from biological changes does not stop with adolescence, but continues through adulthood and undergoes alteration again in later life. These changes in stimulus input, combined with the ever-increasing complexity of external demands from the interpersonal world (marriage, raising a family, etc.), continually put new demands on the evolving psychological structures. While, in the impersonal realm, we can talk of reaching an optimal cognitive structure in which no new accommodations are necessary, it is more useful to think of the psychological system as achieving relative stability in its need to accommodate, but as having the ability for further accommodations, which, when integrated with prior accommodations, can take into account new demands from both the internal milieu and the interpersonal world. In other words, the life cycle of the emotional world has a course and time schedule different from those of the relatively more stable, predictable impersonal world.

This factor, however, does not limit the formation of a general model of intelligent functioning for both the impersonal cognitive world and the emotional world. It only means that the internal and external boundaries have different timetables and achieve in varying degrees an optimal system that can assimilate new elements without requiring further accommodations.

If we consider the capacities for internal cognition in the context of a psychoanalytic understanding of mature functioning, the definition of a general model of intelligence may become clear. There are a number of perspectives from which to look at healthy functioning psychoanalytically. We can look at it from the point of view of the drives, and from the point of view of the development of the affects. We can also look at it from the point of view of the development of object relations; the development of important psychological structures such as the ego, superego, and ego ideal; the development of defenses; and the development of certain subfunctions of the ego dealing with synthesis, integration, and differentiation. We shall systematically investigate these to clarify how the "intelligent" individual deals with his internal milieu.

Variables Related to the Internal Boundary of the Ego in the Context of a General Model of Optimal Intelligence

We shall now examine how the psychoanalytically conceptualized internal boundary variables may be organized in the context of our general model of equilibrium states. The highest-order, most "intelligent" organizations will be contrasted with less "intelligent" ones. We shall not be all-inclusive here, but shall try to take into account a number of the variables conceptualized within psychoanalytic psychology in a more specific manner than in earlier sections.

The Drives

In considering the drives in the context of optimal to less optimal organizations, we usually evaluate the degree to which drives (libidinal and aggressive) are adequately fused and have progressed to a genital level of organization. We attempt to determine potential regressions and fixations to assess how potential fixation points are integrated both quantitatively and qualitiatively within the individual's drive organization. At an optimal level, we see a predominantly genital drive organization with perhaps neurotic manifestations representing regressions to pregenital fixation points. With moderate disturbances, we see drive organizations that represent a mixture of genital and pregenital levels condensed together. In more severe psychopathology, we see predominantly pregenital organizations due to arrested development, major fixations, or marked regressions. In the most severe disorders we observe drive organizations that are not only pregenital but often at pre-object levels; that is, the drives, which are defined in part by their aim and object, have the self as an object and often split off or fragment aspects of the self.

From an emotional perspective, we may say that in the most "intelligent" person the drive organization has advanced to a genital or age-appropriate level, there is an optimal degree of fusion between libidinal and aggressive drives, and fixation points are integrated with and are part of a predominantly genital organization. This concept of an optimal drive organization is consistent with our equilibrium model.

An optimal drive organization has a wide field of application in that it has advanced to a genital level and therefore incorporates the most advanced types of drive derivatives while it condenses elements of earlier drive organizations. In terms of mobility, it encompasses drive derivatives from the present and the past, and any regressions are mobile, permitting, for the most part, progression back to the genital level. In terms of permanence and stability, just as the cognitive structure retains a certain integrity because there is enough flexibility to assimilate a wide variety of stimuli without major new accommodations, so, too, can the integrated drive organization accommodate a broad range of drive derivatives and human experience without alterations in the basically condensed genital structure. The structure has a high degree of permanence and stability in that it provides for regressive channels in relation to early levels of development via transformational bridges or through the use of developmentally appropriate defense mechanisms. The most advanced mechanisms are sublimatory channels, though less neutralized types of transformations are often appropriate for mature functioning, such as some reaction formations and some displacements.

To have a genital organization that integrates drive states from all prior levels of development demands a highly organized structure, capable of finding a way to synthesize a number of discordant variables—*a best solution.* Such integration is possible during the concrete operational period, but it is even better accomplished during the formal operational period, when the structure can assimilate a greater richness and variety of drives. During the formal operational period, there is the maximum possibility to integrate and conserve, as can be seen in sublimations and satisfactions. Although during the concrete operational period such solutions are possible and the integrity of the structure can be conserved, the solutions will not necessarily be the best fit with the person's past history, current needs, and future aspirations.

The basic use of reciprocals and inverses, as seen in the concrete operational period, does not afford much flexibility for the vicissitudes of the drives; yet the concrete operational stage permits some operations on representations of drive derivatives. During the preoperational period, only representation is possible to give flexible expression to drive derivatives. Because feedback is the basic regulatory mechanism, we see withdrawal or splitting and fragmentation of drive representations under stress. Prior to the capacity for representation, the flexibility in dealing with drive derivatives is more limited. Under stress we see alterations in somatic functioning or human attachments.

Affects

In considering affects from a psychoanalytic perspective of optimal to less optimal organizations, we need to look at a number of variables. Which affects predominate? Which emerge under stress? What is their developmental level? Are they developmentally immature affects, like emotional hunger, fear, and rage, or are they developmentally more advanced ones, like love, concern, empathy, and anger? What is their flexibility and selectivity? How many kinds of affects are potentially available, and can they be selectively called forth in appropriate situations (fear and rage in one, love and empathy in another)? Or are only a few affects, such as fear and rage, used in most situations?

In terms of these dimensions of affects, our general conception is that at an optimal level a person experiences a rich variety of developmentally advanced affects that are selectively used in response to external or internal stimuli, as well as to conflicts. At a less optimal level there is often a capacity for advanced and selective use of affects when the person is not under stress, but under stress less advanced and less selective use of affects predominate. In more severe disturbances usually a few affects predominate and are representative of pregenital concerns, for example, emptiness, rage, envy, pseudo-warmth. In the most severe disturbances the affect system is not fully developed, resulting either in a lack of affect (flattening or blunting) or in inappropriate affect.

Related to affects is the type of anxiety the person experiences. At the most advanced level there is signal anxiety related to internal structural conflict. At less advanced levels anxiety is related to a combination of internal and external concerns, for example, projection of fears onto the external world. At the least advanced levels anxiety is related to external concerns—fear of castration, punishment, loss of love, separation, object loss, annihilation by the object, or annihilation by being overwhelmed by the instincts.

In terms of the four parameters of emotional intelligence, the field of application and mobility are greater when there is the capacity for experiencing the most developmentally advanced affects and simultaneously integrating them with developmentally earlier affects. In the optimal personality organization, a variety of developmentally advanced affects, as well as less mature affects, can be called forth in a selective manner. The affect organizations and anxiety systems have a high degree of permanence and stability; that is, when regressive manifestations do occur under stress, they are related through certain defenses or other ego functions to the more advanced state and they maintain these connections. They are part of a system, or part of an interrelated set of affect structures. The highest level of affect organization is reflected in the use of a variety of affects—love, empathy, anger, envy—in connection with ability to conserve polarities in feeling states over time, e.g., the person maintains a basically loving feeling in spite of occasional envious or angry feelings.

From our consideration of affects, it is clear that the most advanced, or developmentally mature, state is dependent on formal operations. In the formal operational period, in which combinatorial thinking is possible, the structure can process a wide variety of affects, some of them discordant, and can find a way to integrate and synthesize them, a solution that takes into account the life history of the individual. The type of affect selected can reflect both the current situation and earlier developmental levels, as well as future anticipations. Such selectivity is possible only with the acquisition of combinatorial thinking characteristic of the formal operational stage of development. During the preceding stage of concrete operations, the affects are limited since only simple reciprocals and inverses can be used, and the system cannot tolerate much discordance among two or three different affect states. Prior to the use of interiorized operations, there are severe limitations in the ability of the system to tolerate a variety of affects simultaneously. Here we see the characteristic splitting in relation to ambivalence, or the disorganization of the affect system (a psychological system) into rhythmical motor patterns or motor inhibitions.

Defenses

We can look at the defenses in a similar manner. Clinically, in terms of optimal to less optimal, we tend to categorize defenses according to their developmental level: primitive defenses, such as projection and introjection, versus developmentally advanced defenses, such as sublimation and intellectualization. We also look at their stability (what happens under stress); their flexibility (how well they adapt to new situations); their selectivity (if the most effective defense can be called forth in a given situation); and their effectiveness (if they respond to signal affects to protect ego functions).

Optimally, the defenses are developmentally advanced and organized, and they protect the ego without significantly hampering its functions. Defenses in neurotic formations, for instance, only minimally interfere with memory (repressed memories) or ego flexibility (repetitive reaction patterns). Minor deviations from this optimal position are seen in mixtures of developmentally advanced and immature defenses; the immature defenses, however, are used mainly in response to stress. In more significant impairments, the defenses are developmentally immature (related to preoedipal issues). They hamper the ego markedly to moderately by restricting it, as in multiple phobias or characterological constrictions, such as avoidance of human relationships or extreme passivity, or they leave the ego open to severe affect storms (anxiety or depression). In cases of unusual stress, they may allow disruptions in reality testing. In the most severe disturbances the defenses are very primitive (projection, denial); they are unselective and severely impede such basic functions as reality testing. At best they serve as a fragile defense against psychotic processes.

In terms of field of application and mobility, at the optimal psychological level a person has a developmentally advanced and selective defense system. The field of application and mobility are greatest when the defenses are organized, can deal with a wide range of stimuli (drives and affects), and can move between advanced and less advanced states in a selective manner. The ability to call forth a particular defense that will serve best in a given human situation represents a strategic advantage over the unselective use of defenses. The permanence and stability of the defensive organization are evidenced in optimally healthy individuals by the use of relatively flexible, selective, and developmentally advanced systems of defense to protect the ego. When regressive defenses are used, they are used in the context of a particular situation and are connected to more advanced defenses via certain transformations. Thus, there is a high degree of permanence and stability to the total system, which is rich and complex enough to be selective as well as resistant to permanent regression even under severe stress.

Here, again, we have a model of a rather complex system that can respond to internal or external stimuli in highly selective ways. It has a wide range in terms of field of application and mobility and yet is highly permanent and stable in its overall structural characteristics. Less optimal defensive organizations cannot deal with certain stimuli, such as intense anger, without permitting disruptions in ego functioning or resorting to the use of ego splitting.

The defenses are related to the transformations or solutions available. In terms of variety, richness, flexibility, selectivity, stability, and effectiveness, only when the combinatorial capacities characteristic of the formal operational period are present is there a defensive structure or set of structures that can process multivariables, find a best solution, and conserve the integrity of the ego. In comparison, in the concrete operational period defenses are available as interiorized operations conserving a system, but they are limited to simple clusters of defenses involving inverses and reciprocals. The latency child's defenses are therefore relatively simple. The preoperational child employs even more primitive defenses, and these interfere with basic ego functioning (projections, denials, ego splitting, etc.). At this stage discordant elements are dealt with only through splitting, supported by the feedback mechanism level. At the most regressed defensive level we see the use of basic rhythms, as in autistic states or total withdrawal.

Human Relationships

Another group of internal boundary variables related to drives, affects, and defenses are those internal structures that have to do with the potential for human relationships. These are based on object relations established early in life, of which aspects become internalized to form the basis of internal self- and object representations. Ultimately they coalesce into providing a foundation for basic ego functions and into systems of self- and object representations. Under optimal circumstances, or in optimal human development, the person has achieved an organized system of self- and object representations, which not only forms a basis for certain ego functions and organized representational systems, but also provides the capacity for developmentally appropriate interpersonal intimacy and stability. We tend to think of relationship potential in terms of a genital capacity that incorporates a number of attributes commonly known to clinicians, including the capacity for sharing, loving, genital sex, intimacy, empathy, stability, limit setting, assertiveness, anger, etc. While this conception touches on a number of variables already considered, here we are emphasizing the capacity for human relationships that, on the one hand, are intimate, rich, and varied in feelings and thoughts and, on the other hand, enable the person to feel a sense of individuality and independence. Hence the emotionally mature person simultaneously has the capacity for closeness with another loving object and the capacity to maintain the boundary between self and other, and self- and object representations. The internal representations and the real relationships that occur and are based on them are able to exist and maintain themselves in the context of genitality through a variety and range of internal drive and affect states and vicissitudes of interpersonal relatedness.

The degree to which a person achieves a stable capacity for a broad-ranging set of human relationships is dependent in part on the evolution of this capacity through the course of development. We tend to think of a person as passing through stages in this capacity from autistic, narcissistic, and anaclitic stages to symbiotic stages; evolving into a stage of relationship based on object constancy; then moving into relationship patterns based on phallic attributes; and eventually evolving into triangular and more complex human relationships and feelings (sharing, loving, empathy, etc.).

Simplified, the capacity for relationships can be divided into five successive developmental stages. The *first stage* is based on autistic patterns, and the world is undifferentiated. The *second stage* is based on symbiotic patterns. The world is differentiated, but there is a merging between self and others. The *third stage* is based on postsymbiotic patterns. There is a differentiation of self from others, along with a tolerance and maintenance of boundaries. The *fourth stage* is based on the capacity for triangular patterns characteristic of the oedipal phase of development; that is, there is a movement from dyadic to triangular relationships, from a two-person to a three-person system, which makes the complexity of human relationships far greater (e.g., the rivalries and intrigues of a three-person system). In the *fifth stage* there is some resolution of the three-person system, with maintenance of appreciation of its complexity. That is, the world does not exist simply as a three-person system based on intrigues, rivalries, and the like, but the increased complexity and appreciation of the world derived from a three-person system remains, and there is enough resolution of the affective issues pertaining to the three-person system to provide an appreciation of complex human relationships in a more neutralized manner.

Another way to conceptualize these patterns in broader terms is in terms of preoedipal and genital object relations, preoedipal representing those prior to the triangular patterns, and genital representing the integration of triangular and post-triangular patterns.

In the optimal situation, at a behavioral level relationship patterns tend to reflect the capacity for intimacy and stability, with pregenital traits being used in the service of genitality. Deviations from this position involve relationships that reflect some capacity for intimacy and stability but are compromised by pregenital patterns (triangular, symbiotic, etc.), which emerge periodically. More severe disturbances reflect markedly unstable relationships based mostly on pregenital patterns (e.g., symbiotic patterns). The most severe deviations from the optimal are either no relationships or relationships based predominantly on anaclitic and symbiotic patterns, with regression into autistic patterns.

At the highest level of organization there is a synthesis and integration of triangular patterns with earlier achievements, resolution of symbiosis, and establishment of object constancy. As for field of application and mobility, the mature person is capable of developing a variety of human relationships in the context of a variety of feeling states; at the same time he has access to earlier developmental states that are connected to the most developmentally advanced patterns via certain transformations. There is a high degree of condensation, with the pregenital or regressive traits integrated under a higher-level organization of self- and object representations.

We thus have a structure with a wide field of application and a high degree of mobility. In addition, at the most optimal level, the mature human being shows a high degree of permanence and stability in his relationships. This is best exemplified by the establishment of object constancy and, later, identity. Permanent and stable delineations of self- and object representations, first in simple organizations and then in more complex ones, maintain their integrity in the face of the vicissitudes of interpersonal relationships (separations, etc.) and of intense drive and affect states. Thus, the parameters of field of application, mobility, permanence, and stability apply in the area of relationship potential.

The optimal organization in relationship potential, a genital post-triangular structure that integrates pregenital trends, is best accomplished when the structure can conserve a variety of discordant elements in the context of past history, present events, and future aspirations. This achievement is most possible with formal operational capacities. With concrete operational capacities it is possible to conserve the self- and object representational organizations, but solutions are limited, and defensive operations compromise the fullest formation of identity; for example, certain affect or drive states are not experienced. In order to conserve the existing organization, certain styles of interpersonal relationships are not possible. Use of the inverse or reciprocal alone limits solutions, compared with use of the inverse, reciprocal, and correlative within one structural system. Preoperational structures, which lack the capacity for interiorized actions, do not have the flexibility to conserve systems of representations, and therefore the representations themselves break down (ego splitting, fragmentation).

Having considered drives, affects, defenses, and relationship potential, we shall now turn to certain other variables, conceptualized by psychoanalytic psychology as psychological structures.

Superego

One such structure is the superego. In a healthy person we tend clinically to view optimal superego development as a superego that is fully structuralized and experienced as internally complete. We also tend to conceptualize an optimal superego structure as one that is integrated with the ego and id and contributes to the regulatory processes, making for finely discriminated regulation in the context of a stable self-esteem system and a capacity for pleasure. This conceptualization accounts for the character and consistency of the introjects, their relationship to a developing identity and sense of self, and their attitudes toward predominant types of drive-discharge expression. In optimal development the character and consistency of the introjects are such that they have an integrated, facilitating relationship to a developing identity and sense of self and permit developmentally appropriate types of drive-discharge expression that allow the person to experience satisfaction.

In a less-than-optimal organization we observe a superego structure that is incompletely developed, experienced as external, and perceived as separate from the ego. The regulatory processes are inconsistent or overly generalized; for example, everything is "bad." There is a high degree of instability in the maintenance of self-esteem and in allowance for pleasure. The character and consistency of the introjects (they may be inconsistent or conflicting) lead to an incomplete, compromised, or negative sense of self and inhibit or lead to aberrant types of drive-discharge expression (perversions, masochism, sadism).

The superego structure is in part based on development in all the categories mentioned, in object relations, as well as in the drives, affects, and defenses. As the description above indicates, the optimal structure not only is at a high level of development—that is, fully structuralized, internalized, and complete—but also is integrated with other elements of the personality, so that there is a smooth, organized system that facilitates further development, for example, in terms of identity, achievement, and satisfaction.

As for the field of application and mobility, the most mature or developmentally advanced superego organization can deal with a variety of external situations, yet maintain its structural integrity, thereby, in one sense, having a broad field of application. But, in a more important sense, it has a broad field of application in that it can deal with a wide variety of id impulses and inputs from other substructures of the personality (e.g., drive-defense-affect organizations) as well as with aspects of the ego ideal. It does not need to split or exclude any of these. Thus, the field of application is broad in relation to both the external world and the internal world. Mobility is similarly broad in that the mature superego can deal with and integrate the present and past and, through the ego ideal, can anticipate aspects of the future.

Permanence and stability were implied when we talked about fully structuralized and stable superego systems. We see this at a behavioral level in that the system of values, ideals, self-concepts, regulatory principles, and self-esteem is relatively stable and permanent under a wide variety of external situations and in the face of a breadth and variety of changing internal stimuli.

A superego that is complete, internalized, and in balance allows for a reasonable amount of drive gratification and self-esteem while exerting finely discriminated regulation. A superego structure at a very high equilibrium state is possible only with the combinatorial capacities characteristic of that state. Only with these capacities can the structure assimilate and integrate a number of discordant variables. In order to achieve a stable system of regulation, self-esteem, and satisfaction, the superego structure must find a solution that integrates a number of variables. To take into account the person's unique life history, current experience, and future aspirations in the context of a system that permits regulation, self-esteem maintenance, and some sense of satisfaction demands a high level of synthesis. Such a "sculpture" is highly specific; it is possible only in a system that offers solutions with multiple combinations of variables.

As noted above, the incompletely developed superego is experienced as external, separate from the ego, inconsistent in its regulation, and highly unstable in its maintenance of self-esteem; also, allowance for pleasure is clearly at a much lower level of equilibrium. The structure cannot bring together in a cohesive manner discordant sets of variables. There is a lack of internalization and structuralization. Instead, there is externalization or splitting based on the independent use of reciprocals or inverses, or there are primitive structures based on feedback mechanisms, without a capacity for internal representations. The externalized superego, for example, is one in which half of the discordant sets of variables are projected onto the external world. Such a projection is usually based on some interiorized action such as inverses or reciprocals, but without a capacity for relating the inverses and reciprocals in one system, as in a full combinatorial system. The more primitive states, based on preoperational thinking, are usually reflected clinically in what appears as a lack of superego functioning, where the person needs constant feedback in order to maintain regulation and self-esteem.

While the personality organization can be conceptualized in many ways, for clarity we shall divide the other elements of the personality into three categories: ego functions related to ego intactness, ego functions related to relatively autonomous and conflict-free spheres of the ego, and ego functions related to ego flexibility.

Ego Intactness

Clinically, in terms of ego intactness, we tend to look at the ego apparatuses that make for the basic organic integrity of the ego—the perceptual, auditory, and motor apparatuses and the apparatuses coordinating them, such as memory, which have to do with the integrity of the mental apparatus. We also include the basic ego functions, such as reality testing, predominance of secondary-process thinking, and presence of ego boundaries, as well as the more subtle aspects of ego functioning, such as the capacity for integrating affect and thought and the ability for organized thinking. In a healthy person the organic ego apparatuses and basic ego functions are fundamentally intact, and interferences from neurotic formations are minimal to none. Deviations from this position involve interference with ego capacities either by physical or psychological factors, as in severe neurological dysfunctions (e.g., organic brain syndromes), or by ego defects, as in psychotic processes (e.g., defects in reality testing). The ability for reality testing, the predominance of secondary-process thinking, and the presence of ego boundaries perhaps need no amplification in terms of the way they correspond to or represent a higher order of emotional intelligence than that of an ego structure hampered by ego defects.

In terms of field of application and mobility, an intact ego can take into account and integrate the real external world as well as aspects of the internal world. At the same time, it can maintain the permanence and stability of an integrated, organized structure even under the vicissitudes of the drives and affects and despite changes in the external world. Thus, in terms of equilibrium, the intact ego structure is clearly more advanced than the defective one.

If we further consider the intactness of the ego in terms of the basic ego apparatuses and basic ego functions, we can see that a structure in which interferences from neurotic formations are minimal to none is not only consistent with a high-level equilibrium state, but requires at least concrete operational capacities, if not full formal operational capacities. If feedback mechanisms are the basic principle regulating an equilibrium state, then the only way to maintain the integrity, or the permanence and stability, of a structure when the discordance of the variables in the system becomes too great is by continually walking down one road and then down another, that is, through a process similar to the mechanism of ego splitting. Once there is the capacity for interiorized actions, as in the concrete operational stage, perturbations in one direction can be simultaneously compensated for with movement in another direction. Interiorized operations permit the simultaneous dealing with discordant sets of variables within one system, thus allowing for some flexibility. In this manner, the basic intactness of the ego can be conserved even with perturbations in the system. However, to be able really to protect basic ego functions—that is, to conserve the integrity of the structure—the combinatorial capacity characteristic of formal operations is needed, where not only are there interiorized operations, but these interiorized operations can deal with real variables and an unlimited number of hypothetical possibilities, and can find potential solutions that integrate past, present, and future.

Capacities Related to the Relatively Conflict-Free and Autonomous Ego Sphere

The functional capacities related to the relatively conflict-free, autonomous sphere of the ego involve a number of abilities, including the ability to observe and experience at the same time; the ability to regress in the service of the ego; the ability to learn; the ability to see connections between things, events, and ideas; creativity; curiosity; intelligence; and the capacity for synthesis, integration, and further differentiation.

In the optimal personality these functions are all rich and flexible and are only rarely restricted by conflict. Intelligence, creativity, and the capacities to observe and experience, to regress, to integrate, and to further differentiate can all be used to enrich the person's experience of his internal and external worlds. Deviations from this position involve restrictions due to conflict or to genetic endowment and cultural background, and exist on a spectrum from mild to severe. At the severe end we see the above-described functions used mainly in the service of drive gratification to cover up ego defects rather than to enrich human experience through integrating new external and internal experiences.

Almost by definition, the field of application and mobility of these functions in the most advanced or optimal state are greater than in the less advanced state. The same is true of permanence and stability. The very terms *synthesizing* and *integrating* imply the ability to put things together in complex configurations connected by a series of transformations (Piaget's definition of a high-order equilibrium state). In fact, the integrated model presented here is really a more differentiated description of the concepts of synthetic and integrative functions of the ego. When we consider those functions related to the relatively conflict-free, autonomous sphere of the ego (cited above), we are considering capacities close to the cognitive sphere.

Perhaps we should focus on a few capacities that are not often taken into account when we talk about cognition, such as the ability to regress in the service of the ego and the ability to observe and experience at the same time. Here, clearly, the combinatorial ability reflective of formal operations provides a great advantage over earlier states in supporting these capacities. With most of these functions, the task is essentially to be doing a number of things at once and yet maintain a connection across them, as in the ability to observe and experience. This fact is best accomplished in the context of a highly developed structure characteristic of the formal operational stage of development in which the inverse and reciprocal operate together within one system. Such a system permits multiple functions to exist simultaneously in interrelationship with one another. The concrete operational stage permits interiorized operations, but only among a limited number of variables, thereby limiting the integrative and synthetic possibilities. Preoperational thinking further compromises these capacities. As illustrated earlier, it is rare for a child to be able to observe and experience at the same time prior to some capacity for concrete operations.

Ego Flexibility

The last category to be described here is ego flexibility. Ego flexibility is defined as the flexibility of the ego in its capacity to utilize a variety of finely discriminated operations, in contrast to the degree to which the ego is rigid, with only a few, poorly discriminated operations at its disposal. Included here are the capacities to form and tolerate internal conflict and a variety of appropriate affects, as opposed to signs of arrested ego development, such as ego constrictions (severe character disorders), externalization of conflict, and altered or restricted modes of drive gratification (perversion). In addition, symptom formation that does not grossly interfere with ego functioning is in contrast to symptoms or affects that lead to a breakdown in ego functions or further constrictions (withdrawal).

At the optimal level the ego is relatively flexible in its response to internal or external stimuli. Neurotic formations interfere only minimally with this flexibility. Deviating from this optimal position is a somewhat rigid ego, where there is still some capacity to tolerate internal conflicts without marked disruption of the ego functioning. One manifestation of this is the walling-off of experience of certain drive or feeling states, with concomitant limitations in behavioral flexibility, as is seen in mixed character and neurotic pathologies (e.g., the narcissistic personality who is incapable of intimacy). Deviating further from the optimal position, the ego tends to be rigid in its operations. Neurotic formations markedly intensify this rigidity and lead to minimal breakdowns in ego functioning, such as temporary loss of reality testing, loss of sense of self, and/or temporary loss of the capacity to integrate thought and affect, as well as states of inhibition or alteration of drive gratification. In the most extreme deviations from the optimal state, the ego is severely constricted and uses only a few, poorly discriminated operations to cover more basic structural defects, as in psychotic or borderline organizations.

This conceptualization of ego flexibility perhaps most closely approximates the construct of emotional intelligence we are attempting to evolve here; that is, the flexible ego is one that has the capacity to utilize a variety of finely discriminated operations (e.g., transformations) in order to carry out a wide variety of operations. It can deal with, tolerate, process, or *assimilate* internal conflict, a variety of appropriate affects, and drive derivatives. Speaking of ego flexibility is another way of describing a structure with a broad field of application: it can assimilate a wide variety of drive and affect states as well as inputs from other substructures of the ego; it can move between the present and the past (mobility); and it can anticipate the future (via the ego ideal subsystem). It can assimilate these inputs from the internal milieu, as well as those from the external world (interpersonal relationships), without employing major new accommodations. In other words, in the optimal state ego flexibility is such that the ego can assimilate a wide variety of elements without having to alter its very structure. The structure thus maintains a high degree of permanence and stability.

Optimal flexibility is characteristic of formal operations. The capacity for the inverse and the reciprocal within one system, together with the capacity for hypothetical thinking, provides a system of transformations that is highly flexible and can deal with and assimilate a wide variety of inputs from the external and internal worlds (impulses, affects, self- and object representations with specific drive-affect dispositions, etc.). A less advanced system—for example, one that uses only the inverse or reciprocal—has to either deny half of a conflict through constructing the inverse, or project half of the conflict through constructing the reciprocal; it is therefore limited in the number of internal wishes and feelings it can serve within one system. As we have seen, before inverses and reciprocals, mental representations are possible, but without interiorized actions to conserve them. They must be conserved by simple feedback mechanisms. An action in one direction may be reversed by an action in another direction. Under such a system, when there is an increase in the number of discordant variables in the system, there is a tendency toward alternating behavioral organizations, as in ego splitting. That is, there is no capacity for interiorized operations in which movements in many directions can be integrated in one structure; loving and hating feelings, for instance, cannot be conserved within one system. Earlier developmental stages may not even have the use of representational capacities, and feelings can only be handled through body processes (e.g., autistic rhythmic patterns, catatonic patterns).

As implied above, a major advance in ego flexibility occurs with concrete operational capacities (interiorized operations). The capacity to do operations (construct the inverse and reciprocal) on internal representations not only makes it possible to integrate discordant representations, but to organize conflicting representations. We see at this stage of development the first organized neurotic structures. While this may represent psychopathology, it also demonstrates the flexibility of the ego to do more than simply displace, condense, or split discordant representations. Now they can be combined and altered through internal transformations. Basic ego functions and developmentally appropriate tasks can be protected through encapsulated neurotic configurations. Concrete operations, however, are limited in two ways. The operations can serve only a certain number of variables at once, and they are related to the real external world or the real internal world. Later on, hypothetical constructs can be taken into account, and the system can conserve an infinite number of variables, many of them discordant, with an infinite number of solutions. This greater ability to conserve discordant variables in a stable structure has already been discussed.

Overview

As the foregoing suggests, the most mature organizations in all the categories rest on a foundation of combinatorial thinking—the highest equilibrium state. In that deviations from the optimal position reflect lower equilibrium states, our general model of intelligent functioning rests on the conception of a hierarchy of equilibrium states, which at the highest level permit the assimilation of a large number of complex variables into a whole, self-regulating system. While we can readily apply this conceptualization to the external boundary—that is, to the aliment or stimuli characteristic of the impersonal environment—it has been suggested here that these same principles can help us understand emotional intelligence at the internal boundary.

It is clear that in the emotional realm we never achieve the optimal states we are capable of in terms of impersonal, external logic. The reasons for this have been suggested earlier. The stimulus nutriments serving as aliment for the structures evolving at the internal boundary are highly variable and rarely reach the organization necessary for optimal development. "Optimal" in this sense must be perceived as an ideal, since it is not usually within the realm of human potential. Because the internal elements and affect-laden interpersonal elements are continually changing throughout the life cycle, even in adulthood, there is also no sense of closure, although there is a relative sense of closure in terms of personality stability at the end of adolescence. Internal boundary cognition is continually evolving, and further maturation is always possible throughout the course of development.

10

DEVELOPMENTAL STAGES OF INTELLIGENCE, ADAPTATION, AND LEARNING

Thus far we have looked at different aspects of development in terms of drives, affects, object relations, and development of substructures. We have observed how these aspects of development exist in a hierarchical developmental sequence. We have also seen how they can be conceptualized in terms of a series of equilibrium states, from lower-order, simple states to higher-order, complex states, and how these states develop sequentially over time, gaining higher levels of intelligence with the process of maturation.

To summarize our discussion thus far: If we conceptualize our model as receiving stimuli from both inside (drives, affects, internal self- and object representations) and outside (affect-laden relationships and stimuli from the impersonal environment), and further, if we conceptualize an evolving psychic structure that processes these stimuli, we can then conceptualize a model in which this structure develops as the organism matures. This development leads to more flexible and complex ways of processing the internal and external stimuli. At some optimal level of intelligence, the psychic structure has the capacity to process (assimilate) a wide variety of internal and external stimuli, existing across time and space. In integrating these diverse stimuli, the psychic structure has the capacity for a high degree of conservation, implying both the permanence of each separate aspect or element within the larger psychic structure and the stability of the entire structure. As will be recalled, this is Piaget's definition of intelligence for the impersonal world and, as has been argued here, one that fits rather well for the internal world.

With regard to the internal world, the optimally developed human organism does not operate simply as a huge computer, integrating various internal and external stimuli, but organizes the information from these stimuli into permanent and stable structures defined by his life experiences. In other words, each human being evolves a unique identity based on the development and integration of psychic structures and constellations of self- and object representations invested with drive-affect dispositions. The particular character and style of these structures are defined by the unique innate potentials of that human being combined with his life experiences. The permanence and stability of the individual elements and of the total structure are what afford a human being his distinctiveness. In this respect, our definition of intelligence in terms of the internal world is somewhat different from our definition of intelligence in terms of the impersonal world. The character of the integration of internal stimuli forms perhaps a relatively more distinct pattern based on the individual's unique constitutional givens and life experiences (life experiences constitute, by our definition, not only actions *on* the individual by his environment, but actions *by* the individual on his environment). As stated earlier, the most significant difference between the internal and external worlds is the greater variability of internal stimuli, including human relationships, in comparison to impersonal stimuli. This greater variability accounts in part for the greater uniqueness and varying stability of the internal boundary structures.

INTELLIGENCE FROM AN INTEGRATED DEVELOPMENTAL PERSPECTIVE

Our next step will be to delineate some of the milestones in human intelligence from an integrated developmental perspective.[1] We shall not attempt to describe comprehensively the steps in the development of human intelligence at the internal

[1] Although physical and neurological development serves as a foundation for the evolving capacities for intelligence, we shall not attempt to document these parallel advances here.

boundary. Rather, we shall point out certain features to be taken into account in putting together the skeleton of an integrated model of human intelligence. After these milestones have been outlined, we shall discuss their implications for normal development and our understanding of psychopathology, defense, coping, and adaptation.

What we are proposing is a structural model, with certain organizing principles that help us understand how internal and external stimuli are integrated. It is a model in which the stimuli that become integrated are of ever-growing complexity and in which the integrating structures are of parallel complexity.

Somatic Intelligence: Phase I

Our first milestone—*somatic intelligence: phase I*—occurs at the earliest stage in life. Internal and external stimuli are processed according to somatic intelligence, the system that relies predominantly on the use of the neurophysiological aspects of the human body. This step is consistent with Piaget's description of the sensorimotor period and with clinical observations of the way infants usually deal with internal and external affective stimulation.

At this stage of development a fundamental organizing principle of equilibrium states is the capacity for basic rhythms and homeostasis. Piaget (1937) has highlighted this in terms of the rhythmical activity infants use to gain experience with their initial reflex patterns. Clinically, rhythmic patterns in infants, from rhythmic movements of their muscles to rhythmic alterations in their basic states, have been an area of important research interest (Sander, 1962). Basic somatic systems, even at this early age, are complex. Various researchers have demonstrated individual differences among babies in terms of state regulation, habituation patterns, crying responses, the establishment of homeostatic cycles and rhythms, and broad measures of temperament (Brackbill, 1958; Brazelton, 1973; Emde, Gaensbauer, and Harmon, 1976; Parmelee, 1972; Thomas, Chess, and Birch, 1968; Wolff, 1966).

Nevertheless, the flexibility of this early system for dealing with internal and external stimuli (which may not be differentiated by the infant) is very limited. Sometimes we observe an infant deal with stress in terms of the interior of his body; at other times we see him deal with it in an outward fashion; and frequently we see him deal with it through repetitive action or rhythmic patterns.

Although during the first two to four months of life a number of processes in neurological, cognitive, and affective development converge around acknowledged nodal points, such as the social smile (Spitz, Emde, and Metcalf, 1970), it appears that this earliest phase of development still does not have the quality of intentionality or "psychological life" that later stages will have. As behavioral determinants, somatic internal coordination and stimulation are relatively more dominant than social interaction, which will become more dominant later on. At this time sleep-wake, hunger, and arousal cycles, for instance, play a large role in determining behaviors. Early distress is related to internal physical and neurophysiological events (Tennes et al., 1972). It should not be overlooked, however, that the infant may relate to and experience external environmental stimuli in ways that are not yet apparent. While it is generally recognized that the harmony between the infant and the caretaking environment plays a vital role in establishing basic rhythms and homeostatic mechanisms, as well as the character of early reciprocal interactions, there is still a great deal to learn about the way in which the very young infant perceives and experiences the world (Klaus et al., 1972; Lewis and Rosenblum, 1974; Sander, 1962; Stern, 1974a, 1974b; Yarrow and Goodwin, 1965; Yarrow et al., 1972).

It appears that at this stage there are few, if any, detour or delay channels. At best the infant may possess some sensory thresholds. The infant's capacity to enter into rhythmic patterns both with important figures in the environment and within himself should not, however, be underestimated as an adaptive tool. This capacity provides the infant important protection during the earliest days, weeks, and months of life, and serves as a foundation for later adaptation. As we observe clinically, the basic somatic mechanisms of shutting out stimulation and of rhythmic patterning remain with us throughout life.

Somatic Intelligence: Phase II

The second step in the development of human intelligence is *somatic intelligence: phase II*—somatic intelligence governed by learning by consequences. As the human organism develops, it begins to show a response to consequences. As indicated earlier, the infant is able to repeat action patterns that bring satisfaction. Eventually the infant can distinguish patterns that lead to certain ends, distinguish means from ends, and can even use intermediary devices to achieve a desired end. The differentiation of means from ends and learning by feedback, as described by Piaget, might be conceptualized more broadly as the capacity for learning by consequences. Our formulation here encompasses differentiation not only of means from ends in the impersonal or inanimate world, but also of self from nonself, because in order to observe one's impact on the environment, one must be able to differentiate oneself from another and from the environment, and experience the differential impact of consequences.

With this increased capacity for differentiation in terms of means-ends relationships and learning by consequences, we see a growing motoric ability along with increasing exploration of the environment. Eventually the toddler reaches a psychological stage, Mahler's (1968) practicing subphase of development, where interest in the environment increases and the toddler with great confidence explores his world.

While during this second phase of somatic intelligence the growing infant/young toddler is beginning to have a capacity for internal representation, it is unclear from current research findings exactly when this capacity for internal representation begins. This capacity probably evolves from relatively undifferentiated to more differentiated internal representations during the course of development. At the crucual 18- to 20-month juncture, when Piaget posits object permanence in terms of the inanimate world, psychological representations in terms of object relations seem to be relatively unstable. (This is also the period of Mahler's "rapprochement crisis.") According to Mahler, stable self- and object representations, or object constancy, do not occur until around age three (Mahler, Pine, and Bergman, 1975).[2] Although at 18 to 20 months the representations are sufficiently organized for certain kinds of clinical observations to be made or experimental procedures implemented, it is most likely that the full capacity for psychological representation develops slowly. Bowen and Woodhead (1955) have shown that an infant in the first year of life will watch a train go behind a screen and expectantly look for it to emerge from the screen. This finding indicates some capacity for psychological representation at a much earlier age than that originally posited by Piaget; the authors' explanation is that this is a simpler task motorically than looking for an object hidden behind a screen. While additional research may clarify the developmental time sequence of the capacity for representation, it is reasonable to assume that this capacity begins in the first months of life. It should also be kept in mind that the processes described here are continuous and gradual; it is only for the sake of conceptualization that we are attempting to delineate steps.

For the purposes of our discussion of phase II of somatic intelligence, we shall assume that there is some capacity for psychological representation, but that it has not yet reached a sufficiently organized state to be considered the dominant mode of intelligent learning. In other words, during this early stage of development the young infant still explores his world by using his somatic system. He learns about internal feeling states through experiences inside the body, and he explores the external personal and impersonal world through his actions on it and its actions on him. In addition, we observe a growing capacity for means-ends differentiation during this period, as indicated by the infant's use of intermediary devices to gain ends in both the animate and inanimate worlds—for example, through the use of imitation in the interpersonal world or the use of a carpet to pull something closer.

That these experiences are at the level of somatic intelligence, rather than the later level of psychological representational intelligence, is evidenced by the fact that later on, when the ca-

[2] Mahler qualifies this somewhat in her own discussion of Piaget's "object permanence" (see Mahler, Pine, and Bergman, 1975, p. 111).

pacity for mental representation has been established, there is a regression at the representational level to magical thinking, a dedifferentiation of means-ends relationships. While a certain amount of logic or causality has been established at the somatic level, the youngster is not able to transfer it to the representational level right away. This observation supports Piaget's hypothesis that early learning is predominantly sensorimotor. It is likely that early learning in terms of the internal world is also primarily a somatic kind of learning. During this stage, schemes are probably internalized in terms of beginning mental structures, but these schemes are of the action patterns used to deal with the environment, with interpersonal relationships, and with the beginning differentiation of internal states. They are not yet representations of either whole objects, animate or inanimate, or the whole self.

As indicated earlier, in phase II of somatic intelligence, with the further differentiation of means from ends, there is enhanced potential for dealing with internal or external stimulation. Learning by consequences provides flexibility to alter behaviors according to consequences. The growing child can change what he does to obtain ends. Even complex patterns can be learned to obtain certain gratifications, as in the process of shaping described by learning theorists (see Greenspan [1975] for a discussion of the concepts of instrumental learning theory in relation to complex human behavior). Learning by consequences thus provides increased flexibility in the specificity of adaptation to a changing and complex environment and is closer than basic rhythms and the capacity for homeostasis to what we think of as intelligent behavior.

The use of learning by consequences develops gradually and is evidenced by a number of observations and experimental findings. The young infant becomes more intentional and interactions with the environment more differentiated. Already, in the early part of the first year, the smiling response becomes less a product of internal stimulation and more a product of complex interpersonal cues (Wolff, 1963). Visual stimuli become more important (Sroufe and Waters, 1976). Later, events can begin to have a negative meaning as the infant selectively frowns and smiles (Brody and Axelrad, 1970; Bronson, 1972;

Tennes et al., 1972). Interactions slowly become more reciprocal and differentiated. For example, the infant will respond to maternal cues like changes in facial expression. A causal sequence of interactions now becomes possible—e.g., mother smiling, baby smiling, mother smiling, etc. (See Brazelton, Koslowski, and Main, 1974; Clarke-Stewart, 1973; Emde, Gaensbauer, and Harmon, 1976; Escalona, 1968; Lewis and Goldberg, 1969; Stern, 1974a, 1974b; Sroufe, Waters, and Matas, 1974.)

As the infant develops through the second half of the first year, behavior at all levels—cognitive, affective, and social—becomes more differentiated and organized. Although the conceptualization of stranger anxiety (Spitz, Emde, and Metcalf, 1970) as an indicator of a certain level of psychological organization may be an oversimplification, this reaction—or, more important, the appearance of different responses to the nonprimary caregiver—does signal the capacity at this time to organize perceptions into more complex units and make discriminations between the primary caregiver and others. The capacity for these discriminations, by inference, leads to the impression that the infant has a greater capacity for differentiating various organizations of internal experience, including both memory and present perceptions. The complex behaviors of surprise and anticipation, for example, appear between nine and ten months (Charlesworth, 1969). In general, affect and cognition appear more connected (Brody and Axelrad, 1966, 1970).

Behavior during the second year of life gradually becomes more organized, original, and intentional. Ainsworth (1973) and Waters, Matas, and Sroufe (1975), among others, have highlighted the existence of more organized behavioral patterns through the study of complex patterns of behavior such as attachment. Whether attachment in itself is the most useful paradigm for the organization of infant behavior is perhaps less important than the fact that investigators have developed high-order behavioral constructs indicating (though perhaps not intentionally) their respect for the infant's greater organizational capacities. Studies of the vicissitudes of attachment and separation have increased our understanding of later behavior and even made some limited predictions possible (see Ainsworth, Bell, and Stayton, 1971; Clarke-Stewart, 1973; Main, 1973; Robertson and Robertson, 1971; Sroufe, Waters, and Matas, 1974). Further support for the complexity of behavior at this time is given by studies of identifiable and empirically useful complex behavioral patterns, such as affiliation, exploration, wariness, and fear (Ainsworth, Bell, and Stayton, 1971; Bischof, 1975; Bowlby, 1969; Bretherton and Ainsworth, 1974).

As development proceeds, the capacity for new levels of organization becomes identifiable, e.g., imitative and identificatory behavior, the beginnings of a sense of self, person and object permanence (Décarie, 1962; Mahler, Pine and Bergman, 1975; Piaget, 1936). While we should not lose sight of the adaptive value of basic rhythms, which continue, the infant now has some capacity both for delay and detour (intermediary devices) and for originality and initiative (Piaget's tertiary circular reactions). This capacity affords greater flexibility in dealing with and, to some degree, determining internal and external experience. Earlier we illustrated this advance in terms of the young child's ability to woo mother's attention in a variety of ways, rather than just being frustrated and crying as in the first month of life. The youngster's use of imitation to satisfy himself for a short time or his actively leading mother to a desired play object are other illustrations.

The toddler's capacity for behavioral organization, initiative, and internalizations (as illustrated by increased imitative behavior) actually represents a transitional stage between somatic and representational intelligence. The organization, originality, and initiative we see in tertiary cicular reactions in the interpersonal and emotional sphere set the foundation for the next level of intelligence.

Representational Intelligence: Phase I

The third step in the development of human intelligence is *representational intelligence: phase I.* The capacity for psychological representation indicates the potential for a new order of intelligence. The child can now mentally represent aspects of impersonal external objects, as well as external emotion- or affect-laden human objects, in whole or in part. In addition, the child is able to represent internal psychological events. These beginning organizations of the self call on various sensory experiences—proprioceptive, visual, auditory, olfactory, etc.

In its unstable form, the capacity for representation may be lost with the absence of the object, particularly the human object, or under the pressure of strong internal experiences (drive derivatives or affects). As mentioned above, in optimal development the capacity for human object constancy becomes stabilized only around age three (Mahler, Pine, and Bergman, 1975). This stabilization is gradual. At the external boundary, the capacity for object permanence has a developmental sequence similar to that of object constancy, but it reaches relative stability much earlier (Décarie, 1962). This difference in timing is most likely related to the greater variability and unpredictability of human objects (changing moods, behaviors, etc.). In any case, the capacity to maintain representations of the self and of both animate and inanimate objects, as well as to maintain the differentiation of self-representations and object representations, probably begins early in the first year and continues to develop throughout life.

It is interesting that psychoanalytic observers and Piaget agree that there is a kind of regression in thinking after the capacity for internal representation becomes established. Piaget refers to a vertical *décalage*, and psychoanalytic clinicians point to an increase in magical thinking. In line with this, Mahler, Pine, and Bergman (1975) describe a regression in the interpersonal dimension as characteristic of the rapprochement subphase of the separation-individuation process. At this time the child has the capacity for constructing mental representations of internal and external objects. He is, however, not yet able to organize them in any logical relationship to each other or to the external world; rather, he uses magical thinking.

Piaget notes that at the sensorimotor level the young infant begins with magical thinking. For example, we observe the young infant pull in the area of his crib where there once was a string, or pull on a string repeatedly even though there no longer is a bell at the other end. Only later, when learning by consequences occurs, does the infant differentiate between pulling on a string and hearing a sound, and pulling on a string when there is no sound. Thus, at the somatic level, the young infant begins to differentiate means from ends. The same process, Piaget posits, is repeated at a new level with the beginning of the capacity for psychological representations. While somatic intelligence continues, the capacity for representational intelligence begins again with magical thinking—hence his term *vertical décalage.*

Psychoanalytic observers describe this type of thinking as primary process, in which the mechanisms of condensation, displacement, incorporation, and projection, among others, are at work. They also describe it in terms of freely mobile cathexes, as opposed to the more stable, fixed cathexes that become invested in secondary-process thinking.

Mahler beautifully describes a regression similar to Piaget's vertical *décalage* crisis (Mahler, Pine, and Bergman, 1975). According to her, the youngster, at 18 to 24 months, after seeming to be "king or queen of his or her universe," undergoes regression in terms of becoming much more dependent. She hypothesizes that this rapprochement crisis occurs in part because the youngster becomes capable of seeing his own true size in relation to the universe; with the greater capacity for psychological representation, he can represent himself and others more accurately and see himself more separately from the "omnipotent" parental objects. Visualizing oneself as small in relation to the universe, Mahler posits, leads to much greater dependence on the maternal object in that the toddler no longer shares an "omnipotent umbrella" with her.

At this point it is important to distinguish two components of the capacity for psychological representation. Representational intelligence: phase I does not involve learning by consequences or means-ends differentiation to any significant degree. It is nevertheless a great leap in intelligent functioning. Now the child can represent stimuli from the inside and the outside; he is not limited simply to dealing with stimulation through patterns using the body. Also, there is now a capacity for organized psychological experience. A representation of the maternal object, for instance, can be held in the child's mind and the youngster can call on this representation even when the mother is absent. If there is stimulation from the interior in terms of yearning for physical contact with the mothering person, memories of the mother's sound, visual image, touch, smell, etc., can be organized through mental representation, and some sense of satisfaction of the need for physical closeness with the mother can be gained. Thus, stimulation from within can be dealt with by a new route. Earlier in life, the best the infant could do was to use imitative activity; before that he could only cry in protest and perhaps begin to quiet himself with rhythmic rocking.

As another indication of beginning representational capacities, it should be mentioned that during the first year many youngsters begin to comfort themselves with a transitional object associated with the nurturing experience, such as a piece of cloth or an old blanket. (See Winnicott's [1953] discussion of the "first not-me possession" and Greenacre [1969].)

At first, when representations are just beginning to be organized, they are susceptible to regression under the pressure of internal affect states. Feelings of displeasure, loss, or anger may bring forth a loss of the capacity for representation and a state of panic in the youngster. Later on, when there is greater stability in the representational system, the child can experience more differentiated affect states and psychological events without the danger of loss of the internalized object. Thus, the flexibility of the internal system increases in terms of being able to tolerate a wider variety of drive-derivative and affect states.

It is important to emphasize that phase I of representational intelligence is simply the capacity for representation. As we have noted, it is not reinforced by additional stabilizing influences and is vulnerable to regression. In addition, during the early phase of representational intelligence, there is not much differentiation between the internal and external boundaries, the animate and inanimate.

Representational Intelligence: Phase II

Representational intelligence: phase II is marked by the gradually increasing ability to learn by consequences again—that is, to differentiate means from ends—but now at a level of psychological representation. Parallel to what Mahler describes in terms of "on the way to object constancy," there is, both in the cognitive impersonal realm and in the emotion-laden interpersonal realm, a growing ability for reality testing. The youngster slowly ceases making the inanimate animate and begins to rely more on secondary-process thinking than on primary-process thinking as he heads from two toward and into four. This evolving capacity for accurate representation is made possible through learning by consequences at the representational level. Experience is not only represented internally, but is the vehicle for learning (e.g., trial and error). The greater capacity for memory and for discrimination that is part of this process will not be dealt with here.

Not only can the youngster now organize internal and external stimuli in psychological representations, but he can, through his evolving capacity for means-ends differentiation, discriminate relatively better between those organizations that are predominantly determined by events based solely on his internal experiences and those based on his external experiences. In other words, the youngster has the ability at the psychological level, as he had before at the somatic level, to differentiate, in a relative sense, self from nonself. That this advance occurs together with the consolidation of object constancy is not surprising; the youngster's ability to hold representations of the object, even when separated from the object and in the face of upsurges from drive-affect organizations, indicates this greater capacity for differentiation of self from nonself.

With this new capacity, anger at the mothering figure for going away does not necessarily mean that she has disappeared permanently. The child feels some assurance that she will be back—even if the separation is *imagined*—because he has learned that his mother returns regardless of what he has been feeling toward her. Nevertheless, some youngsters retain strong fears, and that these fears influence the structure of secondary-process thinking is not surprising. Such fears are multiply determined, and some parents may reinforce their youngster's fantasy. The mother who withdraws every time her youngster is angry, for instance, may facilitate an organization that intrudes upon and influences secondary-process thinking. The youngster remains fearful that his anger or assertiveness will in fact result in the loss of the object. This situation may form the nucleus of a depressive organization later in life.

Let us consider only optimal development for the moment. With the differentiation of self from nonself, there is greater flexibility to tolerate and deal with a wide range of internal and external stimuli. Not only does the child have the capacity for psychological representation of these events or situations, but he can maintain these representations under the pressure of other internal and external events and can differentiate internally derived representations from externally derived ones. Intelligence is therefore greater than earlier in life, since the child now assimilates, accommodates, and conserves a greater variety of stimuli, ranging over time and space, in relatively stable and permanent organizations.

We are not positing here a simple dichotomy between internally and externally derived representations. All representations of external reality are a product of human experience, or internal intelligence, and vice versa. But at this age there is a greater capacity than before for distinction between representations colored by primary-process thinking and the evolving capacity for secondary-process thinking. This new capacity is evidenced by the ability first to delineate the difference between self and nonself and then to organize means-ends relationships in terms of basic principles of causality.

Before continuing, brief mention should be made of the relationship between the capacity for mental representation and language. One way to learn about representational capacity is through language. They should not be confused as synonymous, however. Although we shall not discuss language capacity per se, we take the position here that language evolves in relation to a capacity for mental representation and is one indication of the semiotic function. As with all symbolic activity, maturational events (biological and social) are at its foundation. (For a fuller discussion of the relation between mental representation and language see Piaget, 1968a, pp. 92-93.)

Differences between Somatic and Representational Intelligence: Reality Testing

It has been stressed that when representational intelligence first occurs it is noncausal, or magical, just as somatic intelligence was. Even with representational magical thinking, however, the basic capacity for testing reality remains, because intelligence at the somatic level is still present. Thus, we notice that in normal development children may talk in a primary-process manner and yet be capable of behaving reasonably, particularly if parents set appropriate limits. There is a capacity for responding to appropriate environmental cues—that is, testing reality—even though the representational system is not yet well organized in terms of what we would ordinarily expect of secondary-process thinking. What comes to mind is the statement: "There is method to the madness," which is often made in reference to patients. This claim does not necessarily mean that a patient's seemingly primary-process thinking is manipulative or devious. Rather, it suggests that underneath the primary-process representational capacity, a more fundamental somatic intelligence is operating. Through the process of learning by consequences at the somatic, prerepresentational level, the patient has learned how to obtain what he desires from the environment.

It is important to re-emphasize that differentiation of self from nonself and means from ends first occurs at the level of somatic intelligence. The young infant first begins experiencing his world in terms of his actions on the world and the world's actions on him. Through repetitive actions, together with maturation of the central nervous system, a pattern of differentiation begins. A capacity for learning by consequences is superimposed on the more basic rhythmic-homeostatic adaptational capacities.

This early differentiation of self from nonself and means from ends provides the initial basis of reality testing—what we shall call somatic reality testing. Usually we think of the capacity to test reality in terms of representational intelligence, that is, the construction of thoughts in an adult form. Yet, if we observe the growing infant, we note that prior to achieving organized mental representations of objects, the infant shows a capacity for intelligent behavior with the environment and for some aspects of what we later call reality testing. He can deal with the environment in a realistic way. Learning by consequences is one form of this reality testing. In fact, the young toddler of 12 to 18 months often shows a greater capacity for following the rules communicated by parents and for learning readily by consequences than he does later, in the six months after the initial capacity for representation occurs. As discussed earlier, Piaget refers to a vertical *décalage* and Mahler, in her description of the rapprochement crisis, posits a regression secondary to the capacity for representation.

What we are emphasizing here is that initial, somatic intelligence is based on the effects of the organism's interaction with the environment. With the beginning capacity for representation of objects, there is at first a vertical *décalage* and a loss of some of the capacity for reality testing. Once differentiation of self from nonself and means from ends is re-established at the new level of mental representation, the capacity for reality testing is greatly enhanced. This higher order of intelligence also represents a higher order of reality testing.

It is interesting to note one aspect of the difference between reality testing at the somatic level and reality testing at the representational level. Representational intelligence may have more to do with the experience of reality than with the basic capacity for reality testing. This distinction is best illustrated in borderline and psychotic patients. Some patients have a disturbance in terms of their ability to represent objects realistically. There is a lack of differentiation of self- and object boundaries. Yet these same patients may have a sense of basic prerepresentational reality testing. One patient recently commented that she didn't feel like anything or anyone anymore and was losing her sense of the therapist. This frightening experience occurred under the pressure of certain transference configurations having to do with angry feelings. She continued rather dramatically in this vein. Her experience of reality, of herself, and of the therapist was being shattered, and this was quite threatening to her. Although the same patient, much earlier in her therapy, had shown gross distortions in reality testing, she did not experience these delusional beliefs as frightening, but was quite comfortable with them. It is important to note that during her recent experience, her capacity to test reality was intact, while her experience of reality was frighteningly vulnerable. She is currently at a more advanced stage in her treatment and has a good grasp on reality, even though her internal turmoil and pain are often far greater than before. This situation is not unusual. Grossly regressed psychotic patients, when they are improving, often go through painful depressions and other anxiety-laden experiences as they organize their experience of reality. This reaction occurs after they have gotten back in touch with the foundations of reality; that is, after they have given up some of their delusions. At the later stage in treatment their experience of reality, in contrast to their reality testing, may be impaired.

We are hypothesizing here that there can be a regression at the representational level while the basic capacity to test reality remains intact; what we see then is an impairment in the experience of reality. There is a difference between the patient who says, "I feel as though I were crazy," and the one who is *behaving crazily*, yet feels there is nothing wrong with him. Some patients feel and talk "crazy" but behave in reasonably appropriate ways when they have to perform certain acts; they can carry out the routine functions of everyday life. They can attend to demands, and they can learn by consequences and behave "rationally." This ability indicates a capacity for reality testing even though their experience of reality is grossly disorganized. Other patients, however, may appear more intact superficially, but have lost their capacity for somatic reality testing. In such cases there is a disturbance at the very foundation of learning how to adapt to the environment.

Another example (involving a lesser degree of psychopathology) is the person who is highly competent and effective but has a representation of himself as incompetent and ineffective. The basic capacity for effective competence may have some underpinnings at the somatic level of learning by consequences, in the infant's learning that he has some regular and predictable impact on the environment. Later experiences (e.g., conflicts) in the representational phases may lead to an altered picture of himself but may not necessarily alter the earlier basic capacity. Of course, we also see the reverse: people who have impairments in their basic capacity for effective behavior but who view themselves as competent.

In short, during the first year of life we see a gradual evolution of the capacity to adapt to the environment by use of the somatic means available. Later, as the capacity for representation becomes organized, a new level of intelligence evolves. Even in the second phase of representational intelligence, however, the system is not very flexible. While internal and external events can now be represented and there is a differentiation between self and nonself representations, the ability of this psychological system to deal with the great variety of internal and external events is limited. The representations of self and objects are still vulnerable to regression if internal or external stress is great enough. There is no structural capacity for forming derivative or altered representations to accommodate to conflict or to complex or intense affects. Instead, the system either closes out the stimulation (denial) or it regresses or dedifferentiates. The defenses of this stage (e.g., projection) tend to distort the self-object boundary.

Capacity for Transforming Representations: Phase I

The next stage of intelligence is governed by the capacity to construct *limited, transformed, derivative representational systems.* These new representational systems are related to the existing representational systems in permanent and stable structures. Piaget describes this new capacity for the impersonal realm in terms of the concrete operational child's ability to construct inverse and reciprocal relationships, although not together in the same system.

We suggest that this capacity begins at the internal boundary a good deal earlier (to initiate the oedipal stage) than Piaget has postulated for the external world. Initially, the new representational systems are limited in in terms of internal boundary intelligence, as they are for external boundary intelligence. For example, we observe in the latency child the capacity for constructing a system of reaction formations. The young child whose representations of a significant other—say, a younger sibling—are invested with drive-affect dispositions related to anger, jealousy, and the like, may, for a variety of reasons, construct a reaction formation in which he feels excessive liking and love for this younger sibling. Thus, the child constructs a new representational system based on his original representation of the sibling, but invested with a transformed derivative of the drive-affect disposition, that is, loving feelings. It is important to emphasize that in a true, differentiated reaction formation the new representational system remains tied through transformation to the original representation of the sibling.

This new representation, with its new drive-affect dispositions, is not a split-off representation but part of an integrated system. It is very different from the ego splitting or split representations we may find in normal children at an earlier age, when the capacity for representation is just forming, or in borderline or psychotic patients at a later age. Where there is splitting of representations, the two representational systems are not connected to each other through developmentally advanced transformations. Rather, the representations are completely separate—the "good" brother and the "bad" brother, the "good" mother and the "bad" mother. These attributes are not integrated as part of one person. In a reaction formation, the child consciously acknowledges only the "good" brother; the "bad" brother is repressed. He does, however, have access to some of the repressed feelings, through an understanding of the defenses (transformations) used to disguise them. The important point to emphasize here is that a reaction formation, based on the capacity to construct the inverse ("I hate you" to "I love you"), is part of an integrated system; that is, the new representations are related to the original representations through developmentally appropriate transformations.

The reciprocal may also be used to construct a new representational system related to the original representation. This type of transformation can be illustrated by carrying our example of feelings toward the sibling one step further. One can start off with a hateful, jealous set of feelings toward the sibling at the base of a hierarchical system of psychological representations and from this evolve a series of balanced feelings. From reciprocal relationships, one can love slightly more than one hates, or one can even love sometimes and hate sometimes. Thus, one can alter the drive-affect disposition for reasons of defense (e.g., related to superego formation) and yet maintain the underlying connection to the original drive-affect disposition investing the original representation.

Again, it must be emphasized that when this new representation is part of an integrated system, a series of self- and object representations exists at different hierarchical levels from different stages of development. All these representations are related to one another through transformations; that is, they are in a clear relationship to one another. We see this best in the process of analyzing a predominantly neurotic patient. As the defensive representational systems become experienced in the transference and are analyzed, there is access to other representations and their drive-affect dispositions, which lie at the base of a hierarchically organized structure. We see a quite different picture in borderline patients, who have not evolved integrated representational systems but instead use mechanisms such as ego splitting. Here the process of interpretation of defense does not lead readily to the developmentally earlier drive-affect representations, because where there is ego splitting, there are two separate, dissociated systems unconnected by developmentally appropriate transformational bridges.

As mentioned above, the capacity for transforming representations is consistent with Piaget's description of the ability to construct inverse and reciprocal relationships among objects in the impersonal, inanimate environment. This ability lays the foundation for seriation and classification tasks. What is highlighted here is the conceptualization of these new abilities, particularly in terms of their internal boundary significance, in terms of the capacity to construct new representational systems that have a relationship to existing representational systems through transformations such as the inverse and the reciprocal. Together with the original representations, these transformations provide for a cohesive structure.

As we indicated earlier, in the concrete operational period these new capacities are limited; they become vastly enhanced during the formal operational period. Nonetheless, in terms of the internal boundary, these capacities provide a significant advantage over earlier capacities. Now there is not only the ability to construct initial representations, but to construct new representations that have relationships to these existing representations and form part of a structure. This ability affords greatly increased flexibility. Certain drive-affect dispositions that are in conflict with other elements of the personality may now be altered through the construction of these new representational systems. In addition, the new representational systems provide for the tolerance of a greater variety and breadth (field of application and mobility) of internal and external stimuli simply because these stimuli can be dealt with more flexibly. Yet, though internal experience can be altered, the integrity and permanence of the representations and the basic sense of personal integrity are not altered.

Early in life, when the capacity for self- and object representation is not reinforced by transformations, the youngster does not have much flexibility in dealing with stimulation from the inside or the outside. Mechanisms such as ego splitting, denial, and projection are used, indicating that the youngster cannot tolerate much variety in terms of drive-affect dispositions or much intensity in terms of what he is experiencing from his internal world or from his affect-laden external world. Later on, as he grows and develops, there is a greater capacity for experiencing differentiated drive derivatives and emotional states and for tolerating a wider variety of interpersonal situations and recognizing their subtleties.

How do we account for the enhanced flexibility that we observe at the beginning of the oedipal phase, which evolves further during subsequent stages of development? As noted above, the foundation upon which this enhanced capacity rests is the youngster's capacity for constructing new representational systems, which increases the breadth of the internal and external stimuli experienced, augments the integration of past and present, and affords a much greater resilience in terms of permanence and stability. Experiences now no longer need to be shut out; they can be altered. They now no longer need to be denied, because they can be put into complicated reciprocal relationships with other representational systems that will more closely approximate reality without necessarily having a disruptive impact, as may have been true earlier in life. The new system has a much greater capacity to stretch and alter itself compared with the former system, which was very rigid and allowed little alteration.

It should be highlighted once again that it is these new capacities, which develop first at the internal boundary, that permit entry into the oedipal situation proper in terms of full triangularity. When the youngster can differentiate only self from nonself, he is still pretty much locked into a dyadic system in terms of his view of the world. Only with the ability to construct the new systems of representation can the youngster develop true triangular relationships. Before he acquired this ability, he could not process triangularity in a true sense. Now, through his capacity for constructing complementary series and relationships, as well as inverse relationships and class inclusion relationships, he is able to see relationships in various shades and gradations. He can appreciate and deal with a three-person system. This ability permits him not only to enter the oedipal situation but, as was discussed earlier, under optimal circumstances eventually to resolve it.

Thus, the capacity for constructing new representational systems not only affords greater flexibility for dealing with internal and external stimulation, but provides a foundation for more complex interpersonal relationships. It further stimulates the development of psychological structures and their concomitant adaptational flexibility. Nevertheless, as stated above, this new capacity is limited in that there are only two major transformations for constructing interiorized relationships: the inverse and the reciprocal. The child is at first not able to use both transformations in a system together. He can use them on only a limited number of variables in only a limited number of ways. Focus is on the present, anticipation of the future is not yet possible, and the ability for problem solving is restricted to problems with very limited numbers of variables.

Capacity for Transforming Representations: Phase II

The next stage in intelligence, representing the optimal level of human emotional intelligence, is the capacity for constructing *multiple, transformed, derivative representational systems.* This advance occurs during the formal operational period. Here there is a capacity for creating multiple representational systems related to the original representational systems through a series of complex transformations. The capacity for constructing these multiple representational systems is based not only on the transformations inherent in forming the inverse and the reciprocal, but on those possible in using the inverse and reciprocal together along with the correlative—all in one system. A multiple combinatorial system can not be constructed for the impersonal world, and there is relatively equivalent enhanced flexibility in the realm of internal representations.

The differences between concrete operational and formal operational thinking have already been described. We saw how the multiple combinatorial capacity permits the development of an organization (identity) that assimilates a wide breadth of internal and external stimuli, integrates them over time and space without any major alterations (i.e., new accommodations), and maintains a high degree of permanence of the elements within the system, along with stability of the entire system. In the earlier system, where only inverse or only reciprocal relationships can exist, as the variables to be contended with increase, solutions become more and more limited. In the later system, however, as the variables in the system increase, the potential solutions also increase. Thus, the capacity for constructing multiple representations related to the original representational system represents the optimal state of human intelligence, with the greatest flexibility in dealing with internal and external stimulation.

Viewed from the perspective of the construction of new multiple representational systems, we can understand the psychic structure in terms of a hierarchical model. At the bottom are the developmentally earliest self- and object representations. The construction of new but related representational systems then permits greater flexibility in dealing with the vicissitudes of drive-affect derivatives and external, interpersonal relatedness. These new related representational systems stem from each successive stage of development and are integrated with the representational systems that preceded them. There is thus a hierarchically layered, developmentally based organization of self- and object representations, all related to each other by certain transformations. The advanced structures organizing these transformations permit increasingly greater flexibility by way of lattices connecting the representational systems. While in the first phase of constructing new representational systems, the transformations are limited to the inverse and the reciprocal, in the second phase, the interconnections are essentially limited only to the degree that one's life experience defines and evolves certain patterns of identity that give cohesion and, in a sense, a signature to the pattern of integration. That the points of this intricate latticework are connected to an integrated whole strucure can be readily seen during the psychoanalysis of a rather mature individual with some simple encapsulated neurotic formations. The personality fits together and can be observed and understood through the transformations linking the different elements of the personality.

In this most advanced state, wholeness and permanence predominate, not at the expense of complexity, but consistent with a high degree of differentiation. In more circumscribed personality formations, such as those based on the limited representational systems of the concrete operational stage, the wholeness and permanence of the personality are maintained by restricting the degree of differentiation or the range of the lattice. In other words, there are only a few extended representational systems, with limited options around which identity can be integrated and stabilized. Certain elements of past experience must either be ignored or shut out and certain aspects of current endeavor restricted (e.g., severe obsessive or hysterical character disorders). Even more constricted is the person who has no capacity for forming new representational systems but must rely simply on the capacity for psychological representation. He has very limited flexibility and under stress shows patterns of withdrawal or dedifferentiation. Such persons do not show the cohesion or integration characteristic of those who can form and extend new representational systems. In contrast, they often use primitive defenses, which compromise the integrity of the basic representational system, in order to maintain whatever semblance of a sense of sameness over time is possible for them (e.g.; the borderline conditions). Most limited are states in which the capacity for representation itself is hampered, and regressions to prerepresentational modes of intelligent functioning are seen (e.g., autistic states).

At the two more advanced levels of extended representational systems, the guiding laws are not simply basic rhythms or learning by consequences, even though these two mechanisms of learning continue to maintain a role. As we have seen, the more sophisticated type of intelligence is governed by what Piaget has described as *interiorized operations.* In the realm of emotional learning, these interiorized operations enable the formation at first of limited relationships between different representations, and later, of complex, subtle, multiple relationships between representations (in a manner that lends itself to problem solving).

Overview of Levels of Intelligence

We have delineated a model with a number of milestones in the development of human intelligence:

1. Somatic intelligence governed by basic homeostatic patterns (rhythms).
2. Somatic intelligence governed by learning by consequences.
3. Representational intelligence.
4. Representational intelligence governed by learning by consequences and means-ends differentiation.
5. Representational intelligence with the capacity for forming limited, transformed, derivative representational systems.
6. Representational intelligence, with the capacity for forming multiple, transformed, derivative representational systems.

We have shown how these different stages of development constitute a useful model for understanding both the individual's relationship to the impersonal world and his intelligent functioning at the internal boundary. To repeat: the infant first deals with internal and external stimulation through use of his somatic system and basic rhythms. He then demonstrates learning through a somatic type of intelligence in terms of establishing means-ends relationships. With the next step he develops the capacity for psychological representation, a new form of intelligence. His problem, though, is how to use this capacity for psychological representation to deal with his increasingly complex internal and external worlds and at the same time maintain these representations. Initially he does so by differentiating self from nonself representations, but this only provides a limited flexibility to deal with the ever-growing internal drive-affect organization and increasing demand for a variety of external tasks. To bolster the capacity for representation, maturation makes possible a new capacity that permits the system to deal with a wider variety of internal and external stimulation while protecting and maintaining the basic representations. This is the capacity of transofrming representations, first through forming limited representational systems that are connected to the original representational system via a few transformations, and later through forming more complex multiple systems of representation that are connected to developmentally earlier representational systems via a complicated network involving inverses, reciprocals, and correlatives.

In our discussion here, specific aspects of human development that have been observed clinically are not dealt with, although certain aspects were considered in earlier chapters. It should be clear, however, that our model is consistent with such knowledge. For example, we know that the development of the superego begins at the stage of the first capacity for extended representational systems. The development of the ego ideal and the subtleties of identity formation in adolescence are consistent with the capacity for conserving multiple extended representational systems.

Earlier we described how deviations may occur from the optimal levels of structural organizations at each developmental phase. It is important, in highlighting the landmarks of our model, to repeat that the stimulus nutriments that are assimilated at the internal boundary are of a much higher degree of variability than their counterparts in the impersonal world. The configuration of the impersonal environment is rather predictable over time, given a certain minimal level of complexity. The impersonal world available to one youngster is similar to that available to many youngsters, provided, of course, that there is no severe stimulus deprivation. This is not true for the interpersonal world or for the drive- and affect-laden internal world. Here there is considerable variability in family patterns and dynamics, as well as in the drive-affect dispositions invested in the interpersonal objects. Given this great a variability, we can understand how the internal boundary may develop differently from the external boundary.

In addition, we observed how there may be differences in development at the external boundary because certain issues have not been resolved at the internal boundary (e.g., the lack of resolution of the oedipal situation may constrict the capacity for concrete operational thinking). As indicated earlier, the dynamics of the model are not simple. At times there may even be precocious external boundary development in response to limitations at the internal boundary. Thus, our foregoing discussion of the milestones in processing internal and external stimulation should be seen in the context of the developmental lines at each boundary and the transformational links that connect them.

We must also consider the possibility that selected capacities may partially emerge at a much earlier age than that usually expected. It is my impression from clinical observation that "islands" of precursors of concrete operational thinking appear in certain emotionally relevant (high motivational) areas as early as age two to two-and-one-half. One 25-month-old child, who wanted both to go outside and to eat a cookie, said, "I want to have the cookie first . . . I will go out later." This statement indicates a beginning sense of time, not unusual in this age group. It also, however, demonstrates an emerging capacity for comparing two wishes in terms of which should come first. This may be similar to the later seriation tasks with external objects (e.g., where comparisons of size are made). This child's repeated ability to make such determinations led to the impression that her statements were more than reiterations in an appropriate context of something she had heard.

A related observation involves a 26-month-old child. Angry about not getting something she wanted, she volunteered that certain people shouldn't try to give her lunch—"not Mommy, Daddy, Grandma, PaPa, Hilda [the baby sitter]." When asked again if she would accept lunch from each of these people (they were mentioned by name), she asserted, "*Nobody* . . . I don't want *anybody* to give me lunch." The use of "nobody" and "anybody" in an appropriate context implies an emerging capacity to group people into a class. She declared that no members of this class were acceptable to her.

It should be pointed out that these islands of verbal activity at two to two and a half years may not represent precursors of logical thinking at all; they may indicate only contextually appropriate verbal skills. Such spontaneous comments by young children, however, raise important questions. Do children have capacities for some operativity at a much earlier age than we usually think? Is there a difference in a child using these capacities in a structured experimental setting in comparison with a spontaneous situation where the child has a high degree of motivation? In other words, is there a difference between responses in an impersonal realm and an emotional realm? Studying spontaneous behavior in unstructured situations will undoubtedly provide the data to answer such questions.

In summarizing our model of intelligence we have not again discussed individually the dimensions of time, space, and causality, as we did earlier for external and internal boundary learning. It should be clear, however, that at each new stage of intelligence, at both the internal and external boundaries, there is increased capacity for assimilating a wider variety of internal and external stimuli across both time and space and for integrating them in a causal context.

At the earliest level of somatic intelligence, in which basic rhythms predominate, there is a kind of time-space unity. Time is dealt with through the patterning of the rhythmical actions, be they sleep-wake patterns or rocking paterns. Space tends to be undifferentiated and is experienced in an unintegrated manner according to the level of differentiation of sensory experience—visual space, tactile space, auditory space. The experiences of time and space come together in the mutual rhythmic movements of mother and infant. Causality in this earliest stage tends to be undifferentiated and is experienced in terms of achieving states of equilibrium through rhythmical actions; for example, relief from distress may be obtained through patterns of feeding and sleeping. These patterns are the precursors of a later sense of consequences and more differentiated forms of causality.

With somatic learning by consequences, time, space, and causality take on more distinct properties. For consequence learning to occur, the effects of one's behavior must be readily experienced within a certain time frame and in a spatial context. A sense of causality, in terms of perceiving one's impact on the environment, begins to evolve and sets up the capacity for initial schemes of means-ends differentiation.

With representational learning come great advances in the range of stimulation that can be experienced both spatially and temporally. There is now the capacity for recalling past events through representation, as well as for experiencing, through representation, events that are not present in immediate sensory experience. Notions of causality take on increasingly complex dimensions as a number of objects in various relationships to each other can be represented simultaneously and recalled. Later, with the capacity for transformed, derivative representational systems in logical relation to the original representational systems, there is even greater flexibility as the child is able to assimilate, accommodate to, and integrate increasingly wider ranges of internal and external stimuli across time and space, and to construct and conserve a set of causal relationships.

Levels of Learning

Thus far we have presented a hierarchical model for intelligent fundtioning based on the structural properties existing at different stages of mental organization. The sequence postulated helps us understand the processing of different types of impersonal external stimulation and internal stimulation.

In conceptualizing the different kinds of learning that occur, we have talked about somatic intelligence, representational intelligence, and representational intelligence reinforced by transformed, derivative representational systems. It is useful to summarize the progressive levels of learning in another way: learning by rhythms, learning by consequences, and learning by what Piaget calls interiorized operations and what we shall call *representational-structural learning*. Before the emergence of true structural learning, we see an earlier form of representational learning, corresponding with the beginning capacity to organize experience in terms of mental representations, which have a personal "meaning." Later, at the highest level, Piaget's "interiorized actions" approximate adult forms of logic. In psychoanalytic terms, we refer to the ability to construct transformed, derivative representations and to integrate them with the original representations in the context of secondary-process thinking.

While learning by consequences and interiorized operations (structural learning) are relatively clear, the earliest type of learning, learning by rhythms, is only partially understood and therefore deserves further comment and conceptual expansion. Because the earliest learning involves the infant's entire biological system, as well as his emerging psychological capacities, it may be appropriate to call this *somatic learning* (a broader term). Corresponding with our concept of somatic intelligence, this term conveys the involvement of the entire somatic system, including its capacity for organizing around basic rhythms and cycles. Somatic learning is consistent with and a more comprehensive version of what occurs early in the sensorimotor period, as described by Piaget and Inhelder (1966), and by empirical observations of the way infants use rhythmic patterns to deal with internal and external stimulation.

This earliest and perhaps most basic kind of learning is probably the hardest to define. One approach is by example—i.e., the neonate in a rhythmical rocking pattern with his mother. In the optimal situation there appears to be a "synchrony" or "fitting in" between the infant and the environment (see Winnicott, 1954, 1956). When this "fitting-in" process is appropriate, we often see the baby begin to organize aspects of his somatic functioning. The ability of the neonate to begin to organize sleep-wake and alertness patterns, for instance, is in part related to environmental variables and is not solely a maturational process (Sander, 1962).

That a special type of early learning does exist is also indicated by recent research on imprinting and critical periods, which shows that in certain animal species, even prenatally, selected "environmental experiences" act as inducers, refiners, and maintainers for later behavioral patterns. The ability of the baby duck to respond preferentially to its mother's call, for example, is in part related to experiential factors that have occurred a few days before birth (Gottlieb, 1971, 1976, 1978). The synchrony between a baby's behavior and the maternal voice pattern is further evidence of a type of "fitting in" between the neonate and his environment (Klaus and Kennell, 1976).

It should be pointed out that in addition to somatic, organismic learning, early in life organisms appear to be capable of responding to pain and pleasure and at times their behavior seems shaped by consequences (Gewirtz, 1965, 1969; Lipsitt, 1966). We may also postulate that even the third level of learning—organizing internal representational experience—may begin at this stage, as there is now evidence that imitative behavior occurs during the earliest time of life (Meltzoff and Moore, 1977). These observations should not, however, lead us to assume that learning by consequences or by meanings is predominant early in life. All types of learning may occur at all times, but the most relevant is the predominant type of learning at each developmental phase. Even with the ability for structural learning through interiorized operations, basic somatic patterns and learning by consequences still provide a continuing adaptive foundation for relating to the environment.

At this point it may be useful to speculate in an illustrative manner on the role of these types of learning in the psychotherapeutic process and relationships in general. One ingredient of the psychotherapeutic process and relationships has to do with "basic fit." Some say there are "good vibrations" between a therapist and patient, or between two people. This "fit" may be related to issues arising early in the first year of life, to basic rhythmic patterns between mother and infant (see Stern, 1974a). In other words, aspects of a positive therapeutic experience may be related to recapturing an early feeling of being understood, as in the harmonious patterning of mother and infant. Much has been written on this subject, but we shall not go into it here, except to suggest that early somatic learning based on rhythmic homeostatic patterning may provide a basis for what we have all too often left to ill-defined constructs.

At a second level in all relationships, particularly therapeutic relationships, there is learning by consequences. That is, through providing responses—comments, clarifications, interpretations—we tend to help the patient learn about himself. We also learn from the patient through the feedback he gives us: his responses (associations) to our comments, clarifications, and interpretations. There is a process of mutual learning by consequences in any relationship as two people learn to adjust or adapt to one another in line with the goals of that relationship. Behavior modification techniques, which use the principles of operant learning theory, are based on learning by consequences. Although the operant learning model can be applied to complex human emotions as well as to simple behavior (see Greenspan, 1975), it does not in itself explain enough to provide a full model of human learning.

The highest level of learning is structural learning, which Piaget calls learning by interiorized actions in the concrete and formal sense. We know, for example, that a complex human being can shift his goals in the middle of a learning experience and thereby shift the meanings and impact of consequences. Simple notions of consequence learning are therefore not enough. The fully mature, optimally intelligent human being has the capacity for structural learning, which involves complex linkages between clusters of internal variables, all of which can be related to one another. Here we find the capacity for shifting meanings and for seeing relationships among meanings at a high level of intelligent functioning.

To carry our illustration about the therapeutic process further: much of the learning that occurs, occurs at this advanced level, where the meaning of events and of their connections with other meanings and with life experiences—that is, how groups of variables relate to one another—can be understood in terms of problem solving. Helping the individual reconstruct the early basis for his current difficulties involves just such a process. On the part of the patient, this kind of learning calls for the highest level of the capacity for assimilation and integration. For this capacity to be operative at its optimal level, the capacity for combinatorial thinking characteristic of the formal operational phase is imperative.

Yet it is important to re-emphasize that we never see this kind of learning without the concurrent presence of learning by consequences and the more basic somatic learning. In developing our model we should remember that in the optimal organization, learning is always occurring at all levels and that somatic-rhythmic, consequence, and representational-structural learning occur in the context of somatic, representational, and transformed, derivative representational structures.

The Relationship between Somatic and Representational Patterns in Learning

At this point we need to consider how the different types of learning relate to each other in terms of the levels of intelligence involved. Somatic learning sets into motion certain general organismic processes, such as style of relaxation and achievement of internal harmony. Consequence learning at the somatic level accounts for the further differentiation and, in part, the highly sophisticated discriminatory capacities we observe in the infant and toddler. Representational patterns (which may appear early in the first year) begin to dominate learning toward the end of the second year, as internal and external experience become organized into mental symbols. Eventually, these symbols can be transformed and manipulated according to principles of logic. How, though, do somatic patterns relate in an ongoing manner to representational patterns?

First, somatic patterns form part of the very structure of the representational system. Second, somatic patterns are included in the experiences that eventually become organized (internalized) at a representational level, and, third, somatic experience is constantly perceived by the representational structures and is interpreted and transformed just as external experience is. The early somatic pattern of arousal, for instance, forms the basis for the later intensity of internal representation. The early stimulus threshold (the somatic pattern of shutting out stimulation) lays the foundation for the later tendency of the representational system *not* to represent or experience at this higher level certain noxious sensations (e.g., a type of structural denial).

During the second year of life (when complex interactions

are becoming organized and internalized), the somatic patterns involved in these interactions also become organized and internalized at a representational level. For example, the toddler who experiences intense somatic irritability with stimulation (based on earlier somatic learning) may come to experience any stimulating human relationship as "irritating" and thereby form a mental image (representation) that combines the earlier somatic proclivity with the later complex human experience. A personal "meaning" is established incorporating the earlier tendency (e.g., human relationships are accompanied by irritation.

To take another example: the somatically very active infant may in the second year of life use this activity to express rage. If mother or father withdraws as a consequence of this rage, the toddler may internalize a representation associating activity and rage with loss of human contact. Again a meaning becomes organized that includes both the original somatic proclivity and the later interaction (e.g., activity and withdrawal). Similarly, early somatic pleasure patterns may become connected with complex human relationships, which become internalized and reach a representational level.

The representational system, once organized, shows a distinct tendency to perceive, interpret, and modify experience, including "somatic" experience.[3] For example, if the toddler learns that pleasure leads to separation from caretakers, or if pleasurable experiences are avoided entirely by parents, the representational system, once formed, may either deny (for purposes of defense) or, more ominously, never develop the representational channels or access points for this type of experience.

Consider the work on anorexia nervosa and obesity by Bruch (1973). She postulates that because of experiences in early life, certain infants, toddlers, and young children never become aware of such basic bodily sensations as hunger. In contrast, other children may be hyperreactive to minimal amounts of stimulation. Some adults are acutely aware of sensations such

[3] The sensations from the body exist not only as neurophysiological events, but as somatically learned patterns.

as sexual longing, while others may be totally unaware of such feelings. In some instances, for dynamic reasons, the denial of usually experienced sensations or feelings will occur secondarily. In other instances, because of the lack of confirmatory parental repsonses to the infant's expression of certain internal states, certain bodily feelings or impulses never develop access to awareness. We commonly assume human feelings are repressed secondarily. We do not assume the reverse—that early schemes and patterns related to these biological sensations may never become consolidated, or that the links with the representational, psychological, experiential systems may never be established.

How experiences which existed initially at somatic levels take on representational properites can be seen as a gradual process of differentiation. At some point the differentiation shifts to a higher level and a *new form,* that of representation. Let us consider the infant with a "good-enough" environment and an appropriate "fitting-in" experience. Initially, peacefulness, harmony, and tranquility may be implied by the baby's smile and restful, relaxed state. As complex interactions with the environment develop with the growing autonomy of the toddler, these early undifferentiated pleasurable responses (which have become somewhat more differentiated at a behavioral level) begin to take on meanings. Pleasure now exists in the context of the organization of certain memory traces and is connected with certain patterns of interaction, the representation of the self (multisensory or multimodality), and the representation of the other, or the world. The early pleasurable state, which was inferred by a smile and existed at a prerepresentational level, may now exist as an internal representational experience, highly differentiated in nature and available for evocation as a memory of fantasy. For example, a specific bodily zone, such as the genitals or hands, may now be a source of pleasure in the context of specific interactions with mother or father, such as being bathed or wrestled with.

Defects in the transition from somatic to representational levels may affect the capacity for internal imagery. In relation to alexithymia, Nemiah (1977) hypothesizes that certain psychosomatic and substance abuse patients (as well as certain borderline patients) have a special defect in their capacity for experiencing internal states involving affects. Affects are related to the sympathetic and parasympathetic nervous system and at the same time exist in the context of psychological meaning. Developmentally advanced affects, such as compassion, empathy, love, and anger, have differentiated meanings in contrast to their primitive precursors (comfort, discomfort, protest), which are more directly linked to basic neurophysiological processes. The imitative and identificatory processes of the second year of life are the mediating experiences between the more biologically oriented schemes and the emerging psychological organizations. These processes determine to some degree the nature, character, and structure of the psychological functions and their relationship to somatic experience.

Issues of Specificity and Intensity in Relation to Somatic and Representational Patterns

Freud's (1915) theory of instincts was an important contribution toward delineating the relationship between the somatic or biological and psychological processes. By postulating that drive energy could be transformed and become attached to wishes and ideas, he elaborated a relationship between physiological and mental phenomena. The energic concepts of early psychoanalytic theory have been seriously questioned, however. Psychoanalytic ego psychology to some degree has attempted to resolve these questions by placing emphasis on the formation of ego substructures, which evolve through early object relations. Rather than evolving from the transformation of drive energies, psychic structure is viewed as existing from the beginning as part of "an undifferentiated matrix," and acquiring drive-affect dispositions through maturation and the accumulation of human experience (Hartmann, 1939). In a sense, this approach begs the issue of transformation of drive energy by taking as its starting point mental representations, with drive-affect dispositions accruing to them (Kernberg, 1975). How, then, does one account for the intensity of excitation or degree of pleasure? How does one account for zonal preferences?

Early in his theorizing, Freud proposed that hypercathexis,

the investment of large amounts of energy, could explain increased intensity of sensation. He also postulated that different zones of the body or different modalities may become hypercathected. The skin may become "libidinized," for example. He suggested that at different stages of development different zones become cathected (the oral zone, the anal zone, the phallic zone, etc.). Without recapitulating Freud's theory of instincts, it is worth noting that models that ignore Freud's energic constructs have a difficult time accounting for the phenomena Freud was trying to understand. Neither instinct theory nor the more recent developments in ego psychology and object relations theory have accounted for these clinical phenomena. George Klein (1969) has proposed a model involving cognitive schemes, but he does not deal with the precognitive somatic levels of excitation and other neurophysiological events. A theoretical model that assumes representational capacity and considers somatic events only in their representational or symbolic form overlooks much of what occurs in development in the first year of life—the real issues of somatic-representational, or mind-body relationships.

Our model of levels of intelligence and learning offers a new understanding of intensity and zonal or modal preference. Each baby has his own individual maturational pattern and innate givens in part account for intensity of sensation and zonal preferences. There may, for example, be individual differences in the number of nerve fiber endings in different zones. Maturation combines with environmental experience in the earliest stages to determine early somatically based schemes. The mother who sensitively and pleasurably breast-feeds her baby may help consolidate the baby's already pleasurable experiences around the oral zone. One can envision repeated stimulation of certain zones at pleasurable levels leading to a scheme for this early experience. We do not need to postulate psychic energy disposed at a location in the body; we are merely suggesting that certain repetitive patterns of experience become organized into a somatic scheme (much as Piaget talks about early sensorimotor schemes forming through repetition in the cognitive realm). The repetition itself sets up an organization of early experience. To the degree that this early experience is highly pleasurable, the scheme consolidates the physiological and emerging affective components.

At the level of consequence learning, further differentiaton of these schemes may occur. For example, a mother may selectively reinforce pleasurable experience around certain parts of the body, e.g., the feet. These body parts may then be experienced as zones of pleasure (as well as zones of attachment and contact with the nurturing object).

As experience begins to shift to the third level of learning through the organization of imitative and identificatory processes, we may observe another process by which we can account for intensity and zonal specificity. During this period experience is becoming internalized and takes on meanings. An interaction, which initially was purely at the somatic level of learning (a mother strokes her infant's body and the infant begins organizing schemes of pleasure around bodily stroking), now becomes an experience with meaning. Memory traces of pleasurable interaction emerge. At a mental representational level, both the emotional experience of pleasure, as well as the cognitive experience of how this pleasure occurs, become part of an organized system of memories. As further internalization takes place, an organization of experience emerges that becomes identified as the "self." We can postulate that the representation of the self is at first a "body self." The self that becomes organized is the self that has been experienced. It is the self of perceptions and sensations. This self-representation need not be an *accurate* perception of the self. Thus, if a body zone has been an unusual focus of experience, either of pleasure or pain, it may assume a relatively prominent place in the initial representation of the self. At the level of meanings we may see special emphasis and/or zonal specificities in the formation of the initial representations. In the very structure of the mental representation we now have a way to account for the issues of intensity and zonal specificity.

Yet, once the mental representational system is formed, how are variations in intensity (for example, excitement) explained? How does one account for the relationship between changing somatic experience and representational experience without using a concept such as transformation of energy? Again, we can postulate that just as the representational system organizes itself to perceive the external world, it can perceive sensation from the interior of the body. How and what it perceives depends in part on earlier learning. As indicated, certain sensations can be denied; others can have special importance.

Sensations in the somatic sphere are first experienced and organized in terms of somatic schemes. Later these sensations are perceived at the representational-structural level of learning. Depending on the dynamic relationship to the earlier somatic level of learning, the person may accurately perceive what is going on in his body, may "down-play" what is going on, or may "hyperreact" to it. If, for example, during the stage of internalization, the youngster connects a pleasurable bodily experience to the withdrawal of the nurturing object, the pleasurable experience may take on a frightening meaning and foster the tendency to ignore certain sensations from the interior of the body.

Certain somatic patterns may never become schematized or gain access to the rational realm. With the toddler, for example, interpersonal relationships are minimal and relationships are mostly to the inanimate environment. Emotion-laden somatic schemes and representations are only beginning to form. If a youngster's exploratory and assertive behavior is undermined by an overly controlling mother, he may then turn toward the inanimate world which he can "control." The mother who misperceives or misinterprets her toddler's behavior—exclaiming, "Oh, my little boy is sick and not feeling well," rather than acknowledging "My little boy is assertive and angry"—may encourage distorted representational meanings. In some instances, these structuralized meanings may lead to the overestimation of certain somatic experiences. The mother who overreacts to a youngster's discomfort may facilitate a distorted internalization of experience so that the youngster interprets any, even minimally uncomfortable sensation from the interior of the body as a major illness.

As stated earlier, the intensity of the somatic patterns themselves initially determines the resultant experience. Later transformations within the extended representational structures may further alter the meaning of somatic experience. Thus, the issues of intensity and specificity are related to the initial somatic schemes, the experiences leading up to internalization, the structure and character of the representational system itself, and the later transformations that representations may undergo.

A Speculative Application

To illustrate the potential use of our model of levels of learning in understanding a variety of clinical phemomena, we shall speculate on its application to an area that might not immediately come to mind—the relationship between somatic patterning and the specificity of drug response. It is often difficult to determine without some trial and error which therapeutic pharmacologic agent in a class of agents (e.g., which antidepressant) will be most helpful for a given patient. Some patients, for example, improve with sedating and even mildly depersonalizing phenothiazines, while others become worse with these. Similarly, which nontherapeutic drug a person will become addicted or habituated to seems to be related to individually different proclivities. Some substance abusers become addicted to barbiturates while others choose amphetamines. It has been suggested that the choice of nontherapeutic addictive drugs is related to personality dynamics. Our model may prove useful in understanding drug specificity.

Briefly, our hypothesis is that the drug that has a therapeutic effect or the nontherapeutic drug the person chooses is that drug which creates an internal "core mood state" that in some manner replicates a desired early somatic pattern. During the early stages of infancy and toddlerhood each person experiences a certain "fitting in," a somatic patterning associated with a state of connectedness, wholeness, organization, or well-being. For some this feeling of connectedness, wholeness, and organization may have occurred in the context of their own individual or a dyadic hyperreactive style (e.g., either they or the caregiver or both may have been frenetic). In others this sense of wholeness may have occurred in the context of an apathetic, subdued, even seemingly impersonal "fitting-in" relationship (e.g., a depressed or withdrawn caregiver). For others the only "connectedness" that was organizing may have been with certain visual experiences, sounds, or inanimate stimuli. While the hyperkinetic, mildly apathetic, or impersonal dyadic pattern do not come close to what we would call an optimal interactive style between caregiver and infant, for many persons these patterns were the only way in which they could relate to their human or nonhuman environments—it was the "best they had." For them, this early pattern may have become a "core organizing mood state" during the first years of life. Later in development there are attempts to re-create this core mood state, however idiosyncratic and nonoptimal it may appear to others. The desire to re-create this core mood state may be particularly strong when the integrity of personality functioning is threatened or when dysphoric affects emerge.

It is in this light that we might speculate that the drug responded to is that drug which re-creates the particular core organizing mood state experienced during infancy. This core mood state makes the person feel better, and thus may secondarily assist in alleviating symptoms and dealing with dysphoric affects. In other words, while all drugs have a direct effect on the central nervous system, in many instances this direct effect operates as an intermediary process creating a certain mood state. The person then perceives and responds according to this mood state. If this mood state provides a feeling of organization, fitting in, connectedness, and well-being similar to that experienced in infancy and childhood (i.e., early somatic patterning), then it may have a therapeutic or otherwise sought-after impact on personality functioning.

This hypothesis provides understanding of the impact of what would usually be thought of as solely a somatic event, i.e., the effect of a pharmacologic agent. It is not necessary to think of these events only in relation to their direct effects on the central nervous system. Instead, we can think of these events as affected by patterns of early somatic learning. These patterns of early somatic learning are perceived by and integrated with later patterns of representational learning. It is the meaning of the early somatic event, together with the direct somatic experience, that determines the final behavioral response.

Some Implications for a Unifying Construct

Current understanding of human development is based on focused inquiry from a number of approaches. In this work we have attempted, through integrating concepts from psychoanalytic and Piagetian developmental psychology, to develop a unifying construct which may make it possible to take into account the observations and theoretical frameworks of several of these approaches.

The need for a unifying construct can be highlighted by looking at the various developmental dimensions that *one* discipline, psychoanalysis, has studied: drives, wishes and motives, adaptive capacities, object relations, psychological structures, and psychosocial adaptation. Within each of these lines of psychoanalytic inquiry we see different emphases and models, as each group of investigators studies, in microscopic detail, highly specific phenomena at close range. Similarly, within the realm of understanding cognitive development, we not only have Piaget's approach, which is perhaps the most complete in presenting a general model, but also the work of others, such as Kagan (1978) or Werner and Kaplan (1963).

If we look at empirical studies of infancy and early childhood, we observe a shift away from attempts at establishing norms, to observational and empirical studies of individual differences in infants and their families along multiple developmental lines (e.g., Ainsworth, 1973; Brazelton, 1973; Emde, Gaensbauer, and Harmon, 1976; Escalona, 1963; Sandler, Holder, and Meers, 1963; Sroufe and Waters, 1976; Stern, 1974a). Many of these studies look at different, yet related aspects of development. Emde and his colleagues (1976), for instance, relate some of Spitz's observations (1965) on social behavior to neurophysiological patterns in the developing infant. Such correspondences only confirm that scientiests with a variety of approaches are studying the same basic phenomenon, although they may focus on certain component parts or use particular methods.

The question remains, however: How do we develop a unifying construct which can begin to take into account the data emerging from many sources and settings—from psychoanalytic, cognitive, and neurophysiological studies, from direct observational, naturalistic, laboratory, or controlled settings? Such an integration requires an organizing construct that is at a different level of abstraction, rather than a construct closely tied to a given content area. Within our general construct, different content areas may be integrated and new discoveries may add to the knowledge of human development without diverting the focus for too long a time. (At present a new clinical or theoretical focus often diverts attention from other useful, earlier foci.)

The lack of unifying constructs is perhaps most evident in our inability to see continuities and discontinuities in the progressive development of behavior. While some studies have shown that continuities exist (Ainsworth, 1973; Sroufe and Waters, 1977), and work with clinical populations suggests the existence of certain continuities, other investigators, working with normative populations, have indicated that continuities are the exception rather than the rule (Bell, Weller, and Waldrop, 1971). Debate continues over whether or not predictions can be made from one stage of development to another.

There are various explanations for the failure to demonstrate continuities across stages of development. (1) Variations occur in environmental factors. (2) Behavior transforms itself across stages, precluding simple predictions from one stage to another. (If, however, we know the transformational laws involved in changing behavioral organizations from one stage to another, we may be better able to see continuities.) (3) Variations occur in rate of maturation. (4) Tasks at different stages call on different adaptive capacities. A certain cognitive style, for instance, may lead to vulnerability at one stage and adaptability at another. (5) Too many variables are interacting with one another. (6) Behavior is so plastic and flexible that shifts occur from one behavioral domain to another across developmental stages. For example, a child who appears to be cognitively retarded at one stage of development may then develop adequate cognitive functioning, but show emotional difficulties at another stage of development.

For some or all of the above reasons, certain investigators have been pessimistic about finding continuities in human development. But it may be that this pessimism is based on the lack of high-order constructs for the understanding of behavioral organization at any given time. These constructs need to be of a high-enough order to take into account complexities such as internal and external behavioral transformations and environmental change. There is some evidence that if we shift in this direction, our ability to see the continuities and discontinuities in behavior may improve, as illustrated by the work in progress of Sroufe and colleagues at the University of Minnesota. Using an attachment paradigm similar to that of Ainsorth (1973) to study separation-reunion has enabled them to predict aspects of future behavior, such as peer competence, across a developmental stage. Especially interesting is their attempt to look at aspects of cognitive, affective, and behavioral organization together, in order to observe continuities and discontinuities.

The model presented here not only lends itself toward taking into account the complexity of behavior, but enhances our ability to see continuities and discontinuities in development. If we look at levels of equilibrium or the level of integration at each phase of development, instead of looking at specific behaviors or behavioral constellations, we may be better able to see relationships from one phase to another. In contrast, the attachment paradigm, although it considers a number of related behaviors, still focuses on only one behavioral domain. It uses a single set of complex variables or "indicator behaviors," such as the nature of contingent or reciprocal interaction between the mother and the baby, the way in which the baby discriminates the primary caretaker from strangers, or the way in which the baby reunites with the mother. Instead, we would suggest looking at the level of integration achieved in various domains involving the infant or child and his or her environment.[4]

To provide an empirical prospect for using the notion of equilibrium or level of integration, it is important to specify how we would characterize the level of integration in a given domain at a specific developmental level in terms not only of cognitive but psychological and social variables. We can look at

[4] Anna Freud's (1954, 1965) concept of developmental lines suggests a more comprehensive approach.

the level of integration according to the four parameters outlined earlier, derived from Piaget's original conceptualization of levels of equilibrium. Only in this context will the four parameters be more universal, in that they will apply to wishes, feelings, affect-laden interpersonal relationships, as well as to the impersonal environment.

Range (Field of Application)

The level of integration can be characterized by the range of phase-expected human experience and/or behaviors. In infancy, for example, we may observe a shallow, mechanical attachment to the mother. Within this shallow range of feelings states, the only expression of pleasure may be related to mere relief of frustration. There are no signs of eagerness, joy, or happiness. The mother's responsiveness or contingent reactions to the baby are limited to physical ministrations and do not express the range of human potential. At the other end of the spectrum is a mother-baby interaction where the six-month-old baby demonstrates, through facial expressions and other behaviors, joy and pleasure as well as frustration, anguish, and many subtle states in between, and is able to engage the mother in a deeply experienced, basically pleasurable relationship. The mother responds contingently with differentiated, appropriate affect states and behaviors to the broad spectrum of the infant's behaviors.

In adulthood, we can make similar comparisons in the range of experience expressed. A schizoid adult may maintain a certain intrapsychic equilibrium, but only at the expense of engaging in interpersonal relationships of an affective nature. In contrast, the mature adult is capable of a wide range of phase-appropriate experience including a variety of feeling states and wishes (happiness, glee, joy, empathy, curiosity, assertiveness, anger, disappointment, sadness, mourning, etc.). These internal experiences can be integrated across interpersonal relationships, from intimate family relationships, to relationships at work and in professional life, to more casual relationships associated with hobbies and leisure activities. We can also compare adults in between the schizoid and optimal position in terms of the range of wishes, ideas, thoughts, feelings, internal structures, and interpersonal patterns they can employ. There may, for example, be selected constrictions such as limitations in the capacity for anger, assertion, intimacy, sex, or abstract thought.

In considering the potential range of developmentally expected experience, it is important to be systematic and examine a number of domains. We should, for example, include neurophysiological aspects; cognition (instrumental and conceptual); wishes (e.g., along the pleasure-displeasure continuum); feelings; thoughts; internal representations; internal structures such as the psychological organizations dealing with self-esteem, limit setting, self-delineation, reality testing, impulse regulation, affect organization, tolerance for frustration and stress, creative thinking and behavior, etc.; human relationships (e.g., in terms of dyadic, triangular, and post-triangular patterns); ongoing experience with the world; and manifest behavior.

The range of phase-expected patterns in each area and for some or all of the areas together can then be ascertained, as can their mobility, stability, and permanence. What is being emphasized is that our model lends itself to formulating the level of integration for a specific area or line of development from the organization of neurophysiological patterns to the organization of human relationships, as well as the level for development as a whole, encompassing multiple lines. For empirical purposes, the phase-specific criteria for conceptualizing experiences in the areas under study can be developed according to the character and level of inquiry.

Mobility

The level of integration can be characterized according to ability to integrate the past, engage in the present, and prepare for the future. Some persons, and we observe this in infancy, early childhood, and on through adulthood, evince a psychological organization that integrates the past, while preparing and moving toward the next developmental phases. For example, we see adults who have good continuity in terms of feeling states and memories of past relationships, which have been incorporated into their current psychological makeup and sense of self. We described this ability in discussing the optimal late adolescent and adult in terms of "combinatorial level" structures. On the other hand, we observe persons who have a stable sense of self but are limited in terms of continuity in their feelings and memories with the past.

We also observe persons who, while dealing with current psychological reality, are beginning to cope with the issues of the next developmental phase—for example, late adolescents dealing with separation from their parents and movement into the vocational, sexual, and interpersonal demands of adulthood; latency children showing the first signs of adolescence; preoedipal children entering the triangular oedipal stage. We may compare those who have continuity of the past as well as preparedness for moving into the future with those who do not have continuity with the past, and/or seem reluctant to step into the future. An adolescent, for example, may hold onto the real parental relationships; a latency child may remain at a concrete cognitive level, reluctant to move into the peer relationships and feeling states of adolescence; a preoedipal child with separation fears may be too anxious to move into the triangular situation of expanded relationships.

Even in infants and very young children we can observe these differences. An eight-month-old infant may integrate early homeostatic experiences, where basic rhythmic patterns and the underlying capacity for self-regulation are established, so that we see joy and curiosity in his experiencing of attachment, differentiated reciprocal interaction, discrimination between significant adults, and beginning patterns of internalization. New discriminations occur in the context of inquisitive inspection of new people and secure attachments to the primary caregivers. Movement toward exploration, imitation, and internalization is facilitated by fluid shifts to earlier experiences, which form the basis of security and continuity for new development. In contrast, the youngster who has not integrated the past may be able to differentiate others, but may show immense anxiety, ambivalence, or fear of loss. He does not have a pleasurable, secure attachment and solid patterns of internal regulation to call on as a basis for new development.

Stability

A third parameter that we can look at is the stability of the organizing structure. Can it deal with stress? Are there only transient disruptions, or are there major regressions in functioning? What is the range and intensity of stress it can handle before major disruptions occur? If we consider the optimal adult described in earlier sections, who can integrate a wide ranges of wishes, feelings, and interpersonal relationships across his interpersonal, family, and professional life—how easily is this person's basically cohesive organization disrupted by certain experiences? Similarly, if we consider the eleven-month-old toddler who explores his world from the secure base of a solid and pleasurable attachment with mother—how well does he do when under mild distress due to minor illness, such as a sore throat? How well does he do when there are other stresses such as mother's being preoccupied and slightly less available? Is there a transient distress and then a return to a stable organization which integrates a wide range of behaviors, feelings, and interpersonal relationships, or does the dyad show marked disorganizations and regressions? The baby who abandons his explorative interests at age eleven to thirteen months and becomes clinging, loses the ability to walk, and stops imitating, all because mother has been depressed for two days, differs from the baby who becomes transiently fussy and protests when mother is depressed.

Permanence

A fourth way to characterize the level of integration of a structure is in terms of the degree to which that structure provides for the integrity of its individual elements, e.g., in human development, the integrity of the evolving sense of self. In other words, is there in infancy and on through adulthood, a gradual evolution of a sense of self, a personal signature, some core, evolving permanence? There are, for example, people who experience a wide range of interpersonal wishes, feelings, and interactions across various dimensions, who are quite resilient to stress in maintaining that organization, and who are in touch with the past and anticipate the future. They do not, however, experience a highly differentiated sense of self. In other words, they have not given differentiated, unique personal signature to their personality organization. Obviously, in early infancy one's signature is relatively undifferentiated and becomes more differentiated only as one grows into adulthood.

Some people have a unique sense of self which is conveyed through communications with others, but only at the expense of the range of feelings experienced. For example, if a stubborn or negativistic streak becomes the personal signature, flexibility in the range of behavior and/or feeling is sacrificed as saying "no" and refusing everything dominates. In other cases, as in a protracted identity crisis, stability and range can be maintained, but only by giving up the sense of cohesion that this personal signature affords.

Permanence is less specific in many ways than the other features discussed, but it is nonetheless important. It is the counterpart to "range." In line with this, some people appear to have a wide range of behavior, but at the expense of a cohesive sense of self (e.g., the person with shifting motives, values, etc.).

In terms of the four parameters of organization presented above, we can look at the way the infant establishes initial homeostatic patterns in relation to the environment, at how self-regulation and basic rhythms (sleep-wake, eating cycles) are affected by relationships with primary caregivers. We can examine the range of experience this infant is able to engage in while maintaining some stability in his initial regulating structures, observe how stable these organizations are to stress, and see the ways in which this infant is preparing for future development and beginning to evolve a personal style or signature. Later on, as this infant develops a pattern of attachment, we can again look at the depth, richness, and variety of experience in this attachment (here we can consider the mother's response to the infant as part of a dyadic unit). We can observe the way in which this organization integrates earlier patterns and is adaptive for future development, as well as the way in which the patterns themselves take on the unique personal signature of the developing infant or mother-infant dyad.

While we could continue this description throughout infancy, early childhood, and adulthood, perhaps two further examples will prove especially useful in illustrating the concept of level of integration. At eight to twelve months, when the infant is growing into a toddler and is able to differentiate the primary caregiver from other significant adults, we begin to see the separation and reunion behaviors described so well by Ainsworth, Bell, and Stayton (1974). We must, however, consider the usefulness of looking at even larger domains of behavior than attachment/separation and degree of ambivalence or nonambivalence on reunion. Instead of singling out the infant's acceptance or rejection of the mother after a brief separation, we need to understand the significance of the infant's demonstrating irritation at her for having been away and, at the same time, interest and curiosity in figuring out this piece of maternal behavior. What degree of sadness, despair, and aggression upon reunion is associated with persons who will have, as older children, a capacity to deal with sadness and loss without needing to institute restitutive defensive processes too quickly? In other words, we need to understand the full *range* of what a particular infant-toddler is capable of. Degree of ambivalence is only one parameter of behavior. A more general construct would encompass the full potential of developmentally expected internal and external experience, including various feeling states and interpersonal relationships, as well as the stability (e.g., resistance to stress), mobility (e.g., integration of past), and individuality of personality organization (e.g., the infant's particular style of joy or sadness or ambivalence). Using isolated clusters of behavior, however representative of overall functioning, will still lead to a misunderstanding of those individuals who are both unique and highly adaptive in their functioning.

We mentioned earlier that some studies have shown continuity of behavior—for example, in making predictions of peer competence from earlier separation-reunion experiences with the mother (Sroufe et al., unpublished). As indicated, this work is impressive and supports the idea of using higher-order constructs. However, one wonders if our understanding of the continuity and discontinuity of behavior would be even greater if instead of looking at peer competence, a relatively narrow range of behavior, we looked at wider ranges of phenomena that reflect more of the total personality organization. By age two, for example, we expect the toddler to be able not only to experience and demonstrate a wide range of needs, wishes, and feelings, but to represent some of these symbolically; to demonstrate memory of the past, and to interact interpersonally in a variety of subtle ways. Competence with peers is only one dimension of personality organization at this time. The abilities to reach out for and receive nurturance from parents, show pleasure, express frustration, and experience sadness and passivity are other parts of the total behavioral repertoire of the optimal two-year-old. We should look not only at assertive, competent behavior, but at these other dimensions as well. We know, for example, that in latency extremely "competent" children, who may even be leaders of their peers, can in adolescence have psychotic breakdowns. Often, issues around passivity, intimacy, pleasure, and how dependency needs get met have not been resolved. The importance of investigating the total range of age-expected wishes, feelings, behaviors, and interpersonal capacities cannot be underestimated. The stability, mobility, and personal signature (permanence) of these organizations are also parameters that must be used to characterize levels of personality organization. The basic point here is that characterization along these four dimensions, and perhaps others, will lead to better understanding of the continuities and discontinuities of development.

Given facilitating environmental conditions, it is likely that a highly integrated youngster at one age will remain at a high level of integration at another age. We may wonder, then, whether we need to hold the environment constant in our studies. It is not constant for most youngsters. Our model allows us to take the environment into account. The environment can be characterized along the same dimensions. For example, what is the range of contingent reactions that the environment makes available to the growing child? The environment may be characterized in terms of its ability to provide a developmentally appropriate range of experience that facilitates development. For each stage and each line of development, the environment can be characterized in terms not only of its provision of a developmentally appropriate range of experience, but also of its facilitation of the integration of past, present, and future; its stability; and its capacity to facilitate the delineation of a personal signature. We could then characterize more or less favorable environments, with particular reference to specific infant, child, and adult characteristics in the face of specific developmental tasks. By inserting the environment into the equation, we may be able to observe continuities despite environmental variations.

A careful re-examination of some of the reasons stated earlier as to why it has been difficult for us to observe continuties and discontinuities in human development may also serve to illustrate the use of the construct presented here. That behavior transforms itself across developmental stages and is therefore difficult to follow from one stage to another may be dealt with by using a construct of a high-enough order (level of integration) to allow for changes (transformations) in specific behaviors, character traits, or cognitive styles, while holding the overall conceptualization of the personality constant. For example, a youngster with a wide, developmentally appropriate range of stable, mobile, and permanent psychological characteristics may shift from a slightly aggressive orientation to a more passive orientation, or his cognitive interests may move from one set of stimuli to another. Yet, in certain basic ways, the youngster may remain unchanged—he may still be characterized as a highly mature, flexible, stable, unique youngster. Similarly, a youngster who switches from impulsive behavior wo withdrawn behavior may remain, overall, at an immature, inflexible organizational level.

Variation in rate of maturation does not disturb our model because we are looking more at the way in which a particular level of integration sustains itself and moves the youngster ahead in an age-appropriate manner, rather than at a cross-section of one specific set of behaviors. Nor does the fact that tasks differ at the various stages, and different adaptive capacities may be evoked by these different developmental taks, lead us to separate conclusions about a youngster's capacities for each developmental stage. By looking at the youngster's level of equilibrium or integration, we can consider not only those tasks which are prominent at a given stage, but the full range of behavior at that stage, as well as the tasks that will become prominent at later stages. If a youngster is seen to have difficulty with dependency, or experiencing and expressing passivity, at an age when assertiveness is important and may be appropriate in a socially adaptive context, we would not necessarily consider that youngster to be at a more highly integrated level than a youngster who was comfortable with passivity and dependency and uncomfortable with assertiveness. Although the overly assertive youngster may be more highly praised by nursery school teachers, and the passive-dependent youngster may be singled out as problematic, both may be at a similar level of integration. The importance of this kind of balance is usally borne out in adolscence and adulthood when a fully integrated personality organization is required to deal with developmental tasks.

The fact that there are "too many variables" influencing human development and behavior can also be dealt with by our construct, as it focuses not on one aspect of development or one set of variables, but on how groups of variables are integrated. Thus, although behavior is multiply determined, we can study a "final common pathway": the structural organization achieved in terms of the parameters outlined for level of integration.

The complexity and flexibility of behavior are perhaps also better comprehended with an overall concept of level of integration. We know that a youngster who is cognitively sophisticated in latency may, in adolescence, give up cognitive interests, shift more into interpersonal domains, and become a poor student. We also know that symptoms can shift. A person who has been disinterested in people can suddenly become interested in them and at the same time develop psychosomatic symptoms. The human being is very flexible in terms of internal transformations, from cognitive to emotional realms and across different aspects of cognitive or emotional organization. By looking at an overall level of integration, internal shifts can be observed to occur at a constant level of integration or in the context of a new level of organization.

Without going into detail, it should be recalled that earlier we developed a sequence describing the levels of integration from primitive to advanced. Depending on its range, stability, mobility, and permanence, the total personality organization or one aspect of personality (such as cognition, pleasure-seeking behavior, or attachment behavior) can be characterized according to its developmental level of integration (somatic I or II, representational I or II, or transformed, derivative representational systems I or II). A person may be capable of combinatorial cognitive abilities and yet in certain emotional domains remain at a prerepresentational, somatic-II organization. Or, in the realm of assertive behavior a person may show a range, mobility, stability, and permanence characteristic of derivative representational capacities, but in the domain of dependent behavior may show a range, mobility, stability, and permanence consistent with nonderivative representational abilities.

Finally, it should be pointed out that even where our framework is used to examine a narrow aspect of personality functioning, consideration should be given to the level of integration of the total personality to set the context for the more focused study.

Selected Illustrative Applications: Comments on Psychopathology and Adaptation

Traditional psychiatric nosology uses clustering of symptom complexes to form a diagnostic category; for example, feelings of helplessness and worthlessness, combined with early-morning wakening and other somatic symptoms, may lead to a diagnosis of depressive reaction. In addition to symptom clustering, traditional psychiatric nomenclature is derived from etiological understanding of a disease or illness, as is true for certain organic mental syndromes. Only rarely does the diagnostic classification derive from developmental structural considerations of personality organization.

Psychoanalytic classifications of psychopathology tend to derive from symptom clusterings combined with dynamic understanding of the personality. In considering a depressive reaction for example, dynamic aspects such as turning anger against the self are taken into account, as they would be in considering hysterical or obsessional diagnoses.

While developmental structural considerations have contributed to psychoanalytic understanding of psychopathology and adaptation, their role needs to be further developed. The lack of a full developmentally oriented structural approach to diagnosis is evident when we look at early formulations of different kinds of hysterical reactions. In her designation of the "good" and "bad" hysteric, Zetzel (1968) demonstrates the limitations of the earlier perspective. She points out that although the symptom complexes may be similar, they may in fact be based on problems associated with different stages in development and therefore with different structural considerations. By and large, however, we lack a comprehensive framework for considering diagnostic entities in their developmental structural positions, as well as in relation to specific symptom complexes and dynamic constellations.

In the diagnostic approach we are proposing individually different methods of dealing with internal and external experience or stimulation are considered according to their developmental structural characteristics. The most desirable structure facilitates progressive development though fostering the full range of age- and phase-appropriate human experiences without significant compromises in functioning. Each new capacity in the physical, cognitive, or emotional sphere represents a potential for new adaptation (or maladaptation). For example, the ability to achieve homeostasis in infancy involves not only the capacity to reach a calm state, but the capacity to integrate the full range of phase-appropriate experiences. The latter includes experiencing the world through the various sensory modalities; showing age-appropriate motor responses; being alert (e.g., making eye contact); undergoing the expected state changes with age-appropriate regulation; establishing certain cycles and rhythms (e.g., the sleep-wake cycle, eating cycle, alertness cycle)—all in the context of establishing homeostasis. Each stage of development will be viewed in this way. As we discuss a developmental level of equilibrium in terms of, for example, attachment, it should be remembered we are talking about this capacity in its fullest developmentally facilitating aspects, i.e., a rich, varied, yet stable, human attachment.

Our approach does not exclude etiological or symptom-complex considerations. We advocate a three-column approach. In the middle is the developmental structuralist classification which describes the stage-specific method of organizing and processing experience. To the degree that there are distortions or defects in this structure, we can list symptom configuration (e.g., autistic psychosis) and, where possible, specific etiological agents (e.g., an infection, a traumatic environmental event) in the other two columns. The developmental structuralist approach is, in a sense, the "final common pathway" for the interaction of etiological or causal agents with constitutional patterns. It is a statement about the dynamic and structural characteristics of the personality. As such, according to the principle of multiple determination, we do not expect one-to-one correspondences between the developmental level of organization and specific symptoms, although certain symptom complexes may be more characteristic of one type of developmental disorder than another. In addition, it must be stressed that while our discussion below outlines a series of developmental organizations, for each structural organization, the various causal factors, from genetic and constitutional to dynamic and familial, must be considered in their own right in relation to their effect on this "final pathway," the way in which the evolving personality deals with phase-specific experience. Although some categories are presented here as discrete entities, it should be emphasized that development is not discontinuous. Early experience may lead to impairment in a "later category" if the child's inability to deal with phase-appropriate experience is evident in the functioning described by that category.

Somatic Intelligence I

Using our model, we see that in the earliest period of life, during the first phase of somatic intelligence, the infant handles stimulation from the inside and outside in terms of basic body patterns: the sensorimotor system, the autonomic system, etc. In terms of our understanding of psychopathology that may derive from this early time of life, we need to look at defects in the basic physical integrity of the mental apparatus, that is, the perceptual and processing apparatuses, as well as the motor apparatuses. Any physical defects based on genetic or constitutional factors, or early developmental deviations that express themselves in the somatic system, must be taken into account, particularly as they affect the evolving psychological organization. Thus, our first category would be defects in the physical basis of the mental apparatus. Some of these express themselves so subtly during the course of development that they may not be recognized until the youngster begins school; an example of this would be a minimal lack of integration in the sensorimotor organization.

During this earliest stage of development, when stimulation from the inside and outside is dealt with primarily through the infant's capacity to establish homeostatic rhythms, the somatic system, either in terms of the skeletal-muscular system or aspects of the nervous system, develops patterns to deal with internal and esternal stimulation. Some of these patterns may form the basis of chronic somatic patterns observed in various, later-diagnosed psychopathological entities. We shall thus formulate a specific category entitled *the capacity for somatic homeostasis*.

At birth the infant's first task is to adjust to the extra-uterine environment, both animate and inanimate. The capacity to achieve homeostasis is thus perhaps the first task in which we may observe difficulties in the newborn. As indicated, at an optimal level this task involves the ability to regulate states, establish basic cycles and rhythms (sleep, wake, alertness), organize internal and external experience (through implementation of certain stimulus thresholds, habituation to stimuli, organization of initial response patterns, motor integrity, gaze, etc.), and integrate a number of modalities into more complex patterns, such as consoling oneself and coping with noxious stimuli. Gross physical or neurological defects, subtle physical differences (sloppiness), immaturity of the central nervous system, difficulties in early patterns of integration (Brazelton, 1973; Sander, 1962), certain environmental conditions, organ sensitivities (gastrointestinal problems), allergies—these are a few of the factors that may contribute to a homeostatic disorder. For example, we find excitable infants who cannot habituate to stimulation, infants with specific sensitivities (auditory, tactile), infants with immature motor responses who cannot orient themselves or use the caregiver to calm themselves, or infants kept in a constant state of arousal by a hyperstimulating caregiver. While gross deficits in perceptual apparatuses (e.g., blindness or deafness) make an infant more prone to a disorder of homeostasis, other integrative capacities may predominate and a more optimal homeostasis experience may still become possible (Fraiberg, 1977).

It should be emphasized that the capacity for homeostasis is not simply the capacity for achieving a state of calm or rest. Rather, the optimal capacity for homeostasis involves the integration of developmentally facilitating life experiences in the fullest sense. This means reaching a state of organized experience in the context of taking in stimulation through available sensory modalities and handling internal experience in a rich, developmentally appropriate manner (e.g., cycles and rhythms and states of alertness and relaxation) which then fosters the initiation of human relationships and interest in the world. We can observe the degree to which an infant fully organizes a homeostatic experience without relying on manifest symptoms, such as excessive irritability, withdrawal, and/or response to stress. The infant who is alert, oriented, and engaged in the animate and inanimate world in an organized manner, with established patterns of sleep-wakefulness and eating, may be contrasted with the infant who can only be calm at the expense of an optimal state of alertness and engagement. For the former, a mild stress (illness) may result in a temporary change in sleep pattern, while for the latter, a similar stress may result in intense apathy and lack of engagement in the animate world.

Somatic Intelligence II—Learning by Consequences

In our next stage, the youngster, with the second form of somatic intelligence, further establishes an attachment with the human and inanimate objects in his environment and begins the process of differentiation of self from nonself and means from ends. Stimulation from inside and outside is still dealt with predominantly by the somatic system, often through a symbiotic relatedness to the human object. This phase sees the beginning of learning by consequences, or feedback, which supplements the capacity for basic rhythmic patterns. Although the capacity for internal representations is beginning, this phase is basically prerepresentational in terms of the capacity to represent whole objects, both inanimate and animate.

An arrest in important lines of development during this phase may result in a lack of differentiation of self from nonself at the somatic level, with a consequent lack of development of the capacity for whole-object representations. Such an arrest leaves a person with only beginning capacities for representation of his various, disorganized perceptual experiences with the world. Because at this stage one is just learning to differentiate and regulate aspects of one's own affect states and body sensations in terms of means and ends, we also see basic defects in the ego's capacity to differentiate internal states of drive and affect. In sum, we see basic defects in the capacity for separating self from nonself and in the capacity for dealing with and regulating impulses and affects. The nature and character of these defects, and their degree and severity, depends on the point in development at which severe insults occur. It should be mentioned that insults can occur because of severe environmental stress, genetic proclivities, or constitutional sensitivities that interact with certain kinds of environments. The etiological factors, however, will not be discussed here. What is important to highlight is that self-nonself and means-ends differentiation at the somatic level are the foundation for "somatic" reality testing, a basic sense of causality, and a basic capacity for differentiation and regulation.

A number of discrete tasks (categories) may be postulated for this initial stage of somatic differentiation, including forming a stable attachment (a precursor of human differentiation) and using this attachment for interactions that facilitate differentiation and learning. In addition, the later capacity to imitate, organize behavior, and take initiative is a culmination of somatic differentiation and a preparation for organizing internal representations (psychological events proper).

THE CAPACITY FOR HUMAN ATTACHMENT

Whereas in the first few months of life we can observe the infant's flexibility in achieving homeostasis by two to four months, as Spitz (1965) and Emde, Gaensbauer, and Harmon (1976) point out, we should see a higher level of organization indicative of the evolving capacity for human attachment (e.g., as evidenced by the social smile). This advance reflects the initial capacity for learning by consequences in the sphere of human relationships.

The capacity for attachment originates in the homeostatic experience achieved between the infant and primary caretaker(s), in the quality of the feelings and reciprocal interactions characterizing this human relationship. The reciprocal use of multiple sensory modalities (holding, touching, sucking; proprioceptive, visual, auditory), the degree of contingency in the interactions (e.g., how much caretaker and infant respond to one another [Stern, 1974a, 1974b]), the organization and complexity of the early communication patterns, and the depth and phase-appropriateness of feelings experienced and expressed by the dyad (e.g., warm, joyful satisfaction or mechanical, intermittent excitation), all arc parameters that may be used to gauge the quality of attachment. The degree to which stress—for example, the infant's hunger or mother's being upset—disrupts the optimal quality provides a picture of the integrity of the early attachment patterns.

The most severe attachment disorder appears in the autistic youngster who, because of genetic or constitutional difficulties or severe early environmental trauma, never fully achieves homeostasis and therefore does not move on to the second task of human attachment. We also see disorders of human attachment in children with depressed mothers who cannot reach out to their infants and whose attachment seems shallow and insecure. The infant whose individual constititional differences make physical touch or other kinds of human stimulation painful may also have a proclivity for a disorder of attachment. Anaclitic depression, psychophysiological difficulties (vomiting, rumination), failure to thrive (metabolic depression, marasmus), feeding and sleeping disturbances may all be related to disorders of attachment. While we cannot go into detail at this time, disorders of human attachment should be characterized along the dimensions described earlier and, where possible, with reference to specific causal factors.

THE CAPACITY FOR SOMATIC-PSYCHOLOGICAL DIFFERENTIATION

Once a secure human attachment is achieved through the mutual cueing and reciprocal responses of infant and primary caregiver(s), a process of emotional differentiation occurs similar to the process of means-ends differentiation in sensorimotor development. Through this process, basic schemes of causality are established that form the basis for reality testing. It is important to remember, however, that although the infant experiences internal "emotional" sensations, these do not yet exist at an organized psychological or mental representational level.

Means-ends differentiation may be observed in the somatic-psychological sphere as the infant begins to differentiate one person from another (this reaches a noticeable level at eight months, with the appearance of what has been called stranger anxiety [Spitz, 1965]). We also see the beginning differentiation of somatic-psychological states; hunger, for instance, is distinguished from other need states such as affection or dependency. The infant is also able to decipher distinct moods or communications, such as anger, from the primary caregiver(s). The infant is now less dependent on internal states; he is not just a victim of his own hunger, weariness, or tiredness, but is more of a social, interactive being (Emde, Gaensbauer, and Harmon, 1976; Sroufe and Waters, 1976).

Through social interaction, as well as interaction with the inanimate world, differentiation is facilitated. For example, contingent responses help the infant to appreciate his role as a causal agent and thereby to distinguish means from ends in interpersonal relationships. Not only obvious patterns of interaction, but subtle emotional and emphatic interactive patterns undergo their own differentiation. It is therefore possible for an infant to be able to differentiate in the areas of gross motor responses and general interpersonal causality, and yet remain unable to differentiate at a subtle empathic emotional level. If, for example, an empathic interaction between caregiver and infant is lacking because mother responds in a mechanical and remote manner or projects her own feelings onto her baby, the infant may not learn to appreciate basic causal relationships between people at the level of feelings as compared to acts—to see that feeling angry can cause another to feel bad. Or, because of undifferentiated (noncontingent) or inappropriate (misreading the infant's communication) reactions, the infant may learn to respond somatically to situations in which it would be more adaptive to respond more socially. For instance, the infant may show gastric distress rather than use motor activity to communicate emotional hunger or frustration.

During this stage we also observe the shift from magical causality to consolidation of simple causal links and the beginnings of more complicated means-ends differentiation (use of substitutes, detours, intermediary devices). The foundation for flexibility of coping style has been laid. Somatic-psychological differentiation should thus be studied in the context of phase-appropriate dimensions of differentiation in cognition, human relationships, and affects, as well as in relation to the flexibility to deal with phase-appropriate experience and stress without compromising developmentally facilitating behavior.

An example of an extreme defect in differentiation is the infant who fails to develop age-appropriate contingent behavioral and emotional responses (a basic sense of causality as the foundation of reality testing), either because of his own constitutional factors, earlier development, or because of a withdrawn or overly intrusive (projecting) primary caretaker. A less severe problem exists when only one aspect of emotional differentiation is compromised; for example, anger may be ignored or lead to withdrawal. Symptoms such as sensorimotor developmental delays, apathy or intense chronic fear (stranger anxiety), clinging, lack of exploratory activity and curiosity, flat or nonresponsive emotional reactions to significant caregivers, as well as specific maladaptive patterns of relatedness such as biting, chronic crying, and irritability, may all be related to disorders of somatic-psychological differentiation.

THE CAPACITY FOR INTERNALIZATION (BEHAVIORAL ORGANIZATION AND INITIATIVE)

As the infant becomes able to differentiate clearly and subtly the significant others in his interpersonal sphere, there is an increase in the process of "taking in" or internalizing, evidenced by increased imitative behavior. As this capacity becomes more developed, we see the organization of certain emotional systems, such as affiliation, separation, fear and wariness, curiosity and exploration (Ainsworth, 1973). The study of attachment (Ainsworth, Bell, and Stayton, 1974; Main, 1973) as one complex, "high-order" behavioral organization illustrates the development of constructs that match the infant's overall greater organization at this time.

Initiative and exploration are enhanced by the capacity for combining schemes into *new* behavioral organizations that are goal-directed, with further use of detours, substitutes, delays, and intermediary devices. The infant's capacity to take initiative and organize behavior and feeling states is enriched by, and in part further facilitates, his capacity to internalize. After eight to ten months of age we progressively see more imitative behavior which, in turn, facilitates organized exploratory behavior from the secure base of the primary caregiver(s). The gradual individuation that occurs is perhaps best depicted in Mahler's description of the practicing subphase of the separation-individuation process (Mahler, Pine, and Bergman, 1975).

The capacity for original or new behavior is enhanced by combining known schemes, complex behavioral patterns (tertiary circular reactions), trial-and-error exploration, increased memory, and the gradual shift from imitation to identification. We have a much greater sense of the toddler as an organized, initiating human being; for example, the child will now actually pull his parent somewhere. There is also evidence for a beginning psychological sense of self (Lewis and Rosenblum, 1974).

Basic disorders in behavioral organization and internalization, however, may compromise the beginning of internal "psychological" life. Behavior remains fragmented, related to somatic or external cues. Intentionality and a sense of self are nipped in the bud, so to speak. The capacity to use fantasy and even thought in general may be impaired. In patients who have some capacity to organize and thus do not become borderline personalities, the inability to use thought and fantasy to increase the capacity for dealing with internal and external experience—for example, through detours—may form the basis for a variety of severe character pathologies, including psychosomatic difficulties and impulse disorders. (The final outcome depends on later developmental issues, including later internalizations and superego development.

It is interesting to observe toddlers who are either overprotected and therefore undermined in their initial experience with taking initiative in the human world or who do not have available to them sufficient human contact for periodic human support as they attempt to take initiative. In both these instances, the toddler often shifts from taking initiative in the human world to taking initiative in the inanimate world. The inanimate world can be easily manipulated and controlled; it does not undermine initiative and can be returned to as a base of security in an expectable fashion. Relative overinvestment in the inanimate world may form the basis for the inability or lack of capacity for internal experience (fantasies) regarding the human object world.

A severe disorder at this phase will affect the basic capacity for forming mental representations. We can see the results of such a structural defect in adult patients who evidence states of fragmentation (whose internal representations are disorganized). Specific disorders of this phase involve compromises in the internalization, organization, and originality of behavior. These disturbances range from a complete lack of imitation, intentionality, and organized emotional and behavior systems to circumscribed limitations in certain emotional or behavioral systems (e.g., no assertive behavior or affiliative behavior). Symptoms may include chronic temper tantrums, inability to initiate even some self-control, lack of motor or emotional coordination, extreme chronic negativism, delayed language development, and relationships characterized by chronic aggressive behavior.

Representational Intelligence

During the early phase of representational intelligence, the growing toddler acquires the capacity for mental representations, but initially these are unstable and are subject to regression under the pressure of external stress or upheavals in the realm of drives and affects. Eventually these internal representations become more stabilized and undergo means-ends differentiation, so that self-representations and object representations become differentiated from each other.

It is in association with the beginning of this third stage of human intelligence that we first see psychopathology that is dependent on the maintenance of internal representations. Many of the borderline states, in their different varieties, are based on the loss of integrity of this capacity for differentiation of self- and object representations, as has been well discussed by Kernberg (1975).

These early mental representations have drive-affect dispositions attached to them and are initially very vulnerable to regression. From a structural point of view, the early representations are not protected by any additional structures, as they will be later; thus there is great vulnerability during this stage. It is therefore not surprising that we see beginning deviations in development during this stage that lead to the use of such primitive defenses as projection, incorporation, denial, and splitting of representations—all of which in some way interfere with the basic integrity of self- and object representational systems and/or with their differentiation from each other.

We may see severe character disorders deriving from the latter part of this stage if self-nonself and means-ends differentiation has occurred at the representational level, but there is a severe alteration in the basic structure of the ego in order to protect the integrity of the self- and object representations that are organized. For example, in order to maintain a sense of sameness and continuity, a schizoid style may be adopted in which human relationships, or the degree of affect invested in them is severely limited. This compromise entails a severe alteration in the basic ego structure, so that a major realm of human endeavor is relinquished in order to maintain and protect certain components of self- and object representations. (The dynamic considerations of this process will not be taken up here.)

Another example of psychopathology deriving from this

phase of development is the severe depressive character, which may originate in events occurring toward the end of the establishment of object constancy. In order to protect the integrity of the object representation, the capacity for assertion and anger is given up and a basically depressive and/or passive character structure is adopted. The important point here is that at this stage the capacity for representational intelligence is not reinforced or protected by additional psychological structures, so that the human organism is highly vulnerable and must sometimes use extreme measures to protect the given structural organization. We can, for greater focus, subdivide the tasks of this stage into subcategories.

CAPACITY FOR ORGANIZING INTERNAL REPRESENTATIONS

Around 18 to 24 months, and subsequent to the initial period of internalization and behavioral organization, the youngster becomes capable of object permanence (Décarie, 1962; Piaget, 1936). However, because the youngster can now see himself more accurately in a psychological sense as separate and small, there may be some emotional regression (Mahler, Pine, and Bergman, 1975).

The establishment of an internal sense of self and object and the initial ability to conserve internal representations of animate and inanimate objects are evidenced by the increased behavioral, emotional, cognitive, and interpersonal repertoire of the two-year-old. At this age, we observe the ability to say "No" and the development of personal pronouns. The child can now organize mental images to search for inanimate and animate objects, and has the ability to recall events, as well as memory, for emotional experience. We see the beginning of cognitive insight (combining internalized schemes). A distinction is made between experiences pertaining to the self and the nonself, and the child is now able to identify the various parts of self. He relates to others in a less need-fulfilling manner and shows the beginnings of cooperation and concern for others.

Disorders of this phase are evidenced by the lack of psychological life (internal representations), and may be observed in children with symptoms involving severe regressive behavior (disorganized emotional and motor responses), chronic unrelenting clinging with complete disruption of exploratory behavior, chronic primitive aggressive behavior (biting, scratching, throwing things), chronic fearfulness, and either interpersonal promiscuity or withdrawal. Disorders in the organization of internal mental representations have a profound influence on all areas of basic ego functioning, as we see in adult psychotic and borderline patients.

CAPACITY FOR PSYCHOLOGICAL DIFFERENTIATION

Following the capacity to organize internal mental representations of the object and the self, another differentiation occurs at the new level of mental representation or psychological life. Earlier we referred to somatic-psychological differentiation at the sensorimotor level. A similar differentiation in terms of means-ends relationships now occurs at the level of mental representation, as is evidenced by symbol formation and corresponding capacity for language development.

As noted above, between 18 and 24 months we see the ability for organizing representations. Initially these representations exist in the young child in the context of "magical thinking" or "primary-process thinking." While there are organized perceptions of feelings, behaviors, and aspects of self and nonself, these can be combined or distorted according to need or drive states, thereby distorting reality. Over time there is a differentiation of the self from nonself. Concomitant with this differentiation is a differentiation at a representational or psychological level of various feeling states and behavior. The culmination of this process is the establishment of libidinal object constancy (Mahler, Pine, and Bergman, 1975). This delineation of self- and object representations is the foundation for basic ego functions such as reality testing, the organization and regulation of both impulses and thought, the integration of thought and affect, and an ongoing delineation and sense of self, which is not undermined by brief separations or intense feeling states such as anger.

Disorders of psychological differentiation are seen at two levels. At the more severe level, as indicated, we see disorders consistent with borderline or psychotic states of personality organization. There is a capacity for some organized internal psychological life, but it is extremely vulnerable to vicissitudes of stress (separation, strong feeling states), and primary-process or magical thinking predominates. A fixation has occurred during the stage of psychological differentiation.

At a less severe level, basic differentiation occurs, but at a cost that includes major distortions in personality or character formation. An overall inflexibility of the personality limits full engagement in life's major endeavors. Here we see the severe personality disorders, such as the extremely negativistic, withdrawn, schizoid, paranoid, or very depressed or apathetic youngster.

Thus, during the stage of psychological differentiation we see two kinds of disorders: one consistent with basic defects in the integrity of internalized self-object differentiation, and the other a distortion in the flexibility of the personality structure to deal with the full breadth of internal and external experience. Indications of the first kind of disorder, involing self-object differentiation and the establishment of basic ego functions, can be seen when the shift from fantasy to reality fails to take place; when, under emotional stress, severe distortions in reality-oriented thinking occur; when there is a continued lack of organization and regulation of emotions and impulses; and when chronic patterns of disorganized aggressive or regressive behavior are present. It is symptomatic of distortions in character formation when phase-appropriate negativism only gets worse; withdrawal from human relationships increases; the ability to care for bodily functions does not become established; the tendency to blame others becomes more intense; and the fears of loss of self, security, love, and bodily injury are so severe that progressive development is experienced as dangerous (e.g., intimacy, assertion, curiosity, and self-control are relinquished).

CAPACITY FOR CONSOLIDATION OF BASIC PERSONALITY FUNCTIONS

With consolidation of object constancy at ages three and one-half or four, consolidation of basic personality functions occurs, including reality testing, impulse regulation, and integration and organization of affect and thought. Disorders in the consolidation and further differentiation of basic ego functions are seen in vulnerability to regression, states of anxiety and depression, and moderate to mild characterological constrictions. Self-object differentiation occurs, but cannot withstand the stress of separation or strong affect states, as is seen in the youngster who experiences a high level of separation anxiety and regresses to dependency and clinging. Instead of regressions, we may see phase-specific symptom formations in terms of certain developmental conflicts and/or moderate distortions of character, e.g., mild obsessive-compulsive or hysterical patterns, patterns of impulsive behavior, or patterns of externalization. Moderate characterological distortions serve to keep the person from experiencing certain feeling states, such as anger or intimacy, which for dynamic reasons threaten the stability of self-object differentiation and/or the attachment to the dyadic object. Difficulties at this stage do not usually interfere with development proceeding, for the most part, into the triangular oedipal phase. The final crystallization of character distortions and/or symptoms usually reflects a condensation of oedipal and preoedipal determinants.

Representational-Structural Intelligence—Limited Extended Representational Systems

In the next stage of development we see the capacity for developing new representational systems in relation to the original representational system through inverse and reciprocal transformations. With these transformations, the original system of representations is reinforced and protected by a capacity for altering drive-affect dispositions in related representational organizations. We also see the capacity for forming wider-ranging human relationships and for moving from dyadic to triangular patterns.

Alterations in character structure deriving from this stage are of a more limited nature since ego flexibility is greater than in earlier stages. Here we find the more encapsulated neurotic formations, in which only certain aspects of human endeavor must be limited. For example, in certain neurotic formations only certain memories and kinds of drive derivatives and affects (invested in certain object representations) need to be kept from consciousness. There may be concomitant limitations in behavioral flexibility in dealing with the world, as in certain phobias. In all these conditions, however, the flexibility of the ego structure is less limited than before because the capacity to alter basic drive-affect dispositions through forming inverse and reciprocal representational systems provides the flexible foundation for new, more sophisticated defenses. Also, the basic systems of representation are no longer completely unprotected; they can be altered through the construction of new, transformed, derivative systems of representation. Thus, at this stage, because of the use of the inverse and reciprocal to form a series of reaction formations and rationalizations, only a mild or moderate obsessional character structure or symptom complex develops.

Understanding the different types of concrete operations permits the construction of a hierarchy of steps for increasing flexibility during latency. The initial concrete operational capacity for creating and grouping classes having more than one characteristic (the capacity for setting up inverse relationships) demonstrates only a modicum of increased flexibility in dealing with wishes and feelings, as is evidenced by the continued use of primitive defenses, such as denial and projection, in early latency. The range of variables conserved in the system broadens with the capacity for multiplication and division, and correspondences (one to many) can now be constructed. There is thus added flexibility, as evidenced by the use of multiple defenses at once and the initial construction of complex rationalizations. Derivatives of unconscious experience and ongoing experience can be dealt with through second-order transformations. Finally, with the ability for conducting complex seriation tasks (reciprocal relationships), figuring out symmetrical relationships among groups of variables, and constructing a two-variable matrix with multiplication, the transformations of experience that are possible become vastly enhanced. This advance is evidenced by the sophisticated use of rationalization, beginning capacities for intellectualization, efficient sublimations, and the overall complex grouping of age-appropriate defensive and adaptive maneuvers in late latency and preadolescence.

During this stage of intelligent functioning, though the ego has greater flexibility than before, the alterations it is capable of are still limited. If there is enough internal or external stimulation, the characterological constrictions will become quite rigid because the structural alterations possible are limited by the use of only the inverse or the reciprocal.

Representational-Structural Intelligence—Multiple Extended Representational Systems

At the next stage (from adolescence into adulthood) representational intelligence is reinforced by the capacity for forming multiple new representational systems which allow for hypothetical possibilities and are organized according to inverse, reciprocal, and correlative relationships. This new capacity permits the development of a multiple classification system and provides greater flexibility and options for the ego in dealing with internal and external stimulation.

At this stage, limitations may result in more subtle characterological and neurotic formations, as the degree to which rationalization, intellectualization, and neutralization can occur is much greater then before.[5] A lattice structure, existing in a hierarchical relationship to the original self- and object representations, provides the capacity for considerable neutralization, through the establishment of multiple detours. There are now more potential solutions in dealing with ambiguity, conflict, and a wide variety of stimulation from inside and outside in comparison with the previous stage of intelligent functioning.

As was done for earlier stages, each of the two stages of extended representational systems may be subdivided according to the incremental increase in structural flexibility. For example, the number of variables conserved in an integrated system increases under favorable circumstances as adolescent development proceeds. The late adolescent can integrate seem-

[5] In speaking of neuroses and character disorders at this stage, we are assuming regression to oedipal or preoedipal fixation points. The difference in degree depends on the degree of structural development achieved prior to the solidification of the pathological organization.

ingly contradictory values better than the middle adolescent can. (A more detailed discussion of these stages will be presented in another work.)

The relationship between overall development and cognitive development is illustrated by Inhelder (1966). He has demonstrated that "operativity," or the structural configuration of thought, appears to direct figurative aspects of cognition (representations) as well as language. While the capacity for language and symbol formation increases the mobility of operations, operativity exists as an independent mental capacity. He notes that in neurotic configurations there is a shift in levels of operativity, perhaps related to specific dynamic issues, and in prepsychotic children and adolescents there is both a "deforming assimilation of reality" (p. 315) and a disturbance in operativity. In studying the structural properties of cognition, they were impressed with "a motivational force that is directed toward adapting the person to reality" (p. 315). He believes that the "formation of intellectual structures is closely tied to the adaptive functions of thought . . . the interaction between emotional and cognitive aspects of development" (p. 315).

The Importance of a Structuralist Diagnosis

In summary, in considering psychopathology and adaptive capacity, we must not only look at symptom complexes and dynamic etiological factors, but we must also take into account their derivation from a specific structural, developmental position. We should ask: Were there major arrests at the level of somatic intelligence I, somatic intelligence II, or initial representational intelligence? Did the person advance into the stage of representational intelligence reinforced by the capacity to construct new, related representational systems; and did he advance into the most flexible stage, when representational intelligence is reinforced by multiple, expanded, new representational systems?

A structuralist diagnosis, together with the symptom and dynamic diagnostic considerations, affords greater understanding of the psychopathology and, more important, of the health and adaptative features of the individual. The person who is capable of the highest level of intelligence may be able to handle conflict with a highly condensed neurotic structure, which leaves the remainder of his personality available to deal flexibly with complex experience in the context of past, present, and future.

As indicated earlier, we can classify the major diagnostic entities, from borderline syndromes to hysterical and obsessional neuroses, in terms of the type of structural organization in which these dynamically based psychopathological organizations exist. As Zetzel (1968) has so well indicated in her discussion of the good and bad hysteric, in a primitive preoedipal organization, the defenses that form the basis for hysterical behaviors are related to very different issues from those in a developmentally more advanced organization. We need to know whether the capacity for holding on to organized mental representations is the basic issue at hand or whether other issues of a more complex nature are involved. Although such issues have been considered in terms of deciding whether a patient's problem is primarily oedipal or preoedipal, this approach does not focus clearly on the developmental, structuralist aspect of human adaptation.

Looking at human adaptation or maladaptation in terms of the evolution of a series of structural stages of increasing complexity and sophistication gives us a uniform framework in which to consider various psychopathological entities. Such a unified approach becomes especially important, for example, when we consider narcissistic personality disorders. As Kohut (1971) has pointed out, and Kernberg (1975) has discussed as well, early insults to the personality form the basis of narcissistic disorders. The category of narcissistic disorders, however, includes people with varying degrees of maturation in terms of other lines of development. Our ability to distinguish a more encapsulated narcissistic neurosis from a pervasive narcissistic character disorder would be much enhanced if we determined at which structural level of development most of the personality seems to have been arrested.

Unfortunately, when we look at development this way, we realize that from an emotional perspective very few individuals get beyond the very early adolescent phase of the beginning of formal operational thinking. Few people reach the optimal state of being able to construct the multiple representational systems that provide the optimal degree of integration of internal and external experience. There are far too many individuals with a capacity for only limited extended representations and with consequent vulnerability of the integrity of representational capacity proper.

In line with the above, we can look at the basic intactness of the ego, which derives from the earliest types of somatic and representational intelligence, and the flexibility of the ego as it further develops from transformed, derivative representational systems. This flexibility reaches its optimal level with the capacity for multiple extended representational systems. The specific content and the stylistic ways in which the ego handles internal and external stimulation and/or conflict are based, of course, on the individual signature of that human being—his particular wishes, patterns of identification and grouping of specific defenses, which are based both on his genetic and constitutional givens and on his life experience.

What we are stressing here is that there is a sequential pattern of structural development which affects the level of adaptation or maladaptation. Defects in the somatic levels of intelligence and in the initial representational intelligent capacities are seen in ego defects of a major to moderate degree, for example, in the psychoses, borderline conditions, and some severe character disorders. At the next level, where ego flexibility is enhanced, we see the less severe character disorders and encapsulated neuroses. At the optimal level we find a capacity for integration and identity that can deal with a wide variety of external and internal stimulation and can bring together the past, the present, and anticipations of the future.

Selected Illustrative Applications: Comments on Defense

We shall make only a few comments on the implications of our model for understanding the psychoanalytic theory of defense. Defense mechanisms alter the drive-affect dispositions attached to mental representations of self and object. Through a reaction formation, for example, feelings of hate can be turned into feelings of love. Through the mechanism of displacement, certain drive derivatives and affect dispositions can be switched from one self- or object representation to another. Through the mechanism of projection, drive derivatives and affect states can be shifted from a self-representation to an object representation.

One of the problems with the psychoanalytic theory of defense has been that our understanding of defense mechanisms has been mostly in terms of their dynamic and phenomenological characteristics; that is, the defenses are described in terms of what they do, how they alter the direction or aim or object of a drive derivative or drive-affect disposition. Unfortunately, we have not had an adequate structural understanding of the different basic defenses. We know that projections, for instance, can occur at different levels of development. Freud (1911) has delineated a number of steps in the projections of a paranoid psychotic patient with basically hostile feelings—from I hate you, to I love you, to he loves me, to he hates me. Even given this series of complex steps in the paranoid psychotic patient, the use of projection here derives from a rather primitive ego structure that cannot differentiate self from nonself or inside from outside; the disruption in reality testing is thus of great magnitude. In contrast, we may see more encapsulated uses of projection in well-organized neurotic patients whose reality testing is quite excellent, except within the sphere of their limited neurosis. Here the distortion is usually bolstered by various rationalizations and intellectualizations to give it a feeling of reality. A person with a neurotic encapsulation does not necessarily act on his projections. He may feel that someone is angry at him, but he does not usually act by arming himself with weapons, as a paranoid psychotic person might.

Some of the difficulty in understanding defenses in relation to their structural underpinnings has been dealt with by the addition of new, confusing phenomenological terms. Externalization, for example, has been proposed as a process similar to projection. Most psychoanalytic practitioners, however, have trouble holding in mind or agreeing on the subtle differences between these terms. It seems simpler to point out that some defenses, such as projection, incorporation, denial, and avoidance, are characteristic of the early stages of development. Other, more sophisticated defenses, such as rationalization and intellectualization, are characteristic of later stages of development. We can thus see a developmental hierarchy in which the initial defenses of avoidance, projection, incorporation, and denial lead to capacities for displacement and condensation; then to capacities for isolation of affect, reaction formations, and rationalizations; and finally to capacities for sophisticated sublimations and intellectualizations. Other defenses, such as identification with the aggressor, can exist at multiple levels of development.

What we are suggesting here is that we do the same thing that we did for our understanding of psychopathology: that we hold on to our phenomenological, descriptive understanding of how a defense works to alter a drive-affect disposition, but that, in addition, we locate defenses in terms of their position in the hierarchy of developmental structures described earlier. By looking at defenses as they function in the context of each of these structural organizations, we can get a better understanding of the relative role of a particular defense.

To expand on our earlier example, projection may exist at the level of representational intelligence, where, when the stimulation from inside or outside is too great, ego splitting may occur. In this case, a projection onto the external world involves a basic disruption in the self- and object representations and in the organization and integrity of the sense of self and the sense of the world. The projection thereby leads to a disruption in reality testing, as can be seen in psychotic and borderline individuals. On the other hand, at the level of initial extended representational systems with the capacity for inverse and reciprocal relationships, we see encapsulated projects, which are limited in scope and related to specific drive derivatives or affects. Such projections, which are frequently seen in the fears or nightmares of latency children, do not grossly distort reality testing. A projection that is part of an extended representational system remains in a relationship to basic self- and object representations at the foundation of the personality. It therefore alters drive-affect dispositions in its defensive operations, but does not alter the basic integrity of self- and object representations. Projection at the level of multiple extended representational systems (with the capacity for a "multiple classification table") is couched in subtle intellectualizations and rationalizations that serve defensive purposes but distort reality only minimally. These projections are even more encapsulated and less limiting to the basic flexibility of the ego structure than those of the preceding stage.

By looking at defenses in terms of their structural level, we may also find implications for certain dynamic considerations—for example, what a defense protects the ego from. In the initial stage of representational intelligence, defenses protect the cohesion and the integrity of the sense of self, whereas in the extended representational stages, defenses protect the ego from experiencing anxiety arising out of conflict between intrapsychic structures (e.g., castration anxiety).

In general, we should assume that there are probably many more defenses operating than we have been able to classify, and that the opportunities for drive-affect dispositions to alter themselves in their direction or attachment to objects is far greater than we know. Locating the structural position of defenses in the hierarchy of organizational levels gives us an additional parameter with which to understand how they work.

Some Implications for the Adaptive Point of View

The foregoing model is, in a sense, an extension of the adaptative point of view of psychoanalysis already formulated by Hartmann (1939) and others. What we have attempted here is a more specific consideration of human adaptation, in terms of a hierarchical structural organization of emotional intelligence. We have thus delineated a number of levels of human adaptation: somatic; representational; limited, transformed, derivative representational systems; and multiple, transformed, derivative representational systems.

Our model of adaptation is consistent with psychoanalytic concepts of neutralization of drive energy and with Rapaport's

(1959) concept of a system or hierarchy of detours. According to Rapaport, behavior derived from the top level is relatively more autonomous because of the nature of the detours; at the bottom behavior is associated more directly with drive derivatives. Similarly, in our model, the bottom level is that of somatic intelligence governed by basic rhythms, where there is very little distancing from early drive-affect dispositions, basic physiological stress, or internal or external stimulation. In fact, early in life, direct motivational behavior is more prominent. At the somatic level of learning by consequences the infant has slightly more flexibility for adaptation because he can learn through experience with the world and does not need to rely solely on basic rhythms, even though basic rhythms provide a continuing foundation. With the capacity for representation, there is an ability to organize internal and external stimulation in terms of psychological events. The capacity for relative distancing from primitive states of drive and affect is thus greatly enhanced, as are delay and frustration tolerance. We might describe this as the structural capacity for greater amounts of neutralization, or detour. As the basic capacities for representation are stabilized, and self- and object representations are differentiated at a psychological level (as they were earlier at a somatic level), there is further capacity for delay and detour. When these representations are reinforced by extended capacities for derivative representational systems, the new paths of transformation for drive and affect dispositions afford vastly enhanced potential in terms of new detours and further neutralization. Dynamic events, such as identifications, of course, play a role in this process, but they will not be discussed here.

As we have seen, at the optimal level of multiple representational systems there is an almost infinite number of possible relationships to the original representations, which can then be integrated according to the unique life experiences, current demands, and future expectations of a given individual. Where there is a maximization of the breadth of internal and external experience assimilated and integrated over time and space in a permanent and stable manner, there is a structure that has the potential to remain connected to, yet alter, basic drive-affect dispositions and, at the same time, integrate, through a system of transformations new human experiences. This kind of structure affords the greatest degree of detour, flexibility, and adaptation to multiple demands.

Our model also provides us with insight into new methods of facilitating development. We may, for example, see more clearly how to help a person move from one equilibrium state to another. It also gives us a way of looking at the results of our methods. In addition to looking at dynamic alterations in terms of the relationship between drive derivatives, affects, and ego and superego structures, we now have a specific way to observe structural change in terms of a hierarchy of organizational structures. Thus, when we talk about enhanced ego flexibility, we can specify the advances in this flexibility according to the steps we have outlined in terms of emotional intelligence.

Beyond Defense and Adaptation: The Developmental Structuralist Approach

The developmental structuralist approach takes us beyond traditional concepts of defense and adaptation. In relation to a person's capacities for organizing, integrating, and differentiating human experience (of all types), this approach delineates phase-specific, developmental structures, each defined by a series of governing principles and together collectively organized in hierarchical relationships. It is no longer necessary to separate intellectual and emotional functioning by postulating distinct developmental sequences for each. It is now possible to characterize both cognitive and emotional intelligence within the same frame of reference in terms of the developmental level that predominates in the person's structural organization (i.e., somatic, representational, representational with limited extended representational systems, or representational with multiple extended representational systems).

This approach facilitates our understanding of the person's flexibility in dealing with a wide variety of both internal and external experience. Within this approach it is also possible to describe differences in subcategories of functioning, e.g., responding to intellectual versus emotional problems, dealing with pleasure versus aggression, functioning at work versus in the family. Differences in levels may be clearly delineated because the same frame of reference is used for each domain of functioning. A person may, for example, reach the level of extended representational capacities in dealing with the inanimate world and/or in coping with aggressive feelings, but remain at the limited representational level in dealing with pleasurable feelings and/or intimate relationships. Similarly, some persons may function at different levels of "operativity" in dealing with situations that call for verbal associative patterns and in dealing with visually oriented stimuli.

The developmental structuralist approach may prove an especially useful guide in planning and evaluating various intervention programs. Whether the intervention program emanates from an educational or a psychotherapeutic setting, we can specify a person's level of intelligence in terms of developmental structural characteristics. The delineation of the specific developmental structural organization achieved may then offer clues as to the necessary ingredients of the intervention program. For example, it is unlikely that someone without the capacity for limited extended representational systems will initially be able to use insight (to a significant degree) in the traditional therapeutic sense. Persons arrested at a somatic level of integration may require a combination of approaches, which both directly address the disordered somatic system and help new respresentational capacities develop. Persons with fragile but emerging representational capacities may require help in further developing and differentiating these capacities before regressive experiences can be tolerated. Given that all levels of learning are always operating to some degree, we may find that we cannot ignore the level of representational meaning and that individually different reactions to "pure" somatic interventions may in fact be explained by the relationships between the various levels of learning.

In studying the efficacy of therapeutic approaches this model provides us a way of looking, not only at changes in specific symptoms, behavior patterns, or cognitive styles, but at the overall level of personality integration. Even in evaluating psychotherapeutic approaches that are behaviorally oriented and aim at specific symptom or behavioral changes, we can look at changes in the overall integrative capacity of the personality. We might, for example, ask: Does the patient treated with a specific behavioral therapeutic approach remain at the same overall developmental structural level even with symptomatic improvement, or does he regress to a lower level as a "side effect" of the treatment? Or, together with symptomatic improvement, does this patient progress to a higher level of overall personality functioning? These same questions could be addressed to psychodynamic approaches and educational approaches. Specific personality functions and behaviors can thus be studied against the background of the overall organization.[6]

Our model may be especially useful in setting up and evaluating early growth-facilitating environments. There has been a dilemma in the early childhood field about the degree to which cognitive models, as opposed to psychodynamic models, should be used. Programs that have focused solely on cognitive stimulation have often resulted in a limited ability to foster emotional development (Work, 1972), though in some programs the reverse has occurred. In our model we can look at the general principles of dealing with internal or external stimulation, both animate and inanimate, in terms of levels of equilibrium. If our goal is to facilitate overall development, i.e., to facilitate development in a hierarchical manner from the initial phase of somatic intelligence to representational intelligence enhanced by an expanded capacity for representational systems (in relation to the inanimate impersonal world as well as the animate emotional world), then we now have a general model to help us in this effort. (We shall not specify in detail here how to set up such growth-facilitating environments. We hope, however, that our model will serve as the foundation for a practical, detailed implementation of more integrated attempts to facilitate human development.)

The concept of levels of integration and equilibrium also permits a somewhat value-free approach to understanding lev-

[6] In experimental methodologies the overall personality organization may be viewed as the "context," so to speak, within which the dependent "outcome" variables are being studied.

els of human emotional and cognitive development. It may even be possible to look at cultures in terms of the level of equilibrium or integration reached in different areas. Some cultures may reflect advanced levels in areas around love and giving and primitive levels around issues related to aggression. In other words, complexities of love and giving can be integrated at a high level (without sacrificing subtlety) while issues of aggression are dealt with by more primitive mechanisms, such as splitting. Although some cultures may be relatively advanced in all areas, we may observe some cognitively primitive cultures that can integrate high levels of ambiguity in certain emotional domains and/or cultures whose advanced cognitive levels may not always be matched by their capacity in certain emotional realms.

While the above may provide the basis for fruitful speculation, it should be emphasized that the applications of our model discussed here are mainly for purposes of illustration. Detailed consideration of the issues related to practical applications will be taken up in future works. For illustrative puposes, the levels of learning and intelligence are summarized below in the Appendix in relation to stage-specific tasks and capacities, adaptive skills, and psychopathology.

In conclusion, the model presented here attempts to integrate into a single frame of reference the various dimensions of emotional and impersonal cognitive experiences. It was demonstrated that the principles organizing personality structure are the same for both realms of experience, differing in terms of degree and developmental level attained, rather than in basic structure. As our understanding of human experience deepens and conceptualization of the realms or types of experience increases, there will be a growing necessity for higher-level bridging and integrative constructs.

A major impediment, however, to the development of such constructs and a more complete science of human behavior is the tendency for fragmentation and/or isolation in model development. While focused inquiry and parsimonious model development is necessary as each new realm of human experience is discovered, without unifying constructs, areas of investigation tend to develop unrelated to one another. Eventually, as in unintegrated human development, there are unproductive polarizations and splits, which result in a rigid theoretical and philosophical bias.

The vicissitudes of model building are always characterized by the ebb and flow between attempts at constructing higher-order models and subsequent disappointment and efforts to limit the field of inquiry. As long as each of the multiple lines of development (human relationships, feelings, wishes, cognitive abilities) are interrelated, and human experience is considered in cross-sectional, anticipatory, historical, and developmental contexts,[7] it will prove useful to have both narrowly focused constructs that pertain to the data of the given situation and broadly based, integrating constructs that synthesize realms of experience.

[7] Developmental here implies the complex interweaving of biological and environmental factors that contribute to the development of human experience.

APPENDIX

SCHEMATIC OUTLINE OF LEVELS OF LEARNING AND SUBSTAGES OF INTELLIGENCE

Age	*Levels of Learning*	*Substages of Intelligence: Specific Developmental-Structural Tasks and Capacities*
1 mo.	Somatic	Homeostasis
3 mos.		Attachment
	Consequence	
8 mos.		Somatic-psychological differentiation
12 mos.		Behavioral organization, initiative, and internalization
	Representational	
18 mos.		Representational capacity
25 mos.		Representational differentiation
36 mos.		Consolidation of representational differentiation
3½ yrs. to 9 or 10 yrs.	Representational-structural	Capacity for limited extended representational systems
11 yrs. and beyond		
		Capacity for multiple extended representational systems

A Schematic Outline of Developmental-Structural Levels of Learning and Intelligence: Illustrative Adaptive and Maladaptive patterns

Somatic Level of Learning

Homeostasis

ILLUSTRATIVE ADAPTIVE CAPACITIES

Internal regulation (harmony).
Balanced interest in animate and inanimate world.

ILLUSTRATIVE MALADAPTIVE (PSYCHOPATHOLOGICAL) PATTERNS IN CHILDHOOD

Contributing factors to homeostasis disorders include: gross physical or neurological defects, immaturity of the central nervous system, difficulties in early patterns of integration, certain environmental conditions, organ sensitivities (gastrointestinal problems), and allergies. For example: the excitable infant who cannot habituate to stimulation, the infant with specific sensitivities (auditory, tactile), or the infant with immature motor responses who cannot orient or accept soothing from caregiver.

Even in the absence of manifest symptoms (excessive irritability, withdrawal, etc.) and/or in the face of stress, one can observe the degree to which an infant fully organizes a homeostatic experience. For example: contrast (1) the alert, oriented infant who is engaged in the animate and inanimate world in an organized manner, with established patterns of sleep-wakefulness and eating, with (2) the infant who can be calm only at the expense of optimal alertness and engagement. In the former, mild stress (illness) may result in temporary change in sleep patterns. In the latter, similar stress may result in intense apathy and lack of engagement in the animate world.

ILLUSTRATIVE DERIVATIVE MALADAPTIVE (PSYCHOPATHOLOGICAL) PATTERNS IN ADULTHOOD

Autism.
Primary defects in basic personality integrity (perception, integration, motility, memory, regulation).

Attachment

ILLUSTRATIVE ADAPTIVE CAPACITIES

Rich, multisensory investment in animate world, especially primary caregivers.

ILLUSTRATIVE MALADAPTIVE (PSYCHOPATHOLOGICAL) PATTERNS IN CHILDHOOD

Attachment disorders depend on the relative integrity of early attachment patterns. One measure is the degree to which stress (e.g., infant's hunger, mother's being upset) compromises this integrity.

The most severe attachment disorder is autism. Because of genetic or constitutional difficulties or severe early environmental trauma, the autistic youngster never fully achieves homeostasis and thus does not move on to the second task (human attachment).

Disorders of human attachment also arise when a depressed mother cannot reach out to her infant, when the quality of her relatedness seems shallow and insecure.

Another source of vulnerability is the infant whose constitutional differences make physical touch or other kinds of human stimulation painful.

Anaclitic depression, psychophysiological difficulties (vomiting, rumination), failure to thrive (metabolic depression, marasmus), and feeding and sleep disturbances may all be related to this type of disorder.

ILLUSTRATIVE DERIVATIVE MALADAPTIVE (PSYCHOPATHOLOGICAL) PATTERNS IN ADULTHOOD

Primary defects in the capacity to form human relationships, in internal (intrapsychic) emotional life, and in intrapsychic structure in relation to the animate world, with subsequent defects in somatic-psychological differentiation (see next level).

Consequence Level of Learning

Somatic-Psychological Differentiation

ILLUSTRATIVE ADAPTIVE CAPACITIES

Flexible, contingent, reciprocal, multisystem (sensory/motor/affective) interactions with inanimate and animate world, especially primary caregivers.

ILLUSTRATIVE MALADAPTIVE (PSYCHOPATHOLOGICAL) PATTERNS IN CHILDHOOD

Disorders should be studied in the context of the many phase-appropriate dimensions of differentiation, including cognition, human relationships, affects, and the flexibility to deal with stress (without compromising developmentally facilitating behavior).

An extreme defect in differentiation involves the infant who does not respond differently to different environmental events and has not developed age-appropriate contingent behavioral and emotional responses (a basic sense of causality as the foundation for reality testing). This may be due either to his own constitutional makeup, events in his earlier development, or a withdrawn or overly intrusive (projecting) primary caregiver.

A less severe problem exists when only one aspect of emotional differentiation (because of the character of contingent responses) is compromised, e.g., anger is ignored or leads to withdrawal.

Related symptoms include: sensorimotor developmental delays, apathy or intense chronic fear (stranger anxiety), clinging, lack of explorativeness and curiosity, flat or nonresponsive reactions to significant caregivers, as well as specific maladaptive patterns of relatedness such as biting, chronic crying, and irritability.

ILLUSTRATIVE DERIVATIVE MALADAPTIVE (PSYCHOPATHOLOGICAL) PATTERNS IN ADULTHOOD

Primary ego defects (psychosis) including structural defects in: (1) reality testing and organization of perception and thought, (2) perception and regulation of affect, (3) integration of affect and thought.

Behavioral Organization, Initiative, and Internalization

ILLUSTRATIVE ADAPTIVE CAPACITIES

Complex, organized, assertive, innovative behavioral-emotional patterns.

Behavioral creativity and originality.

Integration of behavioral and emotional polarities.

ILLUSTRATIVE MALADAPTIVE (PSYCHOPATHOLOGICAL) PATTERNS IN CHILDHOOD

Disorders may compromise the beginning of internal "psychological" life. Behavior remains fragmented, related to somatic or external cues. Intentionality and sense of self are "nipped in the bud."

Specific disorders range from complete lack of imitation, intentionality, and organized emotional and behavioral systems to circumscribed limitations in certain emotional or behavioral systems, e.g., the child who cannot assert himself or has difficulties with affiliative behavior.

Symptoms may include chronic temper tantrums, inability to initiate even some self-control, lack of motor or emotional coordination, extreme chronic negativism, delayed language development, and relationships characterized by chronic aggressive behavior.

ILLUSTRATIVE DERIVATIVE MALADAPTIVE (PSYCHOPATHOLOGICAL) PATTERNS IN ADULTHOOD

Defects in behavioral organization and emerging representational capacities, e.g., certain borderline and psychotic states, primary substance abuse, psychosomatic conditions, impulse disorders, and affect tolerance disorders.

Representational Level of Learning

Representational Capacity

ILLUSTRATIVE ADAPTIVE CAPACITIES

Formation of complex organizations of internal imagery.

Increased behavioral, emotional, cognitive, and interpersonal repertoire (e.g., the abilities to: say "no," use personal pronouns, recall, organize mental images to search for inanimate and animate objects, remember emotional experience, locate experiences pertaining to self and nonself, use beginning cognitive insight combining internalized schemes, identify various parts of self, relate in a diminishing need-feeling manner, and show beginning cooperation and concern for others).

ILLUSTRATIVE MALADAPTIVE (PSYCHOPATHOLOGICAL) PATTERNS IN CHILDHOOD

Disorders are evidenced by the lack of psychological life (internal representations).

Symptoms may involve severe regressive behavior (disorganized emotional and motor responses), chronic unrelenting clinging with complete disruption of exploratory behavior, chronic primitive aggressive behavior (biting, scratching, throwing things), chronic fearfulness, and either interpersonal promiscuity or withdrawal.

ILLUSTRATIVE DERIVATIVE MALADAPTIVE (PSYCHOPATHOLOGICAL) PATTERNS IN ADULTHOOD

Borderline syndromes.

Secondary ego defects including defects in integration and organization and/or emerging differentiation of self- and object representations.

Representational Differentiation

ILLUSTRATIVE ADAPTIVE CAPACITIES

Capacity for representational creativity and insight.

Differentiation of imagery pertaining to self and nonself in context of rich investment in animate and inanimate world.

Differentiation of various feeling states and behavior and stabilization of mood.

Gradual emergence of basic personality functions, including reality testing, organization and regulation of impulses, organization and regulation of thought, and integration of thought and affect.

Ongoing delineation of sense of self, which becomes more coherent and eventually reaches a point where it is not undermined by brief separations or intense feeling states such as anger.

ILLUSTRATIVE MALADAPTIVE (PSYCHOPATHOLOGICAL) PATTERNS IN CHILDHOOD

Disorders are seen at two levels.

At the more severe level there is a capacity for some organized internal psychological life, but it is extremely vulnerable to stress (separation, strong feeling states). Magical thinking predominates. This becomes visible in a number of ways: failure to shift from fantasy to reality, severe distortions in reality-oriented thinking under emotional stress, a continued lack of organization and regulation of emotions and impulses, or chronic patterns of disorganized aggressive or regressive behavior. Negativism only gets worse; withdrawal from human relationships increases; the ability to care for bodily functions does not become established; the tendency to blame others intensifies; and fears of loss of self, security, love, and bodily injury are so severe that progressive development is experienced as dangerous (e.g., intimacy, assertion, curiosity, and self-control are relinquished).

At a less severe level, basic differentiation occurs, but at a price, such as major distortion in personality or character formation (an overall inability to engage fully in age-appropriate endeavors). For example: the very negativistic, withdrawn, depressed, or apathetic youngster.

ILLUSTRATIVE DERIVATIVE MALADAPTIVE (PSYCHOPATHOLOGICAL) PATTERNS IN ADULTHOOD

Severe alterations in personality structure:

1. Limitation of experience of feelings and/or thoughts in major life areas (love, work, play).
2. Alterations and limitations in pleasure orientation.
3. Major externalizations of internal events, e.g., conflicts, feelings, thoughts.
4. Limitations in internalizations necessary for regulation of impulses, affect (mood), and thought.
5. Impairment in self-esteem regulation.
6. Impairment in tolerance for most human relationships and affects.
7. Tendencies toward fragmentation in self-object differentiation.

The above includes, for example: certain borderline organizations and severe personality disorders (schizoid, paranoid, depressive, inadequate).

Consolidation of Representational Differentiation

ILLUSTRATIVE ADAPTIVE CAPACITIES

Consolidation of basic personality functions, including reality testing, impulse regulations, affect organization, self-esteem maintenance, delineated sense of self, focused concentration, and capacity for learning.

ILLUSTRATIVE MALADAPTIVE (PSYCHOPATHOLOGICAL) PATTERNS IN CHILDHOOD AND ADULTHOOD

More moderate versions of the personality constrictions and alterations at the previous level, e.g., moderate obsessional, hysterical, or depressive character disorders.

Representational-Structural Level of Learning

Capacity for Limited Extended Representational Systems

ILLUSTRATIVE ADAPTIVE CAPACITIES

Enhanced flexibility to conserve and transform complex and organized representations of animate and inanimate experience in the context of expanded relationship patterns with family, peers, others, and inanimate world.

ILLUSTRATIVE MALADAPTIVE (PSYCHOPATHOLOGICAL) PATTERNS IN CHILDHOOD AND ADULTHOOD

Encapsulated disorders including neurotic syndromes:

1. Neurotic symptom formations: (a) limitations and alterations in experience of areas of thought (hysterical repression, phobic displacements); (b) limitations and alterations in experience of affects and feelings (obsessional isolation, depressive turning of feelings against self).

2. Neurotic encapsulated character formations: (a) encapsulated limitations of experience of feelings or thoughts in major life areas (love, work, play); (b) encapsulated alterations and limitations in pleasure orientation; (c) encapsulated major externalizations of internal events (conflicts, thoughts, feelings); (d) encapsulated limitations in internalizations necessary for regulation of impulses, affects (mood), and thought; (e) encapsulated impairments in self-esteem regulation.

Capacity for Multiple Extended Representational Systems

ILLUSTRATIVE ADAPTIVE CAPACITIES

Optimal flexibility to conserve and transform expanded experience of animate (emotional) and inanimate (impersonal) world, including developmentally expectable relationship patterns, heterosexual interests, educational and occupational plans, hypothetical considerations, emerging values and ideals, and a more differentiated sense of personal identity (independent yet continuous with earlier ties).

ILLUSTRATIVE MALADAPTIVE (PSYCHOPATHOLOGICAL) PATTERNS IN CHILDHOOD AND ADULTHOOD

Phase-specific developmental and/or neurotic conflicts with or without neurotic syndromes. (This pattern can also occur at earlier levels.)

REFERENCES

Ainsworth, M. D. (1973), The Development of Infant-Mother Attachment. In: *Review of Child Development Research,* Vol. 3, ed. B. Caldwell & R. Ricciuti. Chicago: University of Chicago Press, pp. 1-94.

——— Bell, S., & Stayton, D. (1971), Individual Differences in Strange Situation Behavior of One-Year-Olds. In: *The Origins of Human Social Relations,* ed. H. Schaffer. London: Academic Press, pp. 17-57.

——— ——— ——— (1974), Infant-Mother Attachment and Social Development: Socialization as a Product of Reciprocal Responsiveness to Signals. In: *The Integration of the Child into the Social World,* ed. M. Richards. Cambridge, Eng.: Cambridge University Press, pp. 99-135.

Anthony, E. J. (1956a), Six applications de la théorie genétique de Piaget à la théorie et à la pratique psychodynamique. *Schweizerische Zeitschrift für Psychologie und ihre Anwendungen,* 15:269-277.

——— (1956b), The Significance of Jean Piaget for Child Psychiatry. *Brit. J. Med. Psychol.,* 29:20-34.

——— (1957), The System Makers: Piaget and Freud. *Brit. J. Med. Psychol.,* 30:255-269.

——— (1958), An Experimental Approach to the Psychopathology of Childhood: Autism. *Brit. J. Med. Psychol.,* 31:211-225.

Arlow, J. A., Freud, A., Lampl-de Groot, J., & Beres, D. (1968), Panel Discussion. *Internat. J. Psycho-Anal.,* 49:506-512.

Bandura, A., & McDonald, F. J. (1963), The Influence of Social Reinforcement and the Behavior of Models in Shaping Children's Moral Judgments. *J. Abnorm. Soc. Psychol.,* 67:274-381.

Begelman, D. A., & Steinfeld, G. J. (1972), Is There an Error of the Standard? A Critique of Piaget's Perceptual Theory. *Genet. Psychol. Monogr.,* 86:81-117.

Bell, R., Weller, G., & Waldrop, M. (1971), Newborn and Preschooler: Organization of Behavior and Relations between Periods. *Monogr. Soc. Res. Child Devel.,* 36 (1-2, No. 142).

Beres, D., & Joseph, E. (1970), The Concept of Mental Representation in Psychoanalysis. *Internat. J. Psycho-Anal.,* 51:1-9.

Berlyne, D. (1965), Recent Developments in Piaget's Work. In: *Readings in the Psychology of Cognition,* ed. R. C. Anderson & D. P. Ausubel. New York: Holt, Rinehart & Winston, pp. 173-193.

Bettelheim, B. (1967), *The Empty Fortress.* New York: Free Press.

Bever, T. G., Smith, M. L., Bengen, B., & Johnson, T. G. (1975), Young

Viewers' Troubling Reponse to TV Ads. *Harvard Bus. Rev.*, 53:109-120.

Bischof, N. (1975), A Systems Approach towards the Functional Connections of Fear and Attachment. *Child Devel.*, 46:801-817.

Blatt, S. J., Allison, J., & Baker, B. L. (1965), The Wechsler Object Assembly Subtest and Bodily Concerns. *J. Consult. Clin. Psychol.*, 29:223-230.

Borke, H. (1971), Interpersonal Perception of Young Children: Egocentrism or Empathy? *Devel. Psychol.*, 5(2):263-269.

——— (1972), Chandler and Greenspan, "Ersatz Egocentrism": A Rejoinder. *Devel. Psychol.*, 7(2):107-109.

Bowen, H. M., & Woodhead, M. M. (1955), Estimation of Track Targets after Pre-view. *Canad. J. Psychol.*, 9:239-246.

Bower, T. (1967), The Development of Object-Permanency: Some Studies of Existence Constancy. *Percept. Psychophysics*, 2:411-418.

Bowlby, J. (1969), *Attachment and Loss*, Vol. 1. New York: Basic Books.

Brackbill, Y. (1958), Extinction of the Smiling Response in Infants as a Function of Reinforcement Schedule. *Child Devel.*, 29:115-124.

Brazelton, T. B. (1973), *Neonatal Behavioral Assessment Scale.* Philadelphia: Lippincott.

——— Koslowski, B., & Main, M. (1974), The Origins of Reciprocity: The Early Mother-Infant Interaction. In: *The Effect of the Infant on Its Caregiver*, ed. M. Lewis & L. Rosenblum. New York: Wiley, pp. 49-76.

Bretherton, I., & Ainsworth, M. (1974), Responses of One-Year-Olds to a Stranger in a Strange Situation. In: *The Origins of Fear*, ed. M. Lewis & L. Rosenblum. New York: Wiley, pp. 131-164.

Breuer, J., & Freud, S. (1893-1895), Studies on Hysteria. *Standard Edition*, 2. London: Hogarth Press, 1955.

Brody, S., & Axelrad, S. (1966), Anxiety, Socialization, and Ego Formation in Infancy. *Internat. J. Psycho-Anal.*, 47:218-229.

——— ——— (1970), *Anxiety and Ego Formation in Infancy.* New York: International Universities Press.

Bronson, G. (1972), Infants' Reaction to Unfamiliar Persons and and Novel Objects. *Monogr. Soc. Res. Child Devel.*, 37 (No. 148).

Brown, A., Matheny, A., & Wilson, R. (1973), Baldwin's Kindness Concept Measure as Related to Children's Cognition and Temperament: A Twin Study. *Child Devel.*, 44:193-195.

Bruch, H. (1966), Anorexia Nervosa and Its Differential Diagnosis. *J. Nerv. Ment. Dis.*, 141:555-566.

——— (1973), *Eating Disorders.* New York: Basic Books.

Chandler, M. (1973), Egocentrism and Antisocial Behavior: The Assessment and Training of Social Perspective-Taking Skills. *Devel. Psychol.*, 9(3):326-332.

——— & Greenspan, S. (1972), Ersatz Egocentrism: A Reply to H. Borke. Devel. Psychol., 7(2):104-106.

Charlesworth, W. R. (1969), The Role of Surprise in Cognitive Development. In: *Studies in Cognitive Development: Essays in Honor of Jean Piaget*, ed. D. Elkind & J. H. Flavell. London: Oxford University Press, pp. 257-314.

Chomsky, N. (1957), *Syntactic Structures.* The Hague: Mouton.

Clarke-Stewart, K. (1973), Interactions between Mothers and Their Young

Children: Characteristics and Consequences. *Monogr. Soc. Res. Child Devel.*, 38.
Cobliner, W. G. (1967), Psychoanalysis and the Geneva School of Genetic Psychology: Parallels and Counterparts. *Internat. J. Psychiat.*, 3(2):82-129.
Cooper, L. (1970), Empathy: A Developmental Model. *J. Nerv. Ment. Dis.*, 151:169-178.
Corman, H. H., & Escalona, S. K. (1969), Stages of Sensorimotor Development: A Replication Study. *Merrill-Palmer Quart.*, 15:351-361.
Décarie, T. Gouin (1962), *Intelligence and Affectivity in Early Childhood.* New York: International Universities Press, 1965.
Dollard, J., & Miller, N. E. (1950), *Personality and Psychotherapy.* New York: McGraw-Hill.
Dudek, S. (1972), Longitudinal Study of Piaget's Developmental Stages and the Concept of Regression, II. *J. Pers. Assess.*, 36:468-478.
——— & Dyer, S. (1972), A Longitudinal Study of Piaget's Developmental Stages and the Concept of Regression, I. *J. Pers. Assess.*, 36:380-389.
Elkind, D. (1967), Egocentrism in Adolescence. *Child Devel.*, 38:1025-1034.
——— (1970), *Children and Adolescents.* New York: Oxford University Press.
——— (1971), Review of Piaget's *The Mechanisms of Perception. Amer. Educ. Res. J.*, 8:393-396.
Emde, R. N., Gaensbauer, T. J., & Harmon, R. J. (1976), Emotional Expression in Infancy: A Biobehavioral Study. *Psychol. Issues,* Monogr. No. 37. New York: International Universities Press.
Erikson, E. H. (1950), *Childhood and Society.* New York: Norton.
——— (1956), The Problem of Ego Identity. *J. Amer. Psychoanal. Assn.*, 4:56-121.
Escalona, S. K. (1963), Patterns of Infantile Experience and the Developmental Process. *The Psychoanalytic Study of the Child,* 18:197-244. New York: International Universities Press.
——— (1968), *The Roots of Individuality.* Chicago: Aldine.
Feffer, M. (1959), The Cognitive Implications of Role Taking Behavior. *J. Pers.*, 27:152-168.
——— (1967), Symptom Expression as a Form of Primitive Decentering. *Psychol. Rev.*, 74:16-28.
——— (1970), A Developmental Analysis of Interpersonal Behavior. *Psychol. Rev.*, 77:197-214.
——— & Gurevitch, V. (1960), Cognitive Aspects of Role-Taking in Children. *J. Pers.*, 28:383-396.
——— & Suchotliff, L. (1966), Decentering Implications of Social Interaction. *J. Pers. Soc. Psychol.*, 4:415-422.
Fellows, B., & Thorn, D. (1973), A Test of Piaget's Explanation of the Miller-Lyer Illusion. *Brit. J. of Psychol.*, 64:83-90.
Flavell, J. (1963), *The Developmental Psychology of Jean Piaget.* Princeton, N.J.: Van Nostrand.
——— (1970), Concept Development. In: *Carmichael's Manual of Child Psychology,* 3rd Ed., ed. P. Mussen. New York: Wiley, pp. 983-1059.
——— Botkin, P., Fry, C., Wright, J., & Jarvis, P. (1968), *The Development of Role-Taking and Communication Skills in Children.* New York: Wiley.
Fraiberg, S. (1959), *The Magic Years: Understanding and Handling the Problems of Early Childhood.* New York: Scribners'.

——— (1969), Libidinal Object Constancy and Mental Representation. *The Psychoanalytic Study of the Child,* 24:9-47. New York: International Universities Press.

——— (1977), *Insights from the Blind: Comparative Studies of Blind and Sighted Infants.* New York: Basic Books.

——— & Adelson, E. (1973), Self-Representation in Language and Play: Observations of Blind Children. *Psychoanal. Quart.,* 42:539-562.

Freeman, T., & McGhie, A. (1957), The Relevance of Genetic Psychology for the Psychopathology of Schizophrenia. *Brit. J. Med. Psychol.,* 30:176-187.

Freud, A. (1951), The Contribution of Psychoanalysis to Genetic Psychology. *The Writings of Anna Freud,* 4:107-142. New York: International Universities Press, 1968.

——— (1952), The Mutual Influences in the Development of Ego and Id. *The Psychoanalytic Study of the Child,* 7:42-50. New York: International Universities Press.

——— (1954), Psychoanalysis and Education. *The Psychoanalytic Study of the Child,* 9:9-15. New York: International Universities Press.

——— (1965), *Normality and Pathology in Childhood. The Writings of Anna Freud,* 6. New York: International Universities Press.

Freud, S. (1900), The Interpretation of Dreams. *Standard Edition,* 4 & 5. London: Hogarth Press, 1953.

——— (1911), Psycho-Analytic Notes on an Autobiographical Account of a Case of Paranoia (Dementia Paranoides). *Standard Edition,* 12:9-82. London: Hogarth Press, 1958.

——— (1915), Instincts and Their Vicissitudes. *Standard Edition,* 14:117-140. London: Hogarth Press, 1957.

——— (1923), The Ego and the Id. *Standard Edition,* 19:12-66. London: Hogarth Press, 1961.

Furth, H. G. (1966), *Thinking Without Language: Psychological Implications of Deafness.* New York: Free Press.

——— (1968), Piaget's Theory of Knowledge: The Nature of Representation and Interiorization. *Psychol. Rev.,* 75:143-154.

——— (1969), *Piaget and Knowledge.* Englewood Cliffs, N.J.: Prentice-Hall.

——— Youniss, J., & Ross, B. (1970), Children's Utilization of Logical Symbols: An Interpretation of Conceptual Behavior Based on Piagetian Theory. *Devel. Psychol.,* 3:36-57.

Galenson, E. (1971), A Consideration of the Nature of Thought in Childhood Play. In: *Separation-Individuation,* ed. J. B. McDevitt & C. F. Settlage. New York: International Universities Press, pp. 41-59.

Gewirtz, J. L. (1965), The Course of Infant Smiling in Four Child-Rearing Environments in Israel. In: *Determinants of Infant Behaviour,* Vol. 3, ed. B. M. Foss, London: Methuen, pp. 205-260.

——— (1969), Some Contextual Determinants of Stimulus Potency. Presented at meeting of the Society for Research in Child Development, Santa Monica, Cal.

Girgus, J., Coren, S., & Fraenkel, R. (1975), Levels of Perceptual Processing in the Development of Visual Illusion. *Devel. Psychol.,* 11:268-273.

Goldschmid, M. (1968), The Relation of Conservation to Emotional and Environmental Aspects of Development. *Child Devel.,* 35:579-589.

Gottlieb, G. (1971), Ontogenesis of Sensory Function in Birds and Mammals. In: *The Biopsychology of Development*, ed. E. Tobach, L. R. Aronson, & E. Shaw. New York: Academic Press, pp. 67-128.

——— (1976), Conceptions of Prenatal Development: Behavioral Embryology. *Psychol. Rev.*, 83:215-234.

——— (1978), Development of Species Identification in Ducklings. IV. Change in Species-Specific Perception Caused by Auditory Deprivation. *J. Comp. Physiol. Psychol.*, 92:375-387.

Gough, H. (1948), A Sociological Theory of Psychopathy. *Amer. J. Sociol.*, 53:359-366.

Gratton, L. (1971), Object Concept and Object Relations in Childhood Psychosis: A Pilot Study. *Canad. Psychiat. Assn. J.*, 16:347-354.

Greenacre, P. (1969), The Fetish and the Transitional Object. In: *Emotional Growth*, Vol. 1. New York: International Universities Press, 1971, pp. 315-334.

Greenspan, S. I. (1975), A Consideration of Some Learning Variables in the Context of Psychoanalytic Theory: Toward a Psychoanalytic Learning Perspective. *Psychol. Issues*, Monogr. No. 33. New York: International Universities Press.

Harris, P. L. (1975), Development of Search and Object Permanence During Infancy. *Psychol. Bull.*, 82:332-344.

Hartmann, H. (1939), *Ego Psychology and the Problem of Adaptation.* New York: International Universities Press, 1958.

——— (1950), Psychoanalysis and Developmental Psychology. *The Psychoanalytic Study of the Child*, 5:7-17. New York: International Universities Press.

——— & Kris, E. (1945) The Genetic Approach in Psychoanalysis. *The Psychoanalytic Study of the Child*, 1:11-30. New York: International Universities Press.

Hoffman, M. (1970), Moral Development. In: *Carmichael's Manual of Child Psychology*, 3rd Ed., ed. P. Mussen. New York: Wiley, pp. 261-359.

Hollós, M., & Cowan, P. (1973), Social Isolation and Cognitive Development: Logical Operations and Role-Taking Abilities in Three Norwegian Social Settings. *Child Devel.*, 44:630-641.

Holt, R. R. (1967), The Development of the Primary Process: A Structural View. In: Motives and Thought: Psychoanalytic Essays in Honor of David Rapaport, ed. R. R. Holt. *Psychol. Issues*, Monogr. No. 18/19. New York: International Universities Press, pp. 345-383.

Hunt, J. McV. (1963), Piaget's Observations as a Source of Hypotheses Concerning Motivation. *Merrill-Palmer Quart.*, 9:263-275.

——— (1969), The Impact and Limitations of the Giant of Developmental Psychology. In: *Studies in Cognitive Development: Essays in Honor of Piaget*, ed. D. Elkind & J. H. Flavell. New York: Oxford University Press, pp. 3-66.

Inhelder, B. (1966), Cognitive Development and Its Contribution to the Diagnosis of Some Phenomena of Mental Deficiency. *Merrill-Palmer Quart.*, 12:299-319.

——— & Piaget, J. (1955), *The Growth of Logical Thinking from Childhood to Adolescence.* New York: Basic Books, 1958.

Kagan, J. (1978), *Infancy: Its Place in Human Development.* Cambridge, Mass.: Harvard University Press.

Kaplan, L. (1972), Object Constancy in the Light of Piaget's Vertical Décalage. *Bull. Menninger Clinic,* 36:322-334.

Kernberg, O. F. (1975), *Borderline Conditions and Pathological Narcissism.* New York: Aronson.

Kessen, W. (1971), Early Cognitive Development: Hot or Cold? In: *Cognitive Development and Epistemology,* ed. T. Mischel. New York: Academic Press, pp. 288-309.

Klaus, M., et al. (1972), Maternal Attachment: The Importance of the First Postpartum Days. *New Eng. J. Med.,* 286:460-463.

——— & Kennell, J. H. (1976), *Maternal-Infant Bonding: The Impact of Early Separation or Loss on Family Development.* St. Louis: Mosby.

Klein, G. S. (1969), Freud's Two Theories of Sexuality. In: Psychology versus Metapsychology: Psychoanalytic Essays in Memory of George S. Klein, ed. M. M. Gill and P. S. Holzman. *Psychol. Issues,* Monogr. No. 36. New York: International Universities Press, pp. 14-70.

Klein, M. (1928), *The Psychoanalysis of Children.* New York: Delacorte Press, 1976.

Knight, R. P., & Friedman, C. R., eds. (1954), *Psychoanalytic Psychiatry and Psychology.* New York: International Universities Press.

Kohlberg, L. (1969), Stage and Sequence: The Cognitive-Developmental Approach to Socialization. In: *Handbook of Socialization Theory and Research,* ed. D. A. Goslin. Chicago: Rand McNally, pp. 347-480.

Kohut, H. (1971), *The Analysis of the Self.* New York: International Universities Press.

Kuhn, D. (1972) Mechanisms of Change in the Development of Cognitive Structures. *Child Devel.,* 43:833-844.

Laurendeau, M., & Pinard, A. (1962), *Causal Thinking in the Child.* New York: International Universities Press.

Lewis, M., & Goldberg, S. (1969), Perceptual-Cognitive Development in Infancy: A Generalized Expectancy Model as a Function of the Mother-Infant Interaction. *Merrill-Palmer Quart.,* 15:81-100.

——— & Rosenblum, L., eds. (1974), *The Effect of the Infant on Its Caregiver.* New York: Wiley.

Lipsitt, L. (1966), Learning Processes of Newborns. *Merrill-Palmer Quart.,* 12:45-71.

Looft, W. (1971), Egocentrism and Social Interaction in Adolescence. *Adolescence,* 6:485-494.

——— & Bartz, U. (1969), Animism Revised. *Psychol. Bull.,* 71:1-19.

Lovell, K. (1959), A Follow-Up Study of Some Aspects of the Work of Piaget and Inhelder on the Child's Conception of Space. *Brit. J. Educ. Psychol.,* 29:104-117.

Lustman, S. (1968), The Economic Point of View and Defense. *The Psychoanalytic Study of the Child,* 23:189-203. New York: International Universities Press.

Mahler, M. S. (1968), *On Human Symbiosis and the Vicissitudes of Individuation.* Vol. I: *Infantile Psychosis.* New York: International Universities Press.

——— Pine, F., & Bergman, A. (1975), *The Psychological Birth of the Human Infant.* New York: Basic Books.

Main, M. (1973), Exploration, Play, and Cognitive Functioning as Related to Child-Mother Attachment. Unpublished Doctoral Dissertation, Johns Hopkins University, Baltimore, Md.

Martin, M. (1968), A Role-Taking Theory of Psychopathy. Unpublished Dissertation, University of Oregon. Ann Arbor, Mich.: University Microfilms, 68:11, 957.

McDevitt, J. B. (1971), Discussion of "A Consideration of the Nature of Thought in Childhood Play" by E. Galenson. In: *Separation-Individuation,* ed. J. B. McDevitt & C. F. Settlage. New York: International Universities Press, pp. 70-74.

Mead, G. H. (1934), *Mind, Self and Society.* Chicago: University of Chicago Press.

Mehler, J., & Bever, T. (1968), Response to Piaget. *Science,* 162:979-981.

Meltzoff, A. N., & Moore, K. M. (1977), Imitation of Facial and Manual Gestures by Human Neonates. *Science,* 198:75-78.

Mischel, T. (1971), Piaget: Cognitive Conflict and the Motivation of Thought. In: *Cognitive Development and Epistemology,* ed. T. Mischel. New York: Academic Press, pp. 311-353.

Nagera, H. (1966), *Early Childhood Disturbances, the Infantile Neurosis and the Adult Disturbances.* New York: International Universities Press.

Nass, M. L. (1966), The Superego and Moral Development in the Theories of Freud and Piaget. *The Psychoanalytic Study of the Child,* 21:51-68. New York: International Universities Press.

Nemiah, J. C. (1977), *Alexithymia: Theories and Models.* Proceedings 11th European Conference on Psychosomatic Research. Basel: Karger.

Norris, F., Jenes, H., & Norris, H. (1970), Articulation of the Conceptual Structure in Obsessional Neurosis. *Brit. J. Soc. Clin. Psychol.,* 9:264-274.

Novey, S. (1958), The Meaning of the Concept of Mental Representation of Objects. *Psychoanal. Quart.,* 27:57-79.

Nunberg, H. (1931), The Synthetic Function of the Ego. In: *Practice and Theory of Psychoanalysis.* Vol. 1. New York: International Universities Press, 1948, pp. 120-136.

Odier, C. (1956), *Anxiety and Magical Thinking.* New York: International Universities Press.

Parmelee, A., Jr. (1972), Development of States in Infants. In: *Sleep and the Maturing Nervous System,* ed. C. Clemente, D. Purpura, & F. Mayer. New York: Academic Press, pp. 199-228.

Piaget, J. (1932), *The Moral Judgment of the Child.* New York: Free Press, 1965.

——— (1936), *The Origins of Intelligence in Children.* New York: International Universities Press, 1952.

——— (1937), *The Construction of Reality in the Child.* New York: Basic Books, 1954.

——— (1945), *Play, Dreams and Imitation in Childhood.* New York: Norton, 1951.

——— (1946), *The Child's Conception of Time.* New York: Basic Books, 1970.

——— (1947), The Moral Development of the Adolescent in Two Types of Society, Primitive and "Modern." Presented at the UNESCO Seminar on Education for International Understanding, July 24.

——— (1953), *Logic and Psychology.* New York: Basic Books.

——— (1954), *Les relations entre l'intelligence et l'affectivité dans le développement mental de l'enfant.* Paris: Centre de Documentation Universitaire.

——— (1960), The General Problems of the Psychobiological Development of the Child. In: *Discussions on Child Development,* Vol. IV, ed. J. Tanner

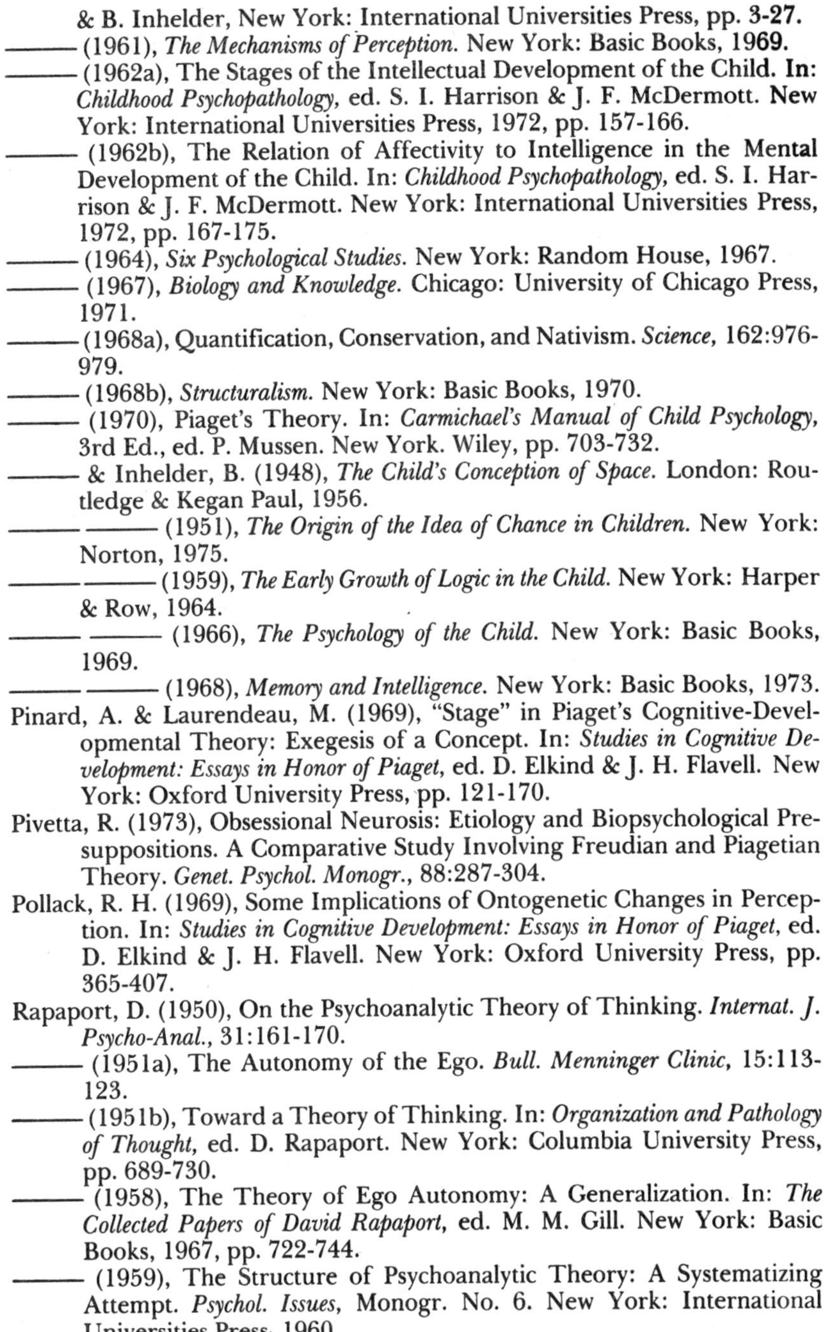

& B. Inhelder, New York: International Universities Press, pp. 3-27.
——— (1961), *The Mechanisms of Perception.* New York: Basic Books, 1969.
——— (1962a), The Stages of the Intellectual Development of the Child. In: *Childhood Psychopathology,* ed. S. I. Harrison & J. F. McDermott. New York: International Universities Press, 1972, pp. 157-166.
——— (1962b), The Relation of Affectivity to Intelligence in the Mental Development of the Child. In: *Childhood Psychopathology,* ed. S. I. Harrison & J. F. McDermott. New York: International Universities Press, 1972, pp. 167-175.
——— (1964), *Six Psychological Studies.* New York: Random House, 1967.
——— (1967), *Biology and Knowledge.* Chicago: University of Chicago Press, 1971.
——— (1968a), Quantification, Conservation, and Nativism. *Science,* 162:976-979.
——— (1968b), *Structuralism.* New York: Basic Books, 1970.
——— (1970), Piaget's Theory. In: *Carmichael's Manual of Child Psychology,* 3rd Ed., ed. P. Mussen. New York. Wiley, pp. 703-732.
——— & Inhelder, B. (1948), *The Child's Conception of Space.* London: Routledge & Kegan Paul, 1956.
——— ——— (1951), *The Origin of the Idea of Chance in Children.* New York: Norton, 1975.
——— ——— (1959), *The Early Growth of Logic in the Child.* New York: Harper & Row, 1964.
——— ——— (1966), *The Psychology of the Child.* New York: Basic Books, 1969.
——— ——— (1968), *Memory and Intelligence.* New York: Basic Books, 1973.
Pinard, A. & Laurendeau, M. (1969), "Stage" in Piaget's Cognitive-Developmental Theory: Exegesis of a Concept. In: *Studies in Cognitive Development: Essays in Honor of Piaget,* ed. D. Elkind & J. H. Flavell. New York: Oxford University Press, pp. 121-170.
Pivetta, R. (1973), Obsessional Neurosis: Etiology and Biopsychological Presuppositions. A Comparative Study Involving Freudian and Piagetian Theory. *Genet. Psychol. Monogr.,* 88:287-304.
Pollack, R. H. (1969), Some Implications of Ontogenetic Changes in Perception. In: *Studies in Cognitive Development: Essays in Honor of Piaget,* ed. D. Elkind & J. H. Flavell. New York: Oxford University Press, pp. 365-407.
Rapaport, D. (1950), On the Psychoanalytic Theory of Thinking. *Internat. J. Psycho-Anal.,* 31:161-170.
——— (1951a), The Autonomy of the Ego. *Bull. Menninger Clinic,* 15:113-123.
——— (1951b), Toward a Theory of Thinking. In: *Organization and Pathology of Thought,* ed. D. Rapaport. New York: Columbia University Press, pp. 689-730.
——— (1958), The Theory of Ego Autonomy: A Generalization. In: *The Collected Papers of David Rapaport,* ed. M. M. Gill. New York: Basic Books, 1967, pp. 722-744.
——— (1959), The Structure of Psychoanalytic Theory: A Systematizing Attempt. *Psychol. Issues,* Monogr. No. 6. New York: International Universities Press, 1960.

Rheingold, H., & Eckerman, C. (1973), Fear of the Stranger: A Critical Examination. In: *Advances in Child Development and Behavior,* Vol. 8, ed. H. Reese. New York: Academic Press, pp. 185-222.

Robertson, J., & Robertson, J. (1971), Young Children in Brief Separation: A Fresh Look. *The Psychoanalytic Study of the Child,* 26:264-315. New York: Quadrangle.

Rubin, K. (1973), Egocentrism in Childhood: A Unitary Construct? *Child Devel.,* 44:102-110.

Sander, L. (1962), Issues in Early Mother-Child Interaction. *J. Amer. Acad. Child Psychiat.,* 1:141-166.

Sandler, J., Holder, A., & Meers, D. (1963) The Ego Ideal and the Ideal Self. *The Psychoanalytic Study of the Child,* 18:139-158. New York: International Universities Press.

Saussure, F. de (1933), Psychologie génétique et psychanalyse. *Rev. Franç. Psychanal.,* 6:364-403.

Schaffer, H., Greenwood, A., & Parry, M. (1972), The Onset of Wariness. *Child Devel.,* 43:165-175.

Selman, R. (1971a), The Relation of Role-Taking to the Development of Moral Judgment in Children. *Child Devel.,* 42:79-91.

——— (1971b), Taking Another's Perspective: Role-Taking Development in Early Childhood. *Child Devel.,* 42:1721-1734.

Silverman, M. (1971), The Growth of Logical Thinking: Piaget's Contribution to Ego Psychology. *Psychoanal. Quart.,* 40:317-341.

Spitz, R. A. (1965), *The First Year of Life.* New York: International Universities Press.

——— Emde, R., & Metcalf, D. (1970), Further Prototypes of Ego Formation. *The Psychoanalytic Study of the Child,* 25:417-444. New York: International Universities Press.

Sroufe, L., & Waters, E. (1976), The Ontogenesis of Smiling and Laughter: A Perspective on the Organization of Development in Infancy. *Psychol. Rev.,* 83:173-189.

——— ——— (1977), Heartrate as a Convergent Measure in Clinical and Developmental Research. *Merrill-Palmer Quart.,* 23:3-27.

——— ——— & Matas, L. (1974), Contextual Determinants of Infant Affective Response. In: *The Origins of Fear,* ed. M. Lewis & L. Rosenblum. New York: Wiley, pp. 49-72.

Stern, D. (1974a), Mother and Infant at Play: The Dyadic Interaction Involving Facial, Vocal and Gaze Behaviors. In: *The Effect of the Infant on Its Caregiver,* ed. M. Lewis & L. Rosenblum. New York: Wiley, pp. 187-213.

——— (1974b), The Goal and Structure of Mother-Infant Play. *J. Amer. Acad. Child Psychiat.,* 13:402-421.

Tanner, J., & Inhelder, B., eds. (1960), *Discussions on Child Development,* Vol. IV. New York: International Universities Press.

Tennes, K., Emde, R., Kisley, A., & Metcalf, D. (1972) The Stimulus Barrier in Early Infancy: An Exploration of Some Formulations of John Benjamin. In: *Psychoanalysis and Contemporary Science,* 1: 206-234. New York: Macmillan.

Thomas, A., Chess, S., & Birch, H. G. (1968), *Temperament and Behavior Disorders in Children.* New York: New York University Press.

Trunnell, T. (1964), Thought Disturbance in Schizophrenia. *Arch. Gen. Psychiat.*, 11:126-136.

——— (1965), Thought Disturbance in Schizophrenia: Replication Study Utilizing Piaget's Theory. *Arch. Gen. Psychiat.*, 13:9-18.

Tuddenham, R. (1966), Jean Piaget and the World of the Child. *Amer. Psychologist*, 21:207-217.

Uzgiris, I., & Hunt, J. McV. (1975), *Assessment in Infancy: Ordinal Scales of Psychological Development.* Urbana: University of Illinois Press.

Vernon, McC. (1967), Relationship of Language to the Thinking Process. *Arch. Gen. Psychiat.*, 16(3):325-333.

Waelder, R. (1936), The Principle of Multiple Function: Observations on Overdetermination. *Psychoanal. Quart.*, 5:45-62.

Waters, E., Matas, L. & Sroufe, L. (1975) Infant's Reactions to an Approaching Stranger: Description, Validation and Functional Significance of Wariness. *Child Devel.*, 46:348-356.

Weintraub, D. J., & Cooper, L. A. (1972), Coming of Age with the Delboeuf Illusion: Brightness, Contrast, Cognition, and Perceptual Development. Devel. Psychol., 6:187-197.

Werner, H., & Kaplan, B. (1963), *Symbol Formation.* New York: Wiley.

White, R. (1959), Motivation Reconsidered: The Concept of Competence. *Psychol. Rev.*, 66:297-333.

——— (1960), Competence and the Psychosexual Stages of Development. In: *Nebraska Symposium on Motivation*, ed. M. R. Jones. Lincoln: University of Nebraska Press, pp. 97-141.

Winnicott, D. W. (1953), Transitional Objects and Transitional Phenomena: A Study of the First Not-Me Possession. In: *Collected Papers.* New York: Basic Books, 1958, pp. 229-242.

——— (1954), Metapsychological and Clinical Aspects of Regression within the Psychoanalytic Set-up. In: *Collected Papers.* New York: Basic Books, 1958, pp. 278-294.

——— (1954), Primary Maternal Preocuupation. In: *Collected Papers.* New York: Basic Books, 1958, pp. 300-305.

Wolff, P. H. (1959), Observations on Newborn Infants. *Psychosom. Med.*, 21:110-118.

——— (1960), The Developmental Psychologies of Jean Piaget and Psychoanalysis. *Psychol. Issues*, Monogr. No. 5. New York: International Universities Press.

——— (1963), Developmental and Motivational Concepts in Piaget's Sensorimotor Theory of Intelligence. *J. Amer. Acad. Child Psychiat.*, 2:225-243.

——— (1966), The Causes, Controls, and Organization of Behavior in the Neonate. *Psychol. Issues*, Monogr. No. 17. New York: International Universities Press.

——— (1967a), Cognitive Considerations for a Psychoanalytic Theory of Language Acquisition. In: Motives and Thought: Psychoanalytic Essays in Honor of David Rapaport, ed. R. R. Holt. *Psychol. Issues*, Monogr. No. 18/19. New York: International Universities Press, pp. 300-343.

——— (1967b), The Role of Biological Rhythms in Early Psychological Development. *Bull. Menninger Clinic*, 31:197-218.

——— (1968), Stereotypic Behavior and Development. *Canad. Psychol.*, 9:474-484.

———, rep. (1971), Panel: Review of Psychoanalytic Theory in Light of Current Research in Child Development. *J. Amer. Psychoanal. Assn.*, 19:565-576.

Work, H. H. (1972), Parent-Child Centers: A Working Appraisal. *Amer. J. Orthopsychiat.*, 42:583-595.

Wynne, L. C. & Singer, M. T. (1963a), Thought Disorder and Family Relations of Schizophrenics. I. A Research Strategy. *Arch. Gen. Psychiat.*, 9:191-198.

——— ——— (1963b), Thought Disorder and Family Relations of Schizophrenics: II. A Classification of Forms of Thinking. *Arch. Gen. Psychiat.*, 9:199-206.

Yarrow, L., & Goodwin, M. (1965), Some Conceptual Issues in the Study of Mother-Infant Interaction. *Amer. J. Orthopsychiat.*, 35:473-481.

——— Rubenstein, J. L., Pederson, F. A., & Jankowski, T. J. (1972), Dimensions of Early Stimulation and Their Differential Effects on Infant Development. *Merrill-Palmer Quart.*, 18:205-218.

Zern, D. (1973), Competence Reconsidered: The Concept of Secondary Process Development as an Explanation of "Competence" Phenomena. *J. Genet. Psychol.*, 122:135-162.

Zetzel, E. (1968), The So-Called Good Hysteric. In: *The Capacity for Emotional Growth.* New York: International Universities Press, 1970, pp. 229-245.

INDEX

ABOUT THE AUTHOR

STANLEY I. GREENSPAN received his M.D. from Yale University School of Medicine in 1966. He received training in adult psychiatry at Columbia Presbyterian Medical Center-Psychiatric Institute, New York City; in child psychiatry at Hillcrest Children's Center, Children's Hospital Medical Center, Washington, D.C.; and in adult and child psychoanalysis at the Washington Psychoanalytic Institute. At present he is Chief of the Mental Health Study Center and Director of the Clinical Infant Development Program at the National Institute of Mental Health. In addition, he is Clinical Associate Professor of Psychiatry and Behavioral Science and Child Health and Development at the George Washington University Medical School and a member of the academic faculty of the Children's Hospital National Medical Center. His previous publications include *A Consideration of Some Learning Variables in the Context of Psychoanalytic Theory* (*Psychological Issues,* Monograph 33).

PSYCHOLOGICAL ISSUES

No. 1—ERIK H. ERIKSON: *Identity and the Life Cycle: Selected Papers.* Historical Introduction by David Rapaport

No. 2—I. H. PAUL: *Studies in Remembering: The Reproduction of Connected and Extended Verbal Material*

No. 3—FRITZ HEIDER: *On Perception, Event Structure, and Psychological Environment: Selected Papers.* Preface by George S. Klein.

No. 4—RILEY W. GARDNER, PHILIP S. HOLZMAN, GEORGE S. KLEIN, HARRIET LINTON, and DONALD P. SPENCE: *Cognitive Control: A Study of Individual Consistencies in Cognitive Behavior*

No. 5—PETER H. WOLFF: *The Developmental Psychologies of Jean Piaget and Psychoanalysis*

No. 6—DAVID RAPAPORT: *The Structure of Psychoanalytic Theory: A Systematizing Attempt*

No. 7—OTTO PÖTZL, RUDOLF ALLERS, and JAKOB TELER: *Preconscious Stimulation in Dreams, Associations, and Images: Classical Studies.* Introduction by Charles Fisher

No. 8—RILEY W. GARDNER, DOUGLAS N. JACKSON, and SAMUEL J. MESSICK: *Personality Organization in Cognitive Controls and Intellectual Abilities*

No. 9—FRED SCHWARTZ and RICHARD O. ROUSE: *The Activation and Recovery of Associations*

No. 10—MERTON M. GILL: *Topography and Systems in Psychoanalytic Theory*

No. 11—ROBERT W. WHITE: *Ego and Reality in Psychoanalytic Theory: A Proposal Regarding the Independent Ego Energies*

No. 12—IVO KOHLER: *The Formation and Transformation of the Perceptual World.* Introduction by James J. Gibson

No. 13—DAVID SHAKOW and DAVID RAPAPORT: *The Influence of Freud on American Psychology*

No. 14—HEINZ HARTMANN, ERNST KRIS, and RUDOLPH M. LOEWENSTEIN: *Papers on Psychoanalytic Psychology*

No. 15—WOLFGANG LEDERER: *Dragons, Delinquents, and Destiny: An Essay on Positive Superego Functions.* Introduction by Roy Schafer

No. 16—PETER AMACHER: *Freud's Neurological Education and Its Influence on Psychoanalytic Theory*

No. 17—PETER H. WOLFF: *The Causes, Controls, and Organization of Behavior in the Neonate*

No. 18/19—ROBERT R. HOLT, Ed.: *Motives and Thought: Psychoanalytic Essays in Honor of David Rapaport*

No. 20—JOHN CHYNOWETH BURNHAM: *Psychoanalysis and American Medicine, 1894-1918: Medicine, Science, and Culture*

No. 21—HELEN D. SARGENT, LEONARD HORWITZ, ROBERT S. WALLERSTEIN, and ANN APPELBAUM: *Prediction in Psychotherapy Research: A Method for the Transformation of Clinical Judgments into Testable Hypotheses*

No. 22—MARJORIE GRENE, Ed.: *Toward a Unity of Knowledge*

No. 23—FRED SCHWARTZ and PETER H. SCHILLER: *A Psychoanalytic Model of Attention and Learning*

No. 24—BERNARD LANDIS: *Ego Boundaries*

No. 25/26—EMANUEL PETERFREUND in collaboration with JACOB T. SCHWARTZ: *Information, Systems, and Psychoanalysis: An Evolutionary Biological Approach to Psychoanalytic Theory*

No. 27—LOUIS BREGER, IAN HUNTER, and RON W. LANE: *The Effect of Stress on Dreams*

No. 28—EDITH LEVITOV GARDUK and ERNEST A. HAGGARD: *Immediate Effects on Patients of Psychoanalytic Interpretations*

No. 29—ERICH GOLDMEIER: *Similarity in Visually Perceived Forms.* Foreword by Irvin Rock

No. 30—MARTIN MAYMAN, Ed.: *Psychoanalytic Research: Three Approaches to the Experimental Study of Subliminal Processes*

No. 31—NANETTE HEIMAN and JOAN GRANT, Eds.: *Else Frenkel-Brunswik: Selected Papers*

No. 32—FRED SCHWARTZ, Ed.: *Scientific Thought and Social Reality: Essays by Michael Polanyi*

No. 33—STANLEY I. GREENSPAN: *A Consideration of Some Learning Variables in the Context of Psychoanalytic Theory: Toward a Psychoanalytic Learning Perspective*

No. 34/35—JOHN E. GEDO and GEORGE H. POLLOCK, Eds.: *Freud: The Fusion of Science and Humanism: The Intellectual History of Psychoanalysis*

No. 36—MERTON M. GILL and PHILIP S. HOLZMAN, Eds.: *Psychology versus Metapsychology: Psychoanalytic Essays in Memory of George S. Klein*

No. 37—ROBERT N. EMDE, THEODORE J. GAENSBAUER, and ROBERT J HARMON: *Emotional Expression in Infancy: A Biobehavioral Study*

No. 38—DAVID SHAKOW: *Schizophrenia: Selected Papers*

No. 39—PAUL E. STEPANSKY: *A History of Aggression in Freud.* Foreword by Roy Schafer

No. 40—JOSEPH DE RIVERA: *A Structural Theory of the Emotions.* Introductory Essay by Hartvig Dahl

No. 41—HANNAH S. DECKER: *Freud in Germany: Revolution and Reaction in Science, 1893-1907*

No. 42/43—ALLAN D. ROSENBLATT and JAMES T. THICKSTUN: *Modern Psychoanalytic Concepts in a General Psychology*—Parts 1 & 2

No. 44—HERBERT J. SCHLESINGER, Ed.: *Symbol and Neurosis: Selected Papers of Lawrence S. Kubie.* Introduction by Eugene B. Brody

No. 45/46—ALAN KROHN: *Hysteria: The Elusive Neurosis*